VOICES OF THE POOR

Can Anyone Hear Us?

"*My colleagues and I decided that in order to map our own course for the future, we needed to know about our clients as individuals. We launched a study entitled 'Voices of the Poor' and spoke to them about their hopes, their aspirations, their realities.*

What is it that the poor reply when asked what might make the greatest difference in their lives? They say, organizations of their own so that they may negotiate with government, with traders, and with nongovernmental organizations. Direct assistance through community-driven programs so that they may shape their own destinies. Local ownership of funds, so that they may put a stop to corruption. They want nongovernmental organizations and governments to be accountable to them....

These are strong voices, voices of dignity."

—James D. Wolfensohn, President, the World Bank Group
Address to the Annual Meeting of the Board
of Governors, September 28, 1999

VOICES OF THE POOR

Can Anyone Hear Us?

Deepa Narayan

with
Raj Patel
Kai Schafft
Anne Rademacher
Sarah Koch-Schulte

*Published by Oxford University Press
for the World Bank*

Oxford University Press

OXFORD   NEW YORK   ATHENS   AUCKLAND   BANGKOK
BOGOTA   BUENOS AIRES   CALCUTTA   CAPE TOWN   CHENNAI
DAR ES SALAAM   DELHI   FLORENCE   HONG KONG   ISTANBUL
KARACHI   KUALA LUMPUR   MADRID   MELBOURNE   MEXICO CITY
MUMBAI   NAIROBI   PARIS   SÃO PAULO   SINGAPORE   TAIPEI
TOKYO   TORONTO   WARSAW

and associated companies in

BERLIN   IBADAN

© 2000 The International Bank for Reconstruction
and Development / The World Bank
1818 H Street, N.W., Washington, D.C. 20433, USA

Published by Oxford University Press, Inc.
198 Madison Avenue, New York, N.Y. 10016

Oxford is a registered trademark of Oxford University Press.

Manufactured in the United States of America
First printing March 2000

Library of Congress Cataloging-in-Publication Data in Process.
ISBN: 0–19–521601-6

Text printed on paper that conforms to the American National Standard for
Permanence of Paper for Printed Library Materials, Z39.48-1984

Contents

Foreword

This book is the first in a three-part series entitled *Voices of the Poor*. The series is based on an unprecedented effort to gather the views, experiences, and aspirations of more than 60,000 poor men and women from 60 countries. The work was undertaken for the *World Development Report 2000/2001* on the theme of poverty and development.

Can Anyone Hear Us? brings together the voices of over 40,000 poor people from 50 countries. The two books that follow, *Crying Out for Change* and *From Many Lands,* pull together new fieldwork conducted in 1999 in 23 countries. The Voices of the Poor project is different from all other large-scale poverty studies. Using participatory and qualitative research methods, the study presents very directly, through poor people's own voices, the realities of their lives. How do poor people view poverty and well-being? What are their problems and priorities? What is their experience with the institutions of the state, markets, and civil society? How are gender relations faring within households and communities? We want to thank the project team led by Deepa Narayan of the Poverty Group in the World Bank, and particularly the country research teams, for undertaking this work.

What poor people share with us is sobering. A majority of them feel they are worse off and more insecure than in the past. Poor people care about many of the same things all of us care about: happiness, family, children, livelihood, peace, security, safety, dignity, and respect. Poor people's descriptions of encounters with a range of institutions call out for all of us to rethink our strategies. From the perspective of poor people, corruption, irrelevance, and abusive behavior often mar the formal institutions of the state. NGOs too receive mixed ratings from the poor. Poor people would like NGOs to be accountable to them. Poor people's interactions with traders and markets are stamped with their powerlessness to negotiate fair prices. How then do poor people survive? They turn to their informal networks of family, kin, friends, and neighbors. But these are already stretched thin.

We commend to you the authenticity and significance of this work. What can be more important than listening to the poor and working with our partners all over the world to respond to their concerns? Our core mission is to help poor people succeed in their own efforts, and the book raises major challenges to both of our institutions and to all of us concerned about poverty. We are prepared to hold ourselves accountable, to make the effort to try to respond to these voices. Obviously we cannot do this alone.

We urge you to read this book, to reflect and respond. Our hope is that the voices in this book will call you to action as they have us.

CLARE SHORT,
Secretary of State for International
Development, U.K.

JAMES D. WOLFENSOHN,
President, World Bank

Acknowledgments

We have many people to thank for their support to this effort. Ravi Kanbur, director of the World Development Report, and Michael Walton, director of the Poverty Group, requested this review and committed financial resources to support this work. This review would not have been possible without the openness of the poor, whose voices we have tried to convey. We are also grateful to the researchers whose work we use in our analysis. We'd also like to thank colleagues in the World Bank for taking the time to hunt down documents for us and for their feedback in the Bank-wide review of the study.

Several people within the Poverty Group provided invaluable assistance, nearly always at short notice! Ben Jones served as the liaison between the group of graduate students at Cornell University and the World Bank. He also played key roles in innumerable ways, including keeping order among the rapidly multiplying successive drafts of chapters. Several people contributed to various chapters: Talat Shah, Tiffany Marlowe, Veronica Nyhan, Sabina Aklire, Ulrike Erhardt, Sirrimatta N'Dow, Gayatri Menon, Radha Seshagiri, Kimberley McLean, Patti Petesch, Jesko Hentschel, and Kristin Hirsch. Special thanks to Kristin Rusch, who worked many late nights patiently editing successive drafts of the book. The book design, copyediting, and production were directed and managed by the Office of the Publisher at the World Bank. The final copyedit was done by Alison Peña. The book has benefited from detailed comments received from three external reviewers, Norman Uphoff and Shelly Feldman, Cornell University, and Leonora Angeles, University of British Columbia. Additional comments were received from Arjan de Haan, Department for International Development, U.K. Thanks to John Blaxall for advice, support, and editing.

The research was financed by grants from the John D. and Catherine T. MacArthur Foundation, Cornell University, the World Bank's Poverty Information Thematic Group, the Gender Policy Research Team, the Poverty Group, and DFID, U.K.

This book is part of the Consultations with the Poor project, led by Deepa Narayan, Poverty Group, World Bank, undertaken to inform the World Development Report 2000/2001 on Poverty and Development.

VOICES OF THE POOR

Can Anyone
Hear Us?

Chapter 1

Listening to the Voices of the Poor

*Poverty is pain; it feels like a disease. It attacks
a person not only materially but also morally.
It eats away one's dignity and drives one
into total despair.*

—A poor woman, Moldova 1997

*The authorities don't seem to see poor people.
Everything about the poor is despised, and above all
poverty is despised.*

— A poor man, Brazil 1995

Introduction

Poverty is pain. Poor people suffer physical pain that comes with too little food and long hours of work; emotional pain stemming from the daily humiliations of dependency and lack of power; and the moral pain from being forced to make choices—such as whether to use limited funds to save the life of an ill family member, or to use those same funds to feed their children.

If poverty is so painful, why do the poor remain poor? The poor are not lazy, stupid, or corrupt—why, then, is poverty so persistent? We explore this problem from two perspectives: one is from the realities, experiences, and perspectives of poor women and men themselves; and the other is from an institutional perspective focusing on the informal and formal institutions of society with which poor people interact. Our analysis is based on a review of 81 Participatory Poverty Assessment (PPA) reports that are based on discussions with over 40,000 poor women and men. The World Bank conducted these studies in the 1990s in 50 countries around the world.

The book is not an evaluation of particular public action programs, economic policies, or trade regimes. It simply offers a view of the world from the perspective of the poor. It provides rich descriptions of poor people's realities, drawing on their experiences of poverty and the quality of their interactions with a range of institutions, from the state to the household. This book is about their voices. Voices of the poor send powerful messages that point the way toward policy change.

Many books could be written from the PPA studies, focusing on particular contexts and unique relationships in a particular institutional context at a particular time in history. In order to take action at the local level, the details and contours of the patterns of poverty have to be understood in each location, for each social group, for each region, for each country. For example, even in one location in one country poor people themselves make important distinctions between social groups: the dependent poor, the resourceless poor, the temporary poor, the working poor, and God's poor, all of whom have different priorities.

Our book is about the common patterns that emerged from poor people's experiences in many different places. As we moved more deeply into analyses of poor people's experiences with poverty, we were struck repeatedly by the paradox of the location and social group specificity of poverty, and yet the commonality of the human experience of poverty across countries. From Georgia to Brazil, from Nigeria to the Philippines, similar underlying themes emerged: hunger, deprivation, powerlessness, violation of dignity, social isolation, resilience, resourcefulness, solidarity, state corruption, rudeness of service providers, and gender inequity.

The manifestation of these problems varied significantly, but we often found ourselves saying, "We have read this before." Sometimes even the words and images poor people evoked in describing their realities were uncannily similar, despite very different contexts.

To cite one example, single mothers with young children use similar imagery to describe hanging onto their children while somehow still scraping together a living. In South Africa (1998) a widow said, "I was tossed around, getting knocks here and there. I have been everywhere, carrying these children with my teeth." In Georgia (1997) a mother described the pain of leaving small children alone in the home while she "runs like a dog from house to house, selling some sort of clothing or product just to make two lari a day."

We write about the common patterns we found across countries because these have important implications for poverty reduction strategies. The study is part of the *Consultations with the Poor* project undertaken to inform the World Bank's *World Development Report on Poverty 2000/01* and to set a precedent for the participation of poor men and women in global policy debates. The *World Development Report (WDR) on Poverty 2000/01* will evaluate changes in global poverty since the Bank's last WDR on Poverty in 1990, and will propose policy directions for the next decade.

Our analysis leads to five main conclusions about the experience of poverty from the perspectives of the poor. First, poverty is multidimensional. Second, the state has been largely ineffective in reaching the poor. Third, the role of nongovernmental organizations (NGOs) in the lives of the poor is limited, forcing the poor to depend primarily on their own informal networks. Fourth, households are crumbling under the stresses of poverty. Finally, the social fabric—poor people's only "insurance"—is unraveling. These issues are addressed in detail in the following chapters, but an overview of each conclusion is presented here.

Poverty is multidimensional. The persistence of poverty is linked to its interlocking multidimensionality: it is dynamic, complex, institutionally embedded, and a gender- and location-specific phenomenon. The pattern and shape of poverty vary by social group, season, location, and country. Six dimensions feature prominently in poor people's definitions of poverty.

First, poverty consists of many interlocked dimensions. Although poverty is rarely about the lack of only one thing, the bottom line is always hunger—the lack of food. Second, poverty has important psychological dimensions, such as powerlessness, voicelessness, dependency, shame, and humiliation. The maintenance of cultural identity and social norms of solidarity helps poor people to continue to believe in their own humanity, despite inhumane conditions. Third, poor people lack access to basic infrastructure—roads (particularly in rural areas), transportation, and clean water. Fourth, while there is a widespread thirst for literacy, schooling receives little mention or mixed reviews. Poor people realize that education offers an escape from poverty—but only if the economic environment in the society at large and the quality of education improve. Fifth, poor health and illness are dreaded almost everywhere as a source of destitution. This is related to the costs of health care as well as to income lost due to illness. Finally, the poor rarely speak of income, but focus instead on managing assets—physical, human, social, and environmental—as a way to cope with their vulnerability. In many areas this vulnerability has a gender dimension.

The state has been largely ineffective in reaching the poor. Although the government's role in providing infrastructure, health, and education services is recognized by the poor, they feel that their lives remain unchanged by government interventions. Poor people report that their interactions with state representatives are marred by rudeness, humiliation, harassment, and stonewalling. The poor also report vast experience with corruption as they attempt to seek health care, educate their children, claim social assistance or relief assistance, get paid by employers, and seek protection from the police or justice from local authorities.

In many places poor people identify particular individuals within the state apparatus as good, and certain programs as useful, but these individuals and programs are not enough to pull them out of poverty. The impact of a corrupt and brutalizing police force is particularly demoralizing for the poor, who already feel defenseless against the power of the state and the elite. There are gender differences in poor people's experiences with state institutions that reflect societal norms of gender-based power inequity. Women in many contexts report continued vulnerability to the threat of sexual assault. Despite negative experiences, when outsiders arrive the poor—for the most part—are willing to trust and listen one more time, with the hope that something good may happen in their lives.

The role of NGOs in the lives of the poor is limited, and the poor depend primarily on their own informal networks. Given the scale of poverty, NGOs touch relatively few lives, and poor people give NGOs mixed ratings. In some areas NGOs are the only institutions people trust, and in some cases they are credited with saving lives. Where there is strong NGO presence new partnerships between government and NGOs are beginning to emerge.

However, poor people sometimes also report that, besides being rude and forceful, NGO staff members are poor listeners. Surprisingly, the poor report that they consider some NGOs to be largely irrelevant, self-serving, limited in their outreach, and also corrupt, although to a much lesser extent than is the state. There are relatively few cases of NGOs that have invested in organizing the poor to change poor people's bargaining power relative to markets or the state. Because the studies were conducted in some countries with the world's largest NGOs (some of which are also the world's most successful NGOs), there are important lessons to be learned. The main message is still one of scale, however—even the largest and most successful NGOs may not reach the majority of poor households.

Thus poor men and women throughout the world must trust and rely primarily on their own informal institutions and networks, while recognizing the limitations of these institutions even under the best of circumstances. Informal associations and networks may help the poor to survive, but they serve a defensive, and usually not a transformative, function. That is, they do little to move the poor out of poverty.

There are important gender differences in the nature and use of informal networks. Because poor women are often excluded from involvement in community and formal institutions, they invest heavily in social support networks that may offer them a hedge in fulfilling their household responsibilities. When everything around them starts to deteriorate, the poor continue to invest in burial societies to ensure that they are at least taken care of in death.

Households are crumbling under the stresses of poverty. The household as a social institution is crumbling under the weight of poverty. While many households are able to remain intact, many others disintegrate as men, unable to adapt to their "failure" to earn adequate incomes under harsh economic circumstances, have difficulty accepting that women are becoming the main breadwinners and that this necessitates a redistribution of power within the household. The result is often alcoholism and domestic violence on the part of men, and a breakdown of the family structure.

Women, in contrast, tend to swallow their pride and go out into the streets to do demeaning jobs, or, in fact, to do anything it takes to put food on the table for their children and husbands. Clearly, this is not necessarily empowering for women. Despite having assumed new roles, women continue to face discrimination in the labor market and gender inequity in the home. They often confront oppressive social norms in both state and civil society institutions in which they live and work, and many have internalized stereotypes that deny their worth as women. Gender inequity within households seems remarkably intractable; economic empowerment or income-earning does not necessarily lead to social empowerment or gender equity within households. Nonetheless, in some places the studies reveal glimmers of more equitable power relations within the household.

The social fabric, poor people's only "insurance," is unraveling. Finally, from the perspective of poor men and women, the social fabric—the bonds of reciprocity and trust—is unraveling. There are twin forces at work. The more powerful and internally cohesive groups reinforce social exclusion of particular groups, while social cohesion (the connections across groups) breaks down. Economic dislocation and sweeping political changes have produced conflict at the household, community, regional, and national levels. This conflict has three important consequences. First, once societies start unraveling, it is difficult to reverse the process. Second, the breakdown of social solidarity and social norms that once regulated public behavior leads to increased lawlessness, violence, and crime, to which the poor are the most vulnerable. Finally, because the poor lack material assets and depend on the social insurance provided by the strength of their social ties, a breakdown of community solidarity and norms of reciprocity with neighbors and kin affects the poor more than other groups.

The book's organization follows the points just summarized. The remainder of chapter 1 sets out the work's conceptual framework and a discussion of methodology. Chapter 2 discusses poverty from the perspective of the poor, highlights concerns that are central to poor people's definitions of poverty, and includes a case study of Eastern Europe and the former Soviet Union (case study 2.1). Chapter 3 examines poor people's experiences with the state, and includes case studies of access to health care (case study 3.1) and education (case study 3.2). Chapter 4 addresses the nature and quality of poor people's interactions with civil society—NGOs, informal networks, associations, and kinship networks. The chapter ends with two case studies: one on financial services (case study 4.1), and the second on community capacity and village government in Indonesia (case study 4.2). Chapter 5 considers the household as a key social institution, and discusses gender relations within households and how these relations affect and are affected by larger institutions of society. It includes two case studies, on gender and education (case study 5.1) and gender and property rights (case study 5.2). Chapter 6 focuses on social fragmentation, and includes a discussion of social cohesion and social exclusion. It ends with two case studies, one on the police (case study 6.1), and the other on widows as an excluded group (case study 6.2). Chapter 7 concludes the analysis and proposes some policy recommendations. Appendixes provide details of the PPA studies included, the methodology, and supporting data.

Conceptual Framework: Examining Poverty Through Institutions

We distrust these institutions because they always deceive us.
—Poor men, Guatemala 1994a[1]

Institutions play a critical role in poor people's lives by either responding to or repressing their needs, concerns, and voices. The PPAs analyzed for this study contain assessments of the effectiveness, quality, and accessibility of a range of institutions encountered by the poor, including government agencies, legal and financial institutions, NGOs, community associations, and others. The reports also address institutionalized sociocultural norms, values, and expectations that the poor identify as obstacles or assets in achieving socioeconomic mobility. The most prominent of these institutions is the household, or family, in its various regional and cultural contexts.

By focusing on the quality of interactions and trust between poor women and men and institutions, the PPAs also expose the psychological realities of poverty. Stories of humiliation, intimidation, and fear of the very systems designed to provide assistance pervade the data, and reveal the importance of psychological factors in poor people's life choices and opportunities.

Defining Institutions

When the poor and rich compete for services, the rich will always get priority. —Kenya 1997

Institutions comprise a wide variety of formal and informal relationships that enhance societal productivity by making people's interactions and cooperation more predictable and effective. Some institutions, such as banks, have organizational form, while others have more diffuse patterns of norms and behavior about which there is social consensus. This social consensus includes the expectation of trust or dishonesty in particular social interactions—for example among kin or neighbors when borrowing sugar or looking after each other's children.

Institutions can be understood as complexes of norms and behaviors that persist over time by serving some socially valued purposes (Uphoff 1986). Institutions provide shared understanding of the cultural meaning of activities (Chambliss 1999). The more powerful members of a society have created many institutions in order to regularize and entrench mutually beneficial relationships. Institutions do not necessarily serve the needs and interests of all, but only of enough influential persons to ensure their preservation. Poor women and men are often peripheral to, or even excluded from, societal institutions. As a result, poor people have developed their own institutions, formal and informal, to ensure their basic security and survival.

Institutions include social relationships at the community level, as well as interactions found in development and social assistance organizations. They are found along a continuum, from the micro or local level to the macro or national and international levels. Institutions often have both formal and informal dimensions, with some part of their operation governed by explicit rules, roles, procedures, and precedents, while unwritten rules, roles, and procedures also shape behavior. An understanding of institutions is important in any project attempting to understand poverty, because institutions affect people's opportunities by establishing and maintaining their access to social, material, and natural resources. They also reinforce capacities for collective action and self-help, while their absence can contribute to immobilization and inertia.

In this book institutions that have organizational form are broadly divided into state and civil society institutions. State institutions include national, regional, and local governments; the judiciary; and the police. Civil society institutions include NGOs, trade unions, community-based organizations, social associations, kinship networks, and so forth.

While these two categories are useful for organizing the PPA data, in reality the boundaries between them are fluid and dynamic. For example, although the dimensions of an institution—such as the caste system—may be seen as primarily sociocultural and operating at the micro level, such an institution often has legal dimensions that formalize it and that link it to wider institutions of the state. Furthermore, when caste determines jobs, education, and associational membership at the national level, caste begins to operate at the macro level. Similarly, the place of religious institutions and political parties in the typology will vary from country to country. In countries with one official religion or one official political party the separation between these state and civil society institutions disappears.

The "institution typology" shown in figure 1.1 inevitably homogenizes a diverse set of institutions, and does not include institutions such as marriage or the household. Nevertheless, the typology is useful for exploring the basic questions of institutional interactions, and points to a host of issues examined in detail in later chapters.

State institutions are formal institutions that are state-affiliated or state-sponsored. They are vested with the power and authority of the state and act in its name, projecting the purposes and interests of those who operate state institutions into the domains of individuals or communities. For

Figure 1.1 Institution Typology

	State Institutions	Civil Society Institutions
Macro	National and state governments District administration Judiciary	NGOs Religious and ethnic associations Trade unions Caste associations
Micro	Local governments Local police Health clinics Schools Extension workers Traditional authority	Community-based organizations Neighborhoods Kinship networks Traditional leaders Sacred sites NGOs

most citizens these institutions are the most important points of direct contact with the ruling national power. The effectiveness of these formal institutions is closely connected to the capacity, legitimacy, and degree of public confidence in the state itself. Legal sanction and state control give these institutions authority and power that is not necessarily related to their actual performance. Ideally, a strong and legitimate state fosters institutions that work to equalize existing social and economic inequalities by extending assistance and opportunities to those citizens possessing fewer resources and less power.

Civil society comprises institutions that are not state-affiliated—they occupy the space between the household and the state (Hyden 1997). Rather than deriving their authority from legal recognition—although some do—civil society institutions draw primarily on the collective will of constituent groups. Both at the macro and micro levels, civil society institutions connect people in collective efforts and may keep states accountable. When states are weak or are considered by particular social groups to be illegitimate, civil society institutions may step in as people's primary points of access to social, material, and natural resources.

The growth of independent civic groups such as trade unions, professional associations, an independent press, NGOs, and community-based organizations can affect and be affected by the state and formal sector. States directly influence the power and freedom afforded to these institutions through legal and other means.

The household is outside this typology and is singled out for separate analysis as a critical institution in the lives of the poor. It embodies a complex set of sociocultural and formal legal structures that defines the choices available to its members. The household is particularly important in the construction of gender identities that determine men's and women's different socioeconomic options.

Poverty amid Plenty: Institutions and Access

> We poor people are invisible to others—just as blind people cannot see, they cannot see us. —Pakistan 1993

A fundamental question guiding our analysis is this: What bars the poor from gaining access to resources and opportunities? By listening to poor people and by tracing the processes that structure access and control of resources, we gain valuable insights into the role of institutional relationships in perpetuating conditions of poverty.

Despite an age of unprecedented global prosperity and the existence of a worldwide network of poverty-reduction institutions, poverty persists and is intensifying among certain groups and in certain regions around the world. Socioeconomic mobility is not a universal experience, but varies tremendously across social groups and individuals. Emphasizing aggregate prosperity diverts attention from the variability of access to resources experienced by different individuals and social groups. Almost two decades ago Amartya Sen (1981) addressed this issue in the context of persistent starvation in the midst of plentiful food stocks, noting that different social groups employ different means to gain access and control over food. The simple existence of sufficient food, he asserts, does not necessarily ensure access to that food. The means of securing access, which nearly always involves institutional interaction, are critical. Institutions limit or enhance poor people's rights to freedom, choice, and action (Sen 1984, 1999).

In short, an understanding of the relationship between institutions and those they serve is critical to an understanding of how different social groups and actors secure different capabilities and entitlements. Rights, opportunities, and power—all of which institutions can sanction or restrict—play an important role in the extent to which people can successfully use institutions for accessing resources. Figure 1.2 presents these relations in diagrammatic form. Poor households access opportunities and resources through the medium of civil society and state institutional mechanisms. A poor person's access to opportunities is influenced not only by his or her relationships with institutions outside the household, but also by relationships within the household. The household plays a significant role in

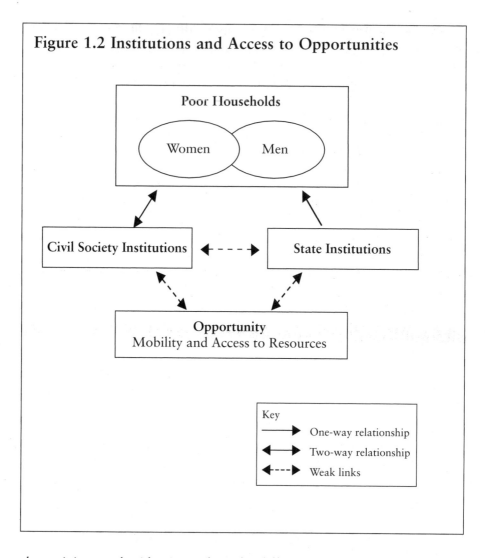

Figure 1.2 Institutions and Access to Opportunities

Poor Households

Women   Men

Civil Society Institutions   State Institutions

Opportunity
Mobility and Access to Resources

Key
⟶ One-way relationship
⟷ Two-way relationship
◀---▶ Weak links

determining gender identity and gender-differentiated access to resources and opportunities.

Consider a poor woman. She may have links with an informal network of women neighbors and friends on whom she relies for emotional support and exchanges of childcare, food, and small amounts of money. Through participation in these horizontal exchanges she both influences and is influenced by the nature of these relationships. She may or may not have contact with NGOs or with other women's groups and associations. She probably has little contact with most formal state institutions, which tend to be a male domain. If she applies to the state for a benefit to which she is entitled, she may or may not get the benefit; she has little influence on the state as an individual. If she and other women facing similar difficulties organize, however, with or without the help of NGOs, the state may be forced to negotiate and take corrective action. Their ability to organize may also change their negotiating power and access to markets.

Two other points are worth noting about a poor household's institutional relations. First, there is usually no direct connection between the informal networks or organizations of poor people and formal institutions. Typically they work quite independently of each other. This means that, unlike rich people's organizations, poor people's organizations have little access to, or influence on, the resources of the state. This is precisely why the work of many NGOs and, more recently, government agencies is to reach out to poor people's groups (for example, water-users' groups and farmers' groups) to build these bridging connections. The relations thus formed are often of unequal partners.

Second, the impact of institutional relationships can be positive or negative. In the former case, such as in joint forest management committees, poor people may gain access to scarce resources; in the latter case, they may suffer greater insecurity, oppression, and conflict—for example, in their interactions with the police. In more benign cases, state representatives may treat poor people differently from rich people. In any case, individual poor households have very little influence on the nature of the state or on provision of state services, whereas state institutions may have a major impact on individuals, especially when the police or justice systems are coercive or repressive.

To bring about change requires changing the strength and nature of the institutional connections among the poor, civil society, and the state. Poor women's institutional relationships are different from those of poor men, and these differences have implications for intervention strategies. Poor people are rarely organized across communities or connected to rich people's organizations or to the resources of the state. The limited resources circulating within their networks and their lack of organization limit poor people's opportunities and access to resources. To achieve greater equity and to empower the poor, institutions of the state and institutions of civil society must become accountable to the poor.

Approaches to Poverty Assessment

At last those above will hear us. Before now, no one ever asked us what we think. —Poor men, Guatemala 1994a

Understanding how poverty occurs, why it persists, and how it may be alleviated is essential if we are to devise effective, appropriate strategies for social and economic development. A variety of different data collection instruments are necessary to understand the cultural, social, economic, political, and institutional realities that determine the opportunities and barriers poor people face in their efforts to move out of poverty.

Since the second half of the 1980s multitopic household surveys have been the key tool for measuring and analyzing poverty. Unlike single-topic surveys (such as employment, income, and expenditure surveys), multi topic household surveys aim to gather information on a wide array of topics intimately linked with household welfare. The most well-known of these surveys, the Living Standards Measurement Surveys (LSMS), were piloted in Côte d'Ivoire and Peru in 1985 and have since been implemented in dozens of countries. Such surveys provide crucial information on living conditions: measures of income, expenditure, health, education, employment, agriculture, access to services, and ownership of assets such as land and so on. Household surveys have been the primary data collection tool in poverty assessments.

However, large-scale surveys can only provide an incomplete picture of poverty since they use—in almost all instances—closed-ended questions. Poverty—its meaning and depth, its manifestations and causes—also depends on factors that cannot be easily captured by such questions. Moreover, many important elements may be missed simply because they are not known to researchers. Such factors can be cultural (who is identified as head of a household, who has the power to allocate resources), social (the extent of domestic violence or informal exchange networks), or political (the extent of corruption and crime). They can also be institutional (documentation requirements, the extent of rudeness by service providers, humiliation experienced by the poor making claims, hidden costs incurred) or environmental constraints (natural disasters, seasonality, and environmental degradation or hazards) or multi-faceted (such as insecurity). Obviously, once an issue is known, surveys can be designed to investigate the prevalence of a problem in a population.

Other forms of data collection are also needed to explore location-specific social, political, and institutional criteria, subjective elements of poor people's experiences of poverty, and the ways in which individuals cope or their highly diversified sources of security and livelihoods (Baulch 1996a, Chambers 1997). Sen (1981, 1999) has frequently argued that absolute poverty includes what Adam Smith called "the ability to go about without shame," but the commodities required to maintain social respectability vary from place to place, and national poverty data overlook them.[2]

Unless very carefully designed, household survey data also obscure gender aspects of poverty, such as women's nonwage-based economic contributions to the household (Tripp 1992); the impact of economic restructuring on the distribution and intensity of women's work (Floro 1995); and the different ways in which men and women respond to social safety nets (Jackson 1996).

Development practitioners and policymakers increasingly acknowledge that a more complete understanding of poverty requires the inclusion of social factors and perspectives of the poor. Sociological and participatory approaches have been proved effective in capturing the multidimensional and culturally contingent aspects of poverty (Booth et al. 1998; Carvalho and White 1997; Patton 1990). The more recent World Bank Poverty Assessments are beginning to include qualitative and participatory methods to complement information from household surveys.

What Is a Participatory Poverty Assessment?

In the early 1990s the World Bank began to conduct Poverty Assessments routinely in order to identify the main poverty problems within a country, and to link the policy agenda to issues of poverty. These Poverty Assessments included quantitative data such as poverty lines, social and demographic characteristics of the poor, and their economic profiles (sources of income, asset ownership, consumption patterns, and access to services).[3] In order to complement these statistical data with an assessment of poverty by its primary stakeholders—poor people themselves—the World Bank also developed the Participatory Poverty Assessment, or PPA.[4]

A PPA is an iterative, participatory research process that seeks to understand poverty from the perspective of a range of stakeholders, and to involve them directly in planning follow-up action. The most important stakeholders involved in the research process are poor men and poor women. PPAs also include decisionmakers from all levels of government, civil society, and the local elite, thereby uncovering different interests and perspectives and increasing local capacity and commitment to follow-up action. PPAs seek to understand poverty in its local social, institutional, and political context. Since PPAs address national policy, microlevel data are collected from a large number of communities in order to discern patterns across social groups and geographic areas, and across location and social group specificities.[5]

These Participatory Poverty Assessments are a recent but growing phenomenon.[6] In 1994 only one-fifth of the Bank's country-level Poverty Assessment reports incorporated PPA material. In 1995 one-third included PPAs, while between 1996 and 1998 PPAs were included in fully half of all Bank Poverty Assessments (Robb 1999). It is this PPA component of the overall Poverty Assessments that we have analyzed.

The methodologies used in the PPAs vary. Depending on the number of field researchers, fieldwork ranged from 10 days to eight months in the field (the majority were two to four months); sample sizes ranged from 10 to 100 communities; and cost ranged from \$4,000 to \$150,000 per PPA (Robb 1999). They were most often conducted by an academic institution or an NGO, in collaboration with the country's government and the World Bank.

Two underlying principles make the participatory approach different from other research approaches. First, the research methodology engages the respondents actively in the research process through the use of open-ended and participatory methods. Second, participatory research assumes that the research process will empower participants and lead to follow-up action. This puts special ethical demands on researchers who use participatory methods for policy research.

Participatory approaches, though difficult to quantify, provide a valuable insight into the multiple meanings, dimensions, and experiences of poverty (Wratten 1995). PPAs capture information that standard Poverty Assessments are likely to miss for two reasons. First, unlike survey research, the sets of questions used in PPAs are not predetermined. Rather, open-ended methods such as unstructured interviews, discussion groups, and a variety of participatory visual methods are more commonly used.[7] This allows for the emergence of issues and dimensions of poverty that are important to the community but not necessarily known to the researchers. Second, PPAs take into account power asymmetries both within the household and within communities. Whereas conventional household surveys focus on the household as the unit of analysis, PPAs approach men and women as dissimilar social groups that have distinct interests and experiences. Thus PPAs have the potential to illuminate power dynamics between men and women, and between the elite and the poor. PPAs do not replace traditional household surveys and macroeconomic analyses, but instead provide important complementary information.

Methodology of the Study

This report reflects the first attempt to synthesize the findings from a broad set of PPA studies through systematic content analysis of the experiences, priorities, and reflections of poor women, men, and children.

Issues Addressed

Some of the basic questions we address include:

1. **How do the poor understand and define poverty?**

How do poor men and women experience poverty? How do poor people define poverty according to their own experiences? How do these definitions differ across lines of gender, class, ethnicity, and region? What policy implications may be drawn from this information?

2. **What are the roles of formal and informal institutions in the lives of the poor?**

How do poor people assess the effectiveness, quality, and accessibility of formal and informal institutions? What roles do institutions—including governmental agencies, legal and financial institutions, social and community organizations, and NGOs—play in the lives of the poor? What are the psychological dimensions of people's interactions with institutions?

3. **How do gender relations within the household affect how poverty is experienced?**

Does the structure of gender relations within the household shift as members respond to changing social and economic conditions? What can we learn about gender relations from the studies? What are the implications for poverty reduction strategies?

4. **What is the relationship between poverty and social fragmentation?**

How has broad political and economic restructuring affected the lives of the poor and society at large? How have social cohesion and social exclusion been affected? How are people coping and surviving?

The Data Set

We began with a broad set of questions, and throughout our research we iteratively refined our questions based on the emerging data. We sought to describe and explain poverty through the voices of the poor. Eighty-one reports were selected for analysis, representing data collected in 50 countries around the world. Almost all were conducted or commissioned by the World Bank since 1993. They were selected from over 300 reports submitted in response to a call for poverty-focused studies that incorporate social analyses and participatory methods.[8] Selection was based on the degree to which the reports used open-ended methods, and on the degree to which they incorporated PPA data and other qualitative assessments into their overall analysis. Not all the reports were called PPAs. Reports with the richest and densest social and qualitative information were selected for the initial analysis. Only a few of the reports successfully combined social analysis, institutional analysis, and participatory methods. For a listing of countries and regional distribution, see appendix 1, and for a listing of PPA reports and authors see appendix 2.

Sampling techniques ranged from nationally representative samples to purposive sampling based primarily on poverty, agro-ecological diversity, and rural and urban diversity. Sample sizes varied from less than one hundred to 5,000 people. Some studies focused only on the poor while others included the nonpoor. Data collection methods included a range of participatory and social analysis tools, household interviews, observation, key informant interviews, as well as household surveys. A summary description of the sample selection procedures and methodology for each report is found in appendix 3.

Systematic Content Analysis

Recurrent themes were uncovered in the reports by a process of systematic content analysis. In its broadest sense, content analysis can be understood as "any methodical measurement applied to text (or other symbolic material) for social scientific purposes" (Shapiro and Markoff 1977:14). Different researchers have emphasized various aspects of content analysis, from its capacity to generate quantitative descriptions by analyzing word counts (Berelson 1954; Silverman 1993), to its ability to help researchers draw inferences from a text by breaking that text down into discrete units of manageable data that can then be meaningfully reorganized (Stone et al. 1966; Weber 1990). Still others emphasize how content analysis is appropriate for inductive approaches to data analysis (Strauss 1987).

Because the reports analyzed for this book vary by author, research teams, time frames, regions, and methods, we were less concerned with generating quantified counts of words or themes than with identifying and locating—through a systematized reading and coding of the reports—recurrent themes connected to the central questions we posed. Furthermore, we were interested in discovering what the patterns of relationships might reveal, especially in terms of changing relations between men and women, and between individuals and institutions. We used an inductive and iterative research process in which our categories of analysis were repeatedly refined by what we found emerging from the data.

The sheer volume of material necessitated use of qualitative data analysis software. Hard copies of the original report documents were scanned to create text files, and Non-numerical Unstructured Data Indexing Searching and Theorizing (QSR NUD*IST), a qualitative data analysis software program, was used to code and analyze the contents of the PPA reports. The index tree, which is the data coding system in QSR NUD*IST, is based on a primary coding index composed of a series of researcher-determined categories, termed "nodes," that are hierarchically organized within the program. In addition to the main index tree, a system of free nodes was used to allow coders to capture points of data that emerged as significant, but that were not included in the original conceptualization of the index tree. This coding system identifies individual or grouped units of text (in this case, paragraphs) from the data set that exhibit characteristics relevant to the investigation of specific research questions.[9] A description of the coding process, nodes contained in the index tree, and examples of outputs on institutional nodes appear in appendixes 4, 5, and 6.

The outcome of this analysis was identification of the recurrent themes described in the remainder of this book. The software did not produce the themes in a mechanical fashion. Human analysis was required at many stages: in the identification of text units to input; in the coding of the units; in the intersection searches and the analysis of what those searches revealed about poor communities; and, finally, in the judgement of what can be said to have emerged from the data, and its implications for policy. Human analysis is the safeguard for the entire process. Many minds worked on the different stages of analysis—data coding, data analysis, the location of examples, and the identification of major themes. The act of questioning whether or not the results made sense, and returning to the data in case of uncertainty (common to both quantitative and qualitative research), guided these processes and averted errors that would have been made by mechanical analysis.

Limitations of the Study

Well-known limitations apply to our research. First, the insights available are limited by the quality of the documents under consideration. The extent to which PPA documents accurately aggregated and reported discussions in the field, and indeed the quality of the information that was generated by the interviews and participatory exercises, directly affect the robustness of this review's conclusions. Every attempt was made to select documents that had rich qualitative data, but the findings remain dependent on data.

Second, the studies were undertaken for different purposes. Data sources varied in size, representativeness, and composition of respondents— hence the study results are not representative at the national level. We make no attempt to count numbers. It is possible that we are overgeneralizing: that is a subject for further research. The 23-country comparative study undertaken as part of the *Consultations with the Poor* project will provide additional evidence.

Third, human error can occur during analysis. The accuracy of data codes depends on the perceptiveness of the coder, and the accuracy of the string and intersection searches depends on the person summarizing them. Accuracy was checked by looking for data on a particular issue in nonrelated string searches and by going back to the original document to ensure that the issue had been examined exhaustively.

Finally, there remains in both quantitative and qualitative work the possibility of human bias. While the researcher who becomes conscious of it can reduce this bias, its absence can never be proven. This risk was reduced by researchers running independent string searches, holding frequent and mutually challenging group meetings, and checking emerging patterns with number counts, as well as by returning to the original documents.

There are other limitations that relate to the nature of fieldwork, understanding what is unspoken, the dangers of generalization, and the problems of raised expectations and ethics.

Encounters in the field

> *We went to Aga Sadek Sweepers Colony in Dhaka and were told that we needed to get the permission of the leaders of the youth club. The next day we returned but could not find our guides. One of us started a group of young men on sketch mapping and the other talked to children about their problems. The youths were quite unwilling to draw a sketch map because one who came from Khulna recalled a case when they were asked to draw a map of their area and two weeks later the government came and evicted the whole area. They eventually agreed when we explained that exact measurements were not needed and only the places of importance like schools, club, and temple should be included. We even suggested that they could keep the original and we would make a copy in our notebooks. As the children were listing their problems, we were rudely interrupted by a Mr. Munna. He said that lots of people came and talked and promised things but never came back. We explained that we were not promising anything. The five or six people with Mr. Munna started to get aggressive. We went to the youth club for help, but they had all sneaked away. We asked the group if we could take the sketch map with us, but they wanted to keep it.* —Field notes, Neela Mukherjee, Bangladesh 1996

> *We didn't trust the PPA process. Now we understand it, accept it and it has become ours.* —Government official, at end of a two-year PPA process, Kenya 1996

Most of the studies mention the anthropological, sociological, and community development codes of conduct and rules that were followed to ensure quality data. These codes of conduct and rules include establishing contacts with communities prior to entry by calling on chiefs, local authorities, or local leaders, and by obtaining permission or going through other credible contacts. Some reports discuss the ways used to win the support of local leaders and yet preclude them from participating in group discussions that they would automatically dominate. To avoid this problem some researchers approached communities in teams with supervisors talking to the village leaders and other team members conducting group discussions. Many studies mention holding separate group discussions with men and women to ensure that women's voices were heard. Many teams included female fieldworkers to ensure that conversations could be held with women. All teams included researchers who spoke the local languages.

No amount of field training and preparation can ensure that fieldwork is problem-free. The more experienced and well-trained the researchers, the more likely it is that they either resolve or clearly identify problems when they arise, so that findings are used with caution. "In some areas researchers encountered some individual reluctance to participate in interviews which was variably attributed to shyness, distrust, fear and, in the case of women, the absence of the husband to give permission" (Guatemala 1994b).

The most direct reporting of the problems that were experienced was found in the field notes of Neela Mukherjee, who led the Bangladesh study (1996). The problems also point to the danger of doing large sample PPAs in a rush.

> It was 2:30 in the afternoon. We were approaching Chibatoli in Hathazari, Chittagong. We asked a villager from the para where we had been working in the morning to introduce us to somebody from the area. This villager accompanied us and together we asked the women to come to talk with us. A few came but many were reluctant because they saw Rukan (my male colleague). They did not want to meet this "outside man." Rukan left and went to talk to some of the village men.
>
> The women, my female colleague (Nazmun), and I started to talk about seasonality and related issues. Then two men who work overseas came and tried to disturb the session. Some women ran away to hide. I took these two men aside and talked to them in order to prevent them from disturbing the women who then were able to continue their analyses with Nazmun.
>
> Rukan was also challenged by other men of the village. They asked him what his intentions were, whose permission we had taken to conduct this work, and why we had not taken the permission of the chairman and members. He was also asked to produce letters of introduction that we did not have. Having completed the seasonality work with the women, we left as there was a high level of suspicion all around.

The process of participation was sometimes hindered due to the presence of dominant men. Women reacted to them with a mixture of fear and respect. Sometimes their influence and effect on the process was so great that we were forced to abandon sessions and move to another location. The nonpoor often made fun of the poor people. For example they jeered, "Write your name and get houses, land, and clothes." —Field notes, Bangladesh 1996

Understanding the unspoken

Women often felt reluctant to talk about some issues such as violence against women inside and outside the home and family planning, except in smaller, more intimate groups. —Bangladesh 1996

Wife-beating is a family problem not to be discussed publicly. —Tanzania 1997

The encounters between PPA researchers and their research subjects are themselves structured by asymmetrical power relations (Pottier 1997; Kauffman 1997). Neither participant in the research dialogue is without expectations or hopes for what may result. It is not surprising that many topics that demand a degree of trust are underreported, particularly within a context in which trust in the state and its affiliates is low. Poor people interviewed for a rapid participatory appraisal may choose not to reveal sensitive information about domestic violence, local government corruption, police intimidation, sexual abuse, and so on without credible guarantees that researchers will not use this information against them. While there is seldom any information within the reports describing instances in which information was withheld from researchers, the examples that do exist are telling.

The problem for our enterprise that seeks to understand the experiences of poverty through the voices of the poor is clear: it is hard to report what the poor don't say. The less time spent in communities, the less likely it is that tacit issues are noticed. Many of the PPAs acknowledge these limitations. Researchers in Mexico, for instance, feel that issues of institutional corruption are underreported, and they recommend future research in this area (Mexico 1995). In Jamaica researchers suspect that an underreporting of sexual abuse and crime is due to the "severe constraints [that] exist for women who want to talk openly about their experiences of rape" (Jamaica 1997). The trust required for subjects to be broached openly cannot be built in a matter of days.

There is, nonetheless, some information available on sensitive topics. The skill and sensitivity of PPA researchers in breaching silences sets the groundwork for important lines of future inquiry. If we take the silence in the data concerning these experiences at face value, we run the risk of presenting a distorted picture of poverty.

Every generalization has an exception

A study of this nature faces the intractable problem of partial generalizations. The PPAs show us the complexity and the heterogeneity of the experiences of poverty. By definition, however, generalizations are not truisms. At the same time, systematic analysis of the PPAs draws out commonalities that cut across age, culture, and continent. This book focuses on such shared themes, especially insofar as they have policy implications.

How does a book communicate recurrent themes in a nuanced way? It would be cumbersome to preface every generalization with the phrase, "In most but not every case ..." Neither the sampling frame nor our analysis of the PPAs allows us to say, "For 80 percent of the poor ..." Instead we have written the generalizations that emerge, without constant qualification. We ask the reader to bear in mind that *none of the generalizations apply to every location or every poor person.* They describe tendencies, but there are exceptions to every rule.

Similarly, some of the poor who contribute to the PPAs are verbally expressive. They use wonderful turns of phrase, and describe their world with freshness and simplicity. We have quoted these voices to illustrate how an individual, or a group, describes and experiences a general theme. Which has greater communicative power—the generalization, "It is widely accepted that female-headed households are more likely to be poor than male-headed households" (Folbre 1991:89–90)? Or the words of a poor Kenyan woman (1997): "I don't have any house or any land or anything because I parted company with my husband and he does not want us"?

We have used quotations to illustrate general trends. The quotations do not prove the trends—no one person's experience could, and we do not expect one quotation to convince the reader of a trend. Having identified the trends by systematic content analysis, we went back to the PPAs and drew out quotations that illustrate these trends and bring them alive. The voices of the poor communicate their experiences, and keep drawing the reader's attention back to their lives.

One final word on generalizations: It may be that the reader will read a phrase such as "NGO staff are poor listeners," and will believe that this is simply wrong. It does not ring true to his or her experience. The reader can remember concrete instances where NGO staff members were very receptive and sensitive people. The reader has read about other examples, or heard of them from friends. It is very likely that, at some time or other, every reader will have that experience regarding a so-called general finding of this report.

The largest single value of this PPA review may occur, precisely, in such surprises. They point out that our own experiences may be more unusual or uncommon than we had assumed. They make us listen. They raise questions for further research. Most importantly, they make us turn again and again to the poor; they make us analyze poverty from their perspective.

Raised expectations and ethics

> *Something will happen, otherwise why have you come?* —Slum dweller, Bangladesh 1995

> *You should say what you think and the truth. This fieldwork group does not intend to build a bridge or dam for us as others did. But they can reflect the difficulties that you face in your life as well as your wishes to leaders, to help us in the long run.* —Deputy Chief of village 13, Son Ham-Huong Son, Vietnam 1999a

Participatory researchers are well aware of their responsibilities not to raise false expectations. They try to do participatory research only when there are plans for follow-up action, or to conduct participatory research in a way that maximizes the probability of follow-up. Researchers in the South African PPA report write:

> *Concerns regarding the use of PRA [Participatory Rural Appraisal] methodology were raised at the preparatory workshop in February 1995. These related mainly to the use of the methods for the purpose of extractive research for policy analysis with no accompanying participatory process. In order to avoid this abuse of communities as research objects, a criterion used in selection of the participatory organizations was that the research be part of ongoing work, and that the organization and communities undertaking the research were in a position to use the results to further local development.* —South Africa 1998

To overcome this ethical issue, many PPAs work with local partners who have on-the-ground development programs. Sometimes this is just not possible. If researchers still decide to go ahead, it is their ethical responsibility to make clear to communities that they have come empty-handed, rather than fear that if they are honest they will not get access to a community. Most researchers report that, once participants realize that the researchers have indeed come empty-handed, the discussions get beyond a "We are all poor" attitude that poor communities sometimes adopt for outsiders, in the hope of getting assistance. It is precisely to get over these initial hurdles that researchers spend several days in communities and use a variety of methods to triangulate information from different sources.

As communities get more and more saturated with researchers who are unable to commit to follow-up action, community groups are beginning to take a stand. Researchers in Guatemala had a range of experiences:

> *A further limiting factor to work in marginal urban areas was the prohibition by local authorities to permit research team entry into a settlement, in the absence of concrete study results such as a future project or payments to informants. In contrast, the region 1 team reported their presence generated such interest and enthusiasm that people stood in line to be interviewed, and they were occupied late into the night talking to communities. In fact, one researcher was threatened at gunpoint by an inebriated man if he did not agree to interview him. The reason stated for the high interest in the study on the part of the Ladino groups was the relative lack of attention to this region where the presence of both government agencies and nongovernmental organizations is severely attenuated.*
> —Guatemala 1997b

In many countries, including Guatemala, Kenya, Tanzania, and Vietnam, poor people agreed to spend time with researchers in the hope that their voices would be carried to those who have the power to affect decisions that affect poor people's lives. In Guatemala poor people express the hope that "At last those above will hear us," and say that "No one ever asks us what we think (before now) and now the president will hear what we say" (Guatemala 1997b).

Some Final Thoughts on Method

We contend that participatory methods can provide unique insights into the complexity, diversity, and dynamics of poverty as a social as well as an economic phenomenon. Furthermore, information from qualitative assessments can give policymakers a deeper, richer, and ultimately better understanding of economic problems, resulting in more effective poverty alleviation strategies.

Box 1.1 Use of Uganda PPA

The Uganda PPA process is led by the Uganda government with multiple civil society partners. Currently, participatory poverty assessment principles are being internalized at three levels: (1) central government, the Ministry of Finance, Planning, and Economic Development (MFPED), and the Ministry of Local Government; (2) local governments, particularly the nine partner districts where the study was conducted; and (3) research institutions, such as the Economic Policy Research Centre at Makerere University. Local ownership of the PPA process and strategic dissemination of findings have led to the following changes.

There is an awareness among politicians and civil servants of the concerns of the poor that has been raised through dialogues, briefing documents, public presentations, regional workshops, and the media.

PPA findings are included in influential government documents, such as the annual Background to the Budget 1999–2000, and the bi-annual Poverty Status Report. The Plan for Modernization of Agriculture now includes the poor as primary producers, focusing interventions on their constraints and priorities for reducing poverty.

The mid-term expenditure framework process used the PPA findings for reviewing public investment programs and sector expenditures. Government allocated additional resources to clean water resources in response to poor people's priorities.

Flexibility in the utilization of conditional and equalization grants by districts has been introduced to respond to the location of specific needs identified in the PPA. Grant utilization procedures have been modified accordingly.

The Poverty Action Fund is reoriented to monitor the effective utilization of conditional grants and the impact on the poor. Poverty indicators identified by poor people have been included in recent national household surveys.

Source: Uganda 1999.

One of the unique characteristics of this research is the breadth of data it encompasses as it draws out cultural, social, political, and historical specificity that make each case unique. The policy challenge that results is to formulate and implement poverty alleviation measures that succeed because they fit the detailed requirements of each case. Therefore, while we may ask, "What are the trends that unify the experiences of the poor across regions?" we must never lose sight of the question these data are truly suited to help answer. That question is, "What is it about how poverty and social inequality are expressed in a given time, place, and circumstance that must be reflected in policy measures?"

Increasing numbers of Participatory Poverty Assessments are being undertaken by governments, with the World Bank and other international agencies. While the methodology can be refined, further studies can only be justified if their findings are used to inform poverty reduction strategies that make a difference in poor people's lives. The three-year Uganda PPA process is one example of how the approach can be used to respond to poor people's priorities and realities (see box 1.1).

Notes

1. To increase readability, when we use material from the PPAs that make up our database we reference only the country and year of the report. A complete list of the authors of the reports appears in appendix 2. We are grateful to the researchers whose work forms our core material and to many colleagues who sent us documents. We are particularly grateful to Nora Dudwick, who made her studies on Eastern Europe and the former Soviet Union available to us.

2. There has been, and remains, an epistemological disagreement between those who define poverty as something subjective, and those who define poverty as objective and as absolute (see Sen 1983, 1985, 1992). In the former case, the poor are those who consider themselves to be poor (a problematic position in the case of the person who describes himself as poor because he has a Cadillac but his neighbor has a BMW—but for defenders see Townsend 1971). There is also a long history of scholars attempting to measure poverty as a multidimensional phenomenon (see Alkire 1999).

3. For an evaluation of Poverty Assessments see World Bank 1997a.

4. The term Participatory Poverty Assessment was coined by Lawrence Salmen at the World Bank in December 1992 in a short paper entitled, "Participatory Poverty Assessment: Applying Beneficiary Assessment Techniques to Poverty Policy Issues." This paper was then expanded into "Participatory Poverty

Assessment: Incorporating Poor People's Perspectives into Poverty Assessment Work" (April 13, 1993), and eventually published in 1995 (Salmen 1995). The earliest PPAs in the World Bank were designed and managed by a small group of social scientists. Larry Salmen worked in Madagascar and Cameroon; Maurizia Tova worked in Burkina Faso (and introduced visual methods); Andy Norton worked in Zambia and Ghana (and introduced PRA methods); and Deepa Narayan worked in Kenya and Tanzania (and combined SARAR, PRA methods, and consumption expenditure surveys on statistically representative national samples). Much of this early work was made possible by bilateral financing, particularly from the British and Dutch governments. Under the leadership of Rosalyn Eyben, DFID, the United Kingdom has played a particularly important role in supporting PPA work in the World Bank. For a discussion of methodological issues from PPAs, see Holland and Blackburn 1998.

5. "The premise [of PPAs] is that involving the poor in the process will contribute to ensuring that the strategies identified for poverty reduction will reflect their concerns, including the priorities and obstacles to progress as seen by the poor themselves" (Norton and Stephens 1995:1).

6. There is a long history of social analysis in the World Bank. As early as 1979 a Bank publication detailed the contribution that social analysis could make to each stage of the project cycle, and by 1980 the Bank had hosted a conference, "Putting People First," that discussed, among other things, the value, mechanisms, and costs of participatory approaches (Cernea 1979, 1985). By 1984 the Bank's Operational Manual Statement 2.20, "Project Appraisal" required that project preparation and appraisal take into account these social dimensions. Lawrence Salmen focused on listening as a tool to improve project design and evaluation in *Listen to the People* (Salmen 1987) and *Toward a Listening Bank* (Salmen 1998). In 1995, under the leadership of Gloria Davis, Social Assessment Guidelines were issued that bring together social analysis and participatory approaches within one framework. Pioneering work has been undertaken in all the regions led by teams of social scientists within countries and the World Bank (see Cernea 1994; Cernea and Kudat 1997).

7. For toolkits on participatory methods, see Narayan and Srinivasan 1994; Rietbergen-McCracken and Narayan 1998; and World Bank 1996b. For an extensive collection of materials on participatory methods at the Institute of Development Studies, Sussex, U.K., search http://www.ids.ac.uk/pra.

8. Several more participatory poverty studies were drawn to the authors' attention during the review of the final draft of this book, too late for inclusion.

9. Text units most often comprised single or multiple paragraphs, but sometimes consisted of only one or two sentences, depending on the formatting of the text appearing in the original report. Coding was very often assigned to several adjacent text units at once. The entire set of text units analyzed in this project totaled slightly over 29,000.

Chapter 2

Definitions of Poverty

Don't ask me what poverty is because you have met it outside my house. Look at the house and count the number of holes. Look at my utensils and the clothes that I am wearing. Look at everything and write what you see. What you see is poverty.

—A poor man, Kenya 1997

Poverty is humiliation, the sense of being dependent, and of being forced to accept rudeness, insults, and indifference when we seek help.

—Latvia 1998

This chapter explores poor people's definitions of poverty as documented in the PPAs. We use an inductive approach to uncover dimensions of poverty that are important to poor people, and to capture their characterizations of poverty. This approach requires us to set aside our prejudices and assumptions about what is important for the poor, about the importance of particular sectors in reducing poverty, about regional or gender differences, and about the best conceptual framework for understanding poverty. As a result, the organization of this chapter and the concepts we use are determined by what emerges from our analysis of definitions of poverty.

There are six main findings:

▸ Many factors converge to make poverty an **interlocking multidimensional** phenomenon.

▸ Poverty is routinely defined as the lack of what is necessary for **material well-being**—especially food, but also housing, land, and other assets. In other words, poverty is the lack of multiple resources that leads to hunger and physical deprivation.

▸ Poor people's definitions reveal important **psychological aspects** of poverty. Poor people are acutely aware of their lack of voice, power, and independence that subjects them to exploitation. Their poverty leaves them vulnerable to rudeness, humiliation, and inhumane treatment by both private and public agents of the state from whom they seek help. Poor people also speak about the pain brought about by their unavoidable violation of social norms and their inability to maintain cultural identity through participation in traditions, festivals, and rituals. Their inability to fully participate in community life leads to a breakdown of social relations.

▸ The absence of **basic infrastructure**—particularly roads (in rural areas), transport, and water—emerges as a critical concern. In the countries of Eastern Europe and the former Soviet Union lack of affordable electrical power is a major concern in the severe winters.

▸ **Illness** is often dreaded, because of the experience that it plunges families into destitution, because of the lack of health care, the costs of available health care, and the loss of livelihood due to illness. While literacy is viewed as important, **schooling** receives mixed reviews, occasionally highly valued, but often notably irrelevant in the lives of the poor.

▸ Poor people focus on **assets** rather than on income, and link their lack of physical, human, social, and environmental assets to their vulnerability and exposure to risk.

The chapter first discusses the multidimensional nature of poverty, material well-being, and psychological well-being. It then focuses on the role of infrastructure and the assets of the poor. The discussion of assets includes physical, human, social, and environmental assets. The chapter concludes with a case study on the large and newly impoverished population in Eastern Europe and the former Soviet Union (case study 2.1).

Poverty Is Multidimensional

The evidence suggests that poverty is a multidimensional social phenomenon.[1] Definitions of poverty and its causes vary by gender, age, culture, and other social and economic contexts. For example, in both rural and urban Ghana men associate poverty with a lack of material assets, whereas for women poverty is defined as food insecurity. Generational differences emerge as well. Younger men in Ghana consider the ability to generate an income as the most important asset, whereas older men cite as most important the status connected to a traditional agricultural lifestyle (Ghana 1995a).

A person's status and location affect perceived causes of poverty. In Madagascar, for example, farmers link poverty to drought, the urban poor link poverty to rising prices and fewer employment opportunities, and the rich link poverty to "deterioration in domestic and international terms of trade, neglect of Malagasy traditions and norms, lack of motivation among certain classes and groups of people, price liberalization and devaluation, lack of education, and absence of governance" (Madagascar 1996).

Poverty never results from the lack of one thing, but from many interlocking factors that cluster in poor people's experiences and definitions of poverty. In the Philippines, in the Mindanao region, women say, "We boil bananas for our children if food is not available. In some cases, when the department of agriculture distributes corn seeds, we cook these seeds instead of planting them" (Philippines 1999). Families borrow money to acquire these seeds, and the cycle of poverty continues, because they are unable to pay off these loans.

In Armenia seasonal changes, lack of savings, and immediate cash needs interact to keep farmers poor:

> To cope, farmers barter or sell crops early in the summer or fall when the prices are low. For example, two kilograms of honey were bartered for a sweater for a young child; and 10 kilograms of cheese were bartered for a pair of shoes. One father explains, "Actually we have no income from August to September. As a result we need to barter goods and use them as money. Last year I harvested my potatoes in mid-August and took them to Khapan to sell. I bought some necessary things for

the children to go to school in September. So we suffered finan-
cially as the potatoes would have brought a better profit had
we sold them later ... We usually barter potatoes and wheat for
coats. But we don't have anything for bartering right now."
—Armenia 1996

In Guatemala a Cackchiquel Indian who works as a hired agricultural laborer says, "During the last eight years we have faced a greater state
of poverty than before in that we can't buy much to eat and we suffer when
it rains because there's no work and everything is very expensive. ... Here
in the community we don't have much hope to live better with what we
earn. There are many needs, but the principal one is food, which is not sufficient, and we don't have a place to live or the means to pay rent"
(Guatemala 1994b).

These interlocking dimensions of poverty come out clearly in the
criteria the poor use to differentiate between categories of rich, average,
and poor, as well in discussions of vulnerability. (See box 2.1 for indicators
of wealth and poverty in Vietnam.)

Poor people give rich and nuanced descriptions of poverty. Some of
their categories will sound familiar to poverty analysts, in fact. In
Swaziland groups distinguish between the "temporarily poor" and the
"new poor." The temporarily poor are defined as "those who could feed
themselves before the drought but are now hungry—previously prosperous
cotton farmers who are now struggling like us," and the new poor as
"previously rich people who have lost their cattle through cattle rustling,
widows whose husbands had left them cattle but who now have nothing to
sell to educate their children" (Swaziland 1997).

There are important differences, as well. The degree of dependency
emerges as an important classification criterion. In Ghana, for example,
poor people not only distinguish between the rich and the poor, but also
between different categories of poor, based on assets and degree of dependency. The rich are described as those who "feed their children properly;
they live in good houses, which they will pass on to their dependents; and
they are able to assist others." At the other extreme are the chronically
hungry, variously described as the extremely poor, the perennially needy,
and the pathetic (Ghana 1995a).

The very poor are divided into two broad groups. The first is "God's
poor," a group that includes factors for which there is no obvious remedy—
disability, age, widowhood, and childlessness. The second group is the "resourceless poor," including immigrant widowers and other landless poor.
In between the two extremes of rich and very poor are the "deprived but
hard-working, the not-so-poor, or not hand-to-mouth category."

Box 2.1 Summary of Household Wealth Indicators as Described by the Poor in Vietnam

Relatively Well-Off Households

▸ Possess solid and stable houses that are usually renovated every 15 years

▸ Have transportation, either a motorbike or a bicycle, or both

▸ Own a television or a radio, or both

▸ Can send their children to school

▸ Never lack money, even after the harvest has been eaten or sold

▸ Are able to save money

▸ Have a garden with useful plants and trees

Average Households

▸ Have a stable house that usually does not need renovating for 10 years

▸ Own a television or a radio, or both

▸ Have enough food all year

▸ Can send their children to school

▸ Have a well, or easy access to water

Poor Households

▸ Live in unstable houses, often made with mud

▸ Have no television or radio

▸ Are not able to save money

▸ May have children who cannot go to school, or who have to leave school prematurely

▸ Usually have enough food until the next harvest, although sometimes lack food for one to two months per year

▸ Are unable to utilize surrounding natural resources to their benefit

Very Poor Households

▸ Live in very unstable houses that often need to be rebuilt every two to three years

▸ Have no wells or easy access to fresh water

Source: Vietnam 1999a.

In Uganda women's groups distinguish between three categories of poor people: the poor, the poorest, and the fully dependent. The poor are described primarily as laborers who work on other people's land or on boats in exchange for food or cash, but who live in a hut on their own tiny patch of land. The poorest have no housing, but work for food and live on the land of the rich. The fully dependent include single mothers, disabled persons, and the elderly who have nothing and cannot work, and so depend entirely on state services or assistance from others (Uganda 1998).

Material Well-Being

Your hunger is never satiated, your thirst is never quenched; you can never sleep until you are no longer tired. —Senegal 1995

It's the cost of living, low salaries, and lack of jobs. And it's also not having medicine, food, and clothes. —Brazil 1995

When I leave for school in the mornings I don't have any breakfast. At noon there is no lunch, in the evening I get a little supper, and that is not enough. So when I see another child eating, I watch him, and if he doesn't give me something I think I'm going to die of hunger. —A 10-year-old child, Gabon 1997

Food Security

Often she has to decide who will eat, she or her son. —Ukraine 1996

The material aspects of poverty are well known. Hunger and food insecurity remain the core concerns. For poor families, meeting their most basic needs for food, water, and shelter can be a daily struggle; this becomes acute when there is unemployment and underemployment, or lack of productive land or other income-earning assets. In Vietnam (1999a) the issue of not having enough to eat arises frequently and is captured in the following saying by a poor man:

In the mornings, eat sweet potatoes, work. At lunch, go without. In the evenings, eat sweet potatoes, sleep. —Vietnam 1999a

In Guatemala poverty is defined by poor people as "having inadequate food and housing" and "having to rely on charity" (Guatemala 1997a). In Cameroon the poor distinguish themselves from the nonpoor in five main ways: "The presence of hunger in their households; fewer meals a day and nutritionally inadequate diets; a higher percentage of their meager and irregular income spent on food; nonexistent or low sources of cash income; and feelings of powerlessness and an inability to make themselves heard" (Cameroon 1995). In Moldova poor people say, "The worst aspects of poverty are hunger, poor health, lack of adequate clothing, and poor housing conditions" (Moldova 1997).

The PPAs are full of accounts of households coping with difficult times by reducing the quality, quantity, and frequency of meals. In Nigeria poverty is equated with preharvest food insecurity and diets that are monotonous and primarily starch-based. The poorest eat only food that is already old and stale (Nigeria 1995). In Swaziland and Zambia the poor depend on famine foods, foods not normally eaten, such as roots and leaves foraged from the bush (Swaziland 1997; Zambia 1994). In Madagascar the poorest are those who are forced to forego meals on a regular basis (Madagascar 1996), while in Guatemala the poorest are those who are forced to eat whatever they are able to find (Guatemala 1993). In slum areas in Phnom Penh, Cambodia, poor people report that they have cut consumption down from three to two, and sometimes to one meal a day (Cambodia 1998). In Ukraine people say that the worst aspects of poverty are hunger and the health effects of malnutrition. In rural Ukraine some respondents claim not to be truly poor because they are not yet starving (Ukraine 1996). In Togo the poor equate poverty with the inability to work because of the effects of malnourishment (Togo 1996).

Employment

The rich have one permanent job; the poor are rich in many jobs. —Poor man, Pakistan 1996

As the state sector contracts, employment opportunities are evaporating. —Ukraine 1996

Being poor is being always tired. —Kenya 1996

Especially for those without access to land or the ability to grow their own food on other people's land, access to dependable wage labor emerges as a major factor defining poverty. Whether in the countryside or in the city, poor people can rarely find permanent, salaried employment. Instead, poor people without land engage in informal, casual, and daily wage labor with no security and low earnings.

In South Africa the poor are characterized as "those who do not have secure jobs," and poor communities are characterized by widespread absence of formal employment. Instead, the poor have "numerous small, often dangerous jobs, rather than one job" (South Africa 1998). In Ethiopia work opportunities are considered unreliable, and vulnerability caused by unemployment is thought to be increasing (Ethiopia 1998). In Ghana the urban poor report a decline in opportunities and crowding in the informal sector due to increases in the number of people trying to survive in this sector (Ghana 1995b). Extended economic deterioration in Senegal has greatly reduced earnings in the informal sector (Senegal 1995). A poor man from Latvia reports that his family abandoned him after he lost his job as a plasterer. He now finds work that earns him a free meal, or sometimes a bit of money (Latvia 1997).

In many cases women are the primary sources of family income, and several countries report that women are engaging in all types of activities. These occupations include paid domestic work, as well as work traditionally considered men's work, such as informal industrial jobs, trading and service enterprises, and any work that requires migrating overseas (Moldova 1997; Georgia 1997; Pakistan 1993).

Psychological Well-Being

The poor person has to exist so he can serve the great one, the rich. God made things like that. —Brazil 1995

Poverty is lack of freedom, enslaved by crushing daily burden, by depression and fear of what the future will bring. —Georgia 1997

While poverty is material in nature, it has psychological effects—such as distress at being unable to feed one's children, insecurity from not knowing where the next meal will come from, and shame at having to go without food—that have strong symbolic value. A father in Guinea-Bissau remarks, "When I don't have [any food to bring my family], I borrow, mainly from neighbors and friends. I feel ashamed standing before my children when I have nothing to help feed the family. I'm not well when I'm unemployed. It's terrible" (Guinea-Bissau 1994). Frequently parents relate that they deal with food insecurity by going hungry so that they will not have to see their children starve. In Brazil parents report that poverty is "to come home and see your children hungry and not have anything to give them"

(Brazil 1995). In Tanzania a mother asks, "How can you face your children day after day hungry?" (Tanzania 1999).

The distress accompanying the decision to abandon babies to increase the likelihood that the baby or the family will survive is acute. In Tbilisi, Georgia, there have been increasing reports of babies abandoned at maternity wards, as well as of mothers selling children to support the remaining children. One respondent heard that a woman sold her child for $500 to support her family, and another witnessed a young woman near Tbilisi's central train station trying to sell her child, telling passers-by, "The child will die of hunger—take him even if you don't pay" (Georgia 1997).

A woman in Uganda remarks, "When one is poor, she has no say in public and feels inferior. She has no food, so there is famine in her house; no clothing, and no progress in her family" (Uganda 1998). The poor often mention turning to God for comfort, solace, and support. A poor man in Pakistan says, "As God gives food to a tiny insect living in the stones, He makes sure we have enough food to live" (Pakistan 1996). In Nepal poor people speak of fear—"fear from the landlord misbehaving, trouble by police. Poor people always fear exploitation by the rich." Women speak of fear to move about alone. "Even the categories of well-being distinguished by poor people highlight the psychological dimension: the miserable poor, facing difficult times; the pulling-along-poor, doing well; and happy people (Nepal 1999).

Being poor can expose one to ridicule. In Latvia poor people "felt humiliated by what they perceived as a pressure to beg for help and to put up with rude, contemptuous, and moralistic behavior on the part of social assistance office staff" (Latvia 1998).

Poor men and women speak of the shame, stigma, and humiliation of poverty. In Latvia parents speak of the shame that children experience in school when they are stigmatized because they receive free lunches, dress in shabby hand-me-downs, or have to use photocopied class materials. "Children who receive free lunches are served at a separate table, receive poorer quality food, and feel humiliated when other children claim they are eating from other people's money even though some parents do community work for the municipality to pay for the lunches" (Latvia 1998). In Ukraine teachers say that it is very easy to distinguish between the children of the rich, who are stylishly dressed, and the children of the poor, many of whom faint during class from hunger (Ukraine 1996). In Armenia and Georgia parents speak about children's psychological trauma of wearing old clothes and being so ashamed that they refuse to go to school (Armenia 1996; Georgia 1997).

Power and Voice

The rich are those who are able to save and sell part of their harvest when prices rise. —A poor man, Niger 1996

You know 'good' but you cannot do 'good.' That is, such a person knows what should be done but has not got the means. —Ghana 1995a

Some have land, but they can't buy fertilizer; if some work as weavers, they aren't well paid; if some work for daily wages, they aren't paid a just wage. —Cackchiquel Indian, Guatemala 1994b

Poverty means working for more than 18 hours a day, but still not earning enough to feed myself, my husband, and two children. —A poor woman, Cambodia 1998

In explaining poverty poor men and women often express a sense of hopelessness, powerlessness, humiliation, and marginalization. In Ghana it is expressed as, "You know good, but you cannot do good." One example given is, "If you have an in-law somewhere and the person dies, you know what to do but you cannot do anything and things will go wrong" (Ghana 1995a).

In Cameroon poverty is characterized as "a feeling of powerlessness and an inability to make themselves heard" (Cameroon 1995). A poor elderly man in Uganda says, "The forces of poverty and impoverishment are so powerful today. Governments or the big churches can only manage them. So we now feel somewhat helpless. It is this feeling of helplessness that is so painful, more painful than poverty itself" (Uganda 1998).

In Madagascar the powerlessness of the small farmers is one clear source of frustration and resentment. "A number of participants fell prey to collectors and administrative agents who take advantage of farmers by offering them low producer prices, which have to be accepted for lack of any alternative. For example, the money a producer of vanilla receives for his produce is roughly 4 percent of the export price and the producer has no negotiation power to raise the value of his crop. Similarly, with litchi and rice crops the collectors set the terms of the market, buying at the lowest price and selling at the highest. Overall the feeling [is] of betrayal and ultimately rejection" (Madagascar 1994).

In Eastern Europe and the former Soviet Union the poor report widespread corruption, powerlessness, and helplessness even when employed by private enterprise or by reorganized and privatized collective farms. In Georgia poor farmers equate privatization with theft. They report that the best land is distributed to those who work for the police, courts, school directors, and businessmen, while the poor receive nonirrigated, saline, and less fertile soil. This land is often 10 to 12 kilometers from their homes, making it difficult for them to work the fields and guard the harvest (Georgia 1997).

In Moldova poor people equate independence, democracy, and the transition to the market with lack of social justice. Workers on collective farms report being cheated out of their share of grains and denied access to tractors and other equipment by those in control (Moldova 1997). In Armenia the poor say, "During privatization, those people who had a patron received five or six cows and the rest received nothing. The whole collective farm was plundered, and the chairman, together with the district leaders themselves, took the remaining 100 head of cattle to Turkey and sold them for $2 a kilo" (Armenia 1995).

The poor often report that they have little influence over their political representatives. In many parts of India the poor are cynical about politicians who promise action and bribe by distributing alcohol, fueling already high rates of alcoholism among some scheduled caste (those Hindus who fall outside the caste system) and tribal groups (India 1997a). In Pakistan local politicians are reported to have used funds for their own purposes (Pakistan 1996). In many countries local politicians are seen as being closely connected with local criminal organization groups and the rich.

Across national borders much of the helplessness and sense of powerlessness of poor people comes from their experience with corrupt, uncaring, and inefficient officers of the state. The Mexico PPA documents several cases of poor people's frustration at being denied social services, jobs, and credit because they lack the necessary documentation (Mexico 1995; see also chapters 3 and 6).

Lack of voice and power is experienced not only in interactions with the state, but also in poor people's interactions with the market, landlords, bankers, moneylenders, and employers. Rich people in Tanzania, for instance, are described as "those who set the prices," while the poor are described as "those who are forced to accept the prices set by others" (Tanzania 1999). An Ecuador report (1996a) notes that poor farmers shoulder debt and therefore cannot afford to store their crops until they can get a good price for them on the market. Instead, farmers are forced to sell their crops immediately, when the prices are low, and in some instances they buy their own food back later at a higher price. In Togo (1996) the poor focus on the "power to buy raw materials without being exploited by wholesale traders." In Zambia (1997) poor farmers speak of being dependent on traders and those with transport for selling produce, being forced to buy inputs at high prices, and feeling powerless to do anything about late payments and fraud. In India, Uganda, Guatemala, Moldova, Thailand, Vietnam, and Ghana the poor speak of their inability to protect themselves from exploitation. The India report notes that "The poor have lost their bargaining power. The basis of dominance is control over productive resources and the basis of subordination is survival" (India 1998b).

Trading on the street can be an experience in powerlessness where the police are silent observers or associated with the gangs and criminal organizations that control the markets. In Ukraine (1996) a vendor explains, "You're standing somewhere and they come up to you and say, 'Bust outta here. No place for you.' I split, find myself another corner and try to sell more quickly. Sometimes they threaten you because of your prices. They say, 'We'll break your face if you lower your prices.' Sometimes I was able to sell quickly and get out. But other times I saw these guys and understood that it's better not to deal with them and then I split right away. In short, it became unpleasant and dangerous" (Ukraine 1996).

In these and in several other countries the poor report that wage laborers are the most exploited because they are forced into poor working conditions and long hours, and they must accept substandard salaries. Because they lack choices and resources, the poor are often forced to ask help from the same people who exploit them: landlords, pawnbrokers, and moneylenders.

Poor women express fear of increased crime, both in public and at home. In Ukraine women and old people say they no longer leave their homes after dark, and "worry when their children return late from school or work" (Ukraine 1996). In Moldova women are afraid to work the night shift because of fear of assaults (Moldova 1997). In South Africa case studies document "rapes of teenage girls, unfiled claims of child support by mothers due to fears of being beaten by the fathers, and even the crippling of a woman following a drunken argument among the couple" (South Africa 1998).

The South Africa PPA also describes gang-related and political violence. Women report feeling vulnerable to physical attacks and sexual assaults when they are out collecting firewood. As a result women give high priority to electrification. In India and in Pakistan women speak of the dangers of sexual assault and harassment by forest officials and others when collecting firewood (India 1993). In Pakistan absence of latrines forces women to use the bush before dawn and after dusk, exposing them to snake bites, sexual harassment, and attacks (Pakistan 1993). In Bangladesh (1996) provision of toilets and bathing places is a high priority among adolescent girls and women because of fear of harassment and inconvenience.

Entering into cycles of indebtedness often contributes to feelings of helplessness and powerlessness among the poor. In Pakistan and India indebtedness and debt are concerns common to both urban and rural communities, and a sense of helplessness and diminished autonomy often accompanies reflections on debt. A PPA from India describes a vicious cycle of indebtedness in which a debtor may work in a moneylender's house as a servant, on his farm as a laborer, or in other activities for a year to pay off his debt. Moreover, the debt may accumulate substantially, due to high interest rates, absence due to illness, and expenses incurred for food or accommodations (India 1997a). Problems with increasing indebtedness are also voiced in Swaziland, especially in connection with the inability to cope with rising prices of food, transportation, education, and health care (Swaziland 1997).

The voices of the poor in developing countries differ from those who have experienced sudden poverty, as have many in the transitional countries of Eastern Europe and the former Soviet Union. All reflect insecurity and material deprivation, yet the experience of long-term poverty is often accompanied by its almost fatalistic acceptance, even if people have not given up the struggle. In contrast, respondents from Eastern Europe and the former Soviet Union are filled with disbelief and demoralization, and are much more likely to make comparative statements contrasting the better past with the intolerable present (see box 2.2).

Cultural and Social Norms

> *Without these simple humane signs of solidarity, our lives would be unbearable.* —A poor woman, Ukraine 1996

> *We are proud of our language, our customs.* —Indigenous group, Panama 1998

Cultural identity is built through "the sharing of common history or common culture, common pride in the past, and, in some, the sharing of a common passion" (Panama 1998). These societal bonds can help to stabilize communities and ease the psychological stresses of poverty. For instance, the Mexico PPA notes the paradox that while indigenous communities of Oaxaca have the least materially, they are happy and less fearful than nonindigenous poor people because they have a range of "traditional communitarian institutions which provide them support in times of need" (Mexico 1995).

Cultural identity is maintained through rituals, celebrations, and festivals, and the poor frequently mention participation in these events. The significance of this cannot be overstated: for many poor people social solidarity is one of the most important assets available to them. To maintain this solidarity and the emotional and physical security it provides, people are willing to make considerable sacrifices and will readily divest themselves of a wide range of material assets in order to ensure that these social bonds are preserved. In Togo the PPA reports that displacement, whether by force or employment, results in "abandonment of symbolic markers, sacred trees, forests, and saps at the root of people's cultural identity and may result in deep alienation" (Togo 1996). Thus, after the most basic needs (such as food and housing) are met, the largest household expenditures tend to be on traditional ceremonies. "Although using

Box 2.2, Cont.

Sudden Poverty

Up to a few years ago I didn't even ask myself the question: What shall I cook? Today there are times I do not have anything to put on the stove and this is very difficult for a mother [crying] ... Before, we were not afraid of getting ill, everything was well regulated and there was health protection. Today we pray to God that nobody gets sick. What could we do?
—A woman, Macedonia 1998

Life has passed for us. I feel badly because of the children. My daughter in order to feed her children takes from time to time old bread from the 'Zito Luks' bakery aimed for cattle. I have never been in such a situation. We have never suffered for food, even though we were poorer when we were young.
—72-year-old woman, Macedonia 1998

People have fallen into despair because they don't see the end of this crisis situation. —Ukraine 1996

There was a time when I had two pigs and about 20 chickens, but now I have nothing. My money is hardly enough to buy bread every day. A few years ago my refrigerator was full of sausage. Now the refrigerator is empty. Perhaps God has punished us for our wastefulness in the past. —A woman, Moldova 1997

scarce resources for social events rather than for, say, health or education may appear an irresponsible behavior, from the point of view of the poor it can be a highly rational choice, provided the expenditures do not become a source of long-term indebtedness. In fact, generous spending (to the point of conspicuous consumption) is a way to gain prestige and to reinforce ties to the community, which in turn will make it easier to obtain assistance in case of need. Hence, ceremonial expenditures may be understood as investments to build social assets and decrease vulnerability" (Togo 1996).

In other words, maintaining social solidarity has extremely high value to the poor, and the inability to reciprocate with gifts or participate in community events can have very harmful consequences ranging from humiliation, loss of honor and psychological distress, to social marginalization and exclusion from important social networks. In fact, violation of social norms is often what poor respondents define as poverty. In the rural areas of Madagascar, for instance, being poor is equated with the inability to "adhere to local customs and norms," whereas a rich person is one who can "afford to remain within the local norms" (Madagascar 1996).

Clothing functions as a powerful social marker, particularly for youth and children. In a number of different reports children report feeling marked by shabby or inadequate clothing and stigmatized by their teachers and children from wealthier families (Bangladesh 1996; India 1997a; Moldova 1997). For young adults in Moldova the "lack of decent clothing, humiliation in front of richer friends, and the inability to participate in a normal social life" are among the principal markers of poverty (Moldova 1997). In Armenia people cite a lack of self-worth and loss of status as a consequence of being unable to maintain basic hygiene (Armenia 1995). In Georgia children who wear old, patched clothing to school are often cruelly taunted, which becomes another reason for their parents to keep them home from school or to enroll them a year late in the hope that their situation may improve. Some Tbilisi youth admit to avoiding university classes because they are humiliated at the daily prospect of appearing dirty and poorly groomed in front of others (Georgia 1997).

State-Provided Infrastructure

Where a road passes, development follows right on its heels.
—Cameroon 1995

We think the earth is generous; but what is the incentive to produce more than the family needs if there are no access roads to get the produce to a market? —Guatemala 1997a

Take the death of this small boy this morning, for example. The boy died of measles. We all know he could have been cured at the hospital. But the parents had no money and so the boy died a slow and painful death, not of measles, but of poverty. —A man, Ghana 1995a

Water is life, and because we have no water, life is miserable.
—Kenya 1997

Poverty is about access and consumption of state-provided commodities, or what some researchers refer to as "social wages" (Baulch 1996b;

Moore and Putzel 1999). Throughout the PPAs poor people discuss the importance of key services such as roads, transportation, water, electricity, health care, and marketplaces.

In several cases the poor in urban areas, though actually poorer than those in comparable rural areas, are viewed as *less* poor because they have access to infrastructure and basic services (Guatemala 1997b; India 1997a). Similarly, a report from India states, "Even the poorer families living in the prosperous villages are comparatively better [off] than the poor living in medium and poorest villages, in terms of social and educational awareness, because these facilities are more accessible to them" (India 1997a).

Community poverty is related to infrastructure and service provision. In a poor rural community surveyed in Nigeria respondents claim that *every* inhabitant is poor precisely because the community lacks basics such as water, electricity, roads, schoolteachers, and more (Nigeria 1995). In Uganda a distinction is made between individual and community poverty, in which community-level poverty is defined as "a lack of key infrastructure for the entire community, for example, schools, roads" and lack of security or harmony (Uganda 1998). Similarly, nearly half of the suggestions from poor Ecuadorian families about how to alleviate poverty concerned the provision of basic infrastructure (Ecuador 1996a).

The absence or poor condition of infrastructure, especially of feeder roads and bridges, is widespread. In many reports the poorest communities are identified as those most isolated and located farthest from roads and from other key infrastructure (India 1997a; Republic of Yemen 1998; Bangladesh 1996; Mexico 1995; Guatemala 1997b; Uganda 1998; Ecuador 1996a; Ecuador 1996b; Cameroon 1995). In India many of the poorest villages are located 15–20 kilometers from the nearest infrastructure; during the rainy season villagers find themselves completely isolated from the more developed areas. "The result is that the members of the unconnected villages remain effectively marginalized from virtually all educational institutions above primary level, from adequate health-care facilities, and from important governmental and nongovernmental institutions" (India 1997a). Respondents in Bangladesh (1996) and Ghana (1995b) also identify the lack of adequate roads, particularly during rainy seasons, as a key problem.

In addition to isolating communities from other infrastructure, the lack of roads can also deny communities political access. Ugandan government officials who are posted in isolated areas perceive it as a kind of punishment (Uganda 1998). Similarly, the Kenya PPA indicates that district leaders tend to avoid villages that are only accessible by bad or dangerous roads. If they go to remote villages at all, it is only for short visits, so there is no time to witness problems directly and talk things over with stake-holders (Kenya 1996).

Roads serve not only as physical connectors but also as communication connectors that expand poor people's options and their power to negotiate. Poor roads greatly limit intervillage and rural-urban trade (India 1997a, Ecuador 1996a). In Cameroon, for instance, 86 percent of those interviewed in the Southwest Province believe that poor transportation infrastructure is a major factor in their inability to increase agricultural productivity and marketing activities (Cameroon 1995). In Uganda the poor report lower bargaining power because of their lack of mobility: "It is because of poor roads that the produce of the farmers is bought at low prices" (Uganda 1998).

Poor transportation infrastructure also compounds problems with obtaining services such as health care and education. Two-thirds of respondents in Mexico City complain of the poor quality and lack of access to health-care clinics, and this problem increases in rural areas. In one rural region, Zacatecas, the average cost for transportation to the nearest doctor is US$41, or the equivalent of a month's wages from the only wage labor in the area: hemp weaving. "In Zacatecas it is not rare to hear of families that have lost all of their animals and gone into debts of from 2,000 to 5,000 pesos (US$365 to $900) due to sickness of a family member" (Mexico 1995). Similar problems exist in the Republic of Yemen where "poor families from remote areas go to health-care facilities only when in extreme need" (Republic of Yemen 1998).

Lack of transportation also affects children. Rural children in Cameroon often do not attend school because schools are located beyond walking distance, and teachers avoid working in the more isolated areas (Cameroon 1995). In Thailand some parents remove their children from school because the combined costs of education and transportation are unaffordable (Thailand 1998). In one of the South African villages the costs associated with transporting children to school are identified as a cause of poverty (South Africa 1998).

In addition to transportation, two other issues distinguish the poor from the nonpoor: water security, and, to a lesser extent, sanitation. Access to water is important for bathing and drinking, as well as for agricultural production. In Bangladesh, lack of safe drinking water is identified as one of the most important problems for the poor (Bangladesh 1996). Similarly, in rural areas of the Kyrgyz Republic only 45 percent of households have running water, and among the most poor over 50 percent rely on lakes, ponds, and rainwater for household water consumption (Kyrgyz Republic 1998). In Vietnam, children define people in poverty as those without drinking water. In India, the poor in one area report, "Here the biggest problem is drinking water. The drinking water is drawn from an open well. Leaves and other wastes fall in it and decay. Water-borne diseases like polio and malaria are very common. No health-care worker visits this village. There are a few hand pumps in this village, but you can see not even a drip of water" (India 1997c).

In India poverty is directly related to overall agricultural productivity, that in turn is dependent on water for irrigation (India 1997b). While the absence of irrigation facilities affects all farmers within an area, farmers with particularly small holdings are most affected. In the surveyed villages lack of these facilities is identified as the root cause of poverty (India 1997b). Richer communities are identified as those that have access to water, making dry-season gardens possible. Households selling produce during dry seasons are able to use these earnings to make improvements on houses, such as the installation of zinc roofing (Ghana 1995a). Also in Ghana, an important community-level asset is a village source of water that can be used as an irrigation source during the dry season. These communities are identified as rich in comparison to those lacking dependable water resources (Ghana 1995a).

In more prosperous areas inadequate supply and the high costs of electricity and telephones are the most frequently cited infrastructure problems. In Georgia (1997) people report that power shortages are most frequent in poor neighborhoods. In 1996 the poor outlying districts of Tbilisi experienced electricity outages that lasted from one day to one month, while surrounding areas received electricity with fewer disruptions. Telephone service, even for emergencies, has become rare in many areas. People complain that even when the phones are not working they are still expected to pay for the service. When they refuse, officials respond, "Electricity sometimes comes at night and then the phone works" (Georgia 1997).

The Assets of the Poor

We have neither land nor work. ... Some of us have land in the reserve, but we can't transport our products from there because it is too far. It is difficult to carry them, and since I don't have land here, and only in the reserve, I am poor.
—Ecuador 1996a

In my family if anyone becomes seriously ill, we know that we will lose him because we do not even have enough money for food so we cannot buy medicine. —Vietnam 1999a

I used to never worry about my illiteracy and the fact that I was not able to send my children to school, as long as we had

something to eat. But now ... I realize that my children are in
trouble for life because they cannot get any decent job if they
don't know how to read and write. —Swaziland 1997

You have to cultivate networks and contacts with people
with power and influence to secure a livelihood and future.
—Pakistan 1993

The poor rarely speak about income, but they do speak extensively about assets that are important to them. The poor manage a diverse portfolio of assets—physical, human, social, and environmental. These assets include a broad range of tangible and potential resources, both material and social, that individuals, households, and communities draw from in times of need or crisis (Togo 1996; Benin 1994; Moser 1998a). Power differences among individuals and groups shape how such assets are controlled and used. The extent to which different resources can be mobilized depends directly on how power is shared within households, communities, and other social institutions. Gender differences in being able to access assets are widespread, affect vulnerability, and have important policy implications. These are discussed in detail in chapters 4 and 5.

The four primary classifications of assets are:

▸ physical capital, including land and material belongings;
▸ human capital, including health care, education, training, and labor power;
▸ social capital, which refers to the extent and nature of social networks such as kinship networks, neighbors, and associations; and
▸ environmental assets, such as grass, trees, water, and non-timber products.

Additionally, assets function at the individual level, the household level, and the community level. Of the four types of assets available to the poor, social capital is probably the least understood. As the recent literature on social capital makes clear, careful examination of the social capital of households, groups, and communities can provide much needed information to policymakers (Grootaert 1998; Woolcock and Narayan 2000).

Assets also may be productive, such as livestock, or purely for investment (jewelry, for instance). Some assets may be both at different times, such as housing that can be rented (productive) or sold (investment). All of these factors are taken into account when assets are drawn on or investments made. How a particular asset becomes incorporated into an individual's or a household's overall strategy for mitigating poverty depends on the nature of the asset, the social context in which it is embedded, and the urgency of need.

Physical Capital

> *Poverty is because of the land; the person who doesn't have any must obligatorily leave to do day labor.* —Ecuador 1996a

> *If one does not own land, a house, household property, or domestic animals, then the person is considered to be poor.* —Uganda 1998

> *Livestock are part of the yearly household reserves; if they get a disease and die we have nothing to support us in between harvests.* —Vietnam 1999a

> *What one shouldn't lack is the sheep, what one cannot live without is food grain.* —China 1997

The ownership of or access to land is commonly identified as a key asset (Uganda 1998; South Africa 1998; Kyrgyz Republic 1998; Benin 1994; Ecuador 1996a). Access to land and land rights, especially in rural areas, is at the core of much of the discussion on poverty. In Ecuador poor people feel that poverty is caused by four interrelated factors: limited access to land on which to raise food; the poor quality of the land, which is sloped and highly eroded; the lack of irrigation facilities; and the limited ability to raise and sell large domestic animals (Ecuador 1996a). A poor man in Guinea-Bissau says, "It's not easy to find land such as these we cultivate ... People say that housing will be built on the land we cultivate. This is a source of great concern, for if all of these projects were carried out, we would be in serious financial straits" (Guinea-Bissau 1994). In the Philippines some indigenous people feel that they are gradually losing control of their ancestral lands. In some areas nonindigenous people get title to indigenous people's lands in connivance with unscrupulous government representatives (Philippines 1999). In Zambia as in many rural areas, poor people express concern about the declining fertility of land (Zambia 1997).

In nearly all of the studies, the ability to provide for oneself and one's family is mentioned by the poor as one of the primary strategies for dealing with material deprivation and reducing overall household insecurity. In Nigeria many rural people grow vegetables around the home to supplement the food they have purchased. Many urban dwellers consider themselves disadvantaged in comparison with their rural counterparts because they have less capacity for self-provisioning (Nigeria 1995). This is true of urban dwellers in Ukraine, where the two most important criteria separating the poor from the destitute are housing and access to a garden plot (Ukraine 1996). In Ethiopia, as well, the poorest families are those who are unable to produce enough food for their own consumption (Ethiopia 1998).

Housing, typically considered an asset, can also be a liability, because it can limit options and drain resources. In Latvia housing had to be re-registered during the postsocialist transition at considerable expense to the owners (Latvia 1998). Maintenance costs can also drain resources. A respondent from Guinea-Bissau explains, "We built [our house] a long time ago, before most of our children were born. But it's made of thatch, so we have to replace the roof each year, and that costs a lot of money. It needs to be replaced each year before the rainy season. Right now the thatch for a house costs approximately 1,200,000 pesos. We want to get zinc for the house. The problem of having to replace the roof periodically would be solved for good" (Guinea-Bissau 1994).

Often, though, what distinguishes the poor from the nonpoor is substandard housing. In Georgia (1997) damaged, seriously deteriorated, even dangerous housing is a serious concern for the poor. The most frequent problems include leaking roofs, cracked and moldy walls, broken windows, rotting floors, blocked toilets, and rusted pipes. One couple who owns their apartment says, "It could hardly be called normal when at night pieces of plaster fall on one's head, during rain the ceiling leaks, the leaks sink through holes in the rotten floor, and the faucet leaks through 24 hours a day" (Georgia 1997). In Bangladesh (1996) the Char people speak about lack of shelter as a major problem because thatched huts are easily destroyed by strong winds during the periodic storms. Of course, housing can also have significant income-generating potential. Some poor families subsist mainly on the income derived from renting out a room in their house (Swaziland 1997).

Personal or household property is an asset insofar as it can be sold in emergencies, and salable property may constitute one of the few safety nets that exists for poor families (Uganda 1998; India 1998a; Georgia 1997; Zambia 1997; Cameroon 1995; Latvia 1998; Ethiopia 1998). In Ukraine virtually none of the poor report having any remaining savings, and most have been forced to sell valuable assets such as cars, jewelry, and electronic equipment (Ukraine 1996). However, property is nonrenewable, and selling personal belongings and property is most often a last-resort coping strategy for dealing with a crisis. In fact, in Swaziland selling assets to pay for immediate household needs is becoming less common as a coping strategy simply because many families have already sold off these assets (Swaziland 1997). In India, "a large number of households today are found to have exhausted all of their valuable assets like gold ornaments and bronze utensils in the course of debt servicing" (India 1998a).

When personal belongings must be sold, several reports note that women's personal belongings are the first to go (Pakistan 1993; Georgia 1997; India 1998a). As the Pakistan report points out, this divestment strategy is "gendered in its impact and an indicator of women's particular vulnerability and lack of decisionmaking power within household" (Pakistan 1993). At the same time, divestment of assets such as jewelry may also represent a rational decisionmaking process in which the assets sold first are those without income-generating potential (Pakistan 1993). A similar pattern emerges in Georgia where it is reported that households tend to divest themselves of assets in stages, beginning with personal property such as jewelry, then furniture, and then their homes. The report continues, "For respondents with nothing left to sell, their own blood provides the final source of income" (Georgia 1997). The same practice is also observed in Latvia (1998).

In some cases, poor people may choose to retain a few scarce assets even during times of hunger, illness, or other hardship. Poverty can be closely associated with the loss of dignity and prestige, which is registered in large part by ownership of possessions that are also symbols of status. In Mali, it is not uncommon for a family to own potentially valuable and salable assets such as jewelry or a bicycle, and yet to decide to go hungry during the preharvest season. As the report explains:

> These choices cannot be dismissed as irrational or selfish, for they reflect the need to diversify investments and to keep one's position in the community in case of a real crisis. Given this cultural context, it becomes very difficult to determine what constitutes poverty. Is a family who has inadequate caloric intake for three months a year poor when it could sell a bracelet and have enough to eat? What about a father who saves money to buy a cow for his son's wedding and does not buy medicines for his sick child? While there are sound explanations for this behavior, traditional poverty measurements, such as household consumption surveys, do not capture them. —Mali 1993

Human Capital

> If you don't have money today, your disease will take you to your grave. —An old woman, Ghana 1995a

> The sick do not have the right to live. —A new saying, residents of Javakheti, Georgia 1997

I am illiterate. I am like a blind person. —Illiterate mother,
Pakistan 1996

*If I had gone to school, I would have got a job and I
would have obtained a husband who has a salaried job.*
—Uganda 1998

*I'm old and I can't work, and therefore I am poor. Even
my land is old and tired, so whatever little I manage to
work does not give me enough harvest for me and my children.*
—Togo 1996

Human capital comprises health, education, and labor. For those lacking material and productive assets, labor power or a healthy body is the core component of most survival strategies, and therefore is perhaps the most important human capital asset (Latvia 1998; Senegal 1995). As explained in the Benin report, loss of a productive adult "whether due to disease, death, divorce, or neglect drastically reduces a household's capacity to overcome external shocks, and is one of the main causes of destitution" (Benin 1994).

The PPAs reveal that, more than anything else, the poor dread serious illness within the family. Illness removes individuals from the labor pool and can push a household into poverty. Where formal institutions provide inadequate safety nets, the illness of one person within the family can affect the economic stability of the entire household. In Togo village children asked to draw a poor person frequently draw someone ill or disabled (Togo 1996). In Ghana good health is seen as a particularly important asset because poor households rely on physical labor for income and lack other assets. "Fieldwork shows that disease, sometimes followed by premature death, is often the cause of extreme poverty, which explains why communities routinely mention poor health (including disability) as one of the characteristics of the poorest people" (Ghana 1995b).

Illness creates a devastating and lasting drain on household resources. In Pakistan a father in Lahore explains that it took him eight years to repay debts acquired after he, his wife, and two of their children had been hospitalized. A mother reports that she has recently withdrawn her daughter from school in order to meet her son's medical expenses. One man says his own parents have sold land in order to pay for the treatment of their grandson. In sum, although many of the Lahore informants have met family health crises effectively, household assets and human resource investments are likely to suffer as a result (Pakistan 1993).

Literacy, or the "thirst for letters," is valued everywhere. In Togo people say that illiteracy limits the ability of individuals to secure employment, follow written instructions, and take advantage of government services or obtain access to credit (Togo 1996). In India, although illiteracy is not reported as the number one reason for poverty, poor people recognize that literacy would help them to manage their lives better. "They understand that illiteracy has made them more dependent, less enterprising, and more vulnerable to the machinations of the educated" (India 1997c).

While literacy is clearly valued, education receives mixed reviews. It is often difficult for families to invest in education. In Swaziland parents make considerable sacrifices, including rationing food to reduce household expenses, so that their children can go to school (Swaziland 1997). In Guinea-Bissau a man says about his children's schooling, "I think that, God willing, they'll do well so they'll be able to get good jobs. I do all in my power to make sure they don't miss class. I hope God will point the way to success for them. If that desire is not realized, patience. Without an education, life is difficult because you can't get a good job" (Guinea-Bissau 1994). In Vietnam (1999a), investment in education is seen as the most important way out of poverty, and a lack of money for education and having a stable job are identified as the overriding problems. In Kenya (1996) in all districts, poor parents place a very high premium on keeping their children in school. To do so, "They would sell their possessions, beg, steal, brew and sell beer, pray, go to church, hawk produce, join self-help groups, cajole teachers into letting the children stay in schools, pay in installments, put their children to work, and sometimes become destitute trying to keep their children in school" (Kenya 1996).

Yet elsewhere the usefulness of education is doubted, particularly when not associated with jobs and wealth. In Eastern Europe and the former Soviet Union there is growing skepticism about the value of education when economic opportunities are shrinking and opportunities seem to come only through connections. In Macedonia schoolchildren say, "School is no good if you don't have connections." Parents agree, but encourage children anyway. They are aware that education no longer leads to jobs or wealth. "Neither the state nor anybody else can offer jobs" (Macedonia 1998).

In Mali (1993), although more than 80 percent of people interviewed believe that schooling is important, schooling has become a disappointment for many. Many parents report that schools have fallen short of helping students to find salaried work, giving them a basic education, and teaching them moral and social behavior. In Burkina Faso, for example, the quality of the available schooling is perceived to be so marginal that "the investment in fees and loss of field labor are perceived as something of a shot in the dark in terms of realistically securing a raise in an individual's or a family's living standards" (Burkina Faso 1994).

The education of girls is mired in a plethora of cultural issues. The common opinion is that education for girls is quite pointless because girls will not learn to care for their homes, and thus their attractiveness as potential wives will be diminished, "effectively ruin[ing] [their] possibilities of a future in the village" (Burkina Faso 1994). Additionally, it is felt that educated girls will desire husbands who are also educated and less likely to find work. "Therefore, young, educated girls will end up in a losing position; they will either not want to marry anybody or nobody will want to marry them, rounding off their social isolation. Eventually they are viewed as the most likely candidates for entering a life of prostitution" (Burkina Faso 1994). In Pakistan the education of girls is seen as raising costs of marriage and hence not valued (Pakistan 1996).

In Armenia both parents and children report that children have given up studying and have instead become merchants and tradesmen because: (1) access to higher education is denied to those without resources; (2) higher education is not a guarantee of higher earnings; and (3) the immediate income needs of the household must be met. In rural areas boys quit school after eighth grade. A student in the Shirka district says, "I lost the will to study because I know that after school I won't be able to go to town to study further because my father won't be able to provide the money that is needed for studying in town. I go to school because there is nothing else for me to do." "Study or not, you will be keeping cows," one father says (Armenia 1996).

Social Capital

The most important asset is ... an extended and well-placed family network from which one can derive jobs, credit, and financial assistance. —Senegal 1995

The prosperity of our village has increased. Before, the two tribes in our village used to be divided. Now they belong to the same group, which brings them together. No two people have the same intelligence or resources, so when people come together they can solve many problems. —Tanzania 1997

Social capital, broadly defined, refers to the benefits of membership within a social network. The accessibility of additional resources through social connections enables poor people to meet everyday needs. In addition, because poor people can rarely afford formal insurance to protect them in the event of crises such as natural disasters, financial crises, health emergencies, unemployment, and the like, reciprocal social relationships provide wells of financial, social, or political support from which they can draw in times of need. Although friends, neighbors, professional ties, and links that extend beyond the community are critical assets for improving welfare, the most frequently mentioned coping mechanism for poor people is the extended family.

The experiences of the poor as described in the various PPAs emphasize the importance of kinship networks for daily survival as well as for crisis management. In Costa Rica approximately 50 percent of those interviewed say that they have at some point received economic assistance from family members in times of crisis and have either reciprocated in kind or are willing to do so (Costa Rica 1997). In Ghana extended families are seen as synonymous with social safety nets (Ghana 1995b). In Niger extended family networks help members deal with hunger and food insecurity (Niger 1996). In Guatemala the family's response to crises is to approach relatives and friends with whom they enjoy a reciprocal relationship. Those individuals give very small loans to cover the cost of medicines, doctors' fees, and transport to medical facilities, or to provide small amounts of foodstuffs in instances of dire necessity (Guatemala 1997b). In Eastern Europe and the former Soviet Union membership in kinship and professional networks is identified as one of the key factors governing how well one managed the financial crisis of the early 1990s (Moldova 1997).

When poor people help one another their scant resources may limit the gains made. Hence, social capital provides a hedge but rarely, by itself, lifts poor people out of poverty. Social capital is a two-way street. While social networks provide benefits such as access to scarce resources, membership also entails having claims made on one's own resources. Poor people from Mali report that accumulating assets at the individual or household level is difficult or impossible because of the claims that family members make on those assets.

These reciprocal ties even affect fertility decisions. If a couple decides to have few children in order to limit the drain on the family's resources, because of the strong norms of reciprocity the couple may end up caring for the children of relatives. "While on the one hand the extended family is a powerful safety net, on the other it discourages behavior that in the long run would reduce poverty, such as productive investments or limited family size" (Mali 1993). A middle-aged man from Guinea-Bissau who has been trained overseas as an engineer notes similar burdens related to education:

> My cousin, a nephew, and two of my wife's brothers will be
> coming next month when I'm going to move into the house
> next door, which has two bedrooms and a living room. You
> know when you return to the country with training for a
> senior post, the whole family thinks you're coming back to
> save them. And so they start sending everyone to your house

arguing that we were able to get an education thanks to the family's support, and that therefore we should provide support to others in turn. In addition I help my father and mother meet their needs. And I need money for ritual ceremonies.
—Guinea-Bissau 1994

As with other forms of capital, levels of social capital are constantly in flux. Without connections to resources beyond poor communities, poor people's networks serve a survival and defensive function, a struggle to meet daily needs.

Environmental Assets: Decline and Shocks

The poor live at the whim and mercy of nature. —Kenya 1997

We are all farmers in this village. When two farmers cultivate together the same plots and at the end of the harvest season, one has made a profit that allows him to get a lot of things and the other hasn't earned a thing, they will say that the second farmer is poor. But next year it could be the reverse. The fact is that we are all poor in this village. —Togo 1996

One of the most critical causes of vulnerability for rural communities is seasonal fluctuation in food and water availability. In some areas of Ghana the *sondure,* "hungry period," may last five or six months due to erratic rainfall and severely degraded soils (Ghana 1995b). Similarly, the Zambia study reports that farm labor demands are highest when problems of food scarcity and malaria are most severe, "both of which circumstances further reduce the availability and energy of labor" (Milimo 1995). During these periods adults frequently migrate, assets may be divested, or debt incurred, all of which may leave households more vulnerable to future shocks (Madagascar 1996). A report from Nigeria notes that "the severity of rural poverty ... is worst shortly before harvest time. The poor run out of stored food and have to purchase at a time when prices are highest, often on credit from moneylenders. After harvest, when prices are low, they have to sell to repay their loans. Their crop is therefore worth little to them and in many very poor families, some of it is sold in advance at very low prices" (Nigeria 1995).

The season brings other risks. Falls and fractures are frequent complaints in the Republic of Yemen where women and children (who may be kept out of school) must travel long distances and often over difficult mountainous roads to fetch water (Republic of Yemen 1998; Kenya 1996).

The rainy season brings its own problems to both rural and urban areas. Grain prices climb, access to casual employment drops, and flooded streets limit informal commerce (Ethiopia 1998; Ghana 1995a; Vietnam 1999b). The winter months are especially hard times for the poor in Macedonia due to their inability to maintain and heat housing (Macedonia 1998).

In addition to the problems of seasonal calamities, a large number of the world's poorest people face challenges because they live in environmentally fragile areas such as arid and tropical lands with limited soil fertility. With no access to other lands, increasing numbers of poor people have also moved to steep hillsides and low-lying coastal areas. Increasing numbers of these fragile sites are caught in a downward spiral of impoverishment and resource degradation that includes erosion, reduced soil fertility, depleted marine and forestry resources, and declining availability of fresh water. The Ghana PPA, for instance, indicates that the poorest rural communities are those "where the natural resource base has become extremely depleted as a result of high population densities" (Ghana 1995a). The Benin report mentions that land-short households can no longer afford to leave some land fallow, which further reduces fertility and yields (Benin 1994). Poor farmers dependent on rain say, "Income is most often a matter of sheer luck" (Senegal 1995).

Many traditional coping strategies such as gathering wood, hunting "bush meat," fishing, and harvesting herbs, fruits, or nuts rely on common resources. Pressure on such resources is intensifying, however, and several studies document that these resources are disappearing (Ghana 1995b). The India report mentions, for instance, that gum collection is no longer profitable due to a drastic decrease in the availability of gum trees (India 1998d). Women are much more dependent on gathering forest resources, and the disappearance of nontimber forest products disproportionately affects their well-being (India 1998a). Shrinking tree coverage in large portions of Benin has meant that poor people can no longer gather wild food and hunt during periods of food shortage (Benin 1994).

Resource degradation is a fact of life for many of the poor people interviewed. "Little by little the environment is dying and people don't understand that the problem comes from the fact that man is killing the environment," says a poor Ladino mother of seven in rural Guatemala. She says the principal reason is that the owners of the forest, the authorities, and the agencies responsible for reforestation are cutting down trees in large quantities (Guatemala 1997b). Resource degradation not only erodes the assets and productivity of individual households, but can also impoverish entire communities. In Tanzania small farmers say, "Ten years ago we harvested 10 sacks of cassava and eight sacks of maize per acre. Today, because of the decline of soil fertility and rain and because we do not use fertilizer or improved seed, some of us get three or four sacks of maize while others harvest nothing" (Tanzania 1999).

The urban poor are also vulnerable to other kinds of environmental risks. With scarce affordable housing, poor families often reside on steep hillsides and marshes that are highly susceptible to mudslides and floods. In some areas of Benin poor people live in "water up to their ankles for three months a year," and must contend with diarrheal diseases and respiratory tract infections, impassable streets, reduced opportunities for petty trades, and constant housing repairs (Benin 1994). In Senegal the urban poor live in what have been called "floating neighborhoods," or unplanned communities with crowded, unsanitary housing in peri-urban areas (Senegal 1995). In urban areas where the poor live in closely built shack settlements, fire is a real hazard due to widespread use of paraffin for cooking and light and the use of cardboard and wood as building materials (South Africa 1998).

Extreme weather conditions such as droughts and floods can devastate communities anywhere in the world (see box 2.3), but it is often poor people residing in marginal areas and precarious housing who are most exposed to such shocks. In 1998 more than 60,000 villages in India were buffeted by heavy rains, landslides, floods, hailstorms, cyclones, and drought. The intense weather patterns exacted a massive financial toll that exceeded the previous combined five years of relief funds. The poor are the worst affected. A cyclone in Gujrat, for instance, destroyed more than 13,000 huts, as opposed to just over 3,000 durable homes.[2]

Disasters can also exacerbate other sources of vulnerability and overwhelm traditional coping mechanisms. The poor of Swaziland and Zambia, in fact, see drought as among their most severe problems (Swaziland 1997; Zambia 1997). Similarly, residents of the Bolangir District in India report that it is impossible to recover from the five-year cycles of drought due to extreme losses of crops, indebtedness, starvation, land-alienation, the sale of assets, and irreparable damage to nearby forest resources. During droughts, household consumption falls by at least one-half (India 1997a, India 1998a).[3] The Benin report (1994) describes the strain of a flood disaster on kinship-based safety nets:

Three years ago it was a very bad year. The flood washed away all of our crops, and there was a lot of hunger around here, to the point that many people actually died of hunger. They must have been at least a dozen, mostly children and old people. Nobody could help them. Their relatives in the village had no food either; nobody had enough food for his own children, let alone for the children of his brother or cousin. And few had a richer relative somewhere else who could help. —Benin 1994

Box 2.3 The 1998 Floods in Bangladesh

Bangladesh suffered its worst floods in living memory in 1998, inundating two-thirds of the country for an unprecedented 11 weeks starting in July. Seasonal flooding is nothing new in Bangladesh, whose river systems (the Ganges, the Brahmaputra, and the Meghna) annually drain a vast basin. The people and the economy of Bangladesh have adapted over generations to seasonal flooding. However, in years when river levels and above-normal rainfall peak together, there have been enormous losses of life, livelihoods, property, and crops.

Over 1,000 individuals died and some 30 million people were affected by the 1998 floods. They severely damaged an estimated 15,000 kilometers of roads, 14,000 schools, and thousands of bridges and culverts. Besides public infrastructure, the floods damaged private assets (including over 500,000 homes), production, and productive inputs, and significantly altered agricultural patterns and lowered farming yields.

Source: Shah 1999.

Assets and Vulnerability

After one poor crop we need three good harvests to return to normal. —Vietnam 1999a

I sold my land and now I have nothing. I can never buy my land back because the prices go up every year. —Tanzania 1999

[I have become like] a stray dog whimpering in front of the closed doors of relatives in the hope that someone might open the door. —A mother of two, Georgia 1997

The PPA analysis reveals that poor people's fears pertain to lack of assets and anxiety about their ability to survive in increasingly unpredictable and insecure environments. This includes economic, social, and environmental uncertainty.

Vulnerability is perhaps best understood as a lack of key sets of assets, exposing individuals, households, and communities to increased or disproportionate risk of impoverishment. Simply put, an increased number and range of assets means less vulnerability, while fewer assets increase the risk of impoverishment (Moser 1998). More than a decade ago, Robert Chambers observed that poverty alleviation policies have tended to neglect the issue of the vulnerability of the poor. That is, instead of examining the particular factors that place individuals, households, and communities at risk of poverty or worsened poverty, policies have focused on levels of consumption or income. Examining vulnerability, however, will bring to light issues of "defenselessness, insecurity, and exposure to risk, shocks, and stress" (Chambers 1989).

It is always the conjunction of many factors that causes vulnerability. A participant from an area in Swaziland that had suffered from both drought and cattle rustling explains:

> *A lot of people were sending their children to school by using the cattle. Come plowing time, the oxen could be used. Come planting time they would sell the cattle to buy seed and fertilizer. Come drought, a few cattle would be sold to tide the family over till the next harvest. Now with so many kraals [corrals] empty [due to theft], the kids will drop out of school, people will have a problem with farm inputs, and we will be more vulnerable to hunger during the drought.* —Swaziland 1997

Vulnerability within the Household and on the Job

> *One farmer's family has worked for a family for three generations, hard physical labor every day. This man has worked since his birth for the same farmer but has nothing, no savings, not even a bicycle. These people can afford nothing but survival.* —South Africa 1998

When poor communities are asked to identify their most vulnerable members, a common initial response is that everyone is poor. Such is the case for a community in Mombasa, Kenya, but on further reflection they select "single mothers, orphans, children, men with large families, unemployed youth, adolescent mothers, casual workers, and women married to irresponsible or alcoholic husbands" as most vulnerable (Kenya 1997). Children, the elderly, widows, the chronically ill, and the disabled are among the groups frequently cited as most vulnerable. Unable to provide for themselves or contribute adequately to the productive capacity of the household, they remain dependent on the aid of others, simultaneously burdening those on whom they depend. When a family is poor, the vulnerable members of the household are often neglected and "the popular perception seems to be that there is little point in attempting to develop their capacities because they are so limited" (India 1997a). Of little surprise, more secure households in Benin are considered those that have a higher ratio of productive and healthy adults (Benin 1994).

Women are frequently identified as among the most vulnerable, often because of child-rearing responsibilities. Cultural norms and legal restrictions that limit women's access to resources as well as their decisionmaking power also heighten their vulnerability (Togo 1996; Swaziland 1997). In rural Bangladesh women are very concerned about ownership of homestead and land because it provides them with some security and collateral for securing loans. With a little homestead land, "women feel they have many options for income-generating activities, including poultry rearing, homestead gardening, and cottage industries. Most of them do not feel they can leave their homes for wage labor. They also fear for their future as widows, and divorcees and deserted wives" (Bangladesh 1996).

Female-headed households, especially those with children who are too young to work or care for themselves, are particularly vulnerable (Republic of Yemen 1998). These households may have lower incomes, fewer work options, and reduced labor power (Pakistan 1993). In some areas of India women within the household are expected to eat only after everyone else has finished eating, and during times of shortage women may be left with virtually nothing to eat at all (India 1998a). In the Philippines women say, "When food becomes scarce, we only eat once a day to allow our children and husbands to eat three times a day" (Philippines 1999).

While assets are usually considered to accrue to the household as a unit, it is often the men within the household who hold exclusive decisionmaking power over how these assets will be used, especially in times of crisis. "It appears that where possible women try to retain some of their income for personal expenditure and for contingencies. However, this is invariably utilized for personal crises such as health costs and food during times of sickness or unemployment, and women become vulnerable when their savings habits are revealed" (Pakistan 1993).

One of the characteristics of vulnerability is dependence, particularly dependence on resources that are exploitative, meager, or unpredictable (see box 2.4). Lack of resources makes a person easy prey. Vulnerability causes fear.

Even when women *do* have some control over productive assets there may be gender differences. In Pakistan, where livestock is an important asset, women raise small animals such as chickens and goats while men

Box 2.4 The Story of Murari

Murari is a 30-year-old man who is presently living in the village of Kedarkui with his family. He began his period of contractual labor in agriculture five years ago for a dominant Thakur caste farmer. The Thakur also acts as a moneylender in many of the surrounding villages. Five years ago Murari took out a loan of approximately Rs. 1,000 that he needed for an unexpected emergency. As a term of the loan, Murari was compelled to work for the Thakur farmer as an agricultural laborer on the moneylender's land for a wage of only Rs. 5,000 a year. This Thakur farmer/moneylender provided Murari and his family with accommodations, food, and some money for miscellaneous expenses, while keeping account of everything that was provided.

At the end of the first two years, Murari owed Rs. 2,500 to the Thakur. After two years of labor he owed 250 percent more to the Thakur than he had initially borrowed due to the interest incurred on the loan, charges for food and accommodation, small loans provided on an ongoing basis, and so on. However, despite this dismal situation Murari was not able to leave the Thakur's farm in search of more profitable work. If he attempted to leave, or flee, it is reported that the moneylender would track him down and the consequences would undoubtedly be serious. After five years of work as an agricultural laborer and house servant for the Thakur, Murari owes over 8,000 Rs. Murari and others like him find that they are virtually powerless once they enter the vicious cycle of contractual labor, where they are compelled to concede to the tyranny and exploitation of the moneylenders. But for many of the poorest villagers, there are no alternative sources of loans and in certain circumstances they have no choice but to accept the exploitative terms of the local moneylenders.

Source: India 1997a.

usually raise cattle. Smaller livestock is sold first, as it is thought to be more easily replaced (Pakistan 1993).

Finally, the occupations available to poor people are often physically risky. Work-related cases of debilitating and fatal injuries, assaults, illnesses, and psychological abuse abound. In Ghana, for instance, unskilled positions such as market truck-pushers or loading boys leave workers extremely vulnerable to sickness, disability (temporary or permanent), and infirmity. In addition, unskilled laborers complain of abuses from managers and employers who fail to uphold verbal agreements (Ghana 1995a).

Another PPA reports that migrant women in India, fleeing the devastation of a drought, work 20 hours a day at such activities as gathering fuel wood to sell in nearby towns, or transplanting paddy saplings (India 1998a). The South Africa report mentions a number of dangerous occupations, including women as old as 75 years old engaged in mixing mud and dung for plastering, or carrying 25-liter drums of water in return for pay. The South Africa report also mentions highly risky jobs such as garbage-picking and prostitution, as well as more traditional occupations. "In the community of Krakeel the major sources of wage-labor are work on fruit farms, and in an apple-processing factory. Both of these sources of income were shown to require the greatest physical effort and carry the greatest health risks of all the occupations that were identified. The factory is built on a dam and the floor gets very wet and cold. One woman pointed out that the swelling and pain in her legs was the result of the conditions she had had to work in the factory" (South Africa 1998).

Women also frequently complain of sexual harassment from co-workers and managers (India 1998a; Pakistan 1993).

Conclusions

There are important insights to be drawn from the PPA data about poor people's definitions and understanding of poverty and their strategies for managing the portfolio of scarce and often contested assets that are available to them. Poverty consists of multiple, interlocking dimensions. Poverty definitions focus on difficulties in securing food and livelihood. What is striking, however, is the extent to which dependency, lack of power, and lack of voice emerge as core elements of poor people's definitions of poverty. Powerlessness and voicelessness also underlie discussions of a heightened sense of vulnerability and the inability of poor people to protect themselves from shocks. Poor people speak extensively about assets and much less about income. These findings have implications for how we measure poverty. One of the challenges is to track and measure changes in power and voice together with other measures of poverty, such as estimates of expenditure and consumption, and access to education and health.

Three findings stand out from the review of poor people's pools of assets and how these assets are managed to reduce vulnerability to shocks. First, assets used by the poor to mediate social, economic, and environmental adversity are multidimensional in nature and are made up of a broad array of tangible and intangible physical, human, social, and environmental resources. Families that lack certain key assets may not necessarily be poor, but nonetheless may be extremely vulnerable in times of need or crisis.

Second, assets available to the poor are scarce and contested resources. The ability to draw on assets in times of need is directly dependent on the power relations governing these resources at a number of levels, from the household to the formal institutional level. There are often strong gender differences. The mobilization of assets almost by definition involves a negotiation of power and control over resources.

Finally, the poor tend to mention income only infrequently, relative to assets such as membership within kinship and social networks, health, labor, land, and other resources that make self-provisioning possible. In fact, the Ghana report states that the "idea of a secure livelihood is frequently more important than the incentive to maximize income" (Ghana 1995a). This is not surprising, given the heightened vulnerability of poor people and poor communities to potentially devastating shocks that are beyond their control. These findings need to be considered carefully from a policy perspective. The data provide compelling evidence that for many of the world's poor, monetary income is only a part of a much broader array of potential assets. Because social relationships are an asset, and because the poor have weak bargaining power, the organizational capacity of poor people and the quality of processes of intervention are critical.

Case study 2.1: Focus on Eastern Europe and the Former Soviet Union

Institutional Collapse, Sudden Poverty

> For a poor person everything is terrible—illness, humiliation, shame. We are cripples; we are afraid of everything; we depend on everyone. No one needs us. We are like garbage that everyone wants to get rid of. —Blind woman from Tiraspol, Moldova 1997

> I feel very unpleasant when you ask me how I would define my own situation. I cannot ... [shrugs his shoulders], but I do know I am poor. —Macedonia 1998

While in many instances the conditions under which people live in this region are better than in much of the developing world, people respond to the harsh social and economic conditions of the last decade with pronounced humiliation, shame, bewilderment, and confusion. After decades of steady employment guaranteed by the state and subsidized food, housing, education, medicine, and standards of living that, if not lavish, were for most at least adequate, the collapse of communism has resulted in the rapid erosion of virtually all social support systems, and has bred mass insecurity among the people of this region as they have watched their savings and accumulated assets dwindle and disappear.

One elderly pensioner in Moldova complained that, "[Before independence] I had two thousand rubles saved in the bank for a rainy day, for my funeral. It was quite enough during those times. Now I have 2 lei. What can I buy with them?" (Moldova 1997). The loss of security they once knew has created a profound sense of hopelessness, depression, and fear of what the future might bring.

The ways in which people define poverty in Eastern Europe and the former Soviet Union vary according to a number of factors, including gender, economic status, and the position of respondents in the socio-economic hierarchy before the social and economic transformations of the late 1980s and early 1990s. The poorest tend to cite the most basic aspects of poverty: hunger, inadequate quantities and quality of food, poor living conditions, and health problems. Following that, the poor tend to cite the inability to provide for their children, to maintain the social traditions that they once enjoyed, and to participate in a meaningful cultural and intellectual life. The transitions to a market economy, to "independence," and to "democracy" have become equated in the minds of many poor people with unprecedented vulnerability and social injustice.

Across the region there are a number of ways in which the poor have developed survival strategies to cope with sudden poverty. An extremely important asset is access to land, either one's own, or within one's family. Even small plots provide the possibility for self-provisioning of food for the family and reducing expenditures. Often food raised can be exchanged for goods and services. Families have been forced to reduce their consumption levels dramatically, often to the point of spending money only on the most basic needs such as food and shelter. Meat and fresh fruits and vegetables have largely been eliminated from the diets of the poor, and replaced with cheaper, less nutritious, and carbohydrate-rich foods such as bread, potatoes, and pasta (box 2.5).

Expenditures on health care have been reduced or eliminated, and there is increased reliance on home and traditional remedies. In addition, selling assets has been a survival strategy employed by the poor across the region. Pensioners, too, rely on the sale of material possessions, perhaps because of a greater accumulation of belongings over a lifetime, but also because of the increased need to pay for costly medical treatment. It is also

Box 2.5 Food: The Ultimate Criterion of Poverty

*Poverty is the fact that sometimes I go hungry to bed in
the evening, because I do not have bread at home.*
—Macedonia 1998

*That person is poor who for 20 days out of the month
eats boiled potatoes without butter, drinks tea without sugar,
and doesn't have enough money to buy subsidized bread.*
—Armenia 1995

*Ivan and Lolita (former collective farm workers nearing
pension age) now survive on what they can grow in their
own garden, on various jobs Ivan finds, and what Lolita
can gather from the forest and sell. They live mainly on
potatoes, going through last winter without any bread at
all. For the last two months they have lived on potato bread:
potatoes are ground up, mixed with oil, and baked. Lolita
cries when she sees a loaf of bread.* —Latvia 1998

*If I consider how other people live, then I feel poor because
I cannot give my child what he needs. If an employed individual still has to worry about buying his or her child bread and
has to scrape to make ends meet—this is not normal.*
—Latvia 1997

*Only God knows how we shall survive over the winter. At
night you wake up because of a stomachache and because of
hunger.* —A former collective farm worker, Moldova 1997

*Poverty for me is the fact that we bought some black flour
with our last money, some flour cheaper than the rest. When
we baked the bread it was not edible. We were speechless
and ate it by force since we did not have anything else.*
—Macedonia 1998

an important way of supplementing pensions that are inadequate, and often sporadically provided (Azerbaijan 1997).

Humiliation and Shame

If I openly admit myself to be poor, life will become psychologically harder. —A 45-year-old female agronomist, Latvia 1998

Much more than reports from other parts of the world, the poverty assessments from the former Soviet bloc underscore the intense shame and humiliation that people feel when confronted by their own poverty and asked to describe their current living conditions. In the former system, poverty was ascribed to laziness and incompetence, and poverty was often associated with criminality. Poverty was mainly perceived to be a result of personal failings or evidence of undesirable family traits and upbringing, and thus it was equated with a lack of social and moral worth. These attitudes can be ascribed in part to the legacy of the communist system, during which time any serious analysis of poverty would have constituted a direct challenge to the authority and legitimacy of the central state whose charge it was to provide welfare for all. Because of this, the position of Soviet ideology was to identify poverty as a social phenomenon associated primarily with deviant groups (Georgia 1997; Azerbaijan 1997).

The association of impoverishment with personal or familial short-comings remains firmly embedded in the collective psyche. In this system, maintaining at least the appearance of prosperity is vital to maintaining the social connections that enable one to secure goods and services (Moldova 1997). To admit to poverty now is therefore very difficult for people who have spent productive working lives, with little or nothing to show for it, and are forced to go to extreme measures to provide sustenance for themselves and their families. To admit to poverty makes an already untenable situation even worse.

Thus people will often try to hide their poverty from their friends and neighbors (Latvia 1997). In response to interviewers' questions many simply denied that they are poor, describing themselves in other terms such as "in the middle," "close to poor," or "underprivileged." As a villager in Armenia says, "If a person is needy, we just say he doesn't live very well" (Armenia 1995). People fear that if their true economic status is known it will damage the honor and respect of the family within the community, and hurt the future chances of their children (Macedonia 1998).

One Latvian interviewee says, "Our situation is somewhere in the middle, [because] there are others for whom it is worse"; yet "there is a lot we would need, but we cannot get anything" (Latvia 1997). In Moldova even people who appeared extremely poor to the interviewers declined to represent themselves as "poor." Instead, they preferred to describe themselves as "close to poor," but not completely poor. A former university lecturer in physics from Tbilisi reports that he was compelled to take a job as a chauffeur in order to support his family. He found work in another city so that he would not have to suffer the humiliation of having people he knew see him driving a limousine. "I would have felt ashamed to work as a driver in the capital, but here no one knows me. All the same, it is difficult. Recently, I ran into my former students; I'm ashamed to this day when I recall how I lied and told them that the car I drive is my own, and that I own this apartment. To this day they think I'm the director of some firm" (Georgia 1997).

Much of the humiliation comes from suddenly being unable to behave in ways consistent with strongly held social norms. When such norms can no longer be upheld, people withdraw and become socially isolated, causing depression and feelings of worthlessness. This psychological toll has had negative effects on the social cohesiveness of communities, kinship groups, and even households.

For instance, being assured of a decent funeral remains a high priority for many, especially among older respondents across the region. Not being able to properly bury and pay respects to a loved one can put the honor of the family in jeopardy. For example, in Georgia funerals take on important symbolic and social significance, serving as occasions in which families demonstrate social solidarity to themselves and others. It is a time to display a family's prestige, honor, and prosperity. Friends of the deceased and the deceased's extended family are expected to attend the funeral and bring gifts. During the socialist period most elderly Georgians were able to save funeral money to offset the considerable costs, but now most have lost the bulk of their savings. The elderly now find themselves caught in the position of having to depend on their families for financial and material support while they live or use up their remaining accumulated savings and leave it to their families to cover their eventual funeral costs (Georgia 1997).

In Armenia funerals continue to have great social significance and play an important role in building social solidarity within the community. Families of the deceased shoulder a responsibility of hosting a big meal to which members of the community are invited. Although guests customarily bring gifts, the financing of a funeral, especially for poorer families, can exhaust resources and send a family into debt (Armenia 1995). People in Azerbaijan report acute embarrassment and anxiety over not being able to provide acceptable funerals for family members. One woman, an internally displaced person, felt shame and embarrassment that she would have to sell her last carpet in which she had intended to be buried (Azerbaijan 1997).

This is not only true of funerals but of other important social occasions as well. Hospitality serves the important social function of helping to build and maintain vital social connections and to establish social standing within the community. In Azerbaijan the ability to entertain guests properly is an important indicator of social status (Azerbaijan 1997), but social events that were once large and extravagant have become small and restricted. In Georgia, where hospitality is a strong social norm, people live in fear of being either hosts or guests, and routinely avoid weddings and funerals. Hosts have nothing to serve guests and guests have nothing to bring to hosts as gifts. All parties find this deeply humiliating.

In Ukraine a 35-year-old driver recalled when families could routinely invite 150 people to celebrate a wedding. Now, when a wedding takes place, few people are told and it is restricted to only a small number of family members (Ukraine 1996). A Moldovan respondent stated: "In northern Moldova the wedding party was an index of a family's welfare. Parents prepared their whole life for this wedding party. They saved money to purchase furniture, refrigerators, and televisions for the young couple. During the Soviet era, it was very shameful for the parents if they couldn't give their children a big wedding. It meant they were poor, and people who were poor were thought of as lazy. Some parents even gave their children a house and car as wedding presents. Weddings then were held either under tents that covered huge land areas, in culture palaces, or in restaurants. Now they are simply held at home" (Moldova 1997).

One woman from Georgia reports that she deals with the inability to afford gifts by disconnecting her phone when she is expecting an invitation. In this way she is able to offer the excuse that her phone is out of order so she learns of the invitation too late (Georgia 1997). A Latvian person told interviewers, "During the past two years we have not celebrated any holidays with others. We cannot afford to invite anyone to our house and we feel uncomfortable visiting others without bringing a present. The lack of contact leaves one depressed, creates a constant feeling of unhappiness, and a sense of low self-esteem" (Latvia 1998).

In Moldova respondents describe poverty as a process of becoming increasingly socially isolated as they have been able to participate less and less in the social ceremonies and traditions that once brought people together and helped to create and maintain the social bonds between people. They feel poverty is gradually destroying these traditions (Moldova 1997). Similarly, in Ukraine the poorest members of society not only cannot afford to invite others to socialize with them, but must also refuse invitations because they also cannot afford even a small gift. A 26-year-old woman who lives with her parents—who are pensioners—and a sister and niece says, "It's been a year since I have seen my girlfriend; I cannot go without at least taking a little gift. We sit at home and don't go anywhere" (Ukraine 1996). "I feel most useless in this society," says a 20-year-old Macedonian man. "I frequently get disappointed. I am looking for a job and I cannot find any. I do not want to ask my parents for money because I know they do not have it. I frequently avoid girls precisely because of this. I am ashamed of finding myself in a position where I would not be able to pay at least for my own drink" (Macedonia 1998). A 51-year-old woman from Macedonia, wife and mother of a 14-year-old son, lost her job after 20 years due to "technical surplus." She says, "I feel my heart aching when somebody comes and we do not even have any coffee to offer. I am ashamed at what we have become" (Macedonia 1998).

Prestige is very important in the former Soviet Union. One's education, job, and the social standing of the family contribute to the amount of prestige one has. Prestige and status remain important assets because of the access to scarce goods and services they provide. Status is an issue at once material and psychological, and its loss can be devastating. Many people will sell belongings rather than leave prestigious jobs (Georgia 1997). Teachers have felt their respect diminish in front of their classrooms because they can no longer afford decent clothing in which to teach. A teacher from Tbilisi reports her humiliation when asked by her 8-year-old student why she looked like a beggar who had been portrayed on television (Georgia 1997).

Coming to Terms with Poverty

> There are some people who live worse than I do, but there are also those who live better. For some I am poor, for others not, but compared to my own former situation, I am a beggar.
> —Armenia 1995

> Each person assesses poverty relative to the lives they used to enjoy, or, depending on the context, relative to the lives around them. —Latvia 1998

People from Eastern Europe and the former Soviet Union tend to think about their current economic position by comparing it with both their earlier standard of living and the current situation of others. Both are ways of attempting not only to rationally comprehend the transformations of their social status, but also to psychologically mediate their experiences. This is one of the most consistent features of the reports from this region.

Comparing the present situation with the past is a way for respondents to externalize responsibility for the current situation. By pointing to specific events that impoverished everybody, by citing examples of those worse off than they are, or the criminality and duplicity of the wealthy, respondents feel that, at least to a certain extent, their impoverishment is not the result of personal failings, but of events utterly beyond their control, such as the transitions associated with independence, or in some cases, with other shocks such as the earthquake in Armenia in 1988 that left thousands homeless (Armenia 1995).

Those over 40 frequently make historical comparisons; they often look back on the socialist era with nostalgia, loss, and regret. One person states, "Then there were no such great differences between people, there was no poverty. There was a middle class that lived well" (Macedonia 1998). Comparing the current situation with that before 1989, one Latvian respondent says, "In any case, there were no problems; we never lived too well, but we did not owe anyone anything" (Latvia 1997). An unemployed single mother with two children states, "I think that others buy new things for themselves; I cannot buy anything. It is not important if a person can survive or not; no one cares!" (Latvia 1997).

In Georgia, where in 1992 prices rose tenfold and by 1993 were increasing 100 to 300 percent each month, a man says that before the hyperinflation he had enough money to buy a car, while now that same amount would buy four loaves of bread (Georgia 1997). This was also the case in Ukraine, where "a family of four living in two rooms might be considered poor if they were unable to save enough money for major purchases such as a summer house, furniture or a washing machine. Such a family, however, could easily afford food, housing, and utility charges, vacations and clothing" (Ukraine 1996). However, now virtually all of these are entirely unaffordable, and simply providing food, health care, and adequate living space for a family is a significant struggle.

Comparing one's position with others (describing poverty synchronically) serves two functions. First, many people point to the worse conditions of others as examples of those who are really poor to avoid being forced to concede their own destitution. "My living situation is very difficult," researchers are told, "but I still have something to eat and something to wear. This morning I saw two women who were eating food they had found in the garbage. This is poverty!" (Moldova 1997).

Second, people may also compare themselves to those wealthier than they are, ascribing that wealth to corruption and dishonesty. Particularly for people over 40, the rules of the new market economy seem to violate the values by which they were raised. Because of the belief that in the former system "business was 'speculation,' and 'speculation' was a dishonest and even criminal way of making money," they compare themselves with their neighbors who have overcome their own psychological barriers to get involved in street trade and commerce (that has come to symbolize the new market relations). They claim they would rather retain their self-respect and the respect of their peers by working for meager salaries in the state sector or selling personal possessions (Georgia 1997).

Maintaining connections to people in government and business and, in general, to those with some control over scarce resources is essential to avoiding poverty, but many are losing any connections they once had as societies become more divided between rich and poor. In Georgia respondents frequently identify "capitalism" and "market relations" with an unswerving pursuit of self-interest with no regard for the effects on those outside of one's own social network (Georgia 1997). A popular joke in Ukraine encapsulates many of the attitudes toward earning money in the new economy and the importance of official connections through which goods and services can be brokered:

> United Nations officials are interviewing three pilots, a
> German, an American, and a Russian, for a UN international
> air force. The German says he has experience and wants a
> salary of $3,000. The American says he has excellent training
> and wants a salary of $6,000. The Russian says he wants
> $9,000. When asked about his experience, the Russian readily
> admits that he's never flown a plane and he has no experience
> in the military. When the astonished UN officials ask why he is
> demanding $9,000, he cheerfully explains, "Simple! $3,000 for
> you, $3,000 for me, and $3,000 for the German. Let him fly!"
> —Ukraine 1996

This joke illustrates how ideologies and attitudes toward earning money have changed as well as how "one person's willingness to bend the rules allows another to earn money purely by capitalizing on the acquaintance" (Ukraine 1996). "We have our problems," says one Latvian man, "how to survive; they have their problems—how to guard their fortunes" (Latvia 1998).

Rural and Urban Areas: Different Assets, Different Needs

> Peasants now live 10 times better than those in the city do,
> but they work 10 times harder. —Agronomist, Armenia 1995

Both the rural and the urban poor raise the issues of food and access to basic services. While references suggest that rural poverty may be less severe than in urban areas because of rural people's possibilities for self-provision, income statistics suggest that poverty is both more widespread and more severe in rural areas than in cities. (See, for instance, Kyrgyz Republic 1998.) As in the rest of the world, rural areas have traditionally had less access to basic services, including transportation, health care, and schools.

In Georgia families in both urban and rural areas report going without food for several days, especially in order to ensure that their children have something to eat. Rural areas mainly experience hunger in the early spring before crops can be planted and after food supplies have been exhausted. In urban areas, however, hunger tends to be more acute and people report subsisting for long periods of time on only bread and tea (Georgia 1997).

Having some small piece of land on which to grow vegetables or having social connections to family or others who can grow food is an important resource for urban families. Indeed, a common opinion among urban residents is that at least people in rural areas stand less of a chance of going hungry. "What benefit do I have from the fact that there is everything in town?" a woman asks. "You see things, but do not have money for anything. If I would live in a village I would be happy. If I had one small piece of land I would plant things, breed cattle and say good-bye to poverty" (Macedonia 1998). There has even been a slight trend in Armenia of urban to rural migration in order to take advantage of extended kinship networks in villages and increased access to land (Armenia 1995).

Nevertheless, the rural poor often report feeling isolated and lack key infrastructure such as transportation, schools, and health-care clinics (Latvia 1998). In Macedonia, for instance, rural residents frequently report that their situation is more severe than that of urban residents due to lack of basic services. "We in the village have a four-grade primary school and one shop," a poor person stated. "Our children should continue their education in the nearest town. We also have to seek medical care in the town. Everything we need we have to go and buy in the city ... and these are additional costs."

Interviews completed in Latvia suggest that urban poverty tends to be more anonymous. People are not as aware of their neighbors' conditions and can ignore the people picking through the garbage for food. Urban residents more frequently tend to equate poverty with being unable to take advantage of the cultural or social activities that they previously enjoyed.

Vulnerability and Despair

Previously, pensioners could help their children and still keep something for themselves, but now you just lie down and die.
—Latvia 1998

Box 2.6 The Situation of the Elderly Population in Eastern Europe and the former Soviet Union

I went to sleep a rich man able to buy several cars. But I woke up a beggar. —Pensioner from Kharkiv, Ukraine 1996

Who is going to provide social assistance to pensioners if they don't even help young people? We pensioners are sick and helpless. We don't produce anything. So who needs us? —Ukraine 1996

We envisaged happy pension days when we would rejoice over our grandchildren and see them grow in settled households. See what we came out with? Instead of our children helping us, they cannot take care and manage their own lives. If it were not for the pension they would have to go out in the streets and beg. —Macedonia 1998

Today you can't die. Not long ago a friend buried her mother. The funeral cost krb 50 million [$226]. To pay for it, they sold her mother's Lenin Medal for $380. How will my children bury me? I am horrified every time I think about it. —Ukraine 1996

You gave birth to them yourself, get rid of this mess yourself!
—Response from officials when mothers requested aid for their needy children, Ukraine 1996

Those for whom the socialist system formerly provided primary support are particularly vulnerable. These groups include the elderly, the disabled, children (and especially orphans), the unemployed, and those who lack adequate social support networks.

Many categories of the elderly are among the most vulnerable segment of the population throughout the region (see box 2.6). Subsisting on the bare minimum provided by state pensions, they often find themselves dependent on their children and extended family whose resources are already spread exceedingly thin. For pensioners, a large problem is actually receiving pensions regularly and on time (Moldova 1997). In Azerbaijan, by 1995 pensions had decreased to 4 percent of their 1991 value (Azerbaijan 1997). One pensioner from Baku, Azerbaijan, used to work as a radiographer and telephone operator, but hyperinflation has rendered her pension and savings practically worthless: "I used to wear a mink coat and now I can't even afford a pair of shoes." She lives on a small pension and is forced to sell her household belongings. She is no longer able to pay for services or buy medicine to treat her tuberculosis. Her diet consists mainly of margarine and pasta (Azerbaijan 1997). Some pensioners are able to find work and supplement their state support, although many cannot find employment or are physically unable to work. Qualitative findings from the Azerbaijan PPA contradict earlier household survey data that showed pensioners with jobs to be among the least vulnerable population groups (Azerbaijan 1997). Salaries tend to be very low and job security uncertain. In Georgia, also, delays in pension payments often pose serious problems to the elderly poor. Pensioners who do not have family networks to fall back on are among the most vulnerable. Large numbers of elderly subsist by begging (Georgia 1997). Many are ill and disabled and cannot work. Others have witnessed their life savings vanish before their eyes because of hyperinflation, and are forced to sell off their personal possessions to survive. Some pensioners are able to self-provide, growing food on small plots of land. Others are unable to do this because of disability or lack of access to land.

Children are also at risk of hunger, and families with many children are often among the poorest (Latvia 1998). In Azerbaijan respondents discuss the increasing prevalence of child labor in which children as young as six are commonly seen on the street engaged in vending and odd jobs (Azerbaijan 1997). In Armenia some children suffer malnutrition, stunted growth, and rickets even though families attempt to ensure that the youngest children are adequately fed (Armenia 1995). A respondent in Latvia says that children are an "expensive pleasure." For single mothers, a child can greatly increase a mother's burdens because of the added logistical restrictions when trying to find or hold down a job (Ukraine 1996). A Ukrainian respondent says, "There's nothing to eat. We're constantly hungry. There's nothing to wear. There's no money to buy the child boots, or notebooks, pens or a book bag. My life is just grief. That's all … I don't even want to live. I gave birth to these kids and I have to raise them. But if I didn't I would have put a rope around my neck and hanged myself a long time ago" (Ukraine 1996).

Additionally, there is now increasing social stigmatization of women with large numbers of children. Many women now try to limit the number of children born. Abortions in Ukraine are available for US$30 to $50, an amount that is prohibitive for poor women. Nevertheless, because abortions are available, many believe it is unconscionable for women to bear so many children during a time of pronounced economic hardship and stress. This attitude is also held among government officials who are in the position of making decisions on how aid is to be distributed to poor families. A respondent, after unsuccessfully trying to get aid, refused to return to the city agency responsible for welfare for families in need. "I only get upset and nothing else. They insult me and reproach me for being a single mother. They told me I'm to blame for having so many children and they're right, I am. But the children aren't guilty of anything!" (Ukraine 1996).

Survey reports indicate that Internally Displaced Persons (IDPs) are among the most vulnerable groups, and there is some animosity toward them due to the aid directed toward them. One person says, "Only refugees and IDPs receive humanitarian aid while we have to sell our goods. I have a negative attitude toward IDPs" (Azerbaijan 1997). Of course, many refugees and IDPs have no assets to sell, as they are forced to leave their homes and all of their possessions, often with just the clothes on their backs (box 2.7).

Attitudes toward Government

What kind of government do we have? One hand gives and the
other takes away! —Ukraine 1996

Attitudes toward the government in Eastern Europe and the former Soviet Union result from a complex combination of factors. Mainly there is widespread anger at what is perceived as horrendous financial mismanagement that has caused hyperinflation and widespread unemployment. The poor blame the government for their impoverishment, widespread unemployment, and the inflation rates that have devalued their savings, wages, and pensions. Poor people believe government officials have exploited their social and political positions for wealth, influence, and personal gain, while ignoring the position of the neediest. At the same time, after a lifetime of dependence on subsidies and entitlements, many still look to the government for solutions to their problems, and hope that it will resume the role it filled in the past. In Georgia, for instance, people frequently described the state as a "parent that should take care of its children" (Georgia 1997). For this reason, many express anger at what they perceive as corruption, mismanagement, and indifference on the part of the government to growing impoverishment (box 2.8).

For many, government support such as pensions, meager though it may be, is the only available source of income. Yet throughout the region people complain about the humiliating treatment they receive when attempting to obtain social assistance. Many become discouraged by bureaucracy, rude and unresponsive officials, and withheld information. A respondent in Macedonia reports, "You have to queue a lot and go from one desk to another. The clerks are very impolite [and] do not inform as they should" (Macedonia 1998). Another spent a month gathering all the necessary documentation to receive social assistance. The result was that he was given a number and told to return in a month's time. He did not return, partly out of shame and partly out of anger (Macedonia 1998). In Armenia some refuse even to apply for a pension because the amount is so minimal its only purpose is to constitute a form of mockery (Armenia 1995).

During the previous regime people gained access to goods and services through connections and often paid for favors with a gift, or modest bribe. This was an accepted and expected way of doing things and it did not pose serious problems. Currently, however, the system of bribery has become more pervasive and extreme, posing hardships above and beyond what most can afford. Employment, health care, and social services all frequently require bribes. A person from Georgia says, "Recently at the

Box 2.8 Attitudes toward the Government

Since the state no longer provides the assistance needed and expected, the overwhelming response is anger, frustration, betrayal, abandonment, and, finally, demoralization.

People place their hopes in God, since the government is no longer involved in such matters. —Armenia 1995

Politicians don't care about the suffering population. —Moldova 1997

Our leaders announced transition to new market relations and then left us to the mercy of fate, not asking whether we were prepared to accept the transition. —Georgia 1997

When I retired I had 20,000 rubles in my savings account. With this money it would have been possible to buy four cars. But what the government did with it— the government we trusted with our money! They re-indexed savings so that inflation ate it! That money is now not enough for bread and water. And still, they give a pension that doesn't even provide minimum survival. If the pension they gave me earlier, 132 rubles, was enough for a comfortable life, well, on today's pension, I can't possibly live or survive. —Ukraine 1996

telephone station they told me, 'Pay $400 and tomorrow we will connect you'—it's market relations!" Another says, "If you don't have the money, it's all the same whether you study or not, but with money, even a moron can enroll in medical school" (Georgia 1997).

While the fall of the Berlin Wall and the accompanying social and political transition are understood by many in the West as changes ushering in a new and unprecedented freedom to the region, many from the former socialist countries experienced the transition as the exact opposite (see also figures 2.1 and 2.2 in appendix 7). In Georgia "people associate their poverty with the lack of freedom—they feel enslaved by their crushing daily burdens, by depression, from fear of what the future will bring" (Georgia 1997).

Notes

1. The numerous academic sources that review the various quantitative methods for measuring poverty include: Sen 1997; Foster and Sen 1997; and Lipton and Ravallion 1995. For a less technical discussion of quantitative poverty measures, see Greeley 1994. For reviews of participatory and qualitative approaches to gathering information on poverty, see Chambers 1994; Salmen 1987; Cernea 1985; and Carvalho and White 1998.

2. The 1998 Gujrat cyclone affected 4.6 million people; left 1,241 people dead; and killed 21,993 cattle. See Bhatt 1999. The figures for the 1999 cyclone in the state of Orrissa are even higher.

3. See Agarwal 1992 for a rich discussion on gender relations and coping with drought and famine in South Asia.

Chapter 3

State Institutions

They have been plundering everything and eating so much that they cannot carry their own stomachs.

—A poor woman, Latvia 1998

For government schemes we have to pay donations.

—A poor man, India 1997b

Loans should be provided when we still have rice to eat.

—A poor woman, Vietnam 1999a

The food aid last year through work on the road has become a husband to me as it helped a lot.

—A poor widow, Zambia 1994

In virtually every country today governments aim not merely to protect their citizens, but also to ensure that even the poorest among them have access to basic services. Typically these services include education, basic health care, and safe drinking water; sometimes they extend much further to include old-age pensions and support for the disabled. Governments set up a variety of state institutions to provide these services, such as police forces, public works, education ministries, public health services, water authorities, and so on. These same institutions are used by external support agencies as channels for projects intended to benefit the poor. But from the perspective of the poor there is an institutional crisis. While there are pockets of excellence, the poor usually experience formal institutions as ineffective, inaccessible, and disempowering. The recurrent themes running through the reports are distrust, corruption, humiliation, intimidation, helplessness, hopelessness, and often anger. While increasing attention is being paid to the issue of good governance as a way of fostering private sector investment,[1] the PPAs reveal poor people's daily experiences and struggles with poor governance at the local level.

Analysis of the PPAs reveals six major findings about state institutions and the poor:

▸ **Formal institutions are largely ineffective and irrelevant in the lives of the poor.** Where government programs of targeted assistance exist, they contribute a little in poor people's struggles to survive, but they do not help them to escape poverty.

▸ **Corruption directly affects the poor.** Poor people have widespread and intimate experience with corruption in health, education, water, forestry, government-provided relief, and social assistance—where it is available. In addition, the poor have little access to the judiciary, and they fear, rather than seek protection from, the police.

▸ **The poor feel disempowered and humiliated.** Poor people's interactions with representatives of the state leave them feeling powerless, unheard, and silenced.

▸ **Collapse of the state increases poor people's vulnerability.** When functioning states collapse, as in Eastern Europe and the former Soviet Union, or go through severe disruption as in East Asia, the poor are particularly vulnerable, and the new poor feel bewildered, crushed, and angry.

▸ **The poor confront many barriers in trying to access government services.** These include bureaucratic hurdles, incomprehensible rules and regulations, the need for documents to which they do not have access, and difficulties in accessing necessary information.

▸ **There is often collusion or overlap between local governance and the elite.** If not outright collusion, local elite at least have direct access to, and influence over, local officials, and resist sharing power in new decentralization and participation policies. There are also examples of caring local elite.

In this chapter we first define key concepts, and then examine the six findings from the PPAs. These dynamics are further explored in two case studies at the end of the chapter that focus on health care and education.

Understanding Institutions

The most important strategy for finding either public or private employment is to use one's "connections" and pay a bribe.
—Georgia 1997

Sociologists, political scientists, and economists have all turned to the nature of society and its informal rules, norms, and expectations, in order to understand the failure of the state to deliver on its promises.

Institutions are legitimized through public sanction and acceptance; this often has legal or statutory dimensions. They operate and exercise authority through rules and regulations that determine "who" is eligible for "what." However, institutions cannot be understood simply through their formal rules, since actual practices often diverge from these rules. Institutional behavior is dynamic, and can be better understood through the "regularized patterns of behavior that emerge, in effect, from underlying structures, or sets of rules in use" (Leach et al. 1997; Giddens 1984). For example, while formal rules may prohibit bribery, "rules in use" commonly require a bribe in exchange for service delivery. Institutions can also reproduce existing social and power inequalities by serving only those who fulfill certain requirements, thus perpetuating current social patterns of gender, race, and ethnicity in society.

Formal institutions structure and are structured by other formal and informal social relationships. As a result, they often claim to be serving the common good, while they actually reproduce unequal relationships of power and authority or marginalize the concerns of particular groups, such as women or the poor (Goetz 1998; Kabeer and Subrahmanian 1996; Narayan 1999). This differential impact of state institutions across social groups may not always be readily apparent. Douglas North (1990) explains:

In the modern Western world we think of life and the economy as being ordered by formal laws and property rights. Yet formal rules, even in the most developed economy, make up a small (although very important) part of the sum of constraints that shape choices; a moment's reflection should suggest to us the pervasiveness of informal constraints. In our daily interaction with others whether within the family, its external social relations or in business activities, the government structure is overwhelmingly defined by codes of conduct, norms of behavior and conventions ... That the informal constraints are important in themselves (and not simply as appendages to formal rules) can be observed from the evidence that the same formal rules and/or constitutions imposed on very different societies produce different outcomes. —North 1990

The experiences recounted by the poor in the PPAs uncover these unwritten rules in use and highlight the ways in which formal institutions are socially embedded, both reflecting and reproducing existing power imbalances. These informal rules, norms, and expectations need to be taken into account when planning services for the poor.

Effectiveness and Relevance

We keep hearing about monies that the government allocates for projects, and nothing happens on the ground.
—South Africa 1998

"L'état est absent"—the state is simply absent from people's lives and strategies for securing their needs.
—Madagascar 1996

Loans should be provided when we still have rice to eat; if we don't have any food, we will spend all the money on food. —Poor woman, Vietnam 1999a

While some government services are reaching some poor people some of the time, across regions formal institutions are commonly described as ineffective and even completely irrelevant in poor people's lives. Both in health-care services and in access to education, the constraints imposed by official and unofficial fees and expenses for school uniforms, books and chalk, transport, ineffective repeat visits to the health clinic or hospital and medicine costs were mentioned repeatedly. In fact, health and education are discussed with such regularity that we focus on them in case studies at the end of this chapter. In some countries (such as

Pakistan), despite the high costs, many poor people go to the private sector where they are at least more assured that they will receive service after all the payments are made. There are few examples of interactions with the judiciary system, which seems to be beyond the reach of poor men and women. There are, however, innumerable examples of police intimidation. (A case study on poor people's interactions with the police appears at the end of chapter 6.)

India has one of the world's largest programs of basic services and public assistance for the poor, lower castes, and tribal groups. These programs provide free schooling, health care, housing, subsidized food, kerosene, water, credit, seeds and relief during natural disasters, pensions for widows, and assistance to the disabled. Our analysis includes excellent, large PPA studies from two different states—Rajasthan and Orissa—that document what often happens to well-intentioned government programs for the poor. While the studies do not constitute an in-depth evaluation of why the system does or does not work, they do illustrate a pattern of problems and the extent to which these programs touch the lives of poor people.

In Rajasthan a participatory assessment of the Baran District Poverty Alleviation Program was conducted in 29 villages selected to be statistically representative of the district. The poor evaluated all programs and institutions affecting their lives. One of these programs, the Integrated Rural Development Program (IRDP), aims to help families below the poverty line with loans and subsidies for livestock, agricultural machinery, funds to open shops, and so on. In the village of Kishanganj people say that the beneficiary selection process left out many families most in need. In the district of Baran as a whole only 40 percent of those selected receive any kind of support at all. People say that "The support is not adequate enough to truly benefit them and the quality of various provisions was substandard and therefore of little use" (India 1997a). Many participants say that the distributed assets (bullock carts, cattle) are in fact more of a liability; hence, many remain unused or are sold, having little impact on the family's well-being. "It is rocky here and it is very hot. So the animals given under IRDP could not survive. All of them died very soon and we could not repay our loans. Those animals needed more water" (India 1997a). Both the TRYSEM program to provide technical skills to youth living below the poverty line, and the Jawahar Rojgar Yojna program to generate employment for those below the poverty line were rated as having little or no impact on the lives of the poor.

Similarly, the Indira Awas Yojna projects provide free housing to the needy. In Baran the program was designed to construct 1,061 houses. Only 350 houses were actually built, and at the time of the research, all of the houses were damaged and not one was occupied because the poor found them "alien to their lifestyle and sociocultural way of living" (India 1997a). Many programs providing housing to the poor use substandard construction materials. Also in the Baran district, government-built water storage tanks remain unused in the three years since they were installed because the hand pumps have been damaged and have not been repaired. The only government program functioning well is the Shaharia Vicks Pariyojna program that provides boarding schools for tribal youths and overall development assistance in tribal villages.

The second PPA was conducted in Bolangir district in a drought-prone western part of Orissa. Again, the findings are based on research conducted in 29 villages chosen to be statistically representative of the district. The PPA also includes an institutional assessment. People generally rate the administrative institutions of the government—including the Revenue Inspector's office, block office, police stations, subdivisional office, and the office of the Zila Parishad—low in terms of efficiency and accessibility. In Padiyabahal village in Khaprakhol, for example, government institutions are rated "medium" to "low" in importance, efficiency, and accessibility. Similarly, in other villages, the government agencies are found to lie at a greater distance from the village compared to the other institutions (India 1998a).

Institutional analysis ratings in Padiyabahal, another Orissa village, illustrate the pattern of ratings by poor men and women. The hospital is rated by the poor as one of the most important institutions—and also as one of the most prohibitively expensive. One PPA states that government "health agencies were seldom used as they are far, there is always a shortage of medicines, and lack of a sympathetic attitude of staff" (India 1998a). People use private pharmacists and traditional doctors instead. Schools, though rated high in importance, are also rated as the second most expensive institution. They receive low ratings in efficiency because of "frequent absence of teachers, nonimplementation of the midday meal scheme, and poor quality education." Sending children to school is considered futile under these circumstances (India 1998a).

The public distribution system (PDS) of food for families below the poverty line (BPL) is found in every village in Orissa. Although the poor consider it important, they rate the program poorly. A BPL card allows the poor to buy rice at Rs. 2 per kilogram. Not all the poor have BPL cards, and rice quotas are issued irregularly, once every three to four months. The poor are unable to buy in bulk because of limited resources. Several cases are cited of poor people selling off their BPL card because they lack the cash to use their cards. Figure 3.1 lists poor people's ratings of government programs in one village.

Farmers rate the block agriculture office's subsidized seed distribution program as very important, though erratic and ill-timed. It makes seeds affordable, but the program has other problems. "When we approach the

Figure 3.1 Analysis of Government Programs, Chikili Village, India

Government Work	Who Did	Year	Which Caste People Were Benefited	Present Condition	Ranking	People Perception
Well	Govt	1965	Adivasi (ST)	is now buried		Did not work Due to Bad construction
Road	Govt.	1962	All Caste	not good	XX XX	Stones [on the side] of the near pola Road have Fallen down Pola is bad
BPL Cards, PDS	PANCH-AYAT	1997	All Caste	Regular Supply	XX XX X	Half of the people have not got CARD Big Farmers are getting Rs.2 Rice While small farmer Rs.4/-
Million Wells Scheme	BLOCK	1994	Adibasi & Ganda (SC)	is working well	XX	Many more poor should get it
Loan for Income generation activities	BLOCK	1983	Adibasi & Ganda (SC)	They are not gebbing now		Waiving off of LOANS was helpfull
Indira Awas Houses	BLOCK	1996	Dal Ganda (SC)	Houses are okay & of use	X	Many more should get it
Literacy Campaign	BLOCK	1996	All Caste	Ignorant started reading	XX XX XX	Got some benefit, why it was stopped we dont know
DPT	BLOCK	1982	All Caste	Now stopped		We need some medical facilities now (ANGANWADI CENTRE)
	BLOCK	1970	All Caste	Now stopped		

Notes: SC: Schedule Caste; PDS: Public Distribution System; BPL: Below Poverty Line Cards; Adibasi: Tribal Groups; Ganda: Tribal Groups; DPT: Diphtheria, Polio, Tetanus; Angannadi Centre: Preschool center

Participants: Gokul Mahakud, Mityanando Mahakud, Pabitra Loha, Pusindra Kabir Tandi block agriculture office for paddy seed," one farmer says, "the official would force us to buy other seeds like Dhanicha, for which we do not have money, and neither do we cultivate these seeds" (India 1998a).

Elsewhere in India people acknowledge that through PDS the government provides subsidized staples such as wheat, sugar, and kerosene to the poor, but that many of the items the poor need to purchase are not available. A PPA reports, "During the course of the survey, the team checked the ration cards of various families and found that there were very few entries, which suggests that the intended beneficiaries are not able to use these systems. Therefore, the PDS are not serving their intended beneficiaries effectively, and it also raises the question of where all the resources are going if they are not being received by the appropriate people" (India 1997a).

The poor list the following reasons for the slow progress and the disappointing results in the implementation of assistance programs in some states in India:

▸ Inordinate delays in the implementation of even the approved programs
▸ Political leaders being more interested in themselves than in the society they have chosen to serve
▸ Lack of participation and involvement of the beneficiaries
▸ Poor managerial competencies at each administrative level
▸ Lack of supervision
▸ Planning from the top ignoring people's assessment of their needs
▸ Pervasive corruption involving the role of government officials and contractors (India 1997c)

Despite problems, poor people participate in government schemes "even if it was not what they wanted because they felt that something is better than nothing and perhaps the schemes could help in some way" (India 1997a). One clear consequence of government agency ineffectiveness is a pervasive distrust of government in general, as expressed in this excerpt from a Madagascar PPA:

In all regions of the study participants expressed a feeling of distrust and betrayal by the government. This can most clearly be seen in the South, where only 12 percent of the participants were in favor of the government. In their opinion the government is not only guardian of their rights but it is also there to assist them during difficult times and in their fight against poverty. However, the remaining 88 percent unanimously expressed distrust toward the government, its representatives,

institutions, and administration. Sixty-seven percent perceived
the government as permeated with corruption. Some com-
plained about the attitude of the government, its indifference
toward their concerns and problems. —Madagascar 1994

In many parts of the world, poor people frequently complain that the
services they need are not available. In South Africa, for example, "Formal
financial institutions are virtually nonexistent in rural areas, and in both
urban and rural communities, the formal institutions that are available are
mostly inappropriate to the requirements of the poor" (South Africa 1998).
A Ghanaian PPA notes that "Governmental safety nets were not mentioned
by any informants as being in any way relevant for the poorest members of
these communities" (Ghana 1995a).

Where services are accessible, their quality and efficiency is often
criticized as substandard and unreliable: "Failed water supply schemes by
Nigeria's state and local governments, as well as under such special programs as Directorate for Food, Roads, and Rural Infrastructure, are extremely common in both rural and urban areas. Often, state water boards
have designed overelaborate and expensive schemes to supply piped
water to house connections and these proved beyond the capacity of local
authorities to construct or to manage. Since communities are not involved
in planning schemes, they can also play little role in managing them"
(Nigeria 1996).

In the Zambia PPA the state-run agricultural extension system,
designed to provide information and inputs to farmers, receives highly
unfavorable ratings by poor farmers. Many farmers view agricultural
services as basically nonexistent or irrelevant (Zambia 1997). Poor farmers
say that either extension agents never visit, or they exhibit favoritism in
their patterns of work. The youth and inexperience of many extension
agents adds to the impression that their knowledge is theoretical and
derived solely from books. Others think that the messages conveyed by the
extension agents are too repetitive and focus too much on maize cultivation
to the exclusion of other cash and subsistence crops. The farmers' meetings
with extension agents are thought to be unnecessarily frequent and, as a
result, are poorly attended. The researchers also assessed the importance of
the agricultural extension system in the lives of farmers through institutional diagramming techniques in which the size and distance of circles
drawn represents the importance and closeness of the institutions in people's lives. "Compared to the church, the headman, the hospital, the district
council and the school, an NGO, and LINTCO (the cotton marketing
organization), the department of agriculture is represented as a mere speck
on the perimeter" (Milimio 1995).

Overall, state institutions appear to be not at all, or only marginally, relevant in the lives of the very poor, except in times of severe crisis. Formal institutions are discussed favorably in the PPAs in some references to food aid and other emergency assistance. A widow in Simanansa, Zambia says, "The food aid last year through work on the road has become a husband to me as it helped a lot" (Zambia 1994). In many cases, however, there are reports of corruption, and a sense that what actually reaches the poor is a diluted form of what was originally allotted. Excerpts from Swaziland, Kenya, and Bangladesh PPAs indicate that government food aid is vital in times of crisis, yet even then it is unreliable. "In Swaziland most people expressed little confidence that the central government agencies were equipped to address the needs of rural communities. In many rural communities food aid and food for work programs were said to have been vital during crop failures or severe drought but were often seen as sporadic and unreliable" (Swaziland 1997).

In Kenya once famine has been officially recognized and the government relief efforts begin, the poor in some of the districts do benefit. However, government-provided relief food becomes an added category in the coping strategies of the poor, rather than the only strategy. This is because the government-provided relief is both irregular and insufficient in quantity by the time it reaches households to meet food needs. In the districts where food relief is mentioned two issues came out consistently: leakage and political interference. In Kitui people report, "Now we just borrow donkeys and go to the relief center ourselves to collect food, otherwise we would never get anything." In Busia people in one area say, "We finally received one bag of maize for the entire sublocation, over 200 households. So we decided to give it to the school, so at least our children would get a few hot meals" (Kenya 1996).

In urban Bangladesh the poor are critical of government relief services. Either people do not receive the amount allocated, or they need to bribe officials to get any relief at all. "Many said that relief should be channeled directly to them and not through local government" (Bangladesh 1996).

In many parts of Eastern Europe and the former Soviet Union, workers speak about deep unfairness in processes used for privatization of state assets. In Moldova farm workers characterize the land privatization as basically increasing the gap between the rich and poor in formerly egalitarian communities. Farm workers felt that the framework for land reform did not provide any cushion and resulted in five to six families in a community buying up the land, leaving the rest working for them just as previously they worked for the Romanian *boyars*. Farm workers at collectives say privatization consists of "collecting numerous poorly understood documents, which they fear the farm managers will only sign if the farmer has already established a 'special relationship' with them" (Moldova 1997).

Insufficient government services cannot be attributed simply to un-motivated or corrupt state employees. A PPA from Gabon notes:

> Several social centers and facilities in Libreville were visited. Discussion with staff members there showed (1) a high degree of motivation; (2) a feeling that staff were powerless in the face of widespread misery, with no resources to help: "All we can do is say nice things to people, and that doesn't help much. We have lots of ideas but no funds. We have to reach into our own pockets to buy someone some milk. We can help these poor people fill out their application forms, but we never know what will be done with them"; (3) a sense of revolt against the low esteem accorded to them and to their work by the authorities. "Social workers are nobodies in Gabon. The big shots don't even know what we're doing. When we try to help the doctors, they tell us we're useless." Staff become discouraged and tend to stick to their offices. "Why bother going out among people if we can't even help the ones who come to us?"
> —Gabon 1997

Not all government programs for the poor get wholly bad reviews. In Nigeria, for example, while opinion leaders in Kwara state noted that many agencies have been providing amenities, such as health clinics, market stalls, immunizations, and employment programs for youth, these leaders also noted several serious problems, such as the large number of government projects started but soon abandoned, and tax monies that seem not to be spent on community betterment (Nigeria 1996). In some cases praise for government projects is unqualified, such as in a PPA from Uganda. "The government has assisted us very much by catering for these four children per family. You may think that is small, but I am told that the government educates about five million children in primary. That is good" (Uganda 1998). In India in an area where the majority of people felt that poverty has declined, the PPA noted that the people's "well-considered" responses attributed the decline in poverty to several things, the first being "state-sponsored development and antipoverty programs" (India 1997c).

Corruption and Distrust

> The state steals from us all the time so deceiving the state is not a sin. —Ukraine 1996

Nobody wants you to come with empty hands.
—Macedonia 1998

For government schemes we have to pay donations.
Those who should be enlisted in the below-the-poverty-
line list are not included, and those who are affluent are
enlisted. —India 1997b

We saw the lorry of food relief arrive and the chief told
us two weeks later that one-and-a-half bags had been
received for distribution to 116 households. —Kwale,
Kenya 1996

Teachers do not go to school except when it is time to
receive salaries. —Nigeria 1997

Discussions of government failure in the PPAs are often interwoven with references to state corruption, which drastically reduces the efficiency and effectiveness of service delivery while breeding distrust and disdain among the poor who encounter it. These trends have dramatic implications for those who rely on formal government services, as the following description illustrates:

> *The reluctance to access loans from formal sources in Orissa*
> *[India] arises mainly due to two reasons. First, the prevalence*
> *of a high level of corruption [as high as 20 percent to 50 per-*
> *cent of the borrowed amount is believed to be lost in greasing*
> *the palms of bank officials for getting loans sanctioned].*
> *Second, excessive delay in the process of loan disbursement*
> *spanning across seasons, which causes too much frustration*
> *and harassment for the loan seekers. By the time a loan from a*
> *bank is sanctioned, the original purpose of credit requirement*
> *becomes redundant. A bullock loan sought in the beginning of*
> *an agricultural season is believed to be of little use if accruing*
> *at the end of harvest. Such untimely loans are usually spent on*
> *unproductive purposes, landing the borrower in an inevitable*
> *debt-trap.* —India 1998a

Corruption in education services appears widespread and cuts off students' opportunities for primary and higher education: "We heard many accounts of village youth in Moldova with excellent grades who tried to enter university. In several cases they were forced to return to their villages because their parents could not pay the large bribes professors demanded to guarantee their admission. One such discouraged mother reported, 'My oldest son graduated as a locksmith from a technical college but could not find a job. He had very good grades and decided to re-educate himself in the Academy of Economic Studies. I was asked to give a bribe of 2,000 lei, but I had no money. As a result, my son failed the entrance examination'" (Moldova 1997).

In a country where privatization is equated with theft due to the high levels of corruption permeating the transition, farm workers have a deep distrust of their own farm managers. Farm workers in Moldova are putting their hope in the "American project" funded by the U.S. Agency for International Development (USAID), which will manage the break-up of 70 collective farms around the country. Despite some reservations about the project, villagers feel that the Americans, as outsiders, will be less prone to corruption than Moldovan officials, and thus land and assets will be distributed more fairly (Moldova 1997).

Corruption in health-care services is common in many regions, and poor people with serious health conditions have no choice but to comply in order to obtain the care they need. In Macedonia, "Most of those interviewed stress [that] 'Nobody wants you to come with empty hands.' Ordinary services presuppose small gifts (coffee, candies, drink, and similar items), but value goes up as the value of the requested services increases" (Macedonia 1998). Further:

- One woman with … gangrene of the foot tried for seven years to get a disability pension. Three doctors composing the commission deciding on the issue of disability, after they learned she had a brother in Germany, determined a bribe in the amount of 3,000 German marks.
- One person interviewed had to repair the doctor's car as compensation for a kidney operation.
- One man who needed a kidney operation had to pay a bribe to get a referral to Skopje.
- According to one of the interviewed, patients at the Oncology Department at the clinical center in Skopje have to pay up to 1,000 to 2,000 German marks for good accommodation and good services.
- Doctors openly told one man from Debar whose wife needed an ulcer operation, "If you have a thick envelope it is all right, if not, scram." In general the opinion prevails that in Skopje hospitals a patient has to pay about 2,000 to 3,000 German marks for one operation (Macedonia 1998).

Examples of corruption in the health delivery system also abound throughout the developing world. Some clinics have no medicines, highly shortened hours, no doctors, and staff who may demand payments from patients in order to register, to be examined by a nurse or a doctor, and to get tests done. These examples are discussed in detail in the case study on health care at the end of this chapter.

State service delivery mechanisms are often described as either delivering nothing or delivering harassment. A PPA from India notes, "If the government passes a loan of Rs. 10,000, only half of it reaches the beneficiary. The rest is taken away by the government people. If we make a hut, the men of the Forest Department will start harassing us for money, asking from where we got the wood and saying it belongs to the Forest Department and so on" (India 1997c).

In Indonesia, a national bottom-up planning process has been subverted. In a study of 48 villages in three provinces all village heads regarded the process as a mere formality. Village officials after a community consultation process submit proposals for priority action. Villages are frequently pressured to revise their proposals in accordance with "suggestions" or "invitations" by government sector agencies. In Central Java, villagers complained that substantial parts of the subsidy were deducted for expenses. In the province of Nusa Tenggara Timur (NTT), in one village 20 percent of the subsidy was received in cash, 50 percent in goods not requested or wanted, and 30 percent was withheld to cover expenses. Another village received 10,000 carp to be collected from the capital city, three days away. The village had not requested fish and had no fishponds (Indonesia 1998).

In Mexico, state institutions are steeped in *clientelismo*. Only some communitarian institutions among the indigenous peoples of Oaxaca seem to be free of corruption. Others depend on leaders who provide favors in exchange for votes (see box 3.1).

When formal institutions break down, people employ a variety of strategies to meet their needs, including working around a system that is perceived to be unjust or exploitative through active sabotage or passive resistance. Especially in cases of state breakdown, few people express hesitation about employing whatever means are necessary to survive, including overtly illegal or dangerous ones. In Ukraine people say, "The government has ripped us off, so why shouldn't people steal a bit on the sly? We don't steal but we don't judge others who do. You have to survive!" (Ukraine 1996).

The PPAs from many regions describe scenarios in which the state is neither trusted nor relied on to deliver the services or goods it claims to provide. Where there is no public confidence in the official sector, the unregulated, unofficial sector easily replaces it, usually exaggerating the inequalities and rivalries already present in society. In this environment it is invariably the poor who lose, and those who have power, influence, and "connections" who gain. As a person in Macedonia comments, "You don't have to be poor in order to be a welfare beneficiary, you just have to pull some strings" (Macedonia 1998).

Box 3.1 *Clientelismo* in Mexico

The custom of providing a service or favor in return for political loyalty is known as *clientelismo*. The PRI party has dominated politics in Mexico for 66 years; this is surely a factor contributing to the importance of *clientelismo*. Fully 80 percent of the respondents in the area of Mexico City state that they engage in *clientelismo* politics to get their houses and urban services (water, electricity, street paving, and so on). Yet, despite widespread participation in this system, it is generally resented. One man interviewed in Mexico City says, "I don't like politics, nor the ties that come with it ... I think no one is interested; they do it to get something, to give something, the house to the children, such as myself. But they have to participate because in so doing they are able to obtain things."

With the exception of those in Oaxaca, where strong traditional communal organizations exist, the majority of those interviewed see help coming from either their families or from the government. Given that relatives of poor people are generally also poor, little recourse can be had from the family alone. The government, however, while generally considered the source of benefits for the poor, is also often separate from the people, either by physical distance or by the fact that local leader-brokers speak and act for the poor rather than encouraging them to speak and act for themselves. Found in all discussions about government are two additional issues. The first is that the people are poorly informed about much of what the government has to offer. Second is a pervasive sense that the government is corrupt. The people see that government programs translate into favors done for certain groups in return for affiliation with the ruling political party. Due to long years of control by one political party, the people have equated government with politics and imbued the state with the same distrust accorded politics.

Source: Mexico 1995.

Disempowerment and Humiliation

We would rather treat ourselves than go to the hospital
where an angry nurse might inject us with the wrong drug.
—Tanzania 1997

It is a selfish land, with no place for the poor. —India 1998a

Reports of corruption are often directly linked to descriptions of the psychological consequences of institutional failure: humiliation, intimidation, and insults have a significant effect on the extent to which people utilize state services at all. Negotiating a way through the corruption and rude treatment endemic in state institutions leaves poor people feeling powerless, voiceless, and excluded from the state services to which they are entitled.

The PPA from Tanzania addresses the rude and humiliating treatment encountered by the poor in the state health sector, where medical services, ironically, may leave patients with psychological scars:

> *While much is already known about the general lack of*
> *availability of even common drugs in health clinics, wide-*
> *spread rudeness of health staff has not previously emerged*
> *as a major issue. People everywhere report that they are*
> *abused at health clinics and would only continue to go*
> *"because we have no choice and need the services." Men,*
> *women, and youths state over and over that they are treated*
> *like animals, "worse than dogs." They report that even*
> *before they could explain their symptoms, they would be*
> *shouted at, told they smelled bad, and were lazy and good-*
> *for-nothing. An older man in desperate need of spectacles*
> *braved the abuse of a nurse for two days until he got his*
> *glasses, but he said he would never again go back and be*
> *so humiliated.* —Tanzania 1997

In Pakistan people report that receiving charity is itself humiliating because they would prefer to work for a living. The embarrassment is compounded in Kasur, where "there was strong resentment at the way in which *Zakat* recipients were called to collect their benefits over loudspeakers, a practice that has become worse since politicians have tried to link social assistance to personal patronage" (Pakistan 1993).

A report from Ukraine suggests that the humiliations endured in contact with government bureaucrats are actually designed to "chase the unemployed away." According to the report, "The Government Employment

Services Office, like all others, suffers from widespread public disdain and criticism. Many people expect [to be] and indeed confirm that they are treated disrespectfully. 'If you're not sure of yourself after your first trip to Employment Services, you're unlikely to ever go back,' says Mikhail Mikhailovich, a 30-year-old man who went there looking for work as a translator. He is referring to the humiliation that one endures from government bureaucrats, infamous for their ferocious and insulting tone, as they try to make the experience of applying so unpleasant that they chase the unemployed away" (Ukraine 1996).

Profound frustration with corruption and maltreatment is compounded by a sense of being voiceless and powerless to complain, since complaining may result in losing services altogether. In Pakistan a widow says, "If anybody complains or protests against this corruption, they are struck off the lists of all support services because it is the same Local Zakat Committee that recommends names for the assistance programs run by different government departments" (Pakistan 1993).

Poor people typically lack access to justice or even police protection. In South Africa, while access to the judicial system is perceived to be extremely important, officials are generally said to be extremely rude and unhelpful. Transport availability and costs are also said to be major factors inhibiting such access to legal services. "It is difficult to get to the court. It costs 10 rands return by taxi from the farm to Patensie, and then 3.50 rands from Patensie to Hankey" (South Africa 1998).

Lack of police protection emerges as a widespread issue. In Georgia farmers say that they live "in a police state, in which police pay for their positions and freely harass citizens. Indeed people often prefer to contact 'criminal authorities' rather than even come to the notice of the police who often extort payments from them" (Georgia 1997). In the Republic of Yemen court services score the lowest satisfaction ratings (16 percent), below that of garbage collection (28 percent) and police services (26 percent). In contrast telephone services receive the highest ratings, 82 percent (Republic of Yemen 1998).

In many societies women have little access to police stations; going to police stations may be a dangerous act in itself. In the Republic of Yemen, for example, women state that they cannot access police stations because the police will laugh at them and their families will not allow it. "A woman cannot go alone, but only with her husband or brother or neighbor. Even if a crime was very serious, and even if the police station were very close, socially it is not accepted for a woman to go to a police station. If there were a police station staffed by women on the other hand, women stated that they could go there, either alone or with male relatives" (Republic of Yemen 1998).

Widespread lawlessness in some areas has led to disillusionment among young people. "Young people have started to believe that honest and law-abiding work leads nowhere, but in fact this is a road that leads to alcoholism, drug abuse, and prostitution. The last two are considered a time bomb in the countryside at present" (Latvia 1997).

Government officials often have different perceptions of poor people and their problems than poor people themselves have. If, in the judgement of service providers, poor people are lazy and undeserving, it is easy to see why their behavior toward the poor would be uncaring. In India, for example, a PPA reports that government staff view the poor as dependent on outsiders, having little initiative, idle, not interested in working, and caught in traditional beliefs. The poor, on the other hand, believe that they are poor because they do not have sufficient resources or income-earning opportunities, they have the worst land, and they are often cheated and exploited by the rich and powerful (India 1997c).

When government officials have limited knowledge about poor people in their areas it is difficult to develop effective programs. In Kenya, sharp differences are noted between the district leaders' understanding of the intensity and spread of poverty in their areas and the perceptions and experiences of village people and the poor. The poor see this gap in perception as an important factor in blocking programs that might otherwise be helping them. "While interviews with village people showed a high degree of awareness about poverty and who the poor are, district leaders tended to give textbook descriptions of poverty and the poor were viewed as an amorphous group" (Kenya 1996).

Almost everywhere, politicians are disdained. Poor people note that when they do receive attention from politicians and state officials it is often connected to an agenda external to their concerns. In PPAs from South Asia and elsewhere the theme is of politicians visiting poor communities only seasonally, that is, during election times. In India, for example: "The poor have also been too often treated as a vote-bank by politicians, rather than as an important constituency that needs to be integrated with the larger society. The combination of these factors has led to quite extreme attitudes, in which members of society either pity the poor or believe that the poor have been too pampered with handouts, increasing the stigma and insecurity of the poor and making it more difficult for them to improve their own conditions" (India 1997a).

In Indonesia, since the major political shifts started in May 1998, "the standard practice of paying voters has been brought into the open" (Indonesia 1998). Becoming a village head or village official usually requires financial contributions. Election campaigns often involve sending out supporters to secure votes through small personal payments to individual voters (Indonesia 1998).

Vulnerability to Collapse of the State

People now place their hope in God, since the government is no longer involved in such matters. —Armenia 1995

It was the rich who benefited from the boom ... but we, the poor, pay the price of the crisis. —Thailand 1998

When poor communities or individuals rely heavily on state institutions for service delivery, the breakdown of the state leaves them vulnerable. This vulnerability is particularly striking in the Eastern European and former Soviet Union PPAs, and in PPAs from regions affected by the East Asian financial crisis. PPAs from the former Soviet Union report a widespread sense that the state has abandoned its citizens, many of whom have been plunged into desperate poverty as a result of political turmoil. The picture of the state that has emerged is one of dishonesty, neglect, and exploitation. In Moldova the poor who are without connections condemn the former Communist Party members who have become rich, as those who "exchanged their party cards for parliamentarians, bureaucrats, local officials, 'Mafia,'" to use their connections to grab material and start their own businesses. Poor people characterize these government officials as "dishonest," "swindlers," "speculators," and "thieves," and insist that politicians do not care about the suffering population (Moldova 1997).

In many countries in Eastern Europe and the former Soviet Union pensions are pitifully insufficient, assistance programs inaccessible, and feelings of humiliation widespread. Poverty is often described as a direct result of government incompetence: "Virtually every respondent lambasted government incompetence for mismanagement of the economy. Regardless of how one became poor, the government is held in such low esteem that respondents viewed it as responsible for the catastrophic drop in the standard of living, far more so than any individual shortcomings" (Ukraine 1996).

An elderly woman in Ukraine claims she is ashamed of being poor but that the feeling of shame is fading. "I'm getting used to it or I've become indifferent. I don't know," she says. Like most others, she blames the government for thrusting her into this impoverished situation. She expects her situation to grow even more desperate. She has already sold most of her possessions. Although she has a small plot, it is located far from any form of transportation. At age 71, she finds it increasingly difficult to carry kilos of potatoes to the bus stop and is considering renting out the plot. Besides her pension, which keeps her from starving, she hopes this could become a second source of income. —Ukraine 1996

In Thailand poor people's comments on the impact of the East Asian financial crisis also underline the vulnerability of those reliant on the state— particularly the very poor—at a time of institutional breakdown.

The crisis has happened so quickly it has left us confused, puzzled, and let down. We have lost our jobs but are given no explanation," says a community leader from the slums of Khon Kaen, Thailand. "It was the rich who benefited from the boom but we, the poor, pay the price of the crisis." Within her community there is a feeling of uncertainty, insecurity, and isolation. "Even our limited access to schools and health is now beginning to disappear. We fear for our children's future," adds her husband. Poor families report having to pull their children out of school to work and a mother says, "What is the justice in sending our children to the garbage site every day to support the family?" —Thailand 1998

In an atmosphere of state collapse all those who were formerly dependent on the state for services suffer. The poor, however, suffer disproportionately, since without resources and power they are ill equipped to negotiate in the corrupt and chaotic environment that replaces the former order.

Barriers to Access: Rules, Regulations, and Information

Not every disabled person can afford the procedures to qualify for disability payments. —Moldova 1997

We have to cross three creeks to reach our schools. These creeks swell up to four feet during rainy periods. When the rains come, our mother fears for our lives. —Grade school children, Kimarayag, Philippines 1999

Where formal state recognition is a precondition for access to state entitlements, the absence of that recognition constitutes a barrier. By requiring identity cards, uniforms, or excessive and unreasonable documentation to access benefits, and by refusing to see and process people's claims, the state formally excludes those who cannot meet its conditions. State regulations may also hinder trade and entrepreneurship by the poor. Those excluded by these requirements are generally the poorest; they mention obstacles of this kind frequently in the PPAs.

While the better-off find ways to circumvent rules, this is more difficult for the poor because of their limited information. In Armenia to get assistance families with elderly members sometimes register themselves as separate households occupying the same apartment so that the pensioner can qualify as "single" and receive kerosene and other forms of assistance. In fact, pensioners living alone who have children living nearby usually have greater assets and so can afford to buy separate apartments for their adult children. Married couples sometimes divorce officially but continue to live together because the divorce qualifies their families for assistance aimed at single mothers. On the other hand, women whose husbands have left Armenia to find work but have not been able to send back money do not qualify for aid targeted to fatherless families (Armenia 1995). The poor also express deep fear of losing their privatized land because of their inability to pay the fee required for land registration.

Even when there are services the rules are seldom designed to make it easy for the poor to participate. In several countries children are pulled out of school because school fees are due when families have the least money. In Ethiopia, for example, the school year runs from September to June—but September is also a month for two important festivals, and these expenses crowd out funds for school fees. Further, children are in school when they are needed for the harvest. In urban areas the poor say that because the children look for work when labor demand is the lowest, in the summer months, this further exacerbates seasonal vulnerability. School holidays also coincide with periods of food stress in families. In one area in India researchers note that, while children do not go to the government school because of the timing of classes, participation is high in the "nonformal" education program conducted by a local NGO. That NGO program is more flexible and "caters to the realities of the village children by allowing them to fulfill their household tasks" (India 1997a). Physical barriers also come in the way of access to education and information. For example, in many rural areas school attendance drops during the rainy season, when travel becomes life threatening.

In Moldova documents are needed for a person to be able to access all kinds of services, including the right to privatize collective enterprises. Moldovans cite numerous examples of being defeated by a system that demands documents to which only state officials have access. A widow in Cahul, for instance, cannot privatize her land because she does not have the right papers, that is, a "workbook" that lists all her previous jobs. "This book should have been in the collective farm offices, or in the district office archives. Officials at this office refused to surrender the book to her; she then applied to the collective farm officials, but they did not help either" (Moldova 1997).

Women as a group can be systematically excluded from a range of services by the state's refusal to recognize their status as individuals. When identity cards are issued only to "heads of households"—meaning men—it severely restricts the extent to which women can function outside of their formal connection to men. In addition, women may face specific barriers created by unreasonable rules before they can access welfare benefits and the like. In South Africa these include court rulings that require women to find men who have absconded in order for the court to enforce payments. Even when men are brought to court, the judicial system remains ineffective in enforcing support for children (South Africa 1998).

In a variety of ways the need for documentation can bar the poor from claiming services and benefits. Lack of documentation creates a "precarious illegality" that is widely tolerated, but leaves the poor vulnerable to exploitation by more powerful groups. In urban slums in Brazil, India, Kenya, Mexico, Pakistan, and Vietnam the lack of identity cards or clear titles to land exposes the poor to the tyranny of "slum-lords." The lack of land titles and food ration cards also leads to increased commodity prices for the poor, that in turn leads to dealing with money-lenders and rich landlords, from whose clutches the poor often have great difficulty ever extricating themselves. In other countries, poor people often lack a labor card, needed to claim unemployment insurance, and they do not receive the minimum wage when hired. Also, any general sub-sidy leaks to the nonpoor, even for products or services such as urban transport, which account for a larger budget share for the poor than for the nonpoor (Brazil 1995).

Unreasonable bureaucratic rules and requirements can make the ben-efits received from the state less valuable than the time and effort invested in claiming them. For instance: "A 65-year-old widower pensioner living 22 kilometers from Donetsk in Ukraine was denied a housing subsidy. Among the documents he was obliged to present was a certificate from Gorgaza, the City Administration of Gas Maintenance. The authorities claimed the certificate he obtained was flawed. To get an acceptable certifi-cate, he had to go to Gorgaza seven times. When he finally became indig-nant at the delays, he was accused of hiding his son's income and denied a subsidy. 'Do you think they are people? They're not people! They're animals!' he says of the authorities responsible for dispensing housing sub-sidies" (Ukraine 1996).

Sometimes the mere process of trying to access benefits can be dangerous. In Georgia internally displaced persons (IDP) have been crushed in crowds waiting for their monthly payments. "Despite their legal entitlement to their modest monthly payments, the actual process of receiving them is often difficult. Displaced people in Tbilisi report that money comes to the savings bank only once a month. Because there is never enough to go around, people start lining up early in the morning. Sometimes the crush becomes so fierce that people are injured; a young female respondent had broken her hand. The displaced feel angry and humiliated, since they consider the money official compensation for the property they had to abandon in Abkhazia" (Georgia 1997).

Lack of information is a critical barrier between the existence of an entitlement and the ability to draw on it. Lack of information about program rules and benefits leaves poor people vulnerable to exploitative middlemen and corrupt officials.

> In India one outstanding theme common to all of the government programs operating in the study area is that there is a severe information gap between the government and the intended beneficiaries. In the view of the villagers there is very little information and awareness about the various governmental poverty alleviation schemes. Even in the cases where there is some degree of awareness of these programs, an understanding of the specificities and the actual mechanisms of the programs is often absent. In most cases the only channel of information that the villagers have access to regarding these programs is through middlemen, which has proven to be problematic. These middlemen often misrepresent the various programs to the intended beneficiaries for their own purposes, which frequently involve extracting a percentage of the allocated funds for their own use. Another salient point that emerged from discussions with the villagers is that in their view many of the government schemes were not actually serving their needs and interests. —India 1997a

> Given the new rules and regulations in Georgia, many people do not even know what assistance they are now entitled to by law, nor do they always know whether the source of aid they have received is the government or private organizations. People receive their information about different forms of assistance from friends, acquaintances, occasionally TV—but never from official sources. Where they used to "pursue their rights" in Tbilisi, or even in Moscow, they no longer know where or to

whom they can appeal for information or restitution. Marneuli residents, for example, were afraid to even approach the medical commission that determines disability, and therefore the right to receive an invalid pension, because they were afraid they would have to pay a large sum. —Georgia 1997

In Latvia only in a few municipalities did respondents report receiving information on kinds of assistance available from the social assistance staff. Because procedures for allocating money are often unclear and appear arbitrary, people react with suspicion and distrust. ... Some potential applicants are held back by distrust and even fear of these institutions. Applicants who have experienced rudeness or contemptuous behavior from the staff do not come back for assistance until they are desperate. ... A neighbor who lives with her unemployed son was shouted at by staff that her situation is her own fault, since she has not managed to bring up a good son. Just as budgets and programs differ regionally, so do attitudes toward the performance of social assistance officers. For example, in Livani respondents felt that local officials were doing their best to distribute assistance fairly, and that local staff treated them with respect. Likewise respondents in Ventspils found the staff there to be "understanding" and "polite." —Latvia 1998

When governments fail to provide reasonable access to information about benefits, opportunities for exploitation and mistrust flourish, as is evident from the example of a woman in the Republic of Yemen trying to get disability benefits for her daughter (box 3.2).

Regulations may inhibit poor people's trading activities, even while liberalization of trade rules may be benefiting the better-off. Restrictive regulations about vending on the streets and harassment by the police and local "strongmen" emerged as an issue in many urban areas. In rural areas, local officials often become the stumbling block in community management and ownership of assets. In Indonesia, in a village in Jambi, after the license of a private company to manage richly endowed caves came to an end the community applied for authority to manage the caves as an enterprise. The forest officials turned down the request, because the community committee did not have, nor could it acquire, evidence of registration as a company or an operating license to establish a work place. Forestry officials say that only a legally established company owned by individuals could exploit the cave (Indonesia 1998).

Box 3.2 Republic of Yemen: Trying to Find Help for Disabled Daughter

Since her daughter's disability Sharifa went back and forth many times to the Ministry of Social Affairs in order to register her daughter's handicap with the Social Welfare Fund. She spent large sums on transportation, and was finally registered and received 1,200 YR. She thought that this sum would continue as a monthly stipend, but she was told it was only a one-time payment. She suspected that she was registered and then the government officials stole her money during the subsequent months, but she is not certain of this, and is not certain of her rights regarding the social welfare fund.

Not succeeding with the government social safety net program, Sharifa tried to get help from one of the powerful *sheikhs* (traditional rulers). To do this, she had to prove that she had a legitimate need by gaining an official paper, or *waraqa*. The process to get the *waraqa* is long and tedious. First, someone must write up her story, then she must get neighbors to testify to the truth of her story, and finally, the *aquel* (elected official) must testify. She finally completed the process, and armed with her *waraqa,* she went to the office of the *sheikh*. She was made to come back several times before finally being brought before him. He put the paper behind his *jambiya* (Yemeni sword) and told her to come back. When she came back, he told her that he couldn't find the paper. She then appealed to the women in the *sheikh's* household, but couldn't get them to listen to her. In a final attempt she found someone from her village working at the office of the *sheikh* as a soldier and sought his help getting her another audience with the *sheikh*. But when she went back to follow up, they continued to say they had lost the paper. At this point she gave up.

Source: Republic of Yemen 1999.

The Role of Local Officials and Community Elite

*The leaders have the power, but they have no interest in
the community. And what the people want is that the leaders
work for their communities, the people don't want promises.*
—Venezuela 1998

The community has no voice; here there are no leaders.
—Panama 1998

While some people state that their poverty is the result of community
"voicelessness" and general lack of leadership (Panama 1998), many
others believe that local leadership is a large part of the problem. The power
wielded by the local elite is often in inverse proportion to the degree to
which they are held accountable for their actions and decisionmaking. If
communities have few ways, or no viable ways, of influencing the actions
of local leadership, if there are no checks on the power of local politicians
and other elite, and if the state is not in a position to monitor and regulate
the power of the local elite, then patronage ties dominate the options available to the poor when accessing resources. When public sectors are dominated by patron-client relationships, individuals and communities lacking
key connections will be unable to make successful claims for government assistance (Togo 1996). In South Africa the creation of homelands during the
apartheid period distorted the role of traditional authorities from the "community spokesmen" to bureaucratic elites who lost their connection with
the people they represented (South Africa 1998).

In Pakistan (1993) in agricultural areas that depend on irrigation,
uncontrolled use of irrigation water has resulted in the waterlogging and
salination of lands. This has led to declining crop yields, which in turn has
led to movement out of the area by poor families. Many blame the problem
on the local elite who control the supply of water and who are perceived to
be indifferent to the impact of water misuse on lands cultivated by the poor.
People also resent the control local politicians have over funds directed
toward localities, and believe they are used only to further the self-interest
of politicians. An exception to this rule is found in the village of Badan.
There, local leadership is trusted, viewed as fair, and reported to distribute
government aid funds equally among those in the village.

In the Republic of Yemen (1998) the local elite is in charge of communities and their interests; contacts and strengths determine what resources flow to the community. One example is in the management of piped
water committees. The committees consist of some technically educated

people from the district city, the local *sheikh* (local chief), and the village's elected local leader. In communities where the *sheikh* has weak connections to local and regional level officials because he belongs to a powerless tribe, community mobilization of resources is low because residents know that their *sheikh* is powerless.

In Jamaica (1997) strong leaders have traditionally been perceived as the most important interlocutors for delivery of services and access to work. However as *dons* (godfathers) have become more and more associated with drugs, unequal distribution of handouts, and gang warfare, *dons* are no longer viewed as paternal godfathers who distribute resources and ensure peace and cohesiveness in the community.

In India the poor experience a range of relationships with the local elite. The elite, particularly those from higher castes, are mostly seen as those who divert government resources for their own use. In some areas local leaders are seen as "selfish and also corrupt" and are cited as one of the reasons for lack of development of the area (India 1997a). Here, too, there are some positive examples, however. The *panch*, an informal committee of the village head and four village leaders, is widely respected for its ability to resolve disputes between villagers fairly. This means that conflicts can be resolved at the local level without resorting to the police or courts. In multicaste villages the Thakurs—the higher-caste landlords—are feared but not respected by the lower service-caste poor and poor laborers. In some areas lower castes feel that since they no longer depend on degraded land for survival but instead earn incomes through migration, the traditional hold of the higher castes on lower castes has eroded (India 1997a).

In Eastern Europe and the former Soviet Union many poor people believe that success comes only to those who use criminal organization connections, or who maintain ties to the former Communist Party elite. While currying favor with the political elite and using small bribes to ease transaction costs was common in the previous regimes as well, a Georgia PPA reports, "today the former system of corruption has become more flagrant and ubiquitous. Poor people are outraged by the contrast between their own lives and those of officials." A citizen of Ajara, contrasting the image advertised by local leadership of Ajara as a "peninsula of prosperity" within Georgia, described the leadership as "moneybags" who "build fashionable hotels and tennis courts for high society, consort with local and foreign businessmen, and waste people's money" (Georgia 1997). In rural communities people point out that local officials almost invariably end up with the best and most expensive plots of land and the largest businesses (Georgia 1997).

To the degree that local officials limit the access of individuals to information and other resources, the poor have a difficult time finding work and escaping poverty (Moldova 1997; Armenia 1996; Georgia 1997). It is important to note that this does not mean that villagers are always completely at the mercy of local leadership; community organizing can be effective. For example, in the Georgian village of Djuta, when local officials delayed the distribution of hay meadows to local farmers, residents took matters into their own hands; they divided the meadows into individual plots and distributed them by casting lots (Georgia 1997).

While negative accounts of corrupt local officials and political elites outnumber positive ones, there are examples within the reports of local leadership being viewed as an important community-level asset. In Livani, Latvia, for instance, officials are reported to play an important role in guaranteeing the equitable distribution of humanitarian assistance (Latvia 1997). Similarly, in India some village leaders have "played an active role in securing the benefit from some poverty alleviation programs for the poor and also improving the infrastructure facilities such as transport facilities" (India 1997c). In fact, as a Nigeria PPA notes, "Many residents of poor communities emphasize the importance of their elite, particularly those members residing and working in urban areas, in securing services for them. Such people are often, indeed, centrally involved in setting up and running 'self-help' organizations." The PPA continues: "Community leaders themselves point to their need to have links with 'godfathers' higher up in the system in order to successfully gain access to benefits for the community. Many leaders say that if they are not active politically, they do not attract government action, which in turn means that community members cannot be enticed to participate in development." A central conclusion drawn from the PPA is that the inclusion of community leaders in government programs is key to the program's success, for respected local leaders who share the views and values of the community at large can rally support for and participation in development programs (Nigeria 1996).

Conclusions

This review of poor people's encounters with state institutions is sobering. Dysfunctional institutions do not just fail to deliver services—they disempower, and even silence, the poor through patterns of humiliation, exclusion, and corruption. Legal and other formal barriers that prevent the poor from gaining access to benefits or trading further compound the problem. Thus, those at society's margins are further excluded and alienated.

The findings raise fundamental questions for programs and agencies that work primarily through state institutions. The answers do not lie in shrinking the state, bypassing the state, or in focusing only on poor people's networks. The answers lie in starting with poor people's realities and experiences with the state in order to design appropriate processes to produce change at the local level. At the same time, agencies need to trace the changes in values, norms, incentives, roles, processes, and policies that are needed at higher levels to support transparency and accountability to the poor at the local level. New thinking is also required to support "clean and motivated" unsung local heroes of the state and civil society, especially at the grassroots level.

Poor men and women recognize the importance of government-provided services and government roles in setting up the framework of rules and regulations, yet they feel powerless to effect change in these institutions. New partnerships are needed between governments (at all levels) and civil society organizations. While this is beginning to happen in the delivery of some sectoral programs, experimentation in direct participation by poor people in local level governance is just starting. To reduce the probability of elite takeover of decentralized programs, poor people's own organizations need to be strengthened within communities and through cross-community networks. Only then can poor women and men exert their rights to information and accountability without negative personal repercussions. Poor women and men want a life of dignity in which they are treated with respect and fairness by state, civil society, and private sector organizations.

State institutions link people to vital services and to participation in civic processes. When functioning effectively, state institutions provide opportunities for socioeconomic mobility and for overcoming power asymmetries. When state institutions deteriorate, services such as health and education become privileges accessed primarily by those who already have resources and power. The following case studies illustrate some experiences reported by poor people in their efforts to access health care and education.

Case study 3.1 Access to Health Care

> *If you don't have money today, your disease will lead you to your grave.* —Ghana 1995a

> *If a poor man gets sick, who will support the household?* —Guatemala 1994b

> *We are ill because of poverty—poverty is like an illness.* —Moldova 1997

When poor people talk about access to formal health-care services, issues of corruption and cost repeatedly arise. For poor families who are already highly vulnerable, the costs of a sudden illness can be devastating, both because of lost income and because of the costs of treatment. While the actual treatment itself can be prohibitively expensive, in many cases there are other hidden costs that add to the overall financial burden of health care. These hidden costs include expenses incurred in traveling to a place where health care can be received, and the psychological costs or stigma of having been treated for certain diseases, such as HIV/AIDS. Costs are also incurred from bribes that must be paid and "gifts" presented to doctors and other health-care workers in order to ensure adequate treatment. The poor identify all of these factors as significant barriers to access. In addition, access to health care is often heavily influenced by gender, with men and women using health care differently.

Costs and Corruption

> We watch our children die because we cannot pay the high
> hospital bills. —Ghana 1995a

Costs and corruption are significant barriers to health-care access. Corruption, which increases the costs of health care significantly, is widely reported in the PPAs. In many countries poor people report that they are asked to pay for medicine that should be available to them at no charge. In Armenia, when free medicines are given out the head doctor of the hospital must countersign prescriptions. These prescriptions are then filled in the facility's drugstore, which is most likely to honor the prescription. Other drugstores may resist honoring prescriptions for free medicines by telling patients that the medicine is out of stock.

A World War II veteran in Yerevan says:

> I had a prescription for free medicines. I went to a pharmacy
> and they told me that they had none. I found the medicines in a
> pharmacy near the Ministry of Health. I didn't want to pass as
> a hooligan, so I dropped in to the Ministry and clarified
> whether I could get the medicine free with this prescription.
> They said yes. So I asked, "If they don't give it to me, can I
> take it by force?" They said, "If you can, take it." So I went to
> the pharmacy and asked to see the box of medicines to verify
> the expiration date. I took the medicines and said that I was
> leaving with it. They wanted to stop me. I told them, "I am not
> a hooligan, if you want, let's go together to the Ministry of
> Health and we can ask there. If I am not correct, they can take
> me to the police." No one came after me. —Armenia 1996

Where health care is no longer free, its rapidly rising costs, especially for serious illness, send many families into destitution while they wait for death. In Georgia there are innumerable cases of people unable to afford operations for sick family members. In the village of Akhalcopeli a man who needs urgent treatment for his stomach ulcer "now lies at home, waiting for death." Similarly: "Nino, who lives in Kazbegi could not pay to have her heart condition treated; it has become steadily worse. But she cannot obtain a certificate of disability (prerequisite to receiving disability payments)—she can neither afford the trip to Tbilisi, nor does she have enough money to pay for the first examination" (Georgia 1997).

> *In Pakistan it was common to find that informants had turned to private sources of care because they feared that a visit to a government facility would prove pointless. Although private sources were said to be expensive, government sources may not be any less so if the dispenser or doctor is abusing his position to make illegal fees and profits. Many household heads, therefore, reported that "they had borrowed large sums of money, sold assets, and/or removed a child from school at least once in the history of their marriage in order to meet the expense of treatment for themselves, a wife or one or more children." Often, several sources of treatment were consulted, either because the disease was particularly alarming or because the first choice was ineffective. As might be expected, less expensive options (such as home care or herbal medicines) were usually tried first and more expensive treatments second. In some cases, however, families went immediately to a qualified private doctor, because of the greater assurance that the private practitioner will have medicine on hand. —Pakistan 1996*

Encounters with corruption lead many poor people to avoid formal services altogether, reserving visits to clinics and hospitals for only the severest emergencies. In Bangladesh the poor report many hidden costs and exploitation by government medical staff including bribery, overcharging, and delay in attending to them (Bangladesh 1996). A PPA report from Kenya notes that the poor are health-conscious and engage in a variety of health-maintenance strategies, but visit government health facilities only as a last resort when they are desperate. This is not because they do not believe in or respect the curative powers of health providers, but because their experience with health facilities has been so dismal over the past few years. Here, again, problems cited by the poor include distance to health-care facilities, unofficial "fees," lack of drugs, and rude health personnel (Kenya 1996).

In some areas charges for health care are unclear. In one government hospital in Ghana official staff members appear unable to give consistent figures for charges for the most basic services. Furthermore, unofficial rents (bribes) are charged for a wide range of small services (Ghana 1995a).

While health care is expensive, forgoing treatment, particularly when treatment is potentially available, can have tragic consequences. A PPA from Uganda describes the death of a young girl whose family could not afford to seek formal medical care at the first sign of illness:

They had no spare money on them, but this was not a special problem as it was one shared by many. They had something to feel happy about, having been among the few to fully pay their 1995 graduated tax and school fees for two out of their five school-age children. Difficulties started in March, when their five-year-old daughter, Grace, had a serious bout of malaria. Given lack of money, their first recourse was with local herbs. Unfortunately, the little girl's condition did not improve. The family borrowed some money and bought a few tablets of chloroquine and aspirin from the local shop. After some improvement, the girl's health sharply deteriorated two weeks later. By the beginning of May, Grace had become very weak. Her parents then sold some chickens for Shs. 2,500 and, with the help of neighbors, took her to Ngora Hospital where she was immediately admitted. She was seriously anemic and required urgent blood transfusion. However, the family was asked to pay Shs. 5,000 that they did not have. They went back home to try and look for money. It was too late. She died on 8 May and was buried the following day.
—Uganda 1998

While rising costs are a common complaint, declining quality is not always so. In Ghana, "Costs of orthodox medical consultations are perceived as high, though it must be said that hospitals are perceived as more competent in general" (Ghana 1995a).

The traditional and informal medical sectors are repeatedly cited as alternatives to expensive or inaccessible formal health-care services in the PPAs. Often women use traditional health care exclusively, while seeking services in the formal sector mainly for male family members. In the Republic of Yemen both poor infrastructure services and social norms in the household restrict access to health care for women:

Lack of public transportation and high costs of private transportation are a major constraint to access. For instance, from Al Moqaaehha village in Hodeida, a visit to the district health center takes one and a half hours by car and costs about 5,000 YR, of which 2,000 is for car rental and the rest for fees, food,

and accommodation in the city ... Stories are told about preg-
nant women losing their babies on their way to the health ser-
vice. In Hazm Al Udeyn center, the cost of hiring a car to the
nearest health facility is 5,000 YR. A significant portion of the
population cannot afford these costs. As a result, poor families
from remote areas go to health facilities only when in extreme
need. In both Ibb and Hodeida, it is not unusual for families to
sell animals or gold to pay for a trip to a district or regional
health center. —Republic of Yemen 1998

In Bangladesh the poor, lacking transportation resources, must be carried to health-care service providers. "The men find it difficult to carry sick people for long distances over the hilly areas, and many patients die during such journeys" (Bangladesh 1996).

Gender and Health

When women are sick, there is no one to look after them.
When men are sick, they can be looked after by women.
—South Africa 1998

Male roles in family health care are not described in much detail in the PPAs. Where they are mentioned, men are typically involved in finances, directing the work of wives as community health nurses, and transporting ill family members or neighbors (Bangladesh 1996). Men are most frequently involved with making financial decisions around health care. Women are typically the providers of health care rather than its recipients, and when resources are scarce they defer treatment of their own disorders in order to get care for their families. It is widely accepted that men are entitled to formal health care and the resources needed to secure it, long before women are entitled to such care.

Access to health care for women may be seriously affected by social norms that restrict women's mobility and public activity. In Pakistan, for example: "The range of care options for some women and their children is restricted by unwillingness to travel alone to a distant facility or by inability to communicate with hospital personnel. In Balochistan women in two households commented that they would not be able to use the hospital unless the men of the household were present to accompany them. In one case the women say they were not "allowed" to go alone, and in the other, the women felt that because they were illiterate they would be unable to describe the problem in words that would be clear to hospital personnel. Women in homes such as these are more likely to use private doctors, compounders, and traditional healers if these practitioners are familiar to them and located in close proximity to their homes" (Pakistan 1996).

In the Republic of Yemen women do not go alone to health services unless they are close by. The agreement of the husband or another male community member (called a *mahram,* that is, a respectable person or protector) is essential before women and children may go to the health centers, since women do not drive, nor are they allowed to travel far alone (Republic of Yemen 1998).

The interconnected barriers to health-care access experienced by poor women have far-reaching consequences for women's health, and, by extension, their quality of life and options for productivity. Women's lower status in many households results in poorer care of their own health and nutritional needs, which in turn affects their ability to feed the family and work. Poor women are often caught in a cycle of malnutrition and preventable disease that stems directly from their place in the household and from gender bias in health-care access. The PPA reports support recent scholarship arguing that gender relations in society and gender stereotyping in health policy and planning dramatically skew women's access to health care. For instance, the PPA from Pakistan (1993) shows that women are the exclusive targets of promotional and preventative programs, even while they are denied care outside their reproductive roles.

Children and Health

Lack of access to medical services traumatized a mother who found herself "holding and singing lullabies to my baby until she died in my arms." —Philippines 1999

Children are among the most vulnerable segments of impoverished populations. Although there have been declines in infant mortality, poor children continue to suffer disproportionately from malnutrition, disease, and lack of adequate health care. The PPA for Latvia notes that "in the past few years the children have become more frail and become ill more quickly. The frailty of today's teenagers' health has become very noticeable." A school nurse commented that "in the last few years the patients more often have health problems such as allergies, cardiovascular problems, blood pressure, and dizziness. In earlier years there was nothing like this" (Latvia 1997). Similarly, the Nigeria PPA notes that in many communities participating in the study, poor people say that the health situation of children is deteriorating. This is linked to poor diet and water supply and an inadequate government health system. When children are sick and resources are scarce, "the male is preferentially treated, since he must survive to carry on family

Box 3.3 "Long Live the Child": Community Health Agents in Ceara State, Brazil

The state government of Ceara has improved the health of young children by providing poor mothers with the information and tools they need to protect their children's health. Community health agents promote breastfeeding; monitor children's growth; teach mothers how to prevent diarrhea-related dehydration using a solution of salt, sugar, and water; educate mothers on the importance of treating drinking water, and teach them low-cost techniques for doing so.

Ceara used to have one of the highest infant mortality rates in the Northeast of Brazil: 95 out of every 1,000 children died before their first birthday. More than half of all mothers surveyed in 1986 had lost a child within the first five months of life due to dehydration brought on by diarrhea.

Among many dramatic changes following the election of a new governor in 1987, the state initiated "Long Live the Child" (*Viva Criança*) a campaign to educate health professionals and the public about primary health care. In the program community members (mostly women) trained in the basics of infant and child health care visit area households monthly (more often, if the household contains a pregnant woman or child under five). The health-care agents travel on foot or bicycle and carry a backpack with basic medical supplies. By 1993, 7,240 health agents were visiting the homes of 4 million people every month at a cost of $500,000. As a result of this program, infant mortality declined 35 percent between 1987 and 1991.

Source: Brazil 1995.

---

traditions." In Benue state, "If the child is not 'special' in any way, the sickness may be interpreted as an 'act of God' and treatment may not be vigorously pursued" (Nigeria 1995).

The most frequently cited barriers to accessing adequate health care for children included cost, distance to health-care facilities, and mixed levels of confidence in the overall effectiveness of treatment provided by clinics and hospitals. In an unusual example from South Africa, however, street children talk about the usefulness of free health services provided by a local hospital. The children describe how they are able to take advantage of this health care, especially in emergency situations (South Africa 1995).

In the PPA reports from the former Soviet Union there are frequent examples of children "falling through the cracks" as state-provided health services deteriorated. "Georgian cities have witnessed the appearance of street children as young as five years old, who beg for money and food, and who engage in theft, prostitution, glue-sniffing, and casual manual labor" (Georgia 1997). Some have run away from families, others from institutions, and others literally have no families. "Many have serious bronchitis, pleuritis, and wounds from injuries and burns, often from operating electric appliances and kerosene heaters in small apartments without adult supervision. Only about half receive immunizations ... The children tend to be frightened, aggressive, and unapproachable" (Georgia 1997).

In Macedonia parents with several children are handicapped in regard to health insurance coupons, which cover costs for only three children. In such cases cards are often swapped among siblings, and since out-patient facilities and health institutions are sensitive to the health needs of children, they reach informal understandings with underinsured patients (Macedonia 1998).

The responsibility for overall family health care, particularly that of children, typically lies with women. State health-care institutions by and large have not adapted to the fact that women, even while they earn incomes, remain responsible for children's health care. In South Africa women in the Lenyenye area made a special plea for clinics to stay open during evenings and weekends in order to allow them to take children for treatment when their daily labor responsibilities were over (South Africa 1998). In some areas in Kenya, "Patients were required to buy children's exercise notebooks to supply the paper in which prescriptions could be written" (1996). There are important exceptions that show how innovative community-state partnerships can reach poor people with health services, for example in Brazil (see box 3.3).

Poverty, Gender, and Sexually Transmitted Diseases

Even if you are faithful, your partner may not be.
—Uganda 1998

Links between increases in poverty and sexually transmitted diseases (STDs) including HIV/AIDS are mentioned in several PPAs. In Thailand the AIDS NGO network expresses concern that the economic crisis may further marginalize HIV/AIDS patients. They also predict that, with increasing prostitution and poor quality health care, HIV/AIDS infection rates will inevitably increase. Many private health-care centers have closed down because they are no longer able to pay the loans they borrowed from abroad, and imported drugs have rocketed in price. People are forced to rely on the strained public health system. "Our fear is for the children, elderly, and AIDS patients," a health worker explains (Thailand 1998).

Migration is linked to STDs in many countries. A health worker in Thailand says, "Migration has brought increased competition for living space and jobs, and we are anxious that migrants will bring more HIV to our community" (Thailand 1998). In Togo long-distance drivers and prostitutes are identified as high-risk groups because of their potential exposure to STDs (Togo 1996). Similarly, trading towns are viewed as dangerous in Senegal: "The proliferation of AIDS and other sexually transmitted diseases remains a real threat, particularly in some trading towns (Kaolack, Ziguinchor), even though prevalence rates are lower in countries such as Côte d'Ivoire or Gambia (which juts into Senegal geographically). The context for efforts to prevent the spread of HIV/AIDS and STDs is one in which family planning remains unavailable to large segments of the rural population" (Senegal 1995). The South Africa PPA reports that "women who become suddenly poor through the loss of a male partner are frequently forced into prostitution to earn a living. In fact HIV/AIDS is largely seen as a women's illness" (South Africa 1998).

The HIV/AIDS epidemic has introduced a new long-term trend in impoverishment. One of the principal effects of AIDS at the individual level is that the household of the victim will become poorer. In South Africa this is attributed to high expenditure on travel, admission fees, fees for healers, clinic fees, and funeral expenses, as well as the loss of labor from the sufferer and the caregivers (South Africa 1998). In Ethiopia the participating communities mention illness of family members as a main cause of vulnerability. In Lideta and Teklehaimanot the most common causes of inability to work are illnesses, such as typhoid, tuberculosis, and HIV/AIDS (Ethiopia 1998). An increase in numbers of orphans is a side effect of the deaths of adult household members from AIDS. In Togo 12,000 children orphaned by parents who died of AIDS were reported in 1994, with numbers expected to grow (Togo 1996).

The stigma associated with a diagnosis of HIV/AIDS naturally limits program effectiveness. Poor communities rarely understand the causes of HIV/AIDS and how to assist those affected. Programs for counseling and treatment need to address the fear of social isolation, which leads many households and individuals to hide the fact of infection (South Africa 1998).

The use of condoms for protection from STDs is problematic among poor men in some parts of the world. The South Africa PPA reports that rural youth find it difficult to obtain condoms, and the negative attitude of clinic staff discourages youths from going to clinics for advice, treatment, and family planning services. "Moreover, men do not like using condoms, claiming that it reduces performance and causes them to tire quickly, and as a result they would be 'careless' when using condoms" (South Africa 1998). In Kenya poor men and boys insist that family planning cannot alleviate poverty; instead, they say, priority should be given to the irrigation of land (Kenya 1997). In Latvia, by contrast, information about reproductive health is widely available in media and schools, and products related to this educational effort can be bought in any country store or pharmacy (Latvia 1997).

In sum, the poor report a range of barriers restricting their use of formal medical services. As a consequence, they often receive inadequate health care, depend on informal sources of care, or simply go without health care. In many places women and children are particularly unlikely to receive sufficient medical treatment and those with STDs or HIV/AIDS are often too ashamed or fearful to seek it.

Case study 3.2 Education

Getting a job has nothing to do with what you learn in school. —Uganda 1998

The future lies in the education of our children. —Uganda 1998

Children have given up studying. They have become tradesmen and merchants. —Armenia 1996

Securing an education is usually a precursor to effective participation in civic and economic life. Yet access to education is also highly gender-biased, according to many of the studies. In a Nigeria PPA, for example, many respondents say that they wouldn't send their girls to school because they believe it breeds "indiscipline and female disloyalty" (Nigeria 1997). In households where resources are limited, boys are often educated before girls, since girls' labor may be required in the household, or girls may be subject to cultural norms that limit the value placed on educating them.[2]

Relevance

By staying out in the street all day [selling peanuts], I saw many of the people who were at the university with me. They also have to do these little jobs to survive. —Togo 1996

Education is losing its allure and teachers their former positions of respect, since diplomas no longer guarantee good jobs. —Armenia 1995

Svetlana, an unemployed Russian woman in Latvia, says that although her son is formally enrolled in school, he frequently skips class and takes part in thefts. Svetlana reported that Misha's teachers used to give her lectures, but they gave up when nothing was achieved. She says, "Why does he need school anyway? It is just money wasted on books. He can read and write well. If you are too smart, you won't get a job" (Latvia 1998).

In Togo a range of institutional forces combines to limit the employment choices available to young people with university degrees:

> *When my father was made a jeune retraite (forced early retirement, as part of structural adjustment policies) back in 1985, I was finishing my university studies. It was a big blow for the whole family, but I thought that with my university degree I could have helped the family. Nothing was coming along, so I started working with my mother, who is a tailor. I'm lucky she taught me how to sew because that way I can earn some money and sew my own clothes. Then my parents moved to the village where life is cheaper, but I wanted to remain in Lomé because here's the only place where I can find a job using my qualifications. I stay in the house that my father had started to build, with two brothers in school to support. I stay there because I couldn't possibly afford to pay rent, but the house isn't finished: there's only one room with the roof and no floors. So I'm losing all my customers, because they say my house is dirty and their dresses will get dirty. I can't blame them, really. I can't even work myself in such conditions. I don't even have a clean table on which to lay the cloth to cut. Sometimes I'm lucky and I find work with a donor or an NGO. They say I'm good, they thank me, but they have no long-term job to offer me. When I work for them, I'm able to pay off some of my debts, or to buy books for my brothers, or to do some more work on the house. Now I have to sell peanuts on the street, making 600 CFAF a day if things go well. At first I was ashamed to do it, and hoped nobody would recognize me. And you know what? By staying out in the street all day I saw many of the people who were at the university with me. They also have to do these little jobs to survive.*
> —Togo 1996

The perceived disconnect between education and securing a livelihood becomes a barrier to investment in education for many poor families. "Especially in rural areas in Ghana, for many families there is no perceived connection between real adult life and education. Education and teaching have little social prestige ('No husband will want an educated wife') or economic value ('School is useless: children spend time in school and then they're unemployed and haven't even learned to work the land'). Given the low quality of instruction and the limited relevance of the curricula, such attitudes are understandable" (Ghana 1995b).

A further example from Uganda underscores the irrelevance of education in the lives of many poor people. "'Getting a job has nothing to do with what you learn in school.' 'School certificates don't guarantee me that the new employee knows anything useful.' 'School was a waste of time.' Lastly, the communities in several studies noted poor physical infrastructure, especially lack of classrooms and materials. Problems with the education system were seen as the failure of the Government to invest properly in education" (Uganda 1998).

A surprising number of those interviewed in Pakistan also say that they do not feel that postprimary education would be of any future benefit to either daughters or sons. Although basic literacy is seen as helpful even to a farmer or day laborer, any further schooling is often thought to be wasted in an environment in which these are the only employment possibilities. "Formal sector jobs are known to exist, but informants said that these positions were available only to those who could pay a bribe that is enormous by the standards of the poor. Figures such as Rs. 20,000–50,000 were quoted for some positions. Many informants said that even if they were able to provide school fees, textbooks, school supplies, and uniforms needed by high school children, they have no hope of being able to pay a bribe of such magnitude [for a job]" (Pakistan 1996).

In Georgia a deteriorating educational system leads to the danger that uneducated poor children will become unemployed adults. In the past children had the "pioneer palaces," houses of culture, clubs, government-subsidized sports activities, and subsidized holidays. Most extracurricular activities now cost money, and poor parents must withdraw their children from their music and dance classes. For youth, especially in villages, the problem is even worse. The lack of educational or employment opportunities, and the decline of village social and cultural life, have contributed to depression, criminality, and increased youth alcoholism (Georgia 1997).

As the quality of public education appears to be declining, the rich are opting out of the public system, leading to the loss of those with some voice in keeping educational systems functioning. "Parents of children in the public system repeatedly voiced their resentment at those, including functionaries, educational administrators and teachers themselves, who send their children to private schools and left the public institutions to decay. In Nigeria teachers who were once held up as role models and beacons of knowledge are now practically considered socially marginal ... The deteriorating incomes and employment conditions of teachers have been accompanied by an erosion of their prestige. In the southwest it is reported that landlords advertise: 'House for rent: no teachers'" (Nigeria 1997).

Class Bias

Education has become the privilege of rich people. If you do not have money, you can "rot" in your house. Despite the fact that the poor do well in primary school, they seldom make it to secondary school because of school fees. —Kenya 1997

Only the children of the poor are in public primary schools now. The big men who run the schools have their children in private schools. —Nigeria 1997

Access to "free" education becomes class-biased when poor families have to invest in school uniforms, textbooks, transportation, and other fees, or when the family needs the child's labor in order to survive, as in this example from Vietnam:

Twelve-year-old HL lives with the three other people in his family. His mother works as a washerwoman, his elder sister is a street vendor, and his elder brother works in Ward 8. In the past HL was in grade 2, but he dropped out because the family had run into debt, and he had to work to help the family survive. HL started working at the age of nine or ten. He got a light job inserting balls into roller wheels (of suitcases for example) earning a monthly wage of 300,000 VND. He works from 7:30 a.m. to 5:30 p.m. He gives all the money he earns to his mother in contribution to the family's debt payment. HL does not know how much the family owes or why. His mother usually returns 10,000 VND to HL when he receives his wages. His only wish is to go to school so that he can know how to calculate money like other people. He often feels a bit sad when he sees children his age going to school. —Vietnam 1999b

[In Georgia] one of the greatest concerns of poor families is the fees introduced by the new school reform, according to which schooling is free through the first nine grades, but a fee

is required for the tenth through eleventh grades. ... In addition to these fees parents are frequently required to contribute wood or money to heat schools, plus monthly sums such as five lari for school renovation, to pay the school guards, or to "top up" the teachers' salaries. In some Javakheti villages education continues mainly thanks to parents, who support the school, supply heating fuel, and contribute to the teachers' salaries. Throughout Georgia, however, the impact of these multiple official and unofficial fees is that increasing numbers of children are leaving school when they complete the ninth grade, if not before. —Georgia 1997

Poor parents can rarely afford to buy textbooks, an issue that emerged in many countries including Armenia. The lack of textbooks has an important impact on children's performance. Many parents remarked that "going to school without books doesn't make sense." One father said, "Last year my son was in the sixth grade. He didn't have half the books he needed. For that reason, he never did well. At the end of the school year, the school director called me. I was told that my son was to be expelled. I talked with my son. He said that he could not study because he had no books. I was to blame because I was the one who should have bought him the books. But I had no money to buy them" (Armenia 1996).

Lack of presentable clothing also keeps children from school. In Ajara, Georgia, parents say "Poorly dressed children refuse to attend school because other children laugh at their ragged clothing. One mother teaches her sons, 10 and 12, at home, for this reason" (Georgia 1997). Being shamed in public about being poor makes the stigma of poverty even harder for children to bear. In Macedonia, for example, "a third-grade teacher expressed to the whole class her belief that a certain student was 'the poorest child in the class.' The girl was so humiliated that she refuses to go to school" (Macedonia 1998).

Finally, buildings—where they exist—may be dangerous in poor communities, especially when the financial responsibility for maintenance is transferred to local communities. In northern Ghana serious funding constraints "prevented a sagging roof from being repaired at the state-run Presbyterian Junior Secondary School at Gambaga. Under the government's educational sector reforms, communities are entirely responsible for all structural maintenance expenditures. Owing to the dire state of poverty, manifested in a high rate of malnutrition, this community is unable to raise the necessary finances. Eventually, in October 1994, the roof collapsed on a roomful of schoolchildren while their class was in session. Twelve children were injured, with one suffering fractures in both legs" (Ghana 1995a).

As the rich pull their children out of poor quality public systems and opt for private schools, cycles of exclusion begin. In Latvia, "parents were concerned that a two-tier educational system was developing, one in which children of well-off families, living in cities and town, would have access to elite, well-equipped schools, while poorer children, particularly in rural areas, would be limited to poor quality nearby schools. Parents were concerned about the fall in the quality of instruction, as many of the best teachers sought better-paid work, leaving behind those unable to find other work" (Latvia 1998).

Corruption

> We find that teachers are charging 10 córdobas for private classes in their homes. We are trying to remove that kind of behavior. Education is not a business, it is a vocation. If it were a business, we would be in a market. —A school director, Nicaragua 1998

> Directors falsify grades for rich students and simply sell them diplomas. —Ukraine 1996

Trust between teachers and parents in Nigeria has been eroded by allegations that teachers misuse money collected by the headmaster, or raised by the community or PTA for school use. Such allegations of embezzlement are quite common. Parents want school management committees to be established to ensure proper accountability (Nigeria 1997). Distrust and lack of respect for teachers and other officials are also problems in Cameroon:

> In Far North province of Cameroon parents reported not sending children to school and/or taking them out of school because "a diploma no longer leads to a job." The standard of teaching is low (PTA teachers typically have seven years of basic education), and there is a general lack of resources. Teachers were generally found to lack motivation due in large part to low pay and poor equipment. Parents criticized teachers for alcoholism, absenteeism, arbitrary grading, and laziness (sleeping in class). In urban areas parents are delaying sending children to school by not enrolling them in nursery schools. Some children are simply staying out of school. In all the regions surveyed except the east, people complained that they had to pay school authorities to gain admission to school for their children. —Cameroon 1995

In Pakistan "free" primary education is actually not free for poor families. On the average, the household's yearly expenditure on school supplies for the poorest is calculated to be about Rs. 317 annually per primary school child, Rs. 745 per middle school child, and Rs. 1,018 per high school child. In addition, in some areas parents report that public school teachers demand payment for each child in the form of "tuition." "If parents do not meet these payments, which are as high as Rs. 40–50 per month, the teachers were reported to beat the student or submit a failing grade for her/him" (Pakistan 1996).

Corruption in educational institutions, high fees, and the need to depend on "connections" to get jobs have created pessimism among students and parents about the value of education. A math teacher in Crimea says, "Rich children don't have to perform well; they know that their parents' money will guarantee their success. The children understand that what's most important isn't knowledge but money" (Ukraine 1996). Another teacher commented that poor students know that they will not be able to continue their studies. "The students have a passive relation to study; they're pessimistic, a kind of lost generation. By eighth grade they know all the prices and how much it costs to enter any given institute. I'm afraid for my own children" (Ukraine 1996).

Children in Institutions, Former Soviet Union

Poverty is the only reason for the children attending boarding school. —Armenia 1999

Among very poor parents in the former Soviet Union countries one commonly discussed strategy to ensure food for children is to institutionalize their children in homes and boarding schools for disabled, orphaned, or mentally disturbed children: "Olga Vadimovna, 31, has two sons, 11 and 9. When her older son was six, she sent him to a state boarding school (*internat*) because she could not afford to raise him. The younger son told an interviewer, 'Like my brother, I too want to go to the *internat*. There they eat four times a day. I want so much to eat.' The children, during interviews, unanimously voiced their preference for the school over home for a single reason—they received more to eat at school" (Armenia 1995).

"Mother, father, and five children live in a storage room at the local post office in Stepanavan. There is almost no furniture in the room. The father's brother is the chief of the post office and let them stay after their house burnt down. Although the mother is employed full time and the father has work on a temporary basis, their salaries are not sufficient to keep them out of poverty. The children are dirty, thin, and pale. Three of them attend Stepanavan No. 21 where they often spend the night. 'It is because they get fed there in the evenings,' explains the mother. She describes how she often only consumes coffee during the day in order to be able to feed her children. They use clothes donated by neighbors and she begs soap from them in order to be able to wash the children. The mother says they would not be able to cope if they did not have the option to send the children to the boarding school" (Armenia 1999).

"Most children's institutions in Georgia are no longer able to guarantee even minimal living conditions for the orphans, disabled, ill, or 'troubled' children they house. Nevertheless, in some cases, parents who feel incapable of even feeding their children may request to send them to a boarding school or orphanage. These children have multiple disadvantages in addition to the initial economic problems that may have motivated their families. Many children live in conditions characterized by an appalling lack of hygiene, cold rooms, inadequate food, and often, poor care" (Georgia 1997).

In brief, for both girls and boys, relevance and the real costs of education emerge as critical problems. Without a perceived benefit from obtaining an education, and with no access to the requisite funds, poor families simply opt out of the system. In so doing, they may be denied the tools necessary for civic participation and informed engagement with formal institutions. Denial of education perpetuates cycles of exclusion, disempowerment, and marginalization.

Notes

1. A 1997 survey found that corruption was the most common out of the 15 problems cited by firms doing business in Sub-Saharan Africa and Latin America and the Caribbean. Corruption was the second most common problem cited in the Middle East and North Africa, and third most common problem in Eastern Europe and Central Asia, and in the Commonwealth of Independent States (Brunetti, Kisunko, and Weder 1997). See also table 3.1 on quality of governance across countries in appendix 7 at the end of the book.

2. This topic is explored in greater depth in case study 5.1 on gender and education at the end of chapter 5.

Chapter 4

Civil Society Institutions

Here to work we have to do a guetza. Here with my neighbor I can help him, he has to come and help me, and in this way we help each other. This we here call guetza: he finishes his work, then comes and helps me and I finish my work [and help him], and this is how we live, direct support from neighbor to neighbor.

—A poor man, Mexico 1995

If you are as poor as I am and can't contribute regularly, you can't participate.

—A poor woman, Togo 1996

This chapter turns from the institutions of the state to institutions of civil society. Civil society refers to those groups, networks, and relationships that are not organized or managed by the state. Civil society, for the purposes of this discussion, covers a wide range of formal and informal networks and organizations including nongovernmental organizations (NGOs), community-based organizations (CBOs), and networks of neighbors and kin.

Social capital is a useful concept in understanding the role that civil society institutions play in the lives of poor people. Social capital, broadly defined, refers to the norms and networks that enable people to coordinate collective action.[1] This capacity varies but can reside in any group, network, or organization—including the state. Civil society clearly lies outside the state, although state laws, such as freedom of assembly and laws governing finance, affect it. Societies vary in the stock of civil society institutions that constitute a part of their social capital.

Poor people invest heavily in social relations for psychological, cultural, and economic well-being. When communities are cohesive and their associational life is vital, they are better positioned to attract government and NGO resources. This chapter explores why this is so, and explores the role that civil society institutions play in poor people's lives, both routinely and in times of crisis.

The relationship between a flourishing associational life and economic development is confirmed by several recent studies. A national survey conducted in Tanzania as part of a PPA finds that, even after controlling for the standard set of economic and demographic variables, villages with higher social capital, as measured by membership in functioning groups, have higher incomes (Narayan and Ebbe 1997; Narayan and Pritchett 1999). Similarly, recent studies in Indonesia (Grootaert 1999) and in Bolivia (Grootaert and Narayan 2000) show that households with higher social capital also have higher incomes, and that social capital has a disproportionate impact on lower income quintiles, and on small landholders rather than large landholders. The characteristics that seem to have the strongest impact on economic well-being are number of memberships, followed by active participation and contributions. Recent studies in Ghana and Uganda establish associations between social capital and social cohesion (Narayan and Cassidy 1999) and in India between watershed management and social capital (Krishna and Uphoff 1999). A social capital survey in Panama concludes that communities with high social capital are close to five times more likely to receive NGO assistance than those with less social capital. This association is particularly strong in access to water systems in rural areas and in indigenous communities. Communities with higher social capital are better able to organize for collective action.

Social capital manifests itself in norms, values, and informal networks, as well as in local organizations such as farmers groups, burial societies, informal lending associations, neighborhood support networks, and mosque associations. It is tempting to assume, especially when the state is weak or dysfunctional, that these mechanisms are a major resource that can be relied on to lift poor communities out of their poverty. The reality is far more complex.

The PPAs indicate that community-based organizations (CBOs) and networks are indeed a key resource for the poor, but often only as coping mechanisms that substitute for the role of the state rather than as a complement to state efforts. Given the limited resources of the poor, if there are no bridging connections across social groups within and outside the community, poor people's social networks will provide only limited resources and opportunities. In rural areas, organizations such as parent-teacher associations, women's associations, or seed-buying groups are disconnected from other similar groups. These bonding social institutions do indeed support and improve life for the poor. But in the absence of bridging social capital, these informal networks do not lead to social movements that challenge inequitable social norms, laws, or distribution of resources, nor do they facilitate new partnerships with the state that sustain improvements in economic well-being for the poor.[2] Some government interventions are beginning to build on local-level institutions. In the final analysis, the PPAs demonstrate that the potential of civil society organizations to represent the interests of the poor in governance still remains largely unrealized.

PPA results concerning the role of civil society institutions in the lives of the poor can be summarized in five findings:

> **Nongovernmental organizations (NGOs) have only limited presence.** NGOs do not figure prominently in poor people's lives. While they are extremely valuable in certain areas, and provide basic services in the absence of state action, they are affected by some of the same flaws as state institutions, albeit to a much lesser extent. Their potential for scaling up by working complementarily with the state is beginning to be tapped, especially in the delivery of basic services such as primary education, forest management, and drinking water. On the other hand, there are few examples of NGOs addressing basic structural social inequity.

> **Community-based organizations (CBOs) often function as important local resources to the poor.** The poor invest heavily and place their trust much more readily in their own CBOs. They do so for survival and security—not necessarily because CBOs are more effective than formal institutions, but because

the poor rarely have access to state institutions. The paradox for the poor is that they benefit more when the groups include the rich, but only up to a point, after which their voices become silenced. The poor also get excluded from many groups because of their limited assets and their inability to pay fees (see chapter 6).

▶ **Neighborhood and kinship networks provide economic and social support.** The qualities of these informal social networks provide important clues to what attributes the poor seek in formal institutions meant to help them. However, long-term stresses can overwhelm informal support systems. Overuse depletes the capacity of individuals and groups to maintain reciprocal relationships. Kinship and community social networks are resilient, but under times of stress they are less capable of functioning as effective and dependable support systems. During such times the radius of trust and cohesion often narrows to the immediate family, and even family bonds can fracture if pressed too hard.

▶ **The rich and the poor, women and men, are organized differently.** First, the groups and networks of the rich, powerful, and elite are cohesive; they cut across communities, and their members are active in social, political, and economic affairs. The networks of the poor, however, are more atomized. Within communities, networks of poor people engage in social activities and rituals, limited economic activity, and very circumscribed political activity. Across communities the poor have relatively little exchange except through intermarriage. Second, there are important differences between the networks of poor men and women. Poor men are embedded in vertical patron-client relations with the state and with landlords, employers, and traders, whereas women, who are largely denied access to these institutions, develop and invest in extensive informal social networks with other poor women.

▶ **Redistributing power is not high on the agenda.** Organizations that help to increase the bargaining power of the poor, or to correct the fundamental power inequities at the household, community, or state level, are conspicuous in their absence from the PPAs. The poor mention membership organizations in only a very few cases. The researchers in the PPAs describe several organizations known worldwide for their excellent work; the poor themselves mention them only infrequently when they talk about institutions that are important in their lives. This is presumably because these organizations, despite their size, do not reach the majority of poor people.

The remainder of this chapter elaborates these findings and is organized in three sections, discussing in turn NGOs, CBOs, and neighborhood and kinship networks. The chapter ends with two case studies—one on financial services for the poor (case study 4.1) and the second on the disconnect between local organizational capacity in communities and the government in Indonesia (case study 4.2).

Nongovernmental Organizations

We have no more malnutrition thanks to the NGO in our village. —A farmer in the Sikasso region, Mali 1993

Nongovernmental organizations (NGOs) around the world embody a rich diversity in terms of purpose, size, structure, and capacity. They run the gamut from small location-specific grassroots organizations to those that are practically indistinguishable from state institutions. In general, NGOs are valued because they are rooted in civil society and have some degree of independence from the formal rules and norms that govern state and market institutions. Typically, they are organized around a core set of values, such as liberty, particular religious beliefs, or the right to education. Over the past decade NGOs have been regarded with great interest by development practitioners, in the expectation that they may become the vanguard of civil society and take a leading role in ensuring more equitable socioeconomic development (Korten 1990). NGOs are often the only outside actors perceived to work in the interests of the poor, and, in the absence of the state, many NGOs have, in fact, taken on a vital role in the provision of basic services to the poor.

However, the PPAs indicate a mixed record for NGOs. On the positive side, there are many localized instances of NGOs reaching groups of the poor with highly valued services. The Sub-Saharan African PPAs in particular contain many such examples. There are several reports of NGOs helping to bring the goods and services of formal institutions into poor communities. There are also increasing examples of NGOs working in partnerships with government to scale up their outreach, particularly in education and in health. For these reasons, NGOs enjoy a measure of trust and confidence that poor people do not generally extend to formal institutions.

There are also stories of problems with NGO coverage, implementation, and ultimate effectiveness. While it is not surprising that NGOs are barely mentioned in the reports from Eastern Europe and the former Soviet

Union because they are so new in the region, they also fail to figure prominently in many other poor communities elsewhere in the world. Furthermore, it is unclear whether NGOs are more successful than formal institutions at reaching the poorest areas. As with other institutions, NGOs are not immune to mismanagement, corruption, or lack of respect, or to actions that inadvertently skew local priorities and power relations. While NGOs are reported as attempting to build local capacity, there are few examples of marked success in the PPAs. Relations between NGOs and governments are often marked by tension: truly complementary relations between the two are rare. There are hardly any examples of NGOs addressing underlying social inequities by actively supporting either poor people's organizations or social movements. When immediate survival needs are great, it makes sense for NGOs to focus on basic survival issues. However, with some exceptions, there is little evidence of NGOs moving forward to address fundamental inequity issues that create the problems in the first place.

The rest of this section addresses three topics. The first focuses on NGOs as resources for poor communities, including the kinds of services they provide and the trust that people place in these organizations. The second addresses the limitations of NGO coverage—whether they reach the poorest, the frustrations the poor experience in dealing with NGOs, and the lack of NGO success in building long-term capacity of the poor for self-governance. The third discusses the emergence of government and NGO partnerships in the context of decentralization, and the tensions underlying these new relationships. There is some evidence that these partnerships may lead to improved local services and local level accountability on a large scale.

NGOs: Resources for Poor Communities

Church-affiliated entities represent probably the most visible and far-reaching safety net presently operating in Benin.
—Benin 1994

A central strength of NGOs is their ability to bring in or access additional financial, technical, and often political resources. Particularly when the state is weak or absent, NGOs can be critical in helping poor people meet everyday needs. This may include providing food during seasonal shortages, introducing safe water and sanitation systems, offering health care and health information campaigns, or improving school buildings or community centers. In Swaziland, for instance, NGOs are active in education and health care, sponsorship of orphans and poor school children, and in the provision of "free medical services ... targeted to street children, the elderly, and HIV/AIDS victims" (Swaziland 1997). In India, in addition to eye camps, health camps, and veterinary camps, NGOs are involved in:

- distributing seeds (often offering varieties that are preferred to those distributed by the government);
- offering watershed management;
- providing access to literacy education;
- organizing or encouraging women's groups;
- teaching income-generating activities; and
- providing relief and direct assistance to the poorest.

In some regions NGOs with the strongest presence are religiously affiliated. This is the case, for instance, in Benin, where these organizations function as one of the most visible and widely distributed institutional safety nets for the poor. "The majority of the orphanages are run by Catholic sisters, the only country-wide nutritional program is managed by Cathwell (Catholic Relief Services), and nuns and priests have set up several programs to assist the sick, the abandoned, and the destitute. In Cotonou the Catholic Church is arguably the strongest presence helping the most vulnerable" (Benin 1994). In Panama (1998) over half the communities acknowledge churches and schools for their support. In Vietnam (1999b) poor Catholic households in need of support turn to the church. In Georgia the Russian Orthodox Church and the International Orthodox Churches Charities run soup kitchens for the elderly and disabled and distribute food and medicines (Georgia 1997). These efforts were praised by local people who noted that "although local Armenian and Georgian priests had organized the distribution, they did not reject any minority, including Jews, Greeks or Russians" (Georgia 1997). In Pakistan (1993) the PPA reports "a deeply entrenched tradition of private charity and welfare reinforced by Islamic religious obligation." Mosques and shrines are valued as sites of charity. Ashrams are mentioned in some places in India as places of refuge for the poor.

Although NGO presence is uneven, in areas where NGOs are active they often receive more positive ratings than state institutions. Some of the trust and confidence in NGOs stems from having extended contacts in particular communities. In Swaziland, for instance, local populations tend to distrust outsiders in general, but are particularly distrustful of government representatives. While there is little confidence in any of the central government agencies to adequately address the needs of poor rural communities, NGOs that have established ongoing relationships with particular communities enjoy a level of trust denied to most other outside organizations (Swaziland 1997).

In Thailand, during the financial crisis, poor people reported feeling disillusioned by the government, but identified NGOs as a potential catalyst for improving their lives. Focus groups in urban slums express feelings of distrust and isolation. Yet "when asked to identify what various institutions can do to overcome their problems, the Bangkok slum group suggested many ways which their own groups and NGOs can help, but very limited suggestions were identified for the government" (Thailand 1998). Focus group participants related that in the past they have received very little support from governmental agencies, and there is little reason to expect that this might change in the near future.

There seem to be two kinds of reasons for the positive reception of NGOs. First, they may be able to respond better to local priorities. In Ghana, for example, NGOs are valued over the government for being able to provide services that reflect community needs. In the areas of health and education, in particular, high appreciation is voiced for NGO efforts. Much of the appreciation stems from the perception that NGOs often possess special expertise that can assist in strengthening local livelihoods. In the village of Komaka community members express strong interest in establishing a grain bank "to create emergency food stocks in the village and thus reduce vulnerability to both drought and the ravages of the 'lean season'" (Ghana 1995a). The overriding opinion is that this is a project in which NGO assistance would be far more valuable and effective than government assistance (Ghana 1995a). In some cases NGOs may have larger resources at their disposal than official agencies. The Togo PPA, for example, reports that NGO expenditures in 1994 were roughly 4 billion CFAF, a figure exceeding the government budget for rural development (Togo 1996). The number of NGOs active in Mali grew from 30 to 250 between 1983 and 1993. While growth in numbers alone can reflect financial incentives to create NGOs, the common perception of NGOs in Mali at the local level is that they contribute significantly to economic opportunities and overall well-being; moreover they function as important social safety nets (Mali 1993).

A second reason for the positive reception of NGOs in some areas is that NGO staff members are viewed as more compassionate than government officials. In the former Soviet Union countries many people describe NGO workers as "more understanding and kind." In Latvia (1998), people have positive attitudes toward both national and international NGOs, even though they do not expect regular or long-term assistance from them. When asked about the NGOs from whom they receive aid, people mention the Salvation Army for its distribution of clothes to large families and to people living alone; Save the Children Fund for cash, clothes, and food; and aid from the churches, if they belong to the congregation. In Georgia many people have benefited from the regular assistance of organizations such as the International Red Cross, and from Médecins Sans Frontières (Doctors Without Borders). Several local NGOs are also cited as providing important assistance to people in need (Georgia 1997).

Limitations of NGOs

Even the nongovernment initiatives have at best provided marginal access to Gandas (tribals). There has been quite limited participation of Ganda women in the development activities promoted by NGOs. —India 1997c

Full information was rarely forthcoming and sometimes aid was diverted to dead souls. —Ukraine 1996

While NGOs have played a key role in making development more participatory, often they have only limited outreach and have not touched the lives of the majority of poor people. In Panama, for instance, a social capital survey concluded that only 10 percent of the communities received support from NGOs compared with 33 percent that reported some support from government sources (Panama 1998). Similarly, in Indonesia, the estimate is 7 percent (Indonesia 1999). Even within the communities where NGOs operate there are accounts of relative unawareness of their activities as well as evidence of NGO-funded investments that have foundered. When a community in India is asked about the role of NGOs in their area, they respond that there are few, although they specifically mention two groups engaged in both development and welfare activities. They rank the contribution of the NGOs to their development and welfare as secondary to the government's efforts (India 1997c). Even in Bangladesh, with the world's largest NGOs, high awareness of NGOs is primarily associated only with microcredit programs.

Similarly, the Togo PPA acknowledges important NGO contributions, but also raises the problems of the uneven presence of NGOs—especially in the poorest communities—and the low sustainability of their interventions. Regardless of NGO presence and activity, over half of the farmers interviewed are not aware of any sources of NGO assistance. In some cases the assistance has ceased because a particular project has finished or because there is no longer any missionary presence in the area. In other cases, however, there is simply no NGO presence whatsoever (Togo 1996). Similarly, while acknowledged as valuable during times of drought and crop failure, NGO activity in Swaziland is viewed as "infrequent and unreliable" (Swaziland 1997).

In the absence of secure financing and the resulting dependence on governments and international agencies, NGOs in many places have become contractors rather than community catalysts. In India even government officials identified "target-led reporting" (which is the pressure to achieve predetermined targets) as an inhibiting factor for performance or quality-led output (India 1998d). In Senegal 80 percent of financing is external; NGOs are dependent on implementing the "pet projects" of external donors. NGO presence is heavily concentrated in certain project areas, leading locals to conclude that NGOs are "vehicles to dispense financing with little local participation" (Senegal 1995). Some NGOs, fed up with their dependency, now consider their highest priority to be achieving financial independence for themselves and their clients (Senegal 1995).

Difficulties with aid programs administered by NGOs are also found in Armenia, where many feel that money spent by NGOs on humanitarian food and fuel assistance is misdirected and can be put to better use in job-creation. There is also a marked lack of information about funding and aid sources. Many people "were also confused and generally negative about the practice of targeting aid and the basis on which decisions about 'vulnerability' were made." Those interviewed are generally most positive about international organizations that used expatriates to distribute and monitor aid because of a widespread and deeply ingrained distrust of national governmental agencies (Armenia 1995).

Like the state, NGOs are not free of the tarmac bias: they tend to reach people who live close to passable roads and miss the very poor. In Latvia, "relatively few respondents had received assistance from NGOs. Those that had tended to live in large towns or cities; in many cases they were already receiving assistance from the municipality" (Latvia 1998). In the Kenya PPA it is noted that only two NGOs are located in the coastal region districts, while the rest are located in Mombasa, accessible for most of the population only by ferry. The NGO activity is concentrated along the highways, near the beach, and near the resort hotels rather than in the large interior area characterized by "drought, lack of water year around, tsetse attacks on livestock, and various forms of wildlife which devastate crops" (Kenya 1996). In Tanzania a chief says, "We have many NGOs working here. They all work in one small circle of communities [he made a circle with his finger on the table]. The largest number of people are ignored. [He spread his arm to indicate the rest of the table]. I don't know why" (Tanzania 1997).

The Bangladesh PPA notes:

We actively sought out "pockets of poor" and it would seem that these pockets are often neglected by government and NGOs alike. Remote and difficult to reach areas such as the

Chars (tribal groups) and parts of Sylhet are particularly neglected. In Sylhet, the conservatism and widespread religious-based distrust of the intentions of NGOs also contribute to the unwillingness of NGOs to work in this area. Most poor people know about NGOs because of their credit provision, either cash loans or provision of latrines, tube wells, and housing on credit basis. Over 80 percent of the NGO services (excluding Grameen Bank) noted were credit. This credit is often too small for productive purposes, repayment terms are not easy, and the behavior of the field workers is often criticized. Very few other NGO activities were noted by villagers and were incidental. For example, one local NGO in Yousuf Matbarer Dangi forms groups and provides training; World Vision provides student support in Burunga; there is a mission hospital in Katabari. One village indicated they had a BRAC [Bangladesh Rural Advancement Committee] school; one local voluntary group is registered with government to provide family planning services in Salim Biswas Dangi.
—Bangladesh 1996

While insufficient geographic coverage is one aspect of not reaching the poor, another aspect is lack of fit between program design and the needs of the poor. In Armenia the NGOs' lack of familiarity with local traditions and conditions results in programs that do not work out as intended. A school program designed to supply children with a daily glass of milk and a high protein biscuit is a case in point. In some schools, teachers present the children with "four to five, or all 45 biscuits at a time, so that the children would not feel humiliated by the offer of a single biscuit." In some schools teachers simply give the children powdered milk to take home because a lack of running water prevents them from making the milk at school (Armenia 1995).

In Zambia, the PUSH (Program Urban Self Help) program involves a number of national and international NGOs. The program aims to build urban infrastructure by giving women food rations. An evaluation revealed that less than 3 percent of households benefited from these programs. Reasons for nonparticipation varied. "Extremely arduous physical labor is resulting in some infrastructural gains but they would be minimal compared to the physical exertion demanded of the women and the costs in terms of time. Women complained that their bodies were breaking" (Zambia 1994).

The reasons for lackluster NGO performance vary, but the PPA reports and other literature on NGOs suggest that uncertain funding and limited management capacities hinder effectiveness and independence of NGOs. This includes difficulties with rotating leadership and effective systems of financial management, planning, monitoring, and evaluation (Fox 1993). Indeed, many have no full-time staff or permanent offices. Some operate on a voluntary basis and some are funded largely by member contributions. Their capacity to make good use of new resources is limited. For these reasons, some of the more successful approaches to scaling up NGOs take a longer-term perspective, allowing them to gather field and administrative experience.

Beyond problems of finances, organizational capacity, and coverage, across regions there are some reports of insulting behavior, corruption, and nepotism within NGOs that have undermined people's general confidence in NGOs. In Bangladesh some of the strongest negative statements about NGOs emerged in connection with credit-granting NGOs. The dissatisfaction centered on credit programs that are perceived to give too small amounts for productive purposes, as well as on rudeness, threats, and use of force to recover credit. The most extreme examples related to the "bad behavior of field staff" (Bangladesh 1996). As a result of poor people's experience with credit-granting NGOs that "terrorize, insult, and lock up defaulters," the poor prefer NGO involvement in tube well installation and in the provision of latrines.

Another sentiment voiced in some places is that there is little altruism in NGOs, and many are established for the personal gain of the founders. "The founders of NGOs are the victims of economic recession who see the establishment of an NGO as the solution to their financial and employment problems. During a regional NGO meeting in July 1992, one of the speakers summarized the problem as follows: 'Those who have taken the initiative are essentially the retrenched civil servants and the unemployed graduates. ... There are several associations that see an NGO as an institution to provide employment to its members, an easy solution to earn money or do some tourism'" (Benin 1994).

In Armenia many poor people feel that relief funds flow into the pockets of NGOs rather than finding their way to poor people. As in many other countries in the region, there is a widespread conviction that local NGO employees direct aid to their families and friends, sell it, and come under pressure from local criminal organizations to divert aid in other ways (Armenia 1995). In Macedonia poor people said that in order to receive humanitarian aid, "they were forced to pay a 'membership fee' which ranges from 250 up to 400 denars depending on the humanitarian or nongovernment organization" (Macedonia 1998). A middle-aged man said, "I became a member of a humanitarian organization and received benefit in oil, flour and noodles. I was promised that in the next shipment I would be **among** the first on the list since my family was poor. I was told that first I had to pay the membership fee, which I paid with borrowed money. From the shipment which was of school commodities, my children did not get anything and they do not go to school now" (Macedonia 1998).

In Georgia many respondents felt that there was large-scale collusion between aid distributors and corrupt business. In Tbilisi, the "neighbor of a Red Cross worker who regularly stored Red Cross shipments of supplies in his apartment said she witnessed middlemen purchasing these goods directly from the apartment to resell to private businesses" (Georgia 1998).

In Ukraine, except for Crimea and Chernobyl, "the question as to whether respondents had received any assistance from charitable organizations was almost seen as black humor" (Ukraine 1996). This was particularly true in eastern Ukraine. Although all had heard of shipments arriving from Western countries, people said it was mostly children's clothes, only some of which could be used, and packages of margarine, butter, or condensed milk. Nearly all argued that humanitarian aid "did not reach those for whom it was intended" because someone was "warming their hands on that aid," evidenced by the fact that the same packages were for sale in the stores (Ukraine 1996). Similar accusations were made by Tartars to whom aid was distributed by the Mejlis, the political organization representing the Tartars.

While faith-based groups are often mentioned as sources of help, in Panama "discussions revealed that Christian sects have occasionally had a divisive effect among indigenous communities. In one Kuna island community, for example, part of the community refuses to recognize the Asambleas de Dios, with their congress not wanting any more churches because the proliferation of churches is seen as fragmenting the community into small units ... If the community is divided, those divisions are reflected in church organizations" (Panama 1998). In Macedonia, while people respect religious humanitarian organizations, it was reported that "most of the families, mostly Moslems, do not apply for help due to the shame, others consider that even these organizations are corrupted and the benefit is distributed among friends" (Macedonia 1998). Georgians expressed mixed sentiments toward the role of religious organizations that required them to switch faiths. The report notes, "This issue perplexed an Azerbaijani family, who finally decided to accept aid from Jehovah's Witnesses, despite initial reluctance to accept a pacifist faith whose tenets they might have to violate if members were called to serve in the Georgian army. They compromised by deciding the 'less important' family members—mother and sister—would use the aid" (Georgia 1997).

Despite their efforts, perhaps the biggest weakness of NGOs is that they generally do not tend to support the long-term capacity for local self-governance. This makes the ultimate institutional legacy of NGO activities questionable. This problem is likely to become more acute as the pressure grows on NGOs to deliver services quickly. In the Busia district in Kenya, in areas where NGOs have been active, the PPA concludes that "There was little or no evidence that any groups formed or assisted by NGOs had achieved any level of autonomy. Nor had they evolved into larger groups or diversified their activities. Thus, while NGO and church inputs are helpful to the individual poor in their struggle to survive, they have not assisted in strengthening the capacity of existing groups to become autonomous" (Kenya 1996).

NGO–State Links

> If I invite 30 NGOs to help me in a decision, I'll have
> 30 different suggestions and one big fight. —Senior
> government official, El Salvador 1997

NGOs provide a vital link between civil society, the state, and the market. Such links can be crucial in making development activities accountable and effective. In India, for example, "The programs that were undertaken by quasi-government institutions in collaboration with NGOs seemed to be more effective than the programs that were purely undertaken by government" (India 1997a).

One important factor creating new opportunities for NGO involvement is the decentralization of government programs. In El Salvador, in 1991, the ministry of education initiated comprehensive reform to increase the accessibility and quality of basic education by decentralizing the school system and promoting community participation in schools. The program has its origins in community-organized efforts to address the educational needs of children during the war period. A community-managed school program, EDUCO (Educación con la Participación de la Comunidad), has been developed in which management of new preschool and primary schools is delegated to parents and community organizations. One hundred and ten NGOs are registered as working in the education sector alone. About half of these offer technical training programs, and the other half offer management training programs. "NGOs are capable of expanding their coverage with subsidies from the private sector" (El Salvador 1997). In Nicaragua NGOs are actively participating with the government in the decentralization program (Nicaragua 1998) and in India NGOs are working with state governments on rural water systems (India 1997c).

While NGOs are independent of the state, their very presence and survival depend on government—on the laws governing NGOs, and perhaps more importantly, on government attitudes toward NGOs. Attitudes can vary from a desire to work in close partnership with NGOs to outright hostility. In El Salvador, as noted above, decentralization policies in education are testing new partnerships among NGOs and the government. While some NGOs find the government to be "authoritarian and inefficient," the government finds NGOs "erratic and unaccountable." Officials also express frustration with large international NGOs "each bringing their own method of conducting affairs ... and the minister is left with people who do and undo things" (El Salvador 1997).

In Armenia tensions and miscommunications sometimes mar the relationships between international NGOs and local authorities. NGOs complain that government lists of "vulnerable" families are very inaccurate, and no reliable statistics can be obtained. In some cases, they feel that "government authorities tried to steer their attentions to less needy areas to satisfy particular constituencies, while needier populations remained underserved" (Armenia 1995).

Local officials sometimes oppose direct NGO distribution of assistance. In Giumri, Armenia, one NGO reports that local officials neither help nor hinder. In other cases, they harass NGOs by cutting off electricity supplies or forcing them out of rented premises. The director of an NGO that ran a low-fee pharmacy reports considerable tension with town authorities, who feel they should control all the local aid "in order to better coordinate it." Local pharmacies and hospitals particularly resent the low-priced pharmacy because it undersells them (Armenia 1995).

In South Asia, particularly in Bangladesh, NGOs have managed over a period of decades to become a force that the government has to take into consideration. Poor people in Bangladesh mention both the Grameen Bank and the Bangladesh Rural Advancement Committee (BRAC) for their credit programs; BRAC is also mentioned for its work in education and scholarship programs for girls. Its educational programs for poor girls have a major impact on government educational policy for poor girls. However, in both Bangladesh and India, while several local NGOs are named as active in various fields, none is singled out as having made a difference in local power relations or inclusion of poor people in local councils or other decisionmaking bodies.

If government involves itself in local organizations but does not share power, it can alienate poor people and destroy the organization. In the Republic of Yemen, for example, the government's increased involvement in local NGOs is cited as a major reason for "the decline of local contributions to local projects in terms of money, time, and labor" (Republic of Yemen 1999). In practice the PPA reports include more examples of government-NGO partnerships than examples of watchdog NGOs holding governments accountable at the local, state, or national level.

Community-Based Organizations

Without age groups in Igede we cannot survive because of general government neglect. —District Head of Owokwu, Nigeria 1996

As the past is more resilient than the future, and as passions are more lasting than interests, indigenous communities tend to be not only more stable over time, but more cohesive than rural and urban communities. —Panama 1998

Community-based organizations (CBOs) are grassroots organizations managed by members on behalf of members (Edwards and Hulme 1992). Poor people everywhere report a heavy reliance on them. CBOs perform vital and quite diverse functions for communities, including the mobilization of labor, infrastructure development, cultural activities, conflict resolution, and management of relations with outsiders, as well as emergency relief. Deeply rooted in local culture, indigenous organizations may sponsor celebrations, rituals, and festivals that bring joy and give meaning to people's lives. They are often the only organizations that poor people feel they own and trust, and on which they can rely.

These positive attributes notwithstanding, CBOs acting alone have generally not been a force for change in local power structures or for significant development gains. Poor people's organizations suffer from many capacity constraints. As Uphoff (1986) notes, "Such organizations can originate spontaneously from local initiative, but while isolated instances of local institutional development can be impressive, their cumulative effect is negligible." When CBOs arise in response to external incentives, there are often difficulties with sustaining local interest. In their now classic study of 150 local organizations across the developing world, Esman and Uphoff (1984) developed scores for rural development performance. They found that local organizations were the most successful with the highest scores when the organization was initiated by rural people themselves or when initiated by local leaders (scoring 153 and 138, respectively). The scores were lowest when the initiation was by government (16) and not much higher when jointly initiated by government and communities (50). However, when outside agencies, either government or NGOs, focused on building local capacity rather than on creating local organizations to implement external programs, the scores were higher (114).

This section is organized in three subsections. The first discusses the role of bonding and bridging organizations and the role of cultural identity as the foundation for bonding and group solidarity. It also discusses the impact of urbanization on group solidarity, and how the basis of solidarity shifts from shared cultural roots and meaning to shared occupations. It highlights two types of CBOs: *tontines* (revolving savings and credit groups) and burial societies. The PPAs report a remarkable absence of bridging associations. While bonding groups are important to survival and for a sense of belonging, in the absence of bridging ties they serve primarily as a defense against destitution rather than as a means of moving the poor out of poverty. The subsection ends with the case of federations of indigenous networks in Ecuador.

The second subsection discusses differences between the networks of the rich and the networks of the poor, and how cohesiveness among the elite often leads to their takeover of CBOs. When the poor belong to mixed community-wide groups they benefit from the greater availability of resources, but they also have less say in decisions that tend to reflect the interests of the elite. The subsection also explores differences between the networks of poor men and poor women. Women continue to be remarkably absent from community decisionmaking roles.

The third subsection focuses on building new partnerships to design interventions that build on the strengths of poor people's institutions, NGOs, and institutions of the state. It ends with a reference to the case study on Indonesia (case study 4.2), highlighting the importance of local capacity building and the difficulties in designing partnerships between community groups, governments, and NGOs.

Bonding and Bridging Organizations

Cohesion can only exist when a sense of identity prevails.
—Panama 1998

If it hadn't been for help from the village, the children would have died of hunger. —Armenia 1995

Community-based organizations typically command confidence because people feel a sense of ownership of them, and feel that these organizations are responsive to their priorities. Indigenous identity, based on caste, ethnicity, clan, gender, and age, lays the foundation for many of these organizations. "Historically, indigenous groups have developed community organizations as a solution for confronting economic, social, and political challenges. Lacking physical capital, and with more problematical access to the institutional resources that build human capital, without the spacious social experience that is behind the sentiment of citizenship, social capital became their capital. Social capital essentially became a homegrown solution among indigenous communities, organized through face-to-face interactions" (Panama 1998).

In Mali researchers find that traditional associations are the main safety nets. Each village generally has three associations, or *tons:* the men's association, the women's association, and the young men's association. The purpose of these tons is "to keep cultural traditions alive, strengthen community ties and, especially, share labor—both in communal fields and in the individual fields of the members. Often the earnings of the association are for consumption items, such as meat for celebrations, but they may also be contributed to community development initiatives, such as building materials or digging wells, and to pay the fines imposed by foresters" (Mali 1993).

Similarly, the age groups (age cohorts tied together through ritual) of Nigeria undertake varied community tasks and often develop sophisticated institutional capacities:

> "Without age groups in Igede, we cannot survive because
> of general government neglect," said the District Head of
> Owokwu. "Age groups are, however, generally self-
> development oriented. They construct roads, act as thrift
> and credit associations, procure farms for their members.
> The age groups actually have an elaborate organizational
> structure that includes a chairman who acts as spokesman
> of the group. There is also a secretary who most times is
> literate in order to keep records of the [happenings] within
> the organization. Actually, the age group also acts as a
> powerful tool of socialization and maintenance of law and
> order for the community. People of the same age have to
> qualify to be members of the group by being upright members
> of the community. They also have to be hardworking, of
> sane mind, and not convicted of any crime." —Nigeria 1995

There are important differences in rural and urban communities. Urban communities, although richer economically, often struggle to find a basis for communal security and solidarity. In Senegal a relative lack of social cohesion in urban areas, when compared with their rural counterparts, is noted. "Economic changes have also spurred changes in the social structure; in the Senegal River Valley for example, pastoral groups have coped with livestock losses by becoming more sedentary, and women have adapted to long absences of their emigrated husbands by becoming more active in farming. In urban areas, the social network has in many cases become weaker, and strained with the growing number of unemployed who come to the cities and stay with relatives while searching for work" (Senegal 1995).

The shift from indigenous to interest-based living, whether in rural or urban areas, is invariably accompanied by a shift in focus from collective gains to individual gains. In indigenous communities people tend to belong to groups that aim to benefit the locality as a whole, whereas urban poor people are more likely to belong to groups for individual income gains. The PPAs bear this out. In Mali urban associations are based on shared characteristics of the members, such as occupation, area of residence, or area of origin. Members of occupational associations help each other by providing tips to increase productivity and earnings or by sharing work opportunities. For example, members of a well-diggers' association will invite an unemployed member to work in their construction site (Mali 1993). In Panama, among rural indigenous communities, identity is based on a common past and a shared history and culture, whereas among the urban communities analyzed, identity is based on occupation and shared common interests. The Panama report notes that indigenous households participate in organizations much more than either their nonindigenous urban or rural counterparts (40 percent, 28 percent, and 30 percent, respectively). Indigenous people are found to participate in community associations, while other rural communities participate more frequently in cooperatives. Cooperatives are the only significantly frequent form of participation among urban residents (Panama 1998) (see box 4.1).

Psychological well-being is independent of economic well-being. When comparing urban to rural areas, at least in terms of community relations, indigenous rural populations appear richer in solidarity and support mechanisms, and appear happier despite greater poverty. They have strong patterned social relations, and a clearer sense of identity. The Georgia report observes, "Poverty has strongly affected patterns of sociability, solidarity, and authority. Although physical conditions are worse in villages than in towns or cities, [village] people felt their neighbors were more willing to lend a helping hand. People offer loans, tutoring, and medical services to neighbors" (Georgia 1997). While in Mexico: "Paradoxically, those that have the least, the indigenous peoples of Oaxaca, are those that fear their present condition the least as well, for they, and only they, have traditional communitarian institutions (*tequio, guetza*) which provide them support in times of need" (Mexico 1995). Similarly, social solidarity among indigenous communities is especially strong in the Panama report. "The [survey] indicates that indigenous communities have a more positive outlook about their situation than urban and nonindigenous rural communities, despite the fact that they have a higher incidence of poverty" (Panama 1998).

Box 4.1 Indigenous Organizations among the Kuna in Panama

The Kuna in particular have a long tradition of organization and thick association networks. On one Kuna island, community members meet every day and hold a traditional congress Fridays and Mondays. In their daily meetings they discuss issues related to the work that everyone owes to the community: airstrip maintenance, house construction, road maintenance, unloading boats. On another island, the community has ordinary meetings once a month and extraordinary meetings when the *Sahila* [chief] goes to the congress or to other islands so that he can give a report to the rest of the community. Smaller groups meet more frequently; women getting together to sweep streets, or to discuss commerce, solve social problems. Another example is the housing committee (*junta de construcción de la casa*), that builds about four houses every three months with about eight people on the committee. Women have a group to prepare for the traditional party held when a girl reaches puberty. They help the family whose fiesta will take place. In the indigenous community of San Ignacio de Tupile, there are as many as eight different community organizations covering issues such as schools, cleaning of local roads, nutrition, and water.

Source: Panama 1998.

Forms of community-based organizations vary infinitely, from revolving loan societies to a simple arrangement for exchanging labor and sharing food. We highlight two types of CBOs: *tontines* and burial societies.

Mobilizing savings through tontines

> *If you engage yourself in many groups, how are you going to work? One needs to survive. ... But if you don't join a group, how can you cope with a difficult life?* —Tanzania 1997

Tontines are an interesting example of CBOs. They are common in several countries in West Africa, and variations are found throughout the world.

Box 4.2 *Tontines:* Pooling Credit and Labor

The *tontine* system in West Africa functions as both a credit network and a labor-sharing system. *Tontines* generally comprise five to 10 people ... who contribute money at regular intervals, with each member in turn receiving the full amount collected. In effect, members who collect the prize during the first rounds benefit from a no-interest credit, while those collecting last simply receive their savings back with no interest. The levels of and intervals between contributions can range from US$.25 a month to over US$10 a week. Other types of *tontines* may be set up with a specific purpose, and they function more like insurance. In Ghana, for example, the *Kugadzadzo* is a savings club to finance funeral expenses (Ghana 1995a). Better-off individuals may belong to multiple *tontines* to provide extra security.

Tontines may also involve sharing labor and other resources among the members. In Benin, *tontines* "enable poorer families to share not only labor and possibly agricultural tools, but also food (often superior food, such as fish sauce) with richer farmers. For the core poor, being members of a *tontine des champs* may well be their only chance to secure regular access to proteins. In addition to playing a redistributive role, labor-sharing clubs are also a form of insurance against illness or other forms of incapacitation because they guarantee continued agricultural production and therefore survival for their members. In this sense, their existence is especially valuable for older people, who might not otherwise be able to cultivate their land" (Benin 1994).

Tontines are often the only local institution, formal or informal, to which the poor have recourse in times of crisis. The Ghana PPA notes that when a member has a desperate need of cash, the others will often rescue him out of a sense of group solidarity (Ghana 1995a). As explained in the Benin PPA, however, "Borrowing is never an easy choice. On the one hand, dignity may prevent people from asking unless the situation is really critical; on the other, becoming a debtor increases vulnerability because it lessens social standing and, perhaps more importantly, the likelihood of obtaining another loan" (Benin 1994).

Box 4.2 illustrates the characteristics and limitations of successful tontines. They appear to be very effective as "voluntary-forced" savings mechanisms and in creating safety nets for the poor.

Dignity in death: burial societies

They will not put you free of charge even in a grave. —An old pensioner in the village of Selce, Macedonia 1998

Burial societies have endured for many generations and can be found throughout the developing world—a testament to the high priority that poor people assign to ensuring that at least in death they are respected and accorded dignity according to local rites. As informal institutions, burial societies function as highly valued safety nets. Funerals are important in reinforcing one's standing in society, and ensuring support for survivors in times of need. Burial societies reinforce trust and reciprocity through pooled and collectively managed funds. "The community of Melan does not have a cemetery, and when somebody dies special transport must be hired to take the deceased and his or her relatives to the next cemetery at a cost of 100,000 sucres (US$50). The community pays half the cost" (Ecuador 1996a).

In Ethiopia, the PPA reports that burial societies are becoming out of reach for poor people: "*Idir-idirs* (burial societies) exist for funeral insurance in four communities, and in two communities, they cover also health and other critical problems. In Mechek no formal *idir* exists but clan members contribute two to three birr at the time of a funeral, that is paid back by the family. In Korate participants mentioned that the membership fee increased from 20 birr to 100 birr, and whereas the poor used to [be able to] afford to be *idir* members by selling fuelwood and grass, the entry cost is now prohibitive" (Ethiopia 1998). In urban areas, given declining incomes, sustaining *idirs* is difficult. However, every community still has at least one *idir,* but with declining membership.

In some West African countries—for example Togo, Senegal, and Benin—it is reported that "tradition and social pressure combine to make conspicuous consumption at ceremonies not a luxury for the very rich, but a duty even for the poor. The cost of funerals and marriages has apparently gone up, following a trend opposite to that of the country's economy. Families will routinely go into debt to finance the best funeral yet in the village, going to such excesses as hiring a generator for the wake, offering abundant food and drinks to everybody, even sewing uniforms for those attending" (Benin 1994).

Concern about funeral expenses and ability to save funeral money is widespread among the poor in Eastern Europe and the former Soviet Union.

Often this means facing the impossible dilemma of either providing health care for a sick relative or ensuring their decent burial. "Families must often gamble on the relative cost of treating a severe illness versus paying for the funeral. When Timur's father became ill, his family could not afford to have him moved to the hospital. The cost of his funeral turned out to be almost as expensive as hospital treatment, however. The family paid 30 lari for the death certificate, 100 lari to have the body prepared, 300 lari for the coffin, 150 lari to register for burial and dig the grave, and 300 lari on a modest wake" (Georgia 1997). For poor people, such expenses for a funeral are weighed heavily because they can serve to maintain or advance one's standing among extended kin and the community as well as to shape access to support during times of need.

Failure to fulfill one's social role can be an extremely shameful and isolating experience: "Recently, Nodar's mother died [in Georgia]. Just after he had arranged her funeral, his neighbor's mother also died, and the neighbor arranged for her own mother's funeral to take place at the same time. The neighbor then begged Nodar to organize his family's funeral procession and burial [for an earlier time]. Because the neighbor could not pay the required $200 for a coffin, she had simply rented one for the showing of the body. Her mother was to be buried without a coffin, however, just wrapped in cellophane. The neighbor was ashamed that people coming to the funeral of Nodar's mother would observe the contrast" (Georgia 1997).

The juxtaposition of social solidarity, financial burdens, and personal pride are well articulated in the PPAs: "Funerals remain the one event which still unites the community. Family members feel great pressure to show their worth by properly honoring the memory of the deceased with a large funeral meal. Although everyone who comes makes a contribution in cash or food, an unexpected death can still mean financial catastrophe for a poor or middle-income average family, forcing it into debt" (Armenia 1995).

Absence of bridging organizations

If one man is hungry and does not have any food, then how can he help another hungry man? —Pakistan 1996

Harnessing the potential of local-level associations and networks for poverty reduction requires an understanding of the nature of crosscutting ties, the extent of bonding and bridging ties, and the extent of substitution or complementarity between local institutions and the state. Societies are built up from social groups within which people interact with each other, share values and resources, and trust each other; in other words, there is bonding. When power is unequally distributed these social groups differ in their access to opportunities and resources. When social groups are disconnected from similar social groups in other communities it is difficult for them to organize around issues to bring about change, and social movement is unlikely. When social groups have no connections with other social groups different from themselves, they are unable to access the resources available to these more powerful groups. In both cases, groups lack bridging social capital.

The results from the PPA analysis suggests that associations of the poor are much more effective at meeting short-term security needs than at fostering change in the underlying rules of exclusion. In large part, this is because limited resources are siphoned off by daily exigencies and ongoing stresses and shocks. Most such informal associations, networks, and traditions of self-help are disconnected from larger collective action and resources of the state or other agencies.

Many countries have traditions for collective community work, such as *swadya* in South Asia, *gotong royong* in Indonesia, and *harambee* in Kenya. While *harambee* once represented an important coping mechanism for the poor, in a climate of high inflation and poorly functioning government services the tradition of *harambee* is stretched thin. People are fed up and say, "Now there is too much *harambee*, we do not want any more" (Kenya 1996). The PPA estimates that there are over 300,000 groups in rural areas, mostly disconnected from any external technical or financial assistance. "Hundreds of cases were recorded everywhere of the poor investing their resources in misguided *harambee* efforts related to water, farming, livestock, education, health, and a range of income-generating activities. School buildings without books, health clinics without drugs, chickens that die before they can be sold, and cotton that does not grow are of little use to anyone" (Kenya 1996).

There are of course exceptions. One striking example is the growth of networks of indigenous organizations that now engage with government at the local and national level in policy decisions in Ecuador.[3] (See box 4.3.) One NGO in Rajasthan, India is working on creating federated structures for women's groups to increase their negotiating power in local markets. Their activities include bulk procurement of raw materials, supplying credit, and teaching women entrepreneurs about the markets (India 1997a).

Differences among Networks

Most PPAs do not differentiate between different kinds of networks, but a few have rich descriptions of the differences between the organizations of the rich and the poor as well as organizations of men and women.

Networks of the rich and poor

> *The leader of the collective farm was and remains a king; he does not obey the law; he does what he wants, when he wants.* —Moldova 1997

There are two important differences between the networks of the rich and the poor. First, since the rich are well connected and, by definition, have more resources, they generally do not need external facilitators or catalysts to organize and mobilize. Second, since they are connected to others with power, their activities do not bring about resistance to change from the powerful unless one well-connected group becomes a threat to another. For example, proposals to increase investment in university education rather than in primary education, or to cut taxes for large businesses, or to reduce

Box 4.4 Tarifero Peasant Farmers Association in Manta, Cahul District, Moldova

In Pirlita farm workers wanting to privatize are frustrated by the many obstacles placed in their way. The 79 households, composed of teachers, *kolkhoz* [collective farm] workers, and pensioners chose a schoolteacher to help them push for privatization. They named their group Tarifero, which means strong as iron. During the first meeting of their leader and the manager of the collective farm the latter promised to implement land reform. In point of fact, though, he distributed only a small portion of the promised area—the oldest and least productive orchards—and began to oppose the group. Members tried to register Tarifero as a formal Peasant Farmers Association, but although they had submitted all the necessary documents for registration, in 1995 the land law changed, and such associations could register only after they received their share of nonland assets. Although they remain unregistered, tax authorities demand they pay taxes as if they have already received their value quota. The collective farm management continues to actively hinder them. It refuses to allow them use of the equipment on the grounds that it can't spare the equipment, forcing them to purchase used equipment for cash. According to Tarifero's leader, "The leader of the collective farm was and remains a king; he does not obey any law; he does what he wants, when he wants."

Source: Moldova 1997.

tariffs for industrial use of water and electricity do not create an uproar in most countries.

Poor men and women, on the other hand, generally do not organize beyond their own communities without long-term external support for networking, creating federations, or mobilizing. Poor people's movements pose a threat to those in power that may result in imposition of restrictions on civil society, direct repression, or engagement and change toward greater equity. The resistance that poor people face is clearly evident in Moldova (1997), as farm workers attempt to privatize land (box 4.4).

The differences between the cohesiveness of the rich and the poor even within the same communities are described in PPAs from India. In

Madhya Pradesh, for example, the higher castes are found to be highly cohesive whereas lower castes have weak linkages, weakened further by the need for seasonal migration to look for work (India 1998c).

While there are feelings of solidarity, the extent of organizing among vulnerable groups varies by activity. Expressed solidarity is highest in social interactions, as in the celebration of festivals and rituals. However, this does not transfer into occupational cooperation. There are some cases of weak cooperation or cooperation among only a few families. For example, in one village in Rajgarh, Chamar (which is a scheduled caste, or Hindus who fall outside the caste system) families "shared the proceeds of sale of the skin of any dead animal in the village" (India 1998c). Some cooperation is noticed among those who migrate from season to season, but the organization is unstable because membership constantly changes. Among the poor there is only a limited amount of lending within the same community. Among the Chamar and Basod (scheduled caste), loans range from Rs. 50 to Rs. 100 for household purposes, and are observed more among women than among men. "Mobilization against the oppressive methods of landlords was very rare" (India 1998c). This is not surprising given the total dependence of poor groups on the landlords. This dependency is beginning to change in areas of high migration and where livelihood strategies are changing. There is little intracommunity cooperation across castes except when the rich are affected by the same problem, for example, in cases where embankment walls are breached. The collaboration and interaction stops as soon as the task of repair is completed.

In contrast, intracaste cohesion is found to be high among the wealthier castes. This cooperation "transcended village boundaries and has an all time presence; the intra- and intercaste cohesion among the vulnerable groups was generally limited to the village or the Panchayat boundaries and was generally present around an issue, existing as long as the issues existed" (India 1998d).

These differences in social networks of the rich and poor help explain why simple procedural interventions introduced by government do not lead to the intended changes.

Takeover by the elite

> These community organizations do not listen at the local level, only help the better-off. —Guatemala 1994a

There are many more examples in the PPA reports of elites taking over local institutions than of elites working to improve the lives of the poor. Given the general cohesiveness of the rich and the relative atomization of the poor, this is not surprising. Indeed, when assessing the specific accomplishments of CBOs, several PPAs give guarded reviews about the extent to which benefits reach poorer community members. Based on data from the central office of cooperative societies, the PPA in Rajasthan finds a number of cooperative societies registered in a particular district. These include the Agricultural Multipurpose Society, Primary Agricultural Cooperative Society, Lift Irrigation Society, Oil Seed Growers Society, Consumer Cooperative Society, and agricultural farming societies. Records reveal that, although in principle membership is open to all, in reality the moderate and prosperous farmers control and manage the cooperatives. "The report concludes that these cooperative societies have mostly benefited the prosperous, while not addressing the needs of the most deprived groups" (India 1997a). The picture is similar in Nigeria: "The main drawback noted with such bodies is that they tend to look after only their members, while a much broader section of the community is in need" (Nigeria 1996). In Guatemala, the poor say, "These community organizations do not listen at the local level, only help the better-off" (Guatemala 1994a). The Cameroon PPA notes that wealthier groups are better able to take advantage of the resources of CBOs:

> *Despite the widespread view that community solidarity is*
> *natural, those who have worked closely with associations*
> *in Cameroon report that social tensions (jealousy, sorcery,*
> *and personal power struggles) can play a divisive role, and*
> *that general cooperation is not automatic. Community-wide*
> *groups may be dominated by the interests of those who are*
> *better off and have more resources—especially time—to devote*
> *to group activities. Small groups made up exclusively of poor*
> *people focus more on their specific needs, but may not have*
> *the linkages necessary to claim needed services or inputs.*
> *Where women are largely confined to the house, their ability*
> *to participate in associations is correspondingly limited.*
> —Cameroon 1995

In a number of countries, including India, Tanzania, and Venezuela, some CBOs have been taken over by political parties. In Venezuela the political parties appear particularly powerful in the life of CBOs. One person remarked, "In the community, the organizations are handled through the neighborhood association. Here in Venezuela the neighborhood associations function through the political parties. The neighborhood leader here is COPEI (Comité de Organización Política Electoral Independiente). I, as a member of the neighborhood association, am part of COPEI and when I need something, I go to City Hall and they listen to me, but if I didn't

belong to any political party, they probably would not listen to me"
(Venezuela 1998).

Communities sometimes take action when faced with government in-
action. Some communities in Venezuela, having grown tired of waiting,
took things into their own hands. "We have built ladders, drainage, wired
alleys, all from our own pockets; we organize and we buy. I'm not going to
tell you we pay for electricity there, the electricity is stolen. When we built
the playing field, we organized it and bought the material we needed"
(Venezuela 1998). In Nigeria, however, the urban elite play a critical role in
bringing resources to rural communities. "Sons abroad" in the cities and
overseas are seen as key allies in poverty reduction. They are the ones who
set up "self-help" organizations in rural areas. The poor feel that without
the involvement of influential leaders, development cannot be stimulated
(Nigeria 1996).

Women's networks

*To mourn, you stay with the dead person for five days if
the dead person is a man and four days if the dead person is
a woman.* —Kigoma, Tanzania 1997

*We women ask for credit only of those who won't tell. We
ask for credit from friends and relatives, sometimes pawning
a piece of jewelry or something precious.* —Togo 1996

The different positions that men and women occupy in social structures have far-reaching implications for women's and men's access to
formal and informal institutions. The most important institutions in poor
people's lives are often gender-segregated. When development interventions
do not factor in these differences, rather than benefiting, women may
emerge as losers from development.

In many parts of the world women cannot own property, do not inherit land, are not documented as heads of households even when they are
the primary income-earners, need to get permission from husbands or another male relative such as a father or brother in order to go out or work,
and have little contact with representatives of the state or with community
leaders.[4] This differential status of men and women is reflected in social
norms, everyday interactions, and even in mourning practices. One important consequence of differential access and exclusion from the powerful
social networks is that women invest heavily in informal social support
mechanisms with other women.

In many societies custom requires that when women get married they
move away from their villages and neighborhoods to their husband's homes

and neighborhoods. Distant from their own social networks, excluded from the husband's social networks and from contact with public institutions, young women seek friends and alliances with other wives who have moved to the same location because of marriage. In many societies there are great differences in the status of mothers-in-law and wives, and wives remain outsiders until the cycle repeats in the next generation as wives become mothers-in-law. In societies where these traditions are strong, this fragments women's networks into those who are from the outside, and those who are on the inside. To survive as outsiders women turn to other outsiders to create informal social networks for emotional solidarity, social support, and financial support for managing their domestic responsibilities.

Women's informal networks also provide support and information. Women's networks often become coping mechanisms. In South Africa, "A discussion group of women in Patensie indicated that women's social support was the network to which they turned when they were abandoned by their husbands. In the event of desertion they explained that a single woman can go to an older woman who will advise her what to do. The group also explained that women are particularly helpful, as they say this could happen to any of them. People will give rands [money] or some vegetables to the deserted woman. Many single mothers indicated that they often borrow from neighbors and relatives" (South Africa 1998). In India the creation of *mahila mandals* (women's groups) is mentioned in some reports as a way of empowering women and raising awareness about their rights (India 1997a).

Women's groups and networks are mentioned in the majority of reports. Women's groups appear to be more prevalent in Sub-Saharan Africa. Some of the most detailed examples of women's groups come from the East African PPAs. The examples show the courage and tenacity of women despite limited resources and limited technical know-how. Both in Kenya and in Tanzania most women's groups in rural areas are disconnected from any sources of technical or financial know-how and resources. In Kenya there are over 23,000 registered women's groups. Grounded in *harambee* and a social welfare tradition, the groups are struggling with economic concerns. Less than 2 percent of the registered groups report social welfare as their primary activity (Kenya 1996). Box 4.5 highlights activities of some women's groups from different regions of the country.

Finally, women's informal networks and groups may decline under conditions of severe economic shock. The PPA in Togo reports a dramatic decline in membership in *tontines* in the poorer regions after the financial crisis because "nobody could afford to save anything." In Benin, among vulnerable groups, *tontine* membership went down as much as 60 percent after the devaluation in January 1994 (Togo 1996).

Box 4.5 Women's Groups Using Social Capital to Generate Income in Kenya

Ombo Women's Group, Kisumu. The group formed in 1983 to begin income-raising activities. All the members belong to the same clan and started with making rope and weeding rich people's farms. Wanting to diversify, they rented two fish ponds from a neighbor, restocked the ponds, purchased fish food, and marketed the fish at the local market. Despite increased fish production, the activity was abandoned because open access to the fish ponds resulted in high levels of stealing fish and a declining fish harvest. The group now focuses on basket making, hiring of vehicles for the very sick for transport to hospitals and, when income is available, extending small loans to members for petty trading and hawking activities.

Nyamira Women's Groups. Both Muchenwa (80 members, of which six are men) and Omoteme women's groups (47 members, of which five are men) started with Kshs. 20 as entry fees. Because of high interest in membership, fees have been increased to Kshs. 500 and 200 respectively. The goal of the groups is to buy commercial plots, rental houses, corn-grinding mills, and household items. The Omoteme Group has assisted in building 20 houses for its members. The Menyenya Women's Group and several like it have a membership fee of Ksh. 20 and rent land to grow vegetables that are then sold to the secondary school. With the meager profits from the vegetables, the groups buy household utensils. Other groups invested in poultry raising, but this was abandoned when poultry diseases killed all the chickens. A private hospital-based livestock extension service is now advising the group on rabbit rearing.

Mandera. Even in the harsh circumstances of Mandera—a dry semi-desert district with the harshest environment of any of the area's studies, and isolated from markets and city centers—women's groups persist in their efforts. In Arda Kalacha, a village in which everyone is categorized poor or very poor, a women's group came into being seven years ago to assist needy people, initiate *harambees*, and help the poor pay for school fees. The group has 30 members. Despite their very limited resources, they continue to extend help to the most destitute in the community who are unable to participate in or contribute to the group's efforts.

Source: Kenya 1996.

Men's networks

In contrast to women's networks, poor men's networks tend to be shaped by their higher social authority and their employment relations. Beyond this, the PPAs have very limited descriptions of poor men's social relations, except to mention poor men's drinking habits (chapter 6).[5] In their employment, poor men are typically embedded in vertical "client-patron" relations. This can be seen most clearly in wage labor where tight markets and increasing mechanization restrict wage labor opportunities for the poor. Under these circumstances it is rare for poor men to organize and collectively negotiate better terms.

In India, for example, the poor are embedded in multiple dependency relations with rich landlords, with whom they seek wage labor as well as loans during times of need. *Haali*—where a poor man pledges labor for a year in return for a loan—is a common way of obtaining credit. The rates in the villages are around Rs. 6,000/ ($180 per year), but when contracts are entered into in times of distress, the amounts can fall to Rs. 4,500. While vertical links provide access to material resources, they no longer seem to provide emotional support to men. In Pakistan older men regret the fact that, while in the old days landlords on whom they depended knew them by name and treated them with respect, nowadays the landlords don't even know their names (Pakistan 1993).

The gender division in social networks carries significant costs for both women and men. In general, while women tend to be isolated from production networks, men are isolated from those informal institutions that provide for emotional well-being. In addition to the social isolation that many poor men feel, like poor women, they too rarely have access to the transformative networks that bring about change in power relations. Poor men are instead often left struggling to maintain their positions in local society. "Honor requires the men to earn enough to support their wives and children and to maintain the family's position in the community by public demonstrations of prosperity" (Armenia 1995).

Women's absence from community decisionmaking

> *Men have a better place in the community.* —El Salvador 1997

> *Mayan society is a man's society.* —Guatemala 1997a

Despite the rhetoric about "women in development," women's participation in community decisionmaking remains highly constrained. In the Republic of Yemen researchers report, "Women do not take part in committees. Participation takes time, and women's workload is heavy, especially when men migrate to the cities or to commercial farms in irrigated areas." Women seem to prefer using their time to raise additional income or to learn to read and write rather than to participate in meetings that offer uncertain returns (Republic of Yemen 1998). Similarly, in El Salvador men dominate the new education management committees. In 1992, 78 percent of the presidents were men. Two explanations are offered: "Men are better known in the communities and have better chances to be selected as representatives; and women's household duties would not allow them time to participate or to be trained to perform management duties"(El Salvador 1997). In Guatemala, because of their exclusion from community councils, women have created their own women's committees (Guatemala 1997a).

In Orissa, India, it is reported that women do not participate in the traditional caste *Panchayats* (caste-based local councils). "Women are not allowed to make any representation and in cases of disputes involving them, they do not get any support from other women of their own caste, as women are barred from attending any such dispute resolution meetings of caste members" (India 1998a). This increases women's vulnerability.

In South Africa, when discussions were being held and women wanted to join in, "at first the men wanted the women to leave because they said that women did not understand the needs of the community. The women argued with the men and eventually it was agreed that the women could stay" (South Africa 1998).

In Vietnam the PPA reports that women's participation in community activities has declined with changes in livelihoods from indigenous systems of shifting cultivation in which women are key actors. "But along with the changes of society when new social systems came into place, the men took over the decisionmaking roles in organizations like the communist party and in local authorities like the committee of the communes" (Vietnam 1999a).

Building New Partnerships

> The mayor, accompanied by the alguacil [sheriff], holds
> open fora where individuals begin by explaining the problem.
> Everyone is entitled to an opinion at this point. Authorities
> try to organize ideas, or what is called "networking the ideas."
> The auxiliary mayor is the moderator. —Guatemala 1997a

Local traditions and practices can be used as the basis of crafting organizations for the poor for governance and service provision in partnership with NGOs or the government. With the peace agreement in December 1996 that ended a 34-year conflict in Guatemala, the indigenous decisionmaking practices by consensus are beginning to be incorporated at each level of government (1997a). While the PPA notes many community-based efforts, the most successful CBO held up as a model of its kind relies on three ingredients for success (Guatemala 1997a). It responds to community priorities; it negotiates projects with line ministries; and it creates tripartite partnerships with the municipality, the government of Guatemala or NGOs, and the community. Through this process it has created its own health center, school, agricultural support activities, and loan fund. This organization, which started in 1975, has spread to 18 communities.

The government of Panama has started a local investment program (Proyecto de Inversión Local) that assigns $25,000 to each district for a community project. In theory, the district's representative schedules a meeting with each local organization to identify a project to be financed with the funds. In rural communities with high levels of associational life, the system is reported to work as planned. In one of the communities visited by the researchers, the community had decided to build an access road to a neighboring hamlet that belonged to the same district (*corregimiento*). "The entire town attended the meeting, and both men and women participated. ... Everyone agreed on the project; there were outsiders who congratulated us for not being selfish." In another town, people have decided to use the money to buy an ambulance and to cooperate with neighboring villages to organize medical visits (Panama 1998).

In Nigeria local government is working with age groups in planning and managing markets. The market in Obusa was virtually built by the age groups. The local government planned the market and allocated the plots to the age groups that build stalls and collect fees on market days. They pay annual rent to the local government (Nigeria 1995).

Effective partnerships require not just changes in procedures but changes in mind-set, so that all partners—including external support agencies—see themselves as learners rather than as experts. In El Salvador, while discussing decentralized education strategies, the Vice-Minister of Education said, "Working with so many consultants that the banks send to El Salvador is difficult. The first comes and advises us we should do things in a certain way. We do it, but then comes the next and changes everything. Every mission there is a new consultant with new ideas and no memory for what has been going on. Often they do not read what the others recommended previously" (El Salvador 1997).

Community-driven programs, in which decisionmaking and resource allocation authority is vested in community groups, are important instruments to respond to community priorities and invest in local organizational capacity. In almost every country the poor say that new ways have to be found that allow poor people to participate and monitor government programs to ensure that these programs really benefit the poor. In Vietnam, when the poor speak of the importance of loans and the corruption in credit supply agencies, they suggest a system of community monitoring. This would involve the poor establishing groups themselves to manage credit programs through appointment of a treasurer, or "moneykeeper," in the community; someone who would keep everyone informed about the money received, who has taken loans and for how long, and so on. The moneykeepers would be responsible for disseminating information about procedures. As well as making the procedures clearer, it is expected that this would also establish a system of community monitoring of the program so that "leaders cannot give money just for their families" (Vietnam 1999a). In Benin (1994) community-based health monitoring systems have been initiated in one region, and communities are involved in collecting information on village health that is discussed every three months in the village assembly. A village committee monitors the implementation of the assembly's decisions. In the Zou region, for example, there are 250 sociosanitary committees that monitor and manage pump repairs, sanitation, and health education.

The Indian experiment with decentralization—with devolution of decisionmaking authority to *gram sabhas* at the village level, and constitutional amendments requiring women to be elected in one-third of the positions of leaders of the *Panchayat*—sets the framework for new partnership between the poor, governments, and NGOs. While change in legislation alone will not necessarily lead to social change, it creates new space for women to emerge as leaders and for civil society to organize and work in partnership with the state to create more responsive governments for the poor. Without support for poor men and women to organize, mobilize, and inform themselves, the potential created by the political changes will remain unrealized. While in some parts of the country rural women are asserting their leadership roles and changing the types of projects being financed by village councils in dramatic ways (Jain 1996), in other parts of Bihar and Uttar Pradesh change may be slower in coming (India 1998b). One PPA from India reports:

> Although Devi was elected village pradhan [chief] to fill a
> quota position reserved for women, the villagers always
> address her husband, Gulab, as the pradhan. It was he who
> was garlanded and congratulated when the election results
> came in, and he attends Panchayat meetings in place of Devi,
> who stays home. It is clear that Devi is pradhan in name
> only, and her election has in no way empowered her or
> women more generally. In other villages, men from scheduled

castes [SC] have been elected to fill SC set-aside positions, but were controlled by their wealthy high-caste patrons. Some cases were found, however, in which the balance of power was said to have shifted due to the activities of an SC prad-han in a way that curbed abuses of power by the higher castes. Thus, while there was variability in the findings, it was learned that a woman or SC pradhan is no guarantee of a shift in power relations. It may be necessary to create more extensive systems of local accountability to ensure that re-served positions are truly occupied by representatives of the deprived and powerless. —India 1998b

The Indonesia case referred to at the end of this chapter (case study 4.2) explores in detail the community's capacity to take collective action, and the difficulties in connecting government programs with community capacity. The study results have been used to design the Kecematan Development Program which seeks to build on community capacity and overcome the problems identified in existing government programs. The funds flow directly from the *kecematan* to the community in response to community proposals. Mechanisms have been designed to ensure trans-parency and accountability of decisions and resource use at all levels through availability of information, and through the training of NGOs and journalists as independent monitors.

Neighborhood and Kinship Networks

So, where do the Togolese turn for help? To their families, of course, and to their clans. —Togo 1996

People who live in the same group (natural settlement) not only cooperate and help each other in productive activities but also support and help each other in family events such as birthday celebrations, weddings, funerals, and religious rituals, and in social life such as first aid and illness. Private loans are often without interest conditions when granted among the households. —China 1997

Beyond groups and associations, networks of neighbors and kinfolk play an important role for most poor people. This is the first line of defense outside the immediate family in times of difficulty or crisis, and reciprocal obligations are strong enough to make it a very reliable defense. Whole communities are dependent on the shared human and material resources of their neighbors, clan, and extended family. Poor people repeatedly state that they borrow money from friends and neighbors to make ends meet, exchange a variety of services, and use the resources of their social networks in innumerable ways in order to survive.

However, it is also clear that there are limits and costs to depending on friends and neighbors for support. The problem, of course, is that these networks have few outside resources to draw on, and the other members of the network are often in exactly the same plight. Especially in times of crisis or stress that increases the vulnerability of the entire community (for example, drought), resources are stretched thin for everyone and thus the "insurance" provided may become only nominal.

Costs and Limits to Reciprocity

> *It is useless for me to use the money I earned abroad*
> *to buy grains to sell during the preharvest season, because*
> *I would have to give them for free to my relatives.*
> —A farmer, Mali 1993

While family networks have great importance as coping mechanisms, the strong sense of reciprocal obligation that makes them successful in times of crisis also makes them resistant to individual entrepreneurship and accumulation. In many parts of Sub-Saharan Africa strong kin obligations interfere with individual motivation to save. In addition, when the network is small and homogeneous, it is likely that problems affecting one member will also affect others. When everyone is affected by an event and resources are limited, kin ties may be of little assistance. "It is not uncommon that in a remote village nobody has enough to eat during the postharvest season, so nobody can offer a free meal to the neighbor's children" (Togo 1996).

In Pakistan the PPA conclude that, while reciprocal relations exist in communities to assist during personal emergencies, they are an unstable base for long-term security. The first order of preference in times of need or crisis is to turn to immediate family. "When these networks are insufficient or unable to respond, assistance is sought within the *biraderi* [kinship network] or *quom* [caste network]. Familial and community obligations toward children, pregnant women, and elderly and invalid dependents are taken very seriously. However, they are often beyond the means of the poorest households, particularly in the context of high levels of unemployment" (Pakistan 1996).

Conclusions

There is no institutional panacea. Informal networks of poor people and bonds of solidarity provide meaning and identity and support during crises. However, the resources of these networks are limited. Community-based organizations are responsive to local needs, but as they grow they may become dominated by the better-off and ultimately exclude the poor. Most CBOs also exclude women from decisionmaking. NGOs are not as widespread as it sometimes appears. While they do much to support basic survival, their track record in accountability to their poor clients is not strong. Few NGOs have successfully addressed local capacity or underlying power and justice issues. Pressure from governments and international donors for quick service delivery, coupled with unstable, short-term financing appears to be undermining the capacity of NGOs, where they exist, to work effectively with poor communities.

It is clear that there is no single institutional solution to the problems of the poor. Crafting institutional designs that blend the values and strength of poor people's institutions with the community organizing skills of NGOs and the resources of state institutions takes on new urgency, given the limits of all these institutions. The big challenge for outsiders—NGOs, governments, the private sector, and international agencies—is to support the capacity of poor people to organize, mobilize resources for priority needs, and participate in local and national governance. In many countries governments are putting into place decentralized structures for local governance. While new structures do create space for poor people's empowerment, long-term commitment to build the capacity of the poor and facilitate collaboration across communities will be required so as to bring about lasting change.

Poor communities are more or less gender-segregated. Unless community organizing strategies are based on an understanding of social cleavages, women are likely to be further marginalized in their communities. There are many cases of successful partnerships between governments and civil society. The challenge is still to scale up small efforts at partnership without losing their responsiveness and accountability to the poor. Responsiveness requires the flexibility to respond to local schedules and local needs, and it requires processes that build local capacity for self-governance. The pressures in large programs are toward standardized procedures and quick disbursement of resources. However the principles are clear, and there is enough on-the-ground experience in large community-driven programs to make fewer mistakes than in the past.

Every human being deserves to be treated with respect. While structural change requires organization and time, mindset and behavioral changes are within the control of individuals. Everyone—NGOs, religious organizations, CBOs, local elite, local leaders, local officials, national and international financiers—all of us should be held accountable for our behavior in our encounters with poor women and men around the world.

Case study 4.1 Financial services

Since there is no self-owned property, we can't get loans.
—Venezuela 1998b

Repayment in labor is the last resort especially for an able adult person. —India 1998d

Participation in the formal financial sector is not an option for most of the poor involved in the PPAs. The microcredit summit estimated that in 1997, 925 institutions reached 12.6 million poor households worldwide. It also estimated that despite the microcredit movement, only 2 to 5 percent of the 500 million poorest households in the world have access to credit through formal institutions (UNDP 1997). Most discussions of credit access in the PPAs focus on informal arrangements. Obtaining credit in the informal sector may entail paying higher interest rates—in India, 36 to 120 percent per annum (India 1997a); in Togo up to 360 percent per annum (Togo 1996). Yet the flexibility and availability of informal credit schemes make them the only choice for the very poor. This case study addresses two prevalent themes in the PPAs: credit access and cycles of debt and poverty.

Access to Credit

In Guatemala local networks are described as the most common alternative to formal credit services. "In marginal urban areas shopkeepers provided credit for food on a limited basis and only when the family was well known to the shopkeeper. Family and friends loaned money to one another to cover emergency health-care costs. Wholesalers gave credit for goods to be sold in the informal economy. Local governance committees provided credit for household construction materials such as tin sheeting" (Guatemala 1994b). Similarly, one of the India studies concludes:

> For the lower economic strata of society whose major requirement is consumption credit, formal credit institutions have no relevance. And even for investment, procedural difficulties and inability to satisfy the collateral requirements drive them away from formal credit institutions. As elsewhere, there are two major categories of moneylenders: (1) trader-moneylender

and (2) landlord-moneylender. There can be a situation where a landlord-moneylender is also active in village and/or Janpad politics, and can integrate his moneylending business with his political activities, and thus influence decisions. Ongoing development efforts do not seem to influence his role or activity in any significant manner and hence, to that extent the moneylender is not a stakeholder. However, any serious effort to intervene in rural microcredit (as has been suggested) would immediately make him a crucial stakeholder. As the moneylender is informal and at the fringes of law, he can immediately respond in many ways to destroy any attempt which affects his business. —India 1998c

In the regions studied in Madagascar fewer than 10 percent of the poor interviewed have access to formal credit, and 98 percent of all agricultural activity is self-financed. Relatives and friends are the most frequent lenders, providing the bulk of short-term credit either in cash or in kind. Most of these loans are interest free (Madagascar 1994).

In some countries, such as Swaziland, access to formal lending institutions may be constrained more by a lack of effective dissemination of information than by the nonexistence of services. "Although borrowing from the bank or from moneylenders was mentioned by a few male participants, and some women mentioned revolving credit schemes, there was generally little knowledge or experience of formal savings and credit. In most of the groups, discussion of the options involved had to be abandoned and the groups discussed instead the use of traditional interhousehold borrowing of food. A number of men had dropped out of agricultural cooperative or credit schemes because their production was insufficient to repay loans" (Swaziland 1997).

The situation in Eastern Europe and the former Soviet Union appears very similar. In Moldova poor people express profound mistrust of banks (Moldova 1997). In Ukraine, as elsewhere, in the absence of access to formal sources of credit people turn to kinship networks. "Families who have fallen on hard times often have friends and neighbors who are somewhat better off and willing to help them make ends meet. Borrowing is a common practice and, given widespread recognition of the number of people working without a salary and the belief that mothers with small children should not be working, there is little stigma attached to it. However, most reported that they tried to avoid borrowing and attempted to repay their debts as quickly as possible to avoid marring a relationship over money" (Ukraine 1996).

Cycles of Indebtedness

When credit is scarce and poverty high, moneylenders wield enormous power and can be extremely exploitative. Box 4.6 presents an example from India that illuminates the complexity of debt and finance cycles for the poor.

Debt cycles are often linked to seasonal migration strategies for providing household income. They can create difficult situations for women left as household heads to deal with sometimes irregular remittances (South Africa 1998). For many villagers in India, migration to the urban locations outside the state in pursuit of livelihood is guided by the need for money to repay debts, covering deficits created by losses in agriculture or meeting expenditures of large magnitude on account of marriages, festivals, ceremonies, and so on. The returns accruing to their ventures outside their village hardly make up for their toil, and the costs include bad health, broken families, and deepening of their debt burden (India 1998a).

Case study 4.2 Indonesia—Community Capacity and Village Government

> People do not perceive themselves as having any real influence. The fact that a village head is an elected official does not, oddly enough, create the feeling among the community that they are the source of his power. —Indonesia 1998

The answer to the question, "Is there capacity in the communities for collective action?" depends on whom you ask. A large study undertaken in 48 Indonesian villages in three provinces—Jambi, Central Java, and Nusa Tenggara Timur—explores this question by examining quantitative data based on in-depth qualitative information about community groups, collective action projects, and village government (Indonesia 1998, 1999).[6] This case study draws on these data to examine three questions: (1) Is there a difference between community-initiated and government-initiated projects? (2) What is the impact of organizational capacity? and finally, (3) What are the linkages between local capacity and government programs? Because community capacity is a key factor in ensuring that poor people have access to information and services, this case study attempts to untangle factors associated with local capacity, including impact of government activities. The study compares government- and community-initiated programs.

Community capacity is the ability of a community to mobilize and carry out collective activities to solve its own problems. Community groups

Box 4.6 A Cycle of Debt and Credit in India

"My household of six members requires at least one *mana* [quantity] of rice every day. However, now that I am carrying so much debt on my head we have no choice but to limit our consumption," says Bhimraj, who came from his ancestral village of Nuapada after his marriage 15 years ago to stay at his in-laws' place. Talking about his household economy Bhimraj softens his voice: "I have no land, so I work as a wage laborer and earn a maximum of Rs. 400 in a month. In the evenings, I go to sell the one liter of milk that I get from my cow, that fetches Rs. 108 to 150 a month for six months. My wife also goes for work and earns Rs. 200–250 a month. My mother-in-law works as a cook in the village school and earns Rs. 100. My brother-in-law is employed in the Keshinga rice mill and he sends Rs. 200 every month to the household. I spend no less than Rs. 800 in buying rice. Every week my expenditure on vegetables and salt is about Rs. 25. Another 200 rupees a month goes on kerosene, cooking oil, and my son's education. So, you can see that I can hardly save Rs. 50 in a month. I have borrowed Rs. 4,000 from Veda of Nuapara by mortgaging one acre of land. I don't see any chance of being able to retrieve my land in the near future. My mother-in-law carries on her head a *Kharif* loan of Rs. 2,000 borrowed from the grain bank. I had also borrowed Rs. 1,200 from the State Bank, which I have yet to repay. I don't know why I got only Rs. 1,200 while Rs. 2,400 was sanctioned against my name. In addition, I had borrowed five pounds of rice from the *mahajan* [moneylender] five years' back for my sister-in-law's marriage, which I need to repay. We had a much better time in my father's house at Nuapara. At least this pressure of debt was not there on the head." He is not sure whether he will be able to educate his other son and his daughter.

Source: India 1998a.

in Indonesia have initiated a wide range of activities with primary focus on credit and the construction of basic infrastructure. Of all community development activities, 53 percent have been initiated by government, 38 percent by communities, 7 percent by NGOs, and 2 percent by the private sector. As seen in table 4.1, community-initiated projects performed better than government-initiated projects on every criterion.

Table 4.1 Comparison of Community and Government Projects

Item	Community-initiated	Government-initiated
Number of projects	319	411
Project initiator	38 percent	53 percent
Reaching beneficiaries	83 percent	67 percent
In full use	85 percent	51 percent
Good maintenance	74 percent	37 percent
No women's participation	29 percent	54 percent

Most community-initiated projects are carried out at the sub-community level, in the hamlet or neighborhood; organizing is based on proximity rather than on occupation or other identity. Women are more involved in community projects, primarily in credit schemes, than in government projects, and poorer households are less active in decisionmaking although not excluded. The most prominent groups in the village are community-initiated. They have multipurpose activities, elect their own leaders, collaborate with other groups, raise and manage funds, and, most importantly, mediate and resolve conflicts at the local level. One-third of the most active groups have existed for more than a decade.

In addition, villages with high organizational capacity (measured on a five-point scale—one is low and five is high) carry out a greater number and a wider variety of community projects, collaborate more across groups both within and across the community, have an effective local government, and have a greater percentage of households that participate in collective activities (see table 4.2). The data do not establish causality, but the strong association is noteworthy.

There are several factors that do not seem to vary with organizational capacity. Organizational capacity does not appear to affect community

Table 4.2 Average Performance Scores of Village Government by Village

Performance	High capacity	Low capacity
Quality of village head	3.49	2.44
Village planning	3.24	2.73
Responsiveness of village government	3.51	2.52

Note: Scores for village organizational capacity range from 1 (low) to 5 (high). The sample was 48 villages.

participation in government projects, nor does it guarantee quality of outputs, either for government or community projects. Organizational capacity seems to be related to multiple bases of leadership, responsive and accountable leaders, multilevel mediation processes, cohesive traditional governance, and supra-village linkages.

Finally, there is a disconnect between community initiatives and institutions and government programs and institutions. Community initiatives and institutions that are the basis of local capacity are not connected to government resources and decisionmaking. In the study villages only 12 percent of community projects receive any government support and another 12 percent receive some government financing. No community groups receive any government financing, and only 2 percent receive any government support. Community organizational capacity has no impact on the quality of government-provided services. This finding is important in light of the fact that villages with high organizational capacity also have better performing village heads. This implies that central government programs do not take into account the knowledge or priorities expressed by village heads.

In the villages studied there are more government projects than community projects, reflecting the assumption that communities lack knowledge and need outsiders' skills. Government-provided projects and services are not accountable to the community, or to village government. The high failure rate of government projects, obvious mismanagement of government funds, and unfair practices in election of village heads to eight-year terms mean that incentives for accountability are low. Villages have little control over financial resources coming from the outside, even in the annual village subsidy from the government for bottom-up planning; regulations favor outside contractors over implementation by locals; and higher government is not responsive to village government's complaints of irregularities in government-initiated projects. Despite these drawbacks, in some places village heads are accountable, responsive, and innovative, and manage to bring development resources to their villages.

Notes

1. For an extensive review of what social capital is and what it does, see Woolcock 1998 and Portes 1998. For detailed empirical evidence in different contexts see Putnam et al. 1993, Tendler 1997, and Grootaert 1999. For debates on

policy implications see Edwards and Foley 1997. For recent research on social capital see Dasgupta and Serageldin 1999.

2. For an extensive discussion on bonding, bridging, and the relationship of substitution and complementarity see Narayan 1999.

3. See also Bebbington and Perreault 1999.

4. For a detailed discussion see Narayan and Shah 2000. The paper provides empirical evidence of women's and men's differential access to formal and informal organizations and implications for policy.

5. A computer search of the NUD*IST database that is merely indicative resulted in 66 references to women's groups and six references to men's groups.

6. The case study is based on two reports by Chandrakirana (1999) and Evers (1998), as part of a Local Level Institutions Study managed by Scott Guggenheim in the Jakarta office of the World Bank.

Chapter 5

Changing Gender Relations in the Household

*In our village, the women cannot do much. They do
agricultural labor, bring fuel wood from the jungle,
and look after children.*

—A village man, India 1997d

*Having 10 daughters but no boy is the same as having
no children.*

—A poor woman, Vietnam 1999a

*Sister, if you don't beat them they'll stop being good.
And if they're good and you beat them, they'll stay
that way.*

—A man, Bangladesh 1996

One of the most important institutions in the lives of poor people is the household.[1] The household is a basic unit of society where individuals both cooperate and compete for resources. It is also a primary place where individuals confront and reproduce societal norms, values, power, and privilege. Gender norms expressed within the household are reinforced and reflected in larger institutions of society. "Gender relations are not confined to the domestic arena—although households constitute an important institutional site on which gender relations are played out—but are made, remade, and contested in a range of institutional arenas" (Kabeer 1997). In other words, this is not simply a story of the household and its members, but about the shaping of gender identities by larger institutions, and the ongoing participation of family members in creating new gender norms.[2]

This chapter is about *gender anxiety*. The household as an institution is strained and in flux. Vast economic, social, and political restructuring has not—with few exceptions—translated into increased economic opportunities for the poor. Under increasing economic pressure, men in many parts of the world have lost their traditional livelihoods, and women have been forced to take on additional income-earning tasks while continuing their domestic tasks. These changes touch core values about gender identity, gender power, and gender relations within poor households, and create anxiety about what is a "good woman" or a "good man." Values and relations are being broken, tested, contested, and renegotiated in silence, pain, and violence. What is striking is that, despite widespread changes in gender roles, traditional gender norms have shown remarkable tenacity, leaving families struggling to meet the often-contradictory demands.

This tension impacts all household members. In the absence of outside support, it is unclear whether the changes will, in fact, lead to more equitable gender relations within the household, or avoid the trauma of abuse, alcohol, separation, divorce, and dissolution of the household. The PPA reports capture the silent trauma going on within poor households that has yet to be factored into poverty-reduction strategies.

Over and over again, in the countries studied women are identified, and identify themselves, as homemakers, the keepers of the family, responsible for the well-being of their children and husbands. The PPAs also relate the entrenched nature of men's identities as breadwinners and decisionmakers even as these roles are undermined and eroded by changing social and economic environments. These socially defined roles of men and women are not only unattainable, they sometimes are in stark contradiction with reality. This is what creates the stress that seems to be endemic in poor households today.

The PPAs show that households are adapting to acute and long-term stress in gender-specific ways: men often seem to react with defeat, while women react by swallowing their pride and taking desperate actions. When men are unemployed or underemployed, women enter low-income, low-status jobs, often at considerable risk, in order to feed their families. As a consequence of their inability to contribute adequately to the family income, men may start feeling redundant and burdensome to households; they experience disorienting challenges to their perceptions of themselves as providers and heads of families, often resulting in anger and frustration. Women, on the other hand, continue to care for their families and gain a shaky new confidence, though their income-earning opportunities remain tenuous. These broad patterns are summarized in figure 5.1.

The Swaziland PPA notes, "The pressures of poverty are experienced very differently by men and women. Men have experienced a threat to their social status, self-respect, and confidence in their economic role as providers for their family, through the loss of their cattle and through increased dependence on the informal earnings of their [wives] to meet basic household needs. Many instances were cited of men who had left the community and deserted their families because of debt they could not repay, or simply because they were unable to provide for their wives and children" (Swaziland 1997).

What is the outcome for households where gender identities are shifting? Some households cope by cooperating and dealing with the shifting identities. For other families, the outcome is violence, family break-up, or divorce.

This chapter is structured around the patterns, linkages, and relationships that emerged from listening to the voices of poor women and men in the PPAs. We first discuss some key concepts that are useful for understanding the findings emerging from the PPA analyses. We then focus on traditional gender norms, gender identity, and traditional divisions of labor, followed by a discussion of the impact of large-scale economic and political change on gender relations and the changing roles of men and women. Finally, two sectoral case studies on education and property rights are presented to demonstrate how gender roles and rights in the household affect and are affected by these larger institutions in society. There is one striking imbalance: we find remarkably little information on men's lives compared to women's lives. Hence the section on men, while revealing, is brief. It appears that, despite a switch in terminology, development thinking is still very much caught in the framework of women in development.[3]

Figure 5.1 Economic Disruption and Gender Anxiety

	Male	Female
Traditional Identity	Breadwinner	Caregiver
Roles	Income-earner	Mother, wife
Reaction (to male job loss)	Stress, humiliation, alcohol, drugs, violence	Stress, conflict, anger, hopelessness, depression
Adaptation	Collapse, defeat	Take action; find risky low-income, low-status jobs, and take care of family
Consequences	Redundant males in households, collapse, family break-up	Shaky new confidence, vulnerability, family break-up
Interventions	Employment creation	Protection, organization, employment
Dialogues	Male-female identity	Male-female identity

Roots of Gender Inequality

> *Men own everything because when they were born, they just found it like that.* —Kanazi village, Kagera, Tanzania 1997

From multiple perspectives women often find themselves in positions subordinate to men. In most societies women are socially, culturally, and economically dependent on men. Violence against women is an extreme expression of male dominance and "one of the most intractable violations of women's human rights" (Davies 1994).

The persistence of domestic violence across many societies suggests that it is not merely a characteristic of particular individuals but is, at a deeper level, related to social structures that maintain unequal socioeconomic relations between men and women.[4] At the core of gender-based violence are the unequal power relations that limit women's choices and reinforce dependency on men. In Cameroon, for example, control and dependency is perpetuated in different ways. Women in some regions require a husband's, father's, or brother's permission to go outside of the home. In addition, "A woman's husband or brother has access to her bank accounts, but not vice versa, providing him with information on her assets. When women in one farmers' group were asked how their husbands used their money, they laughed and said, 'We don't know'" (Cameroon 1995). Davies argues, "The social, political, and economic dependence of women on men provides a structure wherein men can perpetuate violence against women" (Davies 1994). Despite the widespread nature of domestic violence, the subject appears to be socially and politically "untouchable" by state agencies and international institutions.[5] One PPA report stated, "Wife-beating is a family problem not to be discussed publicly. Sometimes the cause is that women are rude and arrogant with their husbands who beat them to discipline them. But some men are just oppressive and like to mistreat their wives" (Tanzania 1997). Unfortunately, men's reactions to their own violence against women is not often recorded in the PPAs.

   When their authority is challenged men seem to experience stress and exert their right to control the women in their lives through threats and violence. Moreover, this violence, depending on prevailing social norms and structures, may even be naturalized by the victim and perceived as acceptable or normal. Rupesinghe and Rubio argue, "An outstanding feature of structural violence is that the victim is also a part of it, in a position of acquiescence or confrontation. We cannot predetermine which of these positions will be taken, because this depends, among other factors, on the degree to which the victim has internalized the predominant culture or the degree of criticism toward it that he or she has developed" (Rupesinghe and Rubio 1994). A PPA from Jamaica reports that "on occasion, when women felt able to speak openly about their experiences, stories of everyday domestic brutality, fear, and a sense of being trapped emerged" (Jamaica 1997).

Traditional Gender Norms

> Like hens, women wait for cocks to crow announcing the
> arrival of daylight. —Proverb, Ghana 1995a

> The cock does not know how to look after chicks, but only
> knows how to feed itself. —Proverb, Jamaica 1997

A norm is a shared expectation of behavior that expresses what is considered culturally desirable and appropriate, while a role is a set of norms attached to a social position (Marshall 1994). Social norms are reinforced through popular culture, radio, television, traditional art forms, proverbs and stories, customs, laws, and everyday practice. Common proverbs such as, "When a girl is born, the karma must be bad" (Durga Pokhrel, personal communication), and in India, "A good girl suffers in silence," indicate that cultural norms are deeply embedded and understood as facts. In general, as a Ugandan man succinctly stated, "Women are taken to be the inferior gender" (Uganda 1998).

Women's presumed "inferiority" is used to justify discrimination and abuse in the household and in society at large; power inequity is reflected and reinforced by traditional and modern laws and institutional practices. A woman's extrahousehold bargaining power with legal authorities, society, and the market impacts her intrahousehold bargaining power (Agarwal 1997). In country after country women explain that their right to inheritance is either nonexistent or limited. When women do have inheritance rights, and assert them, they risk social ostracism from the very same kinship networks on which they base their daily survival.

The ability of men and their families to throw women out of their marital homes with or without a final divorce, without even their own jewelry, reflects a social inequality of power. The threat of divorce is perhaps an even more potent deterrent to women's self-assertion. In North India the idea that "a woman leaves her father's home in a wedding palanquin and only returns in a coffin" is staple fare for many a Bombay film.

Other research in Bangladesh reports women's silence as a self-protecting strategy in the face of few social or economic options. "If I ever argue with him, he hits me," one woman in Bangladesh said. "I don't argue much because he might abandon me, and I would have no place to go. Usually he doesn't beat me unless my shortcoming is serious" (Schuler et al. 1998).

A woman widowed by the genocide in Rwanda reports being treated like a horse on the property of her former husband. She adds, "My husband's parents are like strangers, yet one day they may leave their land there and claim my fields" (Rwanda 1998).

Similarly, in Kenya women report being chased out of their homes by their husbands, without being allowed to take even their utensils with them. In Ukraine, Latvia, and Macedonia women say that they do not bother to report rape because of lack of action by authorities. Around the world women report having little recourse when faced with abuse and threats to property and their lives.

While many women organize, take action, and protest,[6] in the studies analyzed poor women report using individual exit strategies, becoming silent, or using indirect ways of asserting themselves. Women also try to improve their lives by using indirect or discreet, traditionally and culturally appropriate means to negotiate more authority in the household. In South Africa some poor women feel that they can gain more by manipulating men than by rejecting them. They speak of the 'art' of selecting the 'right man,' and of asserting themselves in a relationship. Being able to get your man to hand over his wages at the end of the week was viewed as a major achievement. "This way," one woman stated, "you are in charge and you can decide how to spend the money" (South Africa 1995).

Social norms are remarkably tenacious. Even in the face of changing gender roles, rigid social norms ground men and women in particular identities and expectations. These norms constitute a formidable barrier to survival of individuals, households, and communities. PPAs confirm that traditional gender norms and roles continue to play a role in the perpetuation of poverty.

Gender Identity

> Women can do all the work, except to propose marriage. Nature does not allow women to marry men, just like nature does not allow men to wash dishes, cook, and sweep. People will lose confidence in a man and his wife if they find him in the kitchen. —Older woman, Uganda 1998

> In our culture women tend to feel small. Men have always been the leaders; their voices are final. —South Africa 1998

> Domestic work is usually divided into male and female and is thus performed. Women cook, clean, wash, bring water (where there is no water supply); while men take care of the heating, repairing of the house, and, if necessary, help their wives with the children. —Macedonia 1998

Identity is a person's sense of self. It is a fundamentally relational concept based on social differences. Some aspects of identity are fixed, such as age and race, while others are changeable, such as career, place of residence, and degree of participation in social networks. It follows, then, that identities can be created or changed and used in strategic and pragmatic ways for one's own benefit.

Akerlof and Kranton (1999) connect the psychology and sociology of identity to economic behavior. "Stereotypical characteristics of men are competitive, acquisitive, autonomous, independent, confrontational, concerned about private goods. Parallel stereotypes of women are cooperative, nurturing, caring, connecting, group-oriented, concerned about public goods." Thus gender identity even plays a role in shaping economic outcomes. In Swaziland, for instance, "Most women in the rural communities reported needing the permission of their husband, or their nearest male relative proxy, to seek employment. Often, selling vegetables or crafts was the only culturally approved income-generating activity and, as a result, the competition for these activities was very strong. Many rural women said they believed they were poor precisely because their husbands refused to let them work" (Swaziland 1997).

With marked consistency around the world, data from the PPAs show that men's primary role is breadwinner and decisionmaker, and women's primary role is family caretaker. Moreover, urban-rural differences do not particularly interfere with fundamental norms around female and male roles. In Panama, for instance, "In urban communities, girls stay at home, do homework, watch TV, and do house work, the wash, and sweep floors while boys are allowed to go to the sports fields. The situation is not very different in rural communities, where girls help their mothers sweeping floors and working in the vegetable garden. Later in life, in rural communities men do work, going to the fields and clearing with machete and the like. Women's cooking is not considered work. Women participate in the harvest but not in sowing the seeds" (Panama 1998).

Women are identified and identify themselves as the keepers of the family; they are responsible for the health, education, and well-being of their children and husbands. In this way concepts of identity influence how power and work are organized in households through gender divisions of labor. A PPA from Vietnam defines gender roles simply: "The husband makes the big decisions in investments and housing while his wife is responsible for the children and for the household, including marketing" (Vietnam 1996). In Uganda women say that men control the profits of women's labor and restrict their access to household income. This prompts the saying, "Women plan the income and men plan the expenditure" (Uganda 1998). In many societies women feel that housework is their natural duty. In India, "women's perception regarding the household work reflects their firm belief in traditional gender division of labor. It can be seen that women do all cleaning work within the household and that they think it is their duty to do household work once they are married into another family. Women from Dudkasira and Saltarpalli have expressed that the very purpose of marriage is to bring extra hands into the house to take care of household work" (India 1998a).

Though traditional identities, norms, roles, and behaviors exist and continue to be "a determinant in the cultural and social perpetuation of poverty" (Cameroon 1995), the PPAs show clearly and vividly that tradition is not static. Economic hardship is forcing poor people to adapt to new environments and, in turn, these adaptive actions are forcing wrenching change in gender roles in households in both subtle and obvious ways.

From Breadwinner to Burden: The Changing Roles of Poor Men

Your hands and feet are whole and all right, but you are unable to earn a living. —Unemployed man in Latvia 1998

A happy man is an employed man. —Niger 1996

When men's roles are directly linked to income-earning potential any threat to that potential becomes a threat to gender identity, and spills into gender relations. A South African PPA notes a worrisome "absence of useful social and economic roles for men in the face of the current division of labor within households, high unemployment, and the marginalization of men" (South Africa 1998). Similarly, a Moldova report notes that, "Men used to enjoy higher incomes and be considered the family breadwinner and household head. This is no longer always the case, and men feel displaced when their wives earn more than they [do]. These tensions contribute to family stress and disintegration. Women often blame their husbands for the family's financial situation and criticize them for their lack of success in finding work. Unemployed or underemployed husbands feel emasculated and angry; some confess to losing their tempers and hitting wives and children" (Moldova 1997).

Male identity may intersect with ethnic identity and restrict men's occupational options. In Mali it is found that "for men who do not migrate there are relatively few alternative strategies to pursue ... as cultural taboos often prevent them from engaging in activities reserved for other ethnic groups (for instance, a farmer could not fish, because fishing is reserved to the Bozo group) or for men belonging to a particular caste (for instance, blacksmiths or potters)" (Mali 1993).

When jobs are difficult to come by, men may give up and neglect their families. "Men expressed a sense of social impotence, the inability to fulfill socially important roles as breadwinners for their families ... Many female respondents felt that men had collapsed under the current stresses, while they, because of their sense of responsibility toward their children and their greater psychological adaptability, had taken on greater burdens and become more proactive in their search for solutions" (Latvia 1997).

So strong is the tie between men's self-worth and earning capacity that it may be difficult for men to even acknowledge their dependence on women's incomes. In Pakistan, for example, while interviewing men in rural areas researchers experienced great difficulty in uncovering the extent of women's economic activities. There is both a social stigma about women having to leave the house to work and a sense of shame among men that women have to work to earn incomes. Researchers find that the subject can be broached only after talking about other safe issues such as health. Discussions reveal that, in addition to walking long distances to gather fodder and fuel wood, women work as laborers on nearby landholdings and on rice farms in neighboring provinces (Pakistan 1993).

Household members often unknowingly redefine gender roles as they take action to adapt to changing environments. These actions and opportunities are influenced by the broader institutional environment in which households exist and interact, such as the state, the market, and the community. It may be easier for women to step outside their traditional roles for the sake of their children than for men. For example, in Latvia men may be ashamed to do traditionally women's work, but "society pardons a woman for doing men's work when she does so to feed her children. ... The breadwinner of the family is now anyone—even children—who procures work and income, and this role gives a commensurate authority in the family" (Georgia 1997). When men are considered to be, or in fact are redundant, the stage is set for family conflict. Similarly, it may be more culturally acceptable for women to ask for help than for men. "When the situation is desperate, women will ask as discreetly as possible for gifts from relatives or their women's groups. Men will not do this, but for women it is more acceptable because 'they do it for their children and the children belong to the community'" (Mali 1993).

Due to the traditional expectation that men will provide for a family's livelihood, the adverse effects of unemployment on men and the coping strategies used by them can resonate throughout a family. A young man in Gabon explained, "As time passes ... unemployment begins to undermine the young man's self-esteem. He starts to see himself ... as having failed in his supreme duty as father and head-of-household, and this may drive him to drink and violence. When I don't know how my children are going to eat tomorrow, I tend to get drunk whenever I can. It helps me forget my problems" (Gabon 1997).

Of course, not all men break down. In some societies, despite rigid prescriptions of appropriate gender roles, some men cope with economic stress by adopting new roles in the household, as women become the new breadwinners. In one urban area in Pakistan poor men spend much time carrying their young children with them. However, women still retain primary responsibility for domestic chores (Pakistan 1993).

Women: The New Breadwinners

Whether a woman wants it or not, the man must control the money, and if she refuses she is in danger of being retrenched [sent away from home]. —Woman in Kabarole, Uganda 1998

Where there are jobs, they tend to go to men, not to women. —Mexico 1995

Rather than suffering from poverty, we should better go sweep up the garbage in other people's houses. —Moldova 1997

In their desperation to keep the family together and to provide food for their children poor women have emerged in large numbers in the informal sector, despite the risk and discrimination they face. The Indian study (1997a) documents a typical pattern: "Women receive consistently lower wages than their male counterparts for the same work due to extremely prevalent wage discrimination, especially true in the interior parts of the *tehsils* (districts). While men are likely to spend a significant portion of their income for personal use (for instance, smoking, drinking, gambling), the women in the survey villages tended to devote virtually all of their income to the family (for food, medical treatment, school fees and clothing for the children)." Over and over, what emerges is that women are prepared to do jobs considered too demeaning by men to ensure that their children survive. In Swaziland, for example, while women consider work-for-food programs to be crucial to survival, men do not work on them, as they consider it "degrading, a form of slavery, and inadequate" (Swaziland 1997). As mentioned above, some men instead take the option of leaving the family.

In the Philippines, to cope with periods of difficulty, in the lowlands of Mindanao, "women resort to vending, laundering, sewing and doing other menial jobs. Others seek employment in the town centers. They demeat dried coconut at P30.00 per 1,000 coconuts; they harvest coconuts at P60.00 per 1,000 coconuts; and they harvest rice at 7:1 sharing. They also work as farm laborers. ... During food scarcity they eat root-crops or bananas for breakfast and lunch, and take rice for dinner. Usually the women will miss meals and prioritize available food for the children and husband" (Philippines 1999).

As men become unemployed and underemployed, households increasingly depend on women's incomes from jobs that are often considered marginal or degrading. Women's participation in the informal labor force ranges from 20 percent to 80 percent from country to country

(Charmes 1998). Globally women are not the majority employed in the informal sector, but they produce the majority of informal sector GDP. This is because they take on multiple income-generating roles within the sector. With the exception of Latin America and the Caribbean, the majority of employed women in the developing world are in the informal sector (Charmes 1998).[7]

The informal economic sector is legally unregulated and untaxed, and tends to expand in times of overall economic stress. While the informal sector offers some opportunities for women to earn income, it is also laden with risk, because informal workers are frequently exploited, abused, asked to engage in physically demanding or dangerous occupations, and deprived of legal recourse. Castellas (1997) and Portes (1998) characterize the informal sector as evolving "along the borders of social struggles, incorporating those too weak to defend themselves, rejecting those who become too conflictive, and propelling those with stamina and resources in entrepreneurship." Its characteristics include small-scale economic activity; self-employment (usually including a high proportion of family workers and apprentices); little capital and equipment; labor-intensive technology; low skills; low levels of organization; and limited access to organized markets, formal credit, training, and services (Charmes 1998).

Women are still disadvantaged in labor markets because children are seen as burdens on workers and women are primarily responsible for their care. Sometimes employers are also reluctant to hire younger women in their early 20s "because they fear that she will soon have a child and go on maternity leave. If she already has a child it is assumed that the child will frequently fall ill and she, as the primary if not the only caregiver, will often be absent from work" (Ukraine 1996).

Women's vulnerability in the marketplace takes different forms in different countries. In many of the countries in Eastern Europe and the former Soviet Union expectations of sexual favors from young women seem to be widespread. This also makes it very difficult for women over 25 years old to get jobs. "Women in their early 20s who do get hired often complain of sexual harassment. Employers feel licensed to make such demands on their female employees knowing that the alternative to refusing is simply unemployment. The knowledge that young women face a tremendous uphill battle to find a steady job paying a living wage encourages employers to make outrageous demands of female employees who frequently complain only to one another" (Ukraine 1996).

In Macedonia the unemployed poor also said that the cut-off age for women to be hired was 25 years old, and that being attractive helped them to be hired. Older women (above 25 years old) said, "It happens that we apply to an advertisement requesting cleaning ladies, dishwashers, sales persons, and secretaries. When they learn how old we are they say we are too old to be employed. " An unemployed woman from Skopje said, "I applied several times to an advertisement requiring a cleaning lady and agreed with the owner to meet at a certain place. Sometimes I would wait for an hour and nobody would come. I suppose they would see me from a distance and since I am not young—I am 41 years old and not attractive—they would leave"(Macedonia 1998).

In many parts of Bangladesh (1996) poor women say that lack of employment is their major problem, but women want opportunities for self-employment based in their own homes, because they feel they cannot leave their homes and children. In Nepal the PPA reports wage discrimination against women. When men receive five kilograms of grain in payment, women receive only three kilograms (Nepal 1999).

In Rwanda women adapt to changing economies by using diverse survival strategies, including increasing the rate of domestic work by taking on childcare, gardening, and housekeeping in the homes of the middle-income and rich. Strategies also include adopting traditionally male jobs such as construction work, vending from small booths and kiosks on the roads, selling door-to-door, and participating in formal and informal rotating credit schemes. Often this category of work is unregulated, and women are exposed to theft and police harassment, among other dangers. The Rwanda PPA introduces the phrase "running the marathon": "Women run around because they haven't the means to rent space in the market and to pay municipal taxes. Marathon comes from the coming and going across town to avoid the police, who patrol unauthorized areas" (Rwanda 1998).

The Niger PPA confirms women's adaptability and determination to support their families. "Commercial activity is risky. Bankruptcies occur and capital is hard to come by to start up again. Many men abandon commercial activity, while women often recycle themselves back into the market, even if this entails a smaller-scale activity and less income. Among the poor urban households interviewed, business was limited to petty trade that brings in little money and so is primarily a female activity. The most common business [that] women undertake is the sale of cooked food, especially *la boule*, a mixture of millet flour and curdled milk. A few women had moved to the Benin border or into villages along the river to sell cloth or fresh fish. The women not able to engage in small business activities grind millet for those who are selling it or work as maids" (Niger 1996).

Not only are women contributing economically to the household in nontraditional ways, they are also maintaining their traditional roles as homemakers. A PPA from India notes, "[Women] make a significant contribution to the household chores such as fetching water, collecting firewood, procuring groceries, preparing meals and taking them to the

Box 5.1 Women's Domestic Work in South Africa

Unpaid domestic work is a full-time job for women. They must balance the many tasks including childcare, farming, shopping, cooking, and water collection.

I would like to spend more time with my baby, feeding and washing her, but I have to spend two hours at a time fetching the water. Fieldwork takes up most of the time as we have to get up as early as 4 a.m. to go to the field and leave the baby behind not knowing whether she will be fed in time or not.

At times domestic work makes me feel tired and I cannot look after the baby properly.

In the winter we spend more time in our gardens where we spend a lot of time watering the vegetables, as we have to collect the water from the river.

Source: South Africa 1998.

fields for male members, cleaning, washing clothes, looking after the children. In addition to all the household responsibilities they also do agricultural labor and road construction, spin thread, and make *bidi* (hand-rolled leaf cigarettes), that increases their workload considerably" (India 1997b).

As a result, women's overall work burden has increased relative to that of men. A Nigeria report states, "For both urban and rural women, the time chart shows that within a single hour, a woman is involved with multiple roles. In Akeju Rabin, within a one-hour period, a woman undertook cooking, breastfeeding, picking food items, washing utensils, drying cocoa, and preparing yam/cassava flour" (Nigeria 1996). The demands of paid and unpaid labor consume most of women's days (see box 5.1). Women report feeling isolated because "the workload left them no space for relaxation with friends" (Swaziland 1997). In Ecuador studies indicate that "women in the communities studied had work days of 15 to 18 hours; culturally, leisure is considered unacceptable for women, and they may work at spinning wool even as they walk and talk" (Ecuador 1996a).

Women's workloads also have consequences for their children. In Uganda women's 15 to 18 hours of work per day results in a neglect of children due to time constraints and fatigue. In addition, the younger generation and urban women are increasingly working outside of the home with no reduction in domestic chores. However, when women's work outside the home begins to be profitable, it is no longer identified as women's work, and men take over. In Arua district, "it was revealed that as the cash crop production moved from farming practices to marketing and sale, the involvement of men increased and that of women decreased, such that the women performed the majority of the manual labor while men received the financial returns from the sale" (Uganda 1998).

Women who enter the labor force may find work in nontraditional or traditional occupations. Women are engaged in trade, migrant labor, and to some extent in the sex trade, as well as in traditional occupations such as domestic worker and maid.

Trade: A Growth Opportunity for Women

I was not brought up to be a smuggler, and in the former system such activity was punishable and rightfully ridiculed.
—Macedonia 1998

Charmes (1998) establishes that women in Eastern Europe and the former Soviet Union make up 65 percent of the trading force. The Georgia PPA confirms that "interestingly, women have come to play an important role in trade, even when it involves behavior once considered unseemly for women, such as traveling abroad by themselves and absenting themselves from their families. It may be their very lack of integration into the male world of doing things through long established ties and procedures that has allowed them to move so readily into this new niche. Also, women's responsibility for the daily welfare of children and family has been a strong incentive to swallow their pride and move into such 'unprestigious' activities as street trade" (Georgia 1997).

Women have become active in trade, shuttling goods in the region. In many countries women are less harassed than men are by police and border guards. In Armenia, because many younger men are in hiding to avoid the military draft, people feel it is easier for women to step into the role of trader. In Georgia women travel in small groups between countries such as Russia, Turkey, Hungary, and Poland trading and selling goods. They have to contend with various criminal organizations and corrupt police (Georgia 1997). The most predominant groups among female traders are those who are unmarried, widowed, divorced, or whose husbands are unemployed (Armenia 1995). Increasingly women are hired to run drugs across borders because they are less likely to be suspected by authorities.

Poor households in Macedonia use their own savings and loans from friends and relatives to smuggle goods from Bulgaria and Turkey and resell them on the local streets and in the markets. In Macedonia, "women frequently deal with smuggling. The reason for this is that they raise less suspicion at the border crossings, so they more easily pass the border. But some of the women who earn money in this way consider it demeaning. 'I was not brought up to be a smuggler, and in the former system such activity was punishable and rightfully ridiculed'" (Macedonia 1998).

According to the PPA from Cameroon, women's participation in the informal sector has both positive and negative outcomes: "Increased participation of women in the informal sector has opened up avenues for female empowerment and innovation, and, in the far north has given them increased mobility. Such changes are tempered by increasing [school] dropout rates, early marriage, and prostitution of young girls, an increasingly prevalent mechanism for coping with falling incomes" (Cameroon 1995).

Domestic Workers and Maids

We are not living. We are just surviving. —Group of women, Tanzania 1997

Domestic work is typically done by girls and young women who in effect have been socialized to be domestic workers through gender divisions of labor within the household. A PPA from India explains, "Girls need to help their mothers in carrying out household chores, and the minimum knowledge to run the household can be acquired at home" (India 1998a). These skills can then be carried into labor markets.

In Senegal, for example, young women and girls from rural areas migrate into the cities, as farm labor needs decline. "When demand for their work in the rice fields wanes, many young girls from the Casamance migrate to urban areas in search of (low-paid) work as maids or laundresses (41 percent of all domestics are under age 18)" (Senegal 1995). In Niger, "our daughters work as maids in homes from where they bring their midday and evening meals. Their salary rarely exceeds CFAF 3,000 a month. With this, we scramble to make a little business of cooked dishes; we save a bit for the family, but most is sold. The earnings buy water, soap, and a few condiments. By the end of the month, the salary has barely made ends meet" (Niger 1996).

The low salary of domestic work is sometimes compensated for by in-kind payments. In Pakistan employers will pay school fees for some domestic workers: "However, private charity or patronage often comes with strings attached in the way of obligations to repay the donor in labor, loyalty, or even commitment to supporting a particular political party" (Pakistan 1993).

In some cases, however, domestic work provides a substantial income, and pays better wages than professional work or casual work done by males. For example, in Nicaragua the basic teacher's salary reported is 506 córdobas per month, less than that of a domestic worker. One teacher observed, "A domestic maid is asking 700 córdobas, and she gets extra salary for Christmas and holidays"(Nicaragua 1998). In Pakistan, "Women domestic workers in Dhok Naddi, Rawalpindi make Rs. 600 to 1,000 per month, while unskilled male casual workers make Rs. 700 to 1,000. But men are only guaranteed regular work at this rate during the peak summer season" (Pakistan 1993).

Even with relatively high wages and in-kind compensation, domestic workers often do not make an adequate income to survive, and the PPAs show that they must find additional sources of income. Domestic workers are vulnerable to cutbacks by employers in hours and benefits, or unemployment in the domestic work sector. Some studies found that nonpoor households are cutting down on nonessential expenditures, often seeking savings by reducing the hours requested or benefits for low-paid workers such as maids or laundresses (Senegal 1995). In Ethiopia, "In desperation, some [domestic workers] turn to hidden prostitution to make ends meet."

Workplace harassment and abuse of domestic workers is described in several PPAs, as are parents' efforts to prevent young girls from working as maids to protect them from possible sexual harassment. A PPA from Pakistan describes how older women seek to protect daughters from workplace sexual harassment. "In Dhok Naddi in Rawanpindi District, for example, older women continued in domestic service for as long as their physical strength would allow in order to protect their daughters from the rigors of the work and the sexual harassment that often accompanies it" (Pakistan 1993). In short, despite relatively good wages, domestic work is generally thought of as a bad job with low status, and is often seen as a last resort for female employment.

Female Migrant Labor

We came to Niamey with our children to find food and our husbands. Those who stayed behind in the village, who did not migrate, because they didn't have the money for the trip—our cousins, our brothers—what has happened to them?
—Niger 1996

While certain jobs are still traditionally women's work, gender norms are shifting in the formerly male work enclave of migrant labor, and female labor migration is increasing. Often, female labor migration takes place to take advantage of more lucrative domestic positions in other regions and countries. International domestic work is seen as a solution to poverty for young women as described in this example from Moldova: "Women have increasingly broken into the formerly male domain of seasonal labor migration. ... Greece has become a significant destination for young women, who work as maids and nannies for $400–$600 a month" (Moldova 1997).

Migration can bring several risks to the household. Migrant work can be dangerous for both the migrant worker and the family that is dependent on remittance income. Remittance payments themselves can be irregular. In Nkundusi many women confirm that remittances are small and often irregular (South Africa 1998). In one household, business failure left a Marneuli family with a $2,000 debt incurred by the absent member who disappeared (Georgia 1997). Migration itself is risky, as work may not exist in the country to which the migrant travels. In one PPA women migrants note that "Niamey has changed over the last two years. Today there is no work, no dry food (to send back to the village), no old clothes. People here don't even have enough for themselves" (Niger 1996).

In Mali women's migration in search of income is a recent phenomenon. It is hardly admitted by men, who claim they would never allow their women to leave: "If the women leave, then everybody leaves" (Mali 1993). Women go to the rice fields to barter their crafts, work in the rice fields, or prepare food for the harvesters. They are often paid in kind, mainly in rice. The two or three bags of rice they bring home are sold in the village, while the men's rice is stocked for home consumption. Young women also migrate to towns as maids or washerwomen; their salary goes partly for their dowry and partly to their husbands or fathers.

In addition, some members of families who migrate together may be excluded from receiving social services in their host countries. A man in Vietnam, for example, was the only household member with official permanent registration. The mother and children are classified as long-term temporary residents, without access to free state health care and education:

> Ms. D has lived with her husband and their four children in
> Ward 5 since 1986. ... She goes every day to a different place
> in the city to buy recyclables and sell them for a small profit.
> Her husband has official permanent registration, but she does
> not. Because they were late with their marriage registration, she
> and her children are only classified as long-term temporary
> residents. Her three older children go to evening classes because
> they cannot go to a regular day school. The youngest daughter
> is four years old but she does not attend kindergarten. "How

can I afford that?" D asks. For a week now she has had a pain in her belly near the scar of her last operation. She dares not go to the hospital for a check-up because she is afraid that she will not have the money to pay for it. She does not have a free health checkbook like some other poor people in the neighborhood. She buys some pain-killing pills at a local pharmacy to take. —Vietnam 1999b

When families do not migrate together the family members that remain may be forced to contend with new divisions of labor. A Moldova PPA illustrates shifts in gender roles related to migration: "The prolonged absence of husbands, and in some cases wives, has further challenged the division of labor and power in the family. When husbands leave for a season or even longer … women take over traditionally male responsibilities and decisionmaking. Sometimes prolonged absence turns into abandonment, as men establish new families where they work, and women are left to support their children and themselves as best they can. A few women have, likewise, used trips abroad to search for new husbands. Sometimes, husbands object to their wives' working abroad, fearing her prolonged absence may result in divorce" (Moldova 1997).

Finally, migrant work may lead to family dissolution, as men and women establish new families at their current work location (Moldova 1997). Similarly, in Armenia young wives whose husbands migrate to Russia sometimes find themselves in vulnerable positions. Brothers-in-law and fathers-in-law have seduced young wives left behind; some men have abandoned their families in Armenia, while others have brought their Russian wives back to live with their first wife and family in Armenia. "The Armenian wives tend to swallow their pain and humiliation, knowing that they and their children are dependent on the earnings from Russia. Sometimes the two families establish positive relationships, and the Russian wife has taken the Armenian children to Russia for an education" (Armenia 1995). While migrant work has strained household relations, many women may benefit from related independent incomes (Moldova 1997; Georgia 1997).

Migration and Sex Work

I would not survive, were it not for my lovers. —Georgia 1997

Young girls are no more afraid to leave home to make some money … many women associated with this industry have become the victims of HIV/AIDS. —Cambodia 1998

Increased worker mobility is often related to sex work for both men and women. In Armenia, for example, "some female traders also engage in prostitution while abroad. Family members, even husbands, sometimes turn a blind eye to their wives' prostitution because the income is essential to the family. Although [it is] discouraged by the trading firms working in the Persian Gulf, prostitution in Dubai is very profitable" (Armenia 1995). In Ethiopia, a group in Teklehaimanot also noted an increase in prostitution since 1993, driven by the arrival of more female migrants from rural areas and by a larger number of women from the *kebele*,[8] previously employed as maids, becoming prostitutes for economic reasons (Ethiopia 1998).

Migration for sex work can preserve personal honor in a profession often considered shameful. A single mother from the eastern region of Macedonia explains, "I am 45 years old and I feel incapable of such a thing, but I am forced to do it and bear shame before the children. I do it in neighboring cities to avoid unpleasant situations in the city I live in" (Macedonia 1998). This is also true in Georgia where "Some women find it less shameful to engage in prostitution outside Georgia, particularly in Greece and Turkey, sometimes in connection with the shuttle trade, sometimes sending money home to their families" (Georgia 1997). Sometimes the word "lover" is used as a euphemism in the PPA reports. A divorced Roma woman explains, "I would not survive were it not for my lovers" (who help her with money and gifts) (Georgia 1997). In Swaziland women report exchanging sex for food (Swaziland 1997). In Moldova many newspapers now carry job offers for "nice girls who are not self-conscious," or invitations for weekends or longer vacations, and attach a list of young women available with their photographs (Moldova 1997).

Sex work comes in many forms, including the trade in children and women. This can mean an underground traffic in children, or the sale of women as brides. "In Marneuli some families are said to sell women and girls as brides to buyers in Uzbekistan; in 1989–92, the going price was 3,000 to 5,000 rubles" (Georgia 1997).

In Cambodia sexual exploitation of poor women was reported during group discussions because "Lacking alternative modes of survival, hundreds of young women have opted for this occupation" (Cambodia 1998). Poor women cited three reasons for the dramatic increase. "First, most families face acute shortages of money and everyone will have to work hard. Second, farm work is less and less available and so girls seek nonfarm employment. Third, as instances of domestic violence increase, divorce rates have surged in Cambodia. After separation, she has no means of subsistence, and she has no right to the family land" (Cambodia 1998).

Consequences and Coping

> *He gets up in the morning, he looks at me, and he asks, "Is there any dinner?" If I say there isn't any, he starts drinking.*
> —A female respondent in Tbilisi, Georgia 1997

Economic changes and the changes they effect in gender roles can produce significant household stress, humiliation, and conflict in both men and women. Unable to contribute adequately to the family, men may feel powerless, redundant, burdensome, and may react violently. Women, on the other hand, continue to care for their families and sometimes walk out of abusive relations. Women may gain confidence as they start earning and retaining cash incomes, yet due to their tenuous connections to employment they may also remain vulnerable.

The Georgia PPA reports that many men, unable to keep up with the socially mandated role of breadwinner, find that "their sense of emasculation and failure often leads to a host of physical ailments and sharply increasing mortality, alcoholism, physical abuse of wives and children, divorce and abandonment of families" (Georgia 1997).

Alcohol Abuse

> *Eat and sleep then wake up and go drinking again.* —Women's response to the question, "What kind of work do men in your area do?" Uganda 1998

> *We divorced because my husband was an alcoholic. He started selling property ... to get money for alcohol. We had no shamba [garden plot]. When I stopped him from selling things, he beat me. He chased me, and I came to Korogocho slums.*
> —Kenya 1996

Alcohol is frequently used to manage and alleviate stress and has a strongly negative impact on household members. Men are reported to be drinking more in recent years in Macedonia: "They usually drink when they find somebody prepared to pay for their drinks. Their drinking is painful for those at home, but they [family] have already become used to such scenes like extensive talk, crying, loud music, and so on" (Macedonia 1998).

Reports from Latvia claim that "the most common causes of poverty are the death of the male provider, divorce, and most often male alcoholism" (Latvia 1997). High alcohol costs and the spending of male wages on leisure activities bring additional financial burdens to households

(India 1998a; South Africa 1998). According to one report, alcohol abuse contributes to conflict within the household and beyond: "Alcoholic habits among the males put a tremendous strain on the financial and emotional well-being of the family, and also caused a great deal of conflict within individual households and the community as a whole. … There have been changes in their drinking habits due to the unavailability of traditional *mahua* liquor. … Whereas *mahua* liquor consumption did not create excessive financial burdens on the family, it is not uncommon for a man to spend an entire day's income in a few hours of drinking the more costly 'country' liquor" (India 1997a). In Macedonia a number of women reported having lost spouses to alcohol-related car accidents (Macedonia 1998).

In Vietnam drinking, drug abuse, gambling, domestic violence, and crime are all reported as negative mechanisms used by some men to cope with poverty (Vietnam 1999b). In contrast to the negative coping strategies ascribed to male stress several PPAs describe women as being particularly skilled in dealing with anxiety. Thus, while both men and some women abuse alcohol, "Many respondents of both sexes felt that women had proved psychologically more resilient during periods of economic stress, perhaps because their identity depends more on performance of domestic and child-related tasks. Men, whose identity is more dependent on their ability to earn money, had crumbled more easily, and responded to economic difficulties by retreating into alcoholism and suicidal depression" (Latvia 1998).

Violence

> In all communities, wife-beating was perceived as a common experience in daily life. —Jamaica 1997

Violence against women is a basic abuse of human rights. In addition to the physical injuries, abused women suffer from health and psychological problems. Abused women experience a range of feelings related to the violence, from confusion about what brings on the violence to feelings of hopelessness about the possibility of stopping the violence, to feelings of isolation and depression from being under the violent control of their husbands. Sometimes women consider suicide as an option to escape violence.

In many countries women acknowledge widespread domestic violence. Sometimes, as the issue is acknowledged more openly, as in Uganda, women diagram perceived linkages to violence (see figure 5.2). In Georgia, "Women confessed that frequent household arguments resulted in being beaten" (Georgia 1997).

Figure 5.2 Causes of Wife Battering, Uganda

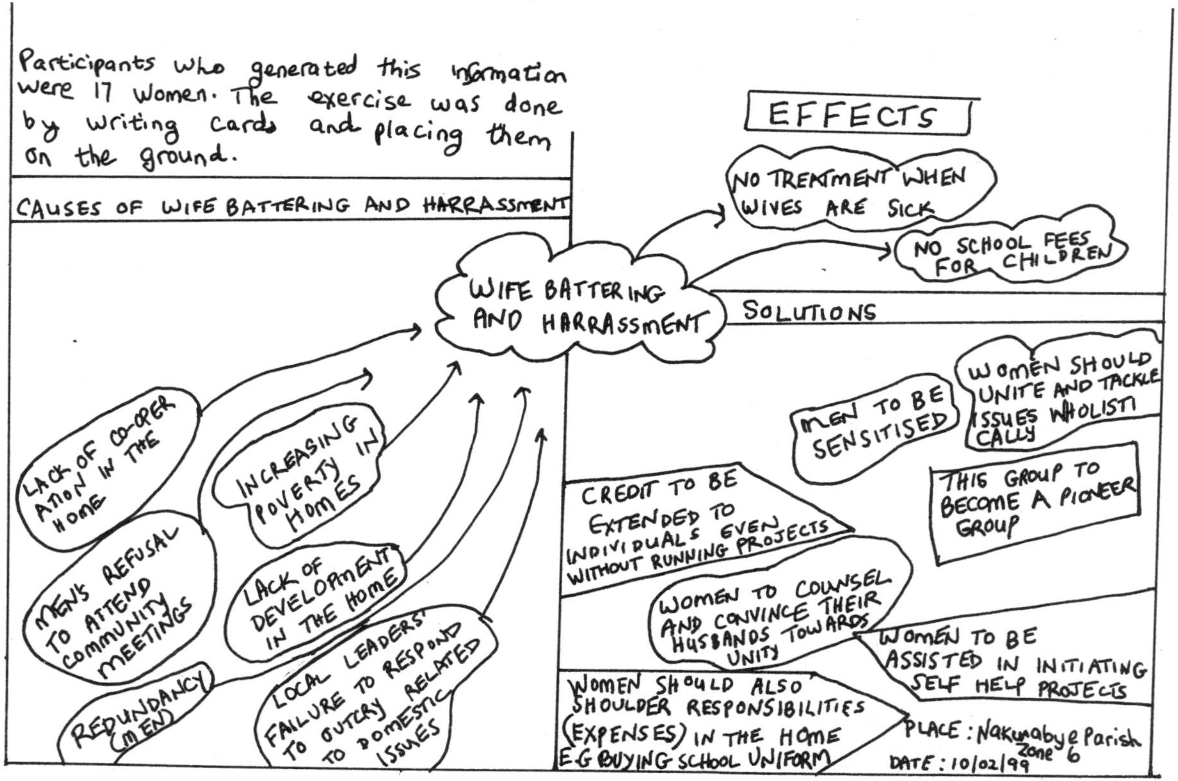

Participants who generated this information were 17 women. The exercise was done by writing cards and placing them on the ground.

CAUSES OF WIFE BATTERING AND HARRASSMENT

LACK OF ANGER IN THE HOUSE

MENS REFUSAL TO ATTEND COMMUNITY MEETINGS

REDUNDANCY (UNEMPLOYMENT)

INCREASING IN POVERTY HOME

LACK OF DEVELOPMENT IN THE HOME

LOCAL LEADERS FAILURE TO RESPOND TO DOMESTIC PROBLEMS

WIFE BATTERING AND HARRASSMENT

EFFECTS

NO TREATMENT WHEN WIVES ARE SICK

NO SCHOOL FEES FOR CHILDREN

SOLUTIONS

WOMEN SHOULD UNITE AND TACKLE ISSUES WHOLISTICALLY

MEN TO BE SENSITISED

THIS GROUP TO BECOME A PIONEER GROUP

WOMEN TO BE ASSISTED IN INITIATING SELF HELP PROJECTS

CREDIT TO BE EXTENDED TO INDIVIDUALS EVEN WITHOUT RUNNING PROJECTS

WOMEN TO COUNSEL AND CONVINCE THEIR HUSBANDS TOWARDS UNITY

WOMEN SHOULD ALSO SHOULDER RESPONSIBILITIES (EXPENSES) IN THE HOME E.G BUYING SCHOOL UNIFORM

PLACE: Nankulabwe Parish, ZONE 6

DATE: 10/02/99

Note: Observations of women in Nankulabwe Parish, Uganda. Focus Group: Sewakiryi, Buyenka, Bankus and Gitta, Uganda 1999.

In all communities included in the Jamaica PPA wife-beating is perceived as a common daily occurrence. On occasions when women feel able to speak openly about their experiences, stories of everyday domestic brutality, fear, and a sense of being trapped emerge. One woman in Greenland, Jamaica talks about how the man she was with for 18 years, whom she loved dearly, continually treated her as a 'beating stick.' In some areas young women say that most women are beaten, but most women hide it. In many areas domestic violence is linked to attitudes of both men and women: women's dependency on men for employment, and frustration and hopelessness arising out of unemployment, cause a cycle of violence, which is usually followed by making up. On rare occasions, "this cycle was broken by the woman's hitting the man or leaving him, or getting him jailed through police involvement" (Jamaica 1997).

Researchers in Bangladesh report that men see wife-beating as their right, and use religious and sociological arguments to legitimize this right. Some men claim that it is condoned in Islamic religious texts. Others describe hitting their wives as a normal way to keep women's unruly natures in check (Schuler et al. 1998). The Bangladesh PPA tells of a 17-year-old woman, married for five years. Her parents had paid about TK 40,000 in ornaments and household goods in dowry. About 18 months before the PPA she was thrown out of her house by her husband after he found that she had not cooked dinner because she was sick: "He scolded her and physically assaulted her for not preparing his meal. Her mother-in-law joined in the abuse, and that evening [she] was sent back to her parents without the baby" (Bangladesh 1996). In order to file for divorce her husband is trying to get a certificate from a doctor to declare her insane. However, the woman's parents' most cherished desire is that her husband will take her back again.

Domination and violence may invade poor households irrespective of whether a woman is working outside the home or not. In Nepal, a major problem reported for women in the communities was dowry because of which "so many women got torched and there were so many deaths and injuries" (Nepal 1999). In villages, discussion groups openly acknowledged that a woman's decisionmaking power within households depended upon the dowry at the time of marriage. "Those girls who bring more dowry command respect and those who do not get beatings and murder is committed" (Nepal 1999).

Children: Vulnerable Inside and Outside the Home

I also have two grandchildren, Miemie (15) and Sharon (17). Sharon's father is in prison serving a 20-year sentence. The mother of these children lives on the farms around Patensie and doesn't look after them. Sharon was raped when she was 14 by a man who has a clerical post at the citrus factory. We only discovered that she had been raped when she told us that she was pregnant. She was in Standard 3 at the time. She came out of school and has been working on the farms with her sister ever since. Her child, Hendrika, is two years old and has been left with me. She doesn't give me any money to support the child and she only comes back at the weekends to see her. I agreed to look after the child as long as it is a Swarts [the family name]. —South Africa 1995

Violence in the home affects children directly and indirectly. Some PPAs document physical and sexual abuse of children, including rape and prostitution. Some evidence suggests that among the most vulnerable to sexual abuse are girls with stepfathers in the home (South Africa 1998). In addition to facing violence in the home—which is not an experience limited to poor children—children of poor families are often forced to work in order to contribute to household income; this puts them at risk of facing abuse on the streets. The South Africa PPA notes that "gender-based differences ... persist even amongst street children." Boys undertake activities such as petty theft and begging and girls take on sex work. "Girls are at great risk of HIV infection and sexually transmitted diseases, whereas boys may face greater risks of assault and abuse" (South Africa 1998).

Family Break-Up

A woman is allowed to move out of the house only with baskets, cooking utensils, bracelets, and her clothes. In rare instances, the man may decide she is worthy of assistance and give her half the crop of that year's harvest. —Tanzania 1997

Family break-up affects men and women differently. In general, men are the financial winners from divorce, and women are the financial losers. Women's assets after a divorce tend to be less valuable than those of men. In addition, laws regarding division of marital property are frequently not implemented. Women then have to rely on social and family networks to start life over again. PPAs often identify divorce as a contributing factor to women's poverty.

A woman in Kagera, Tanzania, says, "A woman can't own anything valuable. On divorce or separation a woman can take a young child with her until he reaches the age of seven. Then she must return him. The children belong to the father. If she has no children, she gets nothing except what she brought when she got married" (Tanzania 1997). In the Tanga region a woman said, "If the fight has not been so bad, a woman may get a few more things, like a radio and a hoe, especially if the family is well-off." In Kasangezi, Kigoma region, a woman said, "In this village men have the bad habit of chasing women away after the harvest, so they can have a good sale for that year, and then try later to get them back" (Tanzania 1997).

In neighboring Kenya women report taking items they had bought with their own money in the event of separation or divorce. After the break-up of a family some women take all the money they can find in the home, and deny taking it if asked, as there would be no evidence. If a woman has a small baby at the time of divorce she is expected to care for it until it stops breastfeeding, and then she must return the child to the man. Sometimes a woman may decide to take her children, which is often not challenged because children are seen as a woman's only asset after divorce (Kenya 1996). In Togo "divorce reduces a household's capacity to overcome external shocks and is one of the main causes of destitution" (Togo 1996).

Some families continue to live together following a divorce for economic reasons. In Moldova some couples who divorce because of alcoholism and domestic violence continue to live together because neither spouse can afford to move out (Moldova 1997). And a household in central Macedonia continues to live together in the house of the former husband because, after the divorce, the woman did not have anywhere else to go with the children (Macedonia 1998).

Family maintenance and child-support payments are reportedly rare. In South Africa one woman who was able to extract R20 from her divorced husband for child support had to give it back when he demanded it (South Africa 1998). Situations are difficult for divorced women in Latvia whose ex-husbands cannot pay child support because of disinterest or unemployment. Benita, aged 43, is a divorced mother living in Riga, Latvia, where she is bringing up two children alone. As a result of "incompetently divided property" after the divorce, her husband received all their joint property, and he provides no support for the children (Latvia 1998).

In Benin men benefit from the valuable labor of their children, except in the few cases where the court may grant women custody or child support. "In the case of divorce the ex-husband will generally take everything with him, including the children, while the parents of the wife still have to refund the bride price. If the children are very young, they will remain with the mother until they become potentially productive, that is, until they are six or seven years old. Payment of child support is a rare exception, although modern courts (only accessible to a small minority) tend to protect the child's interests, occasionally granting custody to the mother, or requesting a family support payment from the father" (Benin 1994).

Unfortunately, legal proceedings following divorce do not ensure fair division of property. In Tanzania some young and more-educated women pursue court battles with the support of women's organizations; these efforts succeed in securing some marital property in a handful of cases. Most women avoid legal action. As one woman explains, "It is tiresome for the legal process to reach conclusion; and there is a possibility that the woman can fail to get her rights. This is because the man can give a lot of money to all the people dealing with legal rights to make sure the woman fails" (Tanzania 1997). Women say that they are allowed back into their natal homes only if they had not brought the shame of public proceedings or become aggressive in trying to claim justice (Tanzania 1997).

Cooperation

Other than food, there aren't any other expenses. Everything else depends on the relationship between a man and his wife.
—A poor woman, Bamako, Mali 1993

If I knew you cannot live without money, I would not have gotten married. We loved each other a lot. Today we only fight. —Macedonia 1998

Obviously not every family breaks down under stress. In Latvia researchers conclude that poverty may affect families in one of two ways: "Either it brings family members together, in some cases even couples on the verge of divorce, as they realize that solidarity is the only way to cope with their economic problems. Or the daily stress of financial problems splits families, particularly those who had experienced discord in the past" (Latvia 1998).

Many families work together to attempt to meet their needs. For example, a farming family with 13 children in Membrillal, Ecuador receives income from the family's combined efforts. "Tomas is primarily a farmer ... he is always in search of ways to earn extra income. His major source of income is coffee, but productivity is low, and prices have dropped consistently for the past three years. This year he and Roberto (a son) went to the Oriente to work for a friend for six weeks. While Carmen considers herself to be a housewife, she harvests coffee in nearby plantations every June and July; this year three of her daughters accompanied her" (Ecuador 1996a).

Households use a wide variety of strategies to "work their way out of poverty" and remain together. The most common strategy for generating family income lies in transforming as many family members as possible into workers. The following story of one family in Brazil demonstrates the degree of cooperation and coordination required among family members to cope. "In this family, consisting of the husband (52), the wife (32), and five children ranging in age from 8 to 13, the husband worked outside the home at two jobs, selling lottery tickets, and guarding a parking lot. The wife spent 38 hours [a week] at home doing housework and 35 hours working outside the home, washing clothes and cleaning houses, and as a manicurist for neighbors. The four boys attended school; the three eldest also worked at a parking lot and undertook minor chores. The 12-year-old girl did not attend school, but rather played a key role in family survival. She spent 40 hours [a week] doing domestic work, freeing her mother for other activities. She also helped care for the family's chickens and even helped her mother at her paying jobs" (Brazil 1995).

In sum, in many households men are an important family resource, but due to low wages, the lack of jobs, and ill health, they are not able to generate sufficient income to help the family out of poverty. In South Africa one man earns R250 a month as a farm worker. The PPA reports, "He earns only a little money. He shows [his wife] all the money, and only uses R12 or R24 to travel home. He does not drink beer. [He is a] good husband, but can't survive on this sum—we help him" (South Africa 1998).

Many men share the view that cooperation is essential to survival. A migrant worker in East London, South Africa, said, "We are different from other men in the township because we have respect for our families. We do not just drink our wages away at month's end" (South Africa 1998).

Female-Headed Households

I don't have any house or any land or anything because I parted company with my husband and he does not want us.
—Kenya 1997

One consequence of family break-up is female-headed households. In some societies female-headed households contend with the daily demands of economic survival in addition to facing ostracism from kinship systems that treat them as outcasts. The Ghana PPA reports that "Female-headed households tend to be genuinely socially marginal under the patrilineal kinship systems that prevail in the north" (Ghana 1995a).

It is widely accepted that female-headed households are more likely to be poor than male-headed households (Folbre 1991:89–90), an observation supported by many reports, including the Kenya PPA: "In 35 villages people were asked to mark all of the female-headed households on a map. Overall, while 25 percent of the study population was categorized as very poor, there were over twice as many female-headed households (44 percent) as male-headed households (21 percent) in this group. While 59 percent of the male-headed households were categorized as poor or very poor, this was true for 80 percent of the female-headed households. The pattern of greater poverty among female-headed households was true for every district and for all 35 villages" (Kenya 1996).

Similarly, the South Africa PPA reports that "many of the poorest households were female-headed where it was left to the grandmother or single female to look after the whole family. Consequently, they were excluded from many of the local income generating activities because they could not afford the joining fee or the time" (South Africa 1995). A researcher in Nigeria observed, "Some categories of individuals are regarded as particularly vulnerable, especially female-headed households, particularly those with children too young to work. Widows and single mothers face special difficulties when their children fall sick, since no one is willing or able to help them. They also lack the necessary farm labor and cannot afford to hire it" (Nigeria 1995).

Not all female-headed households are necessarily poor or the poorest in the community. There are multiple causes of female-headed households and these causes determine the households' ability to cope. Some cultural traditions provide safety nets for women, such as the Islamic social category *mustaheqeen,* which "includes households without earning men … such as widows without family support"(Pakistan 1993). Mustaheqeen translates as "the deserving poor" and as such this group receives *zakat,* an official tax that is disbursed by the government to the poor.

Women head households for several reasons, among them migration of male members, divorce, and men who are present but not contributing financially to the household. Male migration that leads to the creation of female-headed households is usually for certain seasons, but sometimes for longer, leaving women to fend for themselves and their children.

Divorced women are another prominent category of female heads of households, and they are particularly vulnerable to poverty. A man may take his social networks with him, leaving his ex-wife to cope only with her own. In addition, a divorced woman typically has restricted access to the very basic household necessities such as housing and land for food production. Divorced women's access to income is hampered by a range of factors including lack of child support from the ex-husband or his family. They also have limited employment opportunities due to demands of child-rearing and preexisting occupational segregation of women to low-income, low-security jobs. Finally, divorced women may face strong cultural stigmatization due to their divorced status. The combination of unemployment and female-headed household is particularly deleterious for the family. A young and unemployed single mother in Libreville explains, "I have to be both father and mother to my children. I never know what's going to happen. If you don't have any friends, you're on your own. ... The government doesn't know or care about the problems of young mothers—all it can do is talk about birth control! ... We live in constant insecurity—the local thugs have an easy time of it when they know a woman is living alone" (Gabon 1997).

The issue of physical vulnerability of women living by themselves is mentioned in several PPAs. One woman from rural Mali who was abandoned by her husband and could not muster the resources for health care describes the experience of vulnerability. "My husband went away ten years ago and never came back. If my eyes were not sick, I could go to the bush to pick wild fruits. ... Now that my eyes hurt and I can barely see, I don't know what to do. I asked my brothers, but they are too poor to be able to give me anything. I cannot ask my sister or my mother because they are widows, and on top of that my mother is very old and half-paralyzed. So I asked the women's group, but they have nothing" (Mali 1993).

Some women find themselves heads of households when a man is present but is no longer contributing financially to the household. In these cases household survival depends on the income-earning potential of the wife and the children. A woman in Ethiopia, married with six children, has reservations about accepting the representation of households, including her own, as male-headed households. She says, "Although we may take these families to be male-headed, the breadwinners for these households are women." Her own husband lost his business and slid into poverty. Although he struggles to make money by selling meat he buys from butchers, the source of income for the household comes from *kolo* [roasted grain], oranges, and bananas sold by one of the daughters (Ethiopia 1998).

Finally, many women find themselves heads of households when their husbands die. In Nigeria as in many other countries, destitution follows widowhood (box 5.2).

Conclusions

Gender relations are in troubled transition in poor households. This basic fact needs to be a central part of poverty reduction strategies. In economically constrained environments men appear to have great resistance to doing what are often considered demeaning jobs. Women, on the other hand, seem to have greater resilience and hit the streets and do whatever it takes to keep their families together. Many men react to their loss of power as breadwinner by collapsing into drugs, alcohol, depression, wife-beating, or by walking away. Women may find a new confidence through new economic opportunities, although these may be tenuous; they may expose themselves to risk and take on work in the informal sector in

Box 5.2 Widows Organizing in Nigeria

Many PPAs show that households headed by widows are among the poorest and most vulnerable groups in this category. However, the proliferation of widow's associations in Nigeria provides an effective example of how organizing to share stories and resources can result in positive outcomes.

"One of the most successful of these is the Widow's Association in Adikpo ... formed in 1986 [with] a membership of 350. Catholic missionaries were instrumental in assisting its establishment. The association's main functions are those of educating and generally caring in the areas of health and social security for the children of widows. The association is also a thrift and credit organization. The Adikpo Widow's Association has land on which it has citrus fruits and farms from which much revenue is generated. It has also installed a grinding machine, which apart from removing drudgery from grinding corn, brings revenue to the Association. In 1991 the Association won a prize for being the best-organized women's association in Benue State. However, some men interviewed are against the Association. They feel that if women can expect succor after the death of their husbands, they may have a tendency to neglect them and not care whether they live or not! Despite this opposition from some men, this association has grown in membership with the support of church organizations. This accords with the broader finding of this work that informal participatory structures can best obtain their objectives if they receive support and cooperation from formal structures."

Source: Nigeria 1995.

addition to their household responsibilities. Families may cooperate or eventually collapse.

Overwhelmingly, the PPA reports echo the conclusion of Standing (1999) that the feminization of the labor force and the informalization of the economy reflect "the weakening position of men rather than improvement of the economic opportunities for women." Taking on additional income-earning roles has not necessarily led to the social empowerment of women or greater equity and peace in the household. "The impact of employment on women appears to be ambiguous, with some women succeeding in gaining control over the affairs of the household, some women being able to establish their own male-free households, and some women continuing to subsidize men" (South Africa 1998). In some cases the employment of women is viewed as a regrettable necessity, and the dream of achieving prosperity includes the hope that daughters will be spared this necessity (Pakistan 1996).

At the same time some women feel a sense of empowerment with the chance to take on new roles. "Some women reported that female economic independence had grown, improving their coping abilities and their capabilities, especially in terms of work outside the home, and that in rural areas of central Uganda, changes in attitude toward the payment of bride price had occurred. In addition, younger women, particularly from urban areas, noted changes in attitudes toward and of women, as well as some changes in gender roles in recent years" (Uganda 1998).

What is clear from these studies is that the entire household—women, men, and children—pays a high price for adjusting to new gender roles and deeply held notions of gender identity. With few exceptions international development agencies still use an approach focused on "women in development" rather than developing approaches to both poor men and women that acknowledge that men's and women's well-being are intertwined. To help women, it is also critical to understand men's roles and to reach men. Since men still dominate the public space, their involvement is critical in changing institutions. Change is likely when there are alliances between powerful men within organizations and women. And such alliances are more likely to develop if women organize and gain economic power.

Two fundamental issues have to be addressed, one economic and the other social. First, both poor men and women need greater access to economic opportunities, especially for profitable self-employment. This is difficult in an environment of corruption, lack of organizations of the poor, lack of support to battered women, and the breakdown of law enforcement agencies.

Second, in order to assist families both women and men need social and psychological support to explore and navigate change that brings into question their worth as human beings. The issue of gender-based violence needs to be confronted. Deeply entrenched social norms will not automatically change with more women entering low paying jobs. Gender relations must become an integral part of all poverty reduction strategies. This has to be reflected in institutional goals, design, incentives, and criteria of success that are monitored and evaluated. Poor women also require access to legal aid and police that protect rather than assault. Implementing gender strategies implies accepting that women's and men's lives are interlinked. Discussion of gender issues must include both men and women to increase the probability of less traumatic transition toward gender equity. Whether conversations about gender identity and gender relations are appropriate in separate gender groups or mixed groups; whether this should be done by religious leaders, NGOs, governments, or in the workplace is culture- and context-specific. A poor woman in Uganda suggests: "Women and men should sit at a round table to discuss their rights. Unless men are included, these things will not be understood. It will be like bathing in mud again" (Uganda 1998).

Case study 5.1 Gender and Education

In the PPA reports education and household gender issues intersect in six main areas: household literacy; distance and transportation; direct and indirect costs; family security; marriage; and sexual harassment and abuse. The overall result is that girls tend to receive fewer years of formal education than boys do. (See figures 5.4 and 5.5 in appendix 7.)

Household Literacy

> *We would like to go to school with enough books.*
> —Children, Vietnam 1999a

Women are less literate than men, and female illiteracy has far-reaching implications for development because illiteracy further marginalizes women in the public sphere. Women are often simply unable to participate in literacy programs. In Mali, for example, adult female participation in functional literacy programs is extremely weak because women's 17-hour work days prevent them from participating (Mali 1993). In a PPA from India, in a region where the number of girls attending school is less than half the number of boys, information distribution depends largely on literacy; it is therefore not surprising that women are less aware than men of government programs or other services. Similarly, women are less aware of their legal rights, such as their right to own and inherit land (India 1997a).

Distance and Transportation

> *[Schools] are not what they used to be.* —Guinea-Bissau 1994

> *Kwame Lambor comes from a family of 19 children. Each morning he walks the one-and-a-half-mile stretch to his school, the Gambaga JSS. Kwame sometimes leaves home for school without eating. During the rainy seasons he is sometimes*

unable to go to school if the river which he has to cross floods its banks. —Ghana 1995a

Schools are often far away for children, and attendance may require parents to bear the costs of transportation. Moreover, in many regions girls are required to travel with chaperones or else risk violating social norms. Sexual harassment of girls and women traveling independently reinforces such gender norms. In Pakistan, for example, "fear that girls would be teased or harassed en route to school was a constraint for households that could not spare an adult to accompany the child" (Pakistan 1996).

In a PPA from Bangladesh the problem of educating children is identified as the highest priority in some areas, followed by problems of water shortage. Women are particularly concerned about sending children to schools that are long distances from home, across rivers and unsafe hilly terrain. High schools are particularly far away (Bangladesh 1996). In Pakistan distance is named second only to cost as the issue of greatest concern; this issue is compounded for girls, who are unable to travel any distance alone due to cultural norms. Some mothers say they accompany their daughters to school, but mothers with preschool children may be unable to do this. From one focus group we learn, "In an urban slum near Rawalpindi mothers voiced a positive desire to provide higher education for their daughters but said that in order to attend a girls' secondary school their daughters would have to travel (accompanied by a mother) three miles by bus and an additional mile on foot. The entire trip was said to require an hour and a half each way" (Pakistan 1996).

Direct and Indirect Costs

We never finish the book in the prescribed year, yet the fees keep going up. —Uganda 1998

Education costs include both school fees and costs associated with the loss of the child's labor. In addition, families are often asked for bribes and donations to schools. All these costs are a significant disincentive for many poor families. When weighing the cost families frequently choose to educate boys rather than girls.

Often families who wish to educate their children cannot afford to do so. In a Bangladesh PPA men and women report being very supportive of education for girls and boys, and rural women insist that education must be made affordable. These women propose the following: no bribes for education; subsidized books and stationery; less costly admission fees; open and flexible school hours; distribution of wheat; and more schools in remote areas (Bangladesh 1996). In Zambia the seasonal nature of educational fee payments was noted, unfortunately coinciding with the time food stocks are lowest (Zambia 1997). Women in Swaziland face constant stress finding the money to pay for schooling (Swaziland 1997). A woman in Brazil said, "The schools where they were wouldn't let them attend without all the material. I couldn't afford it. First it was the uniform; I managed to get them uniforms, but then it was all the other material. It's very sad. I tell them you have to find some work to pay for your school supplies" (Brazil 1995).

Quite apart from the costs of fees and school supplies many poor families face a loss of children's labor when children are in school. In Mali, although few people claimed that schooling was a burden on domestic life, it became evident from a number of statements that the additional labor provided by the child was sorely missed at home (Mali 1993). The labor of girl children is often described as particularly useful for families, and it is directly related to low female student enrollment. In India girls' time is devoted to household domestic purposes, preventing them from attending school (India 1997a).

In a community in Nigeria parents are upset with government restructuring of education funding. They place responsibility for efficient educational funding firmly on the shoulders of the government. "The government has messed up [the schools]. They should help teachers or hand the schools back to missionaries. ... It is for the government to do it. We have many oil wells, and every day they pump oil overseas without improving our welfare" (Nigeria 1997).

When scarce resources require that parents must withhold education from some of their children, a disproportionate number of these children will be female. In Pakistan, although a number of poor families are educating daughters, in no family did the team find a girl who is educated in preference to her brother (Pakistan 1995). In part this is because girls' labor in the household is typically more valuable than boys' labor. In part it has to do with the family's "investment strategy" for its own future security.

Family Security

We want to be rich women. —Nigeria 1997

PPA descriptions frequently mention that parents seek future security and independence for their children, and this of course influences education decisions. In many cases both marriage and income provision for men and women factor into these decisions. For girls in Armenia education lends status to potential wives and acts as a surrogate dowry. Urban women also mention the need for girls to have higher education "because they need independence ... to be prepared in life" (Armenia 1996). For boys, security and independence are often linked to being an income-provider. There may be great cynicism about the correlation between higher levels of education and higher earnings or employment prospects. A father in Lusarpiur, Armenia, explains, "Because I have no money, I cannot support my son's studies at the institute. There would be food, transport, and lodging expenses—without mentioning bribes of which even a first-grader is aware. What would these expenses be for? So he can earn 10,000 dram salary? Now my son is keeping cows for 10,000 drams a day. Education is not the future" (Armenia 1996).

Some parents also fear that allowing their girls to venture into public spaces such as schools where they will encounter unrelated boys will lead to loss of reputation. Schooling could also encourage daughters to reject their parents' choice of a (possibly illiterate) relative for a husband (Pakistan 1996). Further, many participants believe that girls in school are more likely to become pregnant before marriage. In Mali respondents remark, "Girls who become pregnant out of wedlock have jeopardized their marriage opportunities altogether and, in addition, will be thrown out of school" (Mali 1993). In order to avoid conflicts with school authorities parents prefer to keep their girls home altogether.

In some cases children themselves prefer work to school, and are strategic about their own future plans. In Nigeria two girls in a mixed-gender children's focus group claim that they prefer hawking (informal sales) to school because they can save up money by the time of their marriage. "We want to be rich women," they said. Two boys, aged 7 and 9, who have never been to school, are working on a farm in Maidamashi (Northwest) and do not think they are missing much: "Our parents are farmers and have not found it necessary to send us to school. Farming is a better occupation because potentially it offers a lifetime's livelihood" (Nigeria 1997).

Marriage

My brother completed primary school and went on to college. I look forward to getting married someday. —Nigeria 1996

It is wasting money to educate girls because they will marry and join another family. —South Africa 1998

Families are dissuaded from educating girls and young women in some countries due to marriage systems that place the daughter in the care of the husband's family after marriage. This causes parents to see female education as a waste of money since it is like investing in someone else's family (Togo

1996; Nigeria 1997). As this is explained in Pakistan, "Daughters are destined to be 'other people's property'" (Pakistan 1996).

In other societies educating girls can actually increase the dowry required, as reported in Bangladesh: "The people of Refayetpur in Khustia told us how they assess the likely dowry rates. An educated girl who is unemployed requires the highest dowry. This is because social norms require that the boy is more educated than the girl and boys are not willing to marry girls with higher education than themselves. If the girl is educated and has a job, the dowry rate is the lowest. An uneducated girl without a job commands a dowry in between" (Bangladesh 1996). From the family's point of view, if prospects for a rich match for their daughter are not good in any case, it is not to their advantage to educate her. They will reduce the required dowry if she stays at home and learns useful household skills.

Finally, PPAs frequently mention that educational institutions do not adapt to adolescent pregnancy and marriage customs. Many of the African PPAs report that girls and young women leave school when they become pregnant (Uganda 1998; South Africa 1998). Some young women may also be cast out of their families when they become pregnant.

Sexual Harassment and Abuse

> *I didn't like the school because there were troublemakers, and the teacher hated me and hit me.* —El Salvador 1995

Some young people, overwhelmingly girls, report abuse and sexual harassment in schools by male teachers and students. Educational institutions often have a slow response—or no response—to these problems.

PPAs report that sexual harassment is an impediment to the education of girls. In Pakistan, for example, "Virtually all parents desire literacy for their children, but school enrollments, especially of girls, lag behind the stated desire for education. Parents also express fears that daughters will suffer harassment or loss of reputation by attending school with boys. Poor attendance or supervision by teachers, and consequent classroom rowdiness, exacerbate these dangers. It is suggested that enrollments could be improved if monetary incentives were provided and if teacher performance and girls' security issues were addressed" (Pakistan 1996). In Nigeria it is noted that the unequal distribution of female teachers biased toward urban areas adversely affects girls' school attendance in the rural areas (Nigeria 1997).

In Uganda girls drop out of school at higher rates than boys because the boys harass them in school, and girls fear being "wooed into early sex by men with promises of money and clothes" (Uganda 1998). In South Africa sexual harassment is reported along with pregnancy as contributing to girls' failure to continue education (South Africa 1998). A girl from a village in Macedonia reports, "I did not continue to attend secondary school in Struga because I had to travel every day by bus. Many boys would tease me, and people in the village would talk about me—look at her, alone in a bus or in a van—and that is why I do not want to go" (Macedonia 1998).

Children themselves may decide not to attend school due to poor.security. For example, in one case from Pakistan, parents identify costs as a major impediment, followed by the children's unwillingness to attend school: "[Parents] would enroll them if all expenses were paid—provided the children in question were willing to attend school. Four families mentioned that one or more of their children disliked school and refused to attend. Among these were a girl who had been beaten by a teacher and a pair of sisters who feared harassment from 'wicked boys'" (Pakistan 1996).

When teachers and staff abuse students, communities may find it difficult to remove offenders from their professional positions. In El Salvador a male teacher abused his girl students. As an officially appointed teacher, he could not be fired, so the girls were removed from school for several years. Now, the community runs the school board and hires only female teachers (El Salvador 1997).

Case study 5.2 Gender and Property Rights

> *Even if a woman is given a chicken or a goat by her parents, she cannot own it. It belongs to her husband. A wife may work hard and get a chicken. If it lays eggs, they belong to the husband.* —Uganda 1998

Property rights and property arrangements affect gender relations within the family. In some places women and children are regarded as property themselves and their lives are regulated accordingly through marriage and labor practices. In other places women have control over few assets and the security of their inheritance is tenuous. Lacking access to assets, poor women are more dependent on the environment and diminishing common property resources. This case study explores these issues.

Women as Property

> *Men rape within the marriage. Men believe that paying dowry means buying the wife, so they use her anyhow at all times. But no one talks about it.* —Uganda 1998

Women are often legally considered the property of male family members. In Togo, for example, women cannot inherit, "but the levirate tradition makes it possible for their brothers-in-law to inherit them along with the rest of the deceased husband's estate (including children)." Children are also frequently considered property, particularly girl children in marriage negotiations. Male-centered inheritance systems and residential patterns dictate that a girl must take up residence with her husband and his extended family after marriage, and that her children and benefits of her labor belong to that family (Pakistan 1996). In Tanzania, when it comes to ownership of property following divorce, because a man pays a bride price he is considered to own his wife, the product of her labor, and any children they have together. In Uganda a husband's possession of his wife is reinforced by the payment of a bride price, particularly in the north where it is seen as repayment to the family for loss of the woman's labor. Male ownership of a woman as property under marriage rationalizes marital rape (Uganda 1998).

Girls and young women can be particularly vulnerable as "assets" that can be traded across borders. In Marneuli, Georgia a 16-year-old girl had been raped while doing domestic work, and gave birth to a son. To hide this dishonor and also to improve the family's terrible material conditions, the mother sold her daughter for 5,000 rubles (Georgia 1997).

Security of Home, Land, and Inheritance

> Women with no male children must rely on husbands or other
> male relatives for land access. —Nigeria 1996

Women are often not aware of their legal rights to own and inherit land due to a general lack of awareness of existing laws and regulations, often related to limited literacy (India 1997a). Poor women in Hathazari, Bangladesh, express their main problem as access to land or house, and homestead. "Women are both psychologically insecure and physically distressed with house, land, mortgaging arrangements, and being residents on others' land. With no land or house, men and women find it difficult to borrow capital, which is scarce, expensive, and not provided on easy terms" (Bangladesh 1996).[9]

In many places where the PPAs were conducted it was found that women cannot inherit property. In Uganda inheritance exclusively by males is clearly connected to women's lack of power, control, and decisionmaking in marriage (Uganda 1998). Inheritance in Swaziland is passed through male children, denying women ownership rights and forcing women to be dependent on males for access to land.

In Kenya women suffer twice from land inheritance practices. First, girls are often discriminated against in land inheritance from their birth families. Poor families pass the majority of land to their sons. Second, whether a woman leaves her husband or a man leaves his wife, ownership of the land stays with the man. On his death, in-laws are entitled to seize the land, and may grant the widow limited cultivation and harvesting rights. There were various stories of widow's land inheritance experiences in the Elugulu village in Busia district, for instance. Men state that "when a husband dies and the woman has children with him, she may keep all the household assets." The women told a different story: "The brothers-in-law ... take all the valuable assets, leaving the widow with barely enough to give her a new start" (Kenya 1997).

Women in the Lubombo region of Swaziland express the hardship they face regarding the allocation of land within marriage. "If the wife was out of favor or neglected by the husband, she might find it more difficult to gain use rights to land since "we are too many and there is too little land.' For a woman, even as a female head-of-household, her usufruct access would be facilitated through a male relative, including younger relatives and sons. Should these male relatives be absent or disinterested, the woman's needs were disregarded" (Swaziland 1997).

Women with no male children must rely on husbands or other male relatives for land access (Nigeria 1996). Infertile women may be condemned and treated with disrespect. Mothers with only daughters may suffer neglect from their husbands, face opposition from in-laws, and be denied access to their husband's property; their husbands may take other wives in an attempt to have male children (Nigeria 1996).

In South Africa the form of land tenancy and land tenure (communal tribal land allocation) has increased the uncertainty of women's right of access to land by only recognizing males as titleholders. This has increased women's food insecurity. Women proposed an alternative: "Since most men migrate to urban areas, they should have in place a system like a power of attorney that will enable them to make decisions as members of the household" (South Africa 1998). In Zambia, although no legal restriction on land use exists, women have a difficult time obtaining land from land authorities. Under the statutory system, in some districts married women must provide evidence of their husband's consent to obtain land, while unmarried women are often not recommended for allocation of land if they do not have children. PPA respondents in Zambia suggest a traditional tenure system in the PPA, with rights of long-term occupancy and use allocated to families by chiefs. They fear that land reform and titling will primarily benefit the rich and politically well-connected (Zambia 1997), and urge appropriate consultation before any such programs is undertaken. "There is a great deal of debate about the appropriate land tenure policy for Zambia. There are fears that the rural poor might suffer from establishment of formal tenure systems on traditional land ... because land is their only fixed productive resource" (Zambia 1997).

Control Over Other Assets

The pig is the woman's cow. —Swaziland 1997

As has been already discussed, women in most countries studied have very unequal access to land, homes, or other capital assets, including their own children. Women in the Lowveld region of Swaziland point out that men's ownership of cattle does not help women and children because the men could decide to sell the cattle without family consultation and the money will not necessarily benefit the household. This could apply to the cattle that accompany women as dowry. Women's assets are few. "Besides the utensils of the household and their traditional clothes, the women owned only chickens. None of them owned goats, donkeys, or cattle. Some women in the Lowveld reported that they have a greater say in the decisions about pigs—'The pig is the woman's cow'—because the women are more involved in the husbandry of pigs. With chickens, women were free to slaughter or sell when they decided, but they would nevertheless usually consult with the men" (Swaziland 1997).

Environment and Common Property

Some women gather firewood to sell it to town, while others go deep into the mountains to cut trees to be processed to charcoal. Others gather cogon grass which is sold at P0.50 to P 1.00 a bundle. This usually brings them a daily earning of P3.00, just enough to buy a small amount of salt. —Philippines 1999

The degradation and disappearance of common property resources is a major issue for poor households. Acute water scarcity is a problem for women and men, but the impact on women is especially severe since in almost every culture they are responsible for collecting water. Deforestation similarly impacts women, since usually they are also responsible for collecting firewood and for nontimber forest products for the household.

In India (1997b) women are the main collectors of nontimber products such as *rengal* (a kind of leaf) to make leaf plates. "Due to the low paying nature of nontimber products, many villagers, especially the male, tend to move away from collection of forest products to wage employment. This, in fact, adds additional burden to women, who need to put extra effort to collect the leaves and make plates. Along with this, there are a number of risk factors, especially harassment by forest officials in collecting forest products from reserve forests. Fuel wood collection appears to be the more risky job, often attracting severe penalties and punishments" (India 1997b).

The impact of the drought on women in Swaziland is particularly harsh "because women have to walk further for water and spend more hours each day obtaining food. Many women engaged when they could in informal vending and making crafts to sell, that is crucial for income in the winter. But drought conditions have depleted the grasses on which women depend for their crafts; even cutting grass for thatching as piecework has become precarious and unreliable. ... Women in the Maphilingo community in the Lowveld, for example, now travel in winter and in spring as far as Malkerns for a species of grass they need to produce sleeping mats" (Swaziland 1997). To survive, women also engage in seasonal cotton-picking and harvesting and selling wild green vegetables and aloe plants.

Notes

1. The terms "household" and "family" will be used interchangeably in this chapter.

2. Gender relations vary by social group. For aggregate statistics on gender differences in participation in parliament and women's economic rights, see table 5.3 in appendix 7.

3. For a history of the evolution of gender strategies in development agencies see Moser et al. (1998).

4. According to a WHO (World Health Organization) compilation of 17 primary survey studies undertaken around the world between 1990 and 1997, between 20 and 50 percent of women sampled report physical abuse by their intimate partners (WHO 1997). Although there are mixed data about whether violence in the home is decreasing, increasing, or staying level, a few studies identify an increase in abusive behavior with the length of marriage. In India, in rural Gujrat, for example, 53 percent of newlyweds report verbal abuse as compared to 85 percent of women married for more than 15 years (Visaria 1999).

5. The U.N. Convention on the Elimination of Discrimination against Women (CEDAW), for example, makes reference to violence against women in three articles, but does not explicitly state it is a problem.

6. For a review of women's movements in the developing world, see Ray and Kortweg (1999).

7. Recent surveys show that the informal sector represents 50 percent of GDP in Latin America, 40–60 percent of GDP in Asia, and 75 percent of GDP in Africa. From the perspective of a household, informal sector activities contribute a significant source of income. For example, in Africa informal sector income accounts for nearly 25 percent of rural nonagricultural income, nearly 30 percent of total income, and over 40 percent of total urban income. Moreover, it is likely that the size of the informal sector is larger than official statistics suggest since much of women's paid work is not counted in official statistics.

8. *Kebele* is the lowest level of government administration, or community; *kebele* describes both a geographical area and the committee that runs it.

9. In response to this problem Grameen Bank has started a housing loan program for women. See Narayan and Shah (2000).

Chapter 6

Social Fragmentation

Who can afford to help in this age of crisis?

—A poor man, Pakistan 1993

*In 10 years there will be the selection of the fittest,
and the least principled in the arena will win.*

—An old pensioner, Georgia 1997

*What is mine is mine, and what is yours is yours;
people in this community are very stingy.*

—A poor man, Ecuador 1996a

The fallout from inequity within institutions, the state, civil society, and the household is increasing social fragmentation, resulting in a decline in social cohesion and an increase in social exclusion. Poor people report that, by and large, they have not benefited from new opportunities created by economic and political restructuring. Both in rural and urban areas poor women and men report weakened bonds of kinship and community, as well as direct experience of increased corruption, crime, and lawlessness. While this is often more pronounced in urban areas, it is experienced even in rural areas. In Ghana, for example, groups of rural women note the disappearance of social solidarity as a result of labor migration out of the village over a 10-year period:

> [In the past] men organized themselves in groups through communal labor to assist each other to build and roof houses. Women supported each other to do farm work such as sowing, weeding, and harvesting. A woman who had recently given birth to a baby was always supported by young girls who cared for the babies and by older women who brought firewood and even treated the babies when they fell sick. Individual families tried to support each other. Women would work in groups in search of food to feed their children. They went to the bush in groups to cut firewood and to burn charcoal to sell. Respect and authority was given to the chief and his elders. —Ghana 1995a

Similarly, in the Republic of Yemen the poor speak about decreasing trust and the inability of families to cooperate with one another. "Local merchants and businessmen are accused of being less supportive and betraying traditional solidarity. This makes it difficult to create local committees or to raise money for operation and maintenance of community projects" (Republic of Yemen 1998).

In all societies people live in social groups stratified by ethnicity, caste, race, tribe, class, or clan. When state institutions cannot provide a secure and predictable environment unmitigated power asymmetries can become highly polarized. In response, social groups may rally to provide security for their members. However, a strengthening of ties within individual social groups (bonding) can aggravate existing cleavages and further marginalize those who are already excluded from these groups (exclusion). If intragroup bonding is accompanied by a breakdown of social cohesion among groups, institutions become the agents of partisan interests, rather than the agents of equitable social redress (Narayan 1999).

In such cases, trust in those state and civil society institutions whose role it is to mediate individual and group claims spirals downward. A lack of trust in society's institutions tends to reinforce people's desire to seek security within groups, rather than within society, which in turn exacerbates a cycle of insecurity, social exclusion, and increased levels of conflict and violence. Social fragmentation can permeate society, evidenced in domestic violence at the household level, crime and violence in the community, and massive corruption and civil conflict at the state level. Severe conflict of this type has afflicted over 50 countries since 1980, displacing an estimated 30 million people as a direct result (World Bank 1998).

This chapter first describes the phenomenon of social cohesion, then discusses the reasons for its decline. The second part of this chapter describes the phenomenon of social exclusion, and which groups are most affected by it. The chapter concludes with case studies of poor people's experiences with the police (case study 6.1) and the plight of widows (case study 6.2).

Social Cohesion

> You see those few potatoes in the bag? I have just borrowed
> them from someone, trusting that I will repay with the work of
> my hands. —A mother, Kenya 1997

Social cohesion is the connectedness among individuals and social groups that facilitates collaboration and equitable resource distribution at the household, community, and state level. Social cohesion is essential for societal stability and for easing the material and psychological stress of poverty. It also affirms individual and group identities, and includes rather than excludes less powerful groups. In poor households social connections are used to build social solidarity, to receive and give emotional support, to obtain help in daily tasks, to access small loans and job leads, and to collaborate in order to accomplish otherwise difficult tasks, such as housebuilding, or gathering the harvest. A PPA from India reports that one community had "a considerable degree of social cohesion, which became especially evident in circumstances that were out of the ordinary, such as sudden illness and disease, natural disasters, and accidents. At these times, villagers would pool their resources and energies to provide both financial and moral support to those in need" (India 1997a).

At the community level, cohesion is an asset that provides security, regulates behavior, and improves the standard of living of the community as a whole in matters that include but are not limited to material wealth. The Panama study gives an example of strong cohesiveness sustained by systems of sanctions. In one community this includes imposing fines of five balboas on men who failed to contribute to community work projects "so that the union that comes from work is not lost" (Panama 1998).

At the state level, cohesive societies are likely to be more efficient and more capital-rich, and hence more productive than fragmented societies. Dani Rodrik (1998) finds that the key to national economic growth during periods of external shocks is the presence of state institutions that mediate social conflict. Social cohesion is normally accompanied by political stability, which usually signals the existence of property and citizen rights and encourages private investment from both local and foreign investors.

Robert Putnam et al. (1993) demonstrate that a lack of social capital is not merely "a loss of community in some warm and cuddly sense." Rather, social cohesion and civic engagement are "practical preconditions for better schools, safer streets, faster economic growth, more effective government, and healthier lives. Without adequate supplies of social capital, social institutions falter and lose efficacy." Social cohesion also plays an important role in the way people deal with the psychological aspects of poverty. Giovanni Sartori (1997) states that human beings "endlessly seek identity in some kind of belonging." Social cohesion counters the psychological isolation created by poverty in two ways. First, it affirms the humanity of poor people even in the most degrading physical and economic circumstances. Second, it increases their access to resources through those same social connections.

The decline in cohesion within the community affects not only friends and neighbors, but also affects kinship networks and traditional hospitality. In Ukraine, for example, although family members, relatives, and close friends have become more important than ever as a resource, the rising cost of transportation, telephone service, and even postage stamps, combined with shrinking incomes, has diminished the ability to maintain contact, care for elderly parents, and assist children. Since Ukrainian independence new national borders have split many families (Ukraine 1996). In Armenia it is reported that despite the strength and importance of kinship reciprocity, people are less able to help relatives, and the flow of cash and goods is increasingly confined to parents, children, and siblings (Armenia 1995).

In Apunag, Ecuador, some households report that, in order to save scarce resources for food, they do not participate in celebrations at all. In Maca Chico community rituals have been shortened considerably, while in Melan fiesta expenditures have been converted from a community responsibility to an individual household option. Villagers note that this tends to reduce community solidarity (Ecuador 1996a).

An older poor man in Kagadi, Uganda, says:

Poverty has always been with us in our communities. It was there in the past, long before Europeans came, and it

affected many—perhaps all of us. But it was a different type of poverty. People were not helpless. They acted together and never allowed it to squeeze any member of the community. They shared a lot of things together: hunting, grazing animals, harvesting, etc. There was enough for basic survival. But now things have changed. Each person is on their own. A few people who have acquired material wealth are very scared of sliding back into poverty. They do not want to look like us. So they acquire more land, marry more wives, and take all the young men to work for them on their farms and factories distilling gin. So we are left to fight this poverty ourselves. And yet we only understand a little of it. It is only its effects that we can see. The causes we cannot grasp.
—Uganda 1998

Why Is Social Cohesion Declining?

Youth are most affected; they see no real chance for participation in the development of the country. In spite of their education and energy they are helpless, frustrated, and dangerous.
—Kenya 1997

Around the world social fragmentation is associated with major economic disruptions and frustration that new opportunities are limited to the rich, the powerful, or the criminal; migration in search of employment; and an overall environment of lawlessness, crime and violence combined with failure of systems of police and justice.

Economic Difficulties

This is not the desert of sand, but the desert of unemployment.
—Unemployed man, Pakistan 1993

If a person keeps one chicken [that] lays an egg every day, then he will have 800 drams a month—the salary of a teacher. If he has two chickens and gets two eggs a day, this gives him the salary of a professor. —A village official, Goris, Armenia 1995

The decline in social cohesion is linked to lack of economic opportunities. In Eastern Europe, Central Asia, and the former Soviet Union, the decline is linked to dramatic shifts away from occupations that once provided a living wage. While some of the elites have been able to take advantage of new trading and business openings, the poor have been excluded from those same opportunities. The perceived unfairness of unequal access to opportunities results in frustration and disorder, further exacerbating economic difficulties.

In Armenia the dramatic drop in the value of salaries has forced professionals and the intellectual elite to abandon their jobs, because they are no longer able to live on their salaries. During the summer of 1993 the typical salary of a senior researcher in social sciences was the ruble equivalent of US$25. By November, the average salary had dwindled to US$7. By December, a month after the introduction of Armenian currency, it had shrunk to US$2.50, although it was soon raised to US$5 (Armenia 1995). In Moldova:

> *Poverty has created rifts in communities ... between former friends and neighbors. People are cynical, suspicious, and jealous of other's success, which they most often attribute to dishonest and corrupt behavior. In their own communities the poor feel ashamed and constantly humiliated in their encounters with former neighbors and friends who have prospered. This humiliation is poignant in the case of children and young people, who sometimes prefer to remain at home rather than risk their classmates' mockery at their old clothes. Although poor people extensively rely on each other, at the same time frequent mutual suspicions and animosity, as well as fear of those in authority, often prevent people from cooperating on a community scale to help each other more effectively and improve community conditions. —Moldova 1997*

In Latvia it is reported that the lack of financial resources has forced people to reduce their socializing outside the family circle, so that the family has become their only shelter, and sometimes the only group that can be trusted (Latvia 1998). Unfortunately, economic hardship touches the household as well, and people report that the unending problems of poverty create stress, arguments, and even violence within families. A woman in Latvia says that endless arguments have made her sons "aggressive, ready to fight and defend themselves" (Latvia 1997).

In Ukraine the collapse of public sector employment has resulted in the poor trying to learn the new ways of trading. The word that has emerged is *ratitsa*, literally to spin oneself. "Spinning or hustling to make money refers to the incessant motions of buying and selling, buying and selling, and evokes the tremendous effort needed to work more than one job, and plan ahead in case all attempts at earnings fail." The poor, those most actively seeking employment, say that the reason for poverty is that "they didn't know how to work" in the new post-Soviet market-oriented world (Ukraine 1996).

For the poor in developing countries unemployment seems to have become a fact of life. Cambodia has been shattered by war, yet migrant workers, despite their hardships, are sometimes viewed as the lucky ones, whereas those left in the rural areas are seen as the losers. "These years, the majority in rural communities nationwide are losers, while a small number of families gained ... We have lost control over the fish in the lake and river waters. New mechanized boats have arrived to do fishing on a large scale" (Cambodia 1998). In Pakistan the poor say that new opportunities are beyond their reach (Pakistan 1993). In Nepal, the PPA reports, "People want to work. They have some knowledge and skill but they are not getting a chance to use it" (Nepal 1999). In Jamaica focus groups linked violence largely to economic need (Jamaica 1995). In Kenya and South Africa the poor not only speak extensively about lack of wage opportunities, but explicitly link it to increasing violence (South Africa 1998). In Ethiopia the poor say that because of unemployment, the unemployed "are exposed to *durayenet,* behaviors and acts which are morally unacceptable and disapproved by the family and community at large" (Ethiopia 1998).

Migration

We widows are left alone because the men leave in order to work. —A poor woman, Ecuador 1996a

The cohesion of households, communities, and states begins to erode when men and women are forced to migrate to find employment. Family members left behind for long stretches of time have less time and fewer resources to contribute to and sustain community relations. In Ecuador communities feel that "communal organization has seriously slipped recently, partly reflecting that many male members have migrated to the urban centers on the coast" (Ecuador 1996a). Similarly in India the institutional framework of caste *panchayats* (traditional caste-based councils) across the district was found to be under constant erosion. Caste elders attributed this mainly to migration in search of employment, which greatly reduced the opportunities for community gatherings, and changes in the attitude of the younger generation toward caste norms (India 1998d).

In addition, migration can reduce social cohesion in the host community. In Ethiopia, for example, prostitution increases as women in the urban areas lose their jobs as maids and are joined by more female migrants who arrive from rural areas seeking work, all of whom find no other options (Ethiopia 1998). In Ukraine migrants report difficulties in tapping into existing networks in host cities. One man has trouble because "not being from Kharkiv poses serious disadvantages because he lacks networks of relatives or childhood friends to tap into to locate employment opportunities" (Ukraine 1996).

The South Africa PPA concludes that the forced resettlement of blacks during the apartheid era and high levels of migration, mobility, and pervasive violence contributed to the undermining of social cohesion. "The result is that many communities are extremely divided, with little commonality in terms of needs and aspirations," to the degree that "the notion of community is extremely tenuous in South Africa" (South Africa 1998). The same PPA notes that support by community networks is infrequently mentioned by respondents, and then only in connection with assistance in exchange for labor. The traditional strategy of *ubuntu*, or sharing whatever one has, had been severely eroded by material and social pressures. Many of those interviewed express regret that this custom is no longer followed and note that the loss of *ubuntu* places an extra burden on poor families (South Africa 1998).

In Niger (1996) migration of a whole family is viewed as a sign of great distress. "Both the rich and the poor people migrate: the rich leave with money to start a business; the poor migrate to look for food and work, often returning to the village during the period of cultivation. Poor migrants seek employment in unskilled jobs such as making small crafts or selling tea or water. Sometimes they go back to their village with a few gifts—watches or radios—that they sell to be able to leave again. Some come back only with an illness, AIDS, or venereal disease" (Niger 1996).

Lawlessness

> *When disputes arise between neighbors, there are few legal channels by which to resolve them.* —Moldova 1997

> *Theft from the workplace is not a new phenomenon, but the degree to which it is practiced is.* —Ukraine 1996

> *It is the weapons of war that threaten the peace and security of our people.* —Cambodia 1998

Poor people frequently report a general feeling that lawlessness, or normlessness, has increased, accompanied by significant upheavals in norms of acceptable behavior. It is both a cause and an effect of declining social cohesion. When community networks are stretched too thin and there is insufficient state support, community cohesion begins to unravel as norms of reciprocity quickly become norms of opportunism. Communities without cohesion are often characterized by mistrust between neighbors, and fear accompanied by high levels of interpersonal crime and violence. Lawlessness degenerates into crime, in the absence of functioning police and court systems (see case study 6.1). This may be particularly acute in Eastern Europe and the former Soviet Union and in Latin America.

In Kenya "during difficult times, the poor resorted to stealing from shops or farms in order to survive" (Kenya 1996). In Moldova people report that in the past it was rare for people to steal from their neighbors' homes or fields; nowadays, however, "even the family horse is taken" (Moldova 1997). People report feeling powerless to stop theft. One man reports that he did not have a watchdog because he could not feed it. As a result, his 300-liter oak wine barrel worth 300 lei was stolen. Because he could not identify the culprit, the police closed the case without making any effort to pursue it.

Poor people report an overall sense of lawlessness in Moldova. Many people fear going out in the evening because the streets are filled with "aggressive and intoxicated youth." Brutal attacks on both men and women are common because help is difficult to come by. In one community, "A widow was gang-raped by seven men while her 10-year-old daughter looked on. Three men returned and tried to rape her again, but she managed to escape out of a window. She has since moved in with her sister and is afraid to return to her own home" (Moldova 1997).

When social solidarity breaks down, collective action is difficult and social norms and sanctions no longer regulate behavior. In Panama researchers find that in communities with low social capital, it is difficult to enforce the most basic norms, even when the benefits to the community seem clear. For example, in one community the local *junta* (community-level government) lent money to residents to install electricity in their homes and no one repaid the loans. In another community if there are problems between neighbors, the arbiter is supposed to be the representative of the *regidor*, "but we do not trust [him]"(Panama 1998).

Disciplining a neighbor's child is not a good idea in this community: "One tries to call attention [to children who engage in acts of vandalism] and is confronted with profanity." The lack of trust hinders the organization of activities: "Respect is lost. If someone wants to do something [for community development] ... always someone steals the money." In that same community focus group, participants explain that children are at the edge of violence: "They do not say hello, do not respect [you], they want to beat you up" (Panama 1998). In one indigenous island community the *Sahilas* (chiefs) worry that norms are not being transmitted to the next generation: "Parents do not offer guidance ... young men do not go to the fields [to work]; they want to [hang out] all day long" (Panama 1998).

In Armenia researchers find that "self-help groups and indigenous community structures of power outside government have not yet emerged, especially in rural areas. Sometimes people cooperate on a single task—for example, a small group of refugees traveled from Vaik to present their complaints in Yerevan to the government committee on refugees. Such groups dissolve as soon as their immediate task is completed. Most people rely on their own families or cooperate at best with related households to ensure their immediate survival" (Armenia 1995).

Crime and Violence

The 'Mafia' is huge, literally in every government body. If children used to play at being Cossack raiders, they now play at being 'mafiosi' with short haircuts, imitating bandits.
—Ukraine 1996

At the extreme, general lawlessness escalates to crime and violence, which becomes a vicious cycle, fed by the absence of functioning systems of communal or formal justice and police. In the rural areas theft of one family's belongings by another family was virtually unheard of in the former Soviet Union. Today, in Ukraine rural respondents report that their storage bins have been raided and livestock stolen. One person reports that a relative's seedlings were stolen right out of the ground hours after they had been planted. "This rise in rampant village crime represents a sharp break in community cohesion and fractures rural solidarity" (Ukraine 1996).

In Thailand poor people report feeling unsafe and insecure. They express great concern about their children's futures. Some children have been forced by their parents to drop out of school, not to work, but to guard the home from break-ins. In this environment of declining trust and increasing competition, along with decreased free time, people note the weakening of community groups. Groups report increased conflict within the household, within the community, and in the nation at large, linked to the absence of police (Thailand 1998). In Cambodia, "the use of light weapons (grenades, light rifles, or land mines) has resulted in a society characterized by unpredictable and frequent outbreaks of terror and violence" (Cambodia 1998).

In Jamaica gang violence prevents the installation or maintenance of infrastructure, which in turn exacerbates crime and war and erodes community cohesion. Telephones were widely perceived as a mechanism to reduce violence. But in Maka Walk, "Telephone Company [workers] had been stoned by local youths as they began laying lines, so the installation was never complete. An important indicator of community cohesion in Park Town is the fact, as participants frequently pointed out, that their one telephone box had never been vandalized" (Jamaica 1997). Violence of this kind frequently seems counterproductive even to the interests of the perpetrators.

Psychoanalysts point out that "In the face of powerlessness, violent and destructive behavior such as trashing shops and cars during riots is experienced as transformative. It isn't that people are simply destroying the facilities in their communities. They are psychologically transferring the bad feeling lodged within them to the perceived malign environment, despoiling it as they feel they have been despoiled themselves. They are enacting in their behavior an expression of their inner world which is a reflection of their social experience" (Orbach 1999).

Participants in the Ethiopia PPA made a timeline discussing the waves of rising and falling crime and violence during the 1990s. The group in Teklehaimanot saw crime increase first during 1990–91, when there was a government transition, and during 1994–95, when a rise in unemployment was accompanied by "loose police control." The most recent years,1996–97, have seen a dramatic decline in crime. This was seen as the result of an increase in the numbers of police on the force, especially on the local level (Ethiopia 1998). While the community of Teklehaimanot notes a strong correlation between rises in crime and a weakening of the state and its institutions, they also observe that, when crime is at its lowest, an effective state is complemented by local participation.

In sum, massive economic, political, and social changes have isolated individuals and fragmented communities in many parts of the world. For the poor the situation is especially acute because they have less flexibility to adapt to dislocation. Those whose life insurance is fundamentally social in nature experience increased insecurity and vulnerability. Some poor people have managed to seize opportunities offered by rapid economic change, and others with good luck and hard work have flourished in these same difficult circumstances. In Ukraine, for example, the key to moving out of poverty is summarized as "connections, individual initiative, and talent" (Ukraine 1996). Overall, those who are poor today clearly see themselves as losers rather than winners as vast changes sweep through their countries. Their feelings of loss and vulnerability are perhaps best exemplified in poor people's interactions with a quintessential institution of the state: the police (see case study 6.1).

Social Exclusion

You're not one of us. —Georgia 1997

As people become progressively more isolated, they also cut themselves off from information and assistance that could help them overcome problems and reenter society. —Latvia 1998

There tends to be a social separateness between tribal people and the rest of the village. —India 1997a

Social exclusion emphasizes "the role of relational features in deprivation" (Sen 1997). It refers to the norms and processes that prevent certain groups from equal and effective participation in the social, economic, cultural, and political life of societies (Narayan 1999). It is both an outcome and a process that renders similar outcomes more likely. Social exclusion thus involves at least four factors: the excluded, the institutions from which they are excluded, the agents whose actions result in the exclusion, and the process through which exclusion occurs. Social exclusion is a relational phenomenon, implicating those with power and affecting those without. To complicate the dynamic, power asymmetries are observed even within groups of excluded individuals.

The PPAs demonstrate the close connection between social exclusion and poverty. Most of the excluded groups—including women, children, old people, widows, and AIDS sufferers—are cut off from the networks that provide access to power and resources. This makes them vulnerable and increases their risk of being poor. Being poor is in itself a cause for social exclusion due to the social stigma poverty carries. While it is possible to break the cycle of exclusion, social exclusion can pass from generation to generation. A researcher in Mexico asked children how a person could stop being poor. They responded, "Getting an inheritance," "Receiving money from relatives who live in the United States," and "Having faith and praying every night." When asked why there are rich and poor, they answered, "Destiny," "That's the way God created earth," and "The rich are of the devil and the poor of God." These answers refer to factors beyond their control, beyond personal effort, studying, and working, which are not felt to measurably improve their social or economic class (Mexico 1995).

While exclusion can lead to economic poverty, and while social exclusion and poverty are deeply interconnected, they are not one and the same thing. Discrimination and isolation—the hallmarks of social exclusion—have a profound negative impact on quality of life. There are two aspects of this relationship. First, being poor can lead to social stigmatization and marginalization from institutions, leading to greater poverty. Second, while social exclusion does not always lead to economic poverty, it is always linked to exclusion from institutions of society and always leads to a poorer sense of well-being.

How Are People Excluded?

In rural districts especially when parents are intimidated by the city, or are not Georgian-speaking, they hesitate to seek medical treatment. They don't know where to take their children, and are afraid they cannot afford treatment. —Georgia 1997

Each caste group maintains strict norms about interdining and also accepting water from other communities ... any violation would lead to conflict within the village. —India 1997d

Christine Bradley's framework describes five main mechanisms of exclusion in order of increasing severity: geography, entry barriers, corruption, intimidation, and physical violence (Bradley 1994). These barriers are observed operating in the lives of many of those who participated in the PPAs.

Geography

We are all poor here, because we have no school and no health center. If a woman has a difficult delivery, a traditional cloth is tied between two sticks and we carry her for 7 km to the health center. You know how long it takes to walk like that? There is nobody who can help here, that's why we are all poor here. —Togo 1996

Social exclusion can be a function of geography, and there are often direct correlations between rural isolation and poverty (Ravallion 1995). Many PPAs report that poor people in rural villages cannot easily make trips to access health care or educational facilities in towns. A mayor in El Quiche says, "The problem or the most urgent need in relation to community health is the lack of money to buy medicine and also bringing sick persons from the farthest villages to the municipality for treatment" (Guatemala 1997b). Poor people in outlying areas not only must find a means to traverse the distance to schools, hospitals, and other institutions—they also lose income by undertaking a long trip. The poor often live in the most marginal areas, which compounds the cycles of poverty and exclusion. In Bangladesh the poor live on eroding riverbanks, the first affected by floods. In rural areas the poor are often relegated to unproductive land.

Urban areas also can generate excluded populations. As the Jamaica PPA reports, "A group of youths argued that through area stigmatization everyone in their community was branded either a criminal, or an accomplice to one, so that they are disrespected by outsiders and the police alike and cannot secure a job or learn a trade. They perceived this leading to hunger, frustration, and idleness, which encourages gang war and gun violence, with death or imprisonment as the ultimate price. When contract work was available to the local male work force, crime and violence declined, increasing again once the contract ended" (Jamaica 1997).

Barriers to entry

*Kinh people have been applying and writing papers for a
year now, and still haven't gotten anywhere. The land tenure
situation in Vietnam is precarious without official recognition.*
—Vietnam 1996

*Privatizing land consists of wandering among district and
national offices for weeks and months at a time.* —Farm
worker, Moldova 1997

Transaction costs and documentation requirements are the two most common barriers to entry. Transaction costs are any costs entailed in acquiring a good or service above and beyond its actual price. For example:

*After receiving a heart operation, hernia surgery, and removal
of gallstones in the course of two weeks, Valentina remained in
hospital for four more weeks. During that time, most of her
elderly parent's money was spent on her treatment and medication. Each of the nurses had to be paid 10 lei when she was
in the emergency ward, otherwise they wouldn't have bothered
to bring her meals ... and 10 lei so they would be careful when
they gave her injections. At the end of the treatment, the doctors demanded that Valentina's mother organize a dinner for
them. She acquiesced, selling some household items to purchase
the food, since she feared that Valentina might have to enter
hospital again and would depend on the doctors' good will, if
not their skill, which the mother felt was inadequate.*
—Moldova 1997

Barriers to entry involving state bureaucracy commonly revolve around documentation requirements. The state is often inflexible in helping the excluded gain access to resources. The PPA report from Cameroon notes that "Women's access to national institutions in the Far North is greatly handicapped by the fact that they do not possess national identity cards. Without them, women cannot vote, nor can they initiate a judicial process, nor travel farther than the family enclosure. Because women traditionally have little say on critical issues of inter-household resource allocation and decisionmaking, and owing to the fact that they are illiterate in the language of government administrators, women have little chance of voicing their opinions" (Cameroon 1995).

Documentation as a means of excluding the poor is commonly cited in PPAs as a reason for poor people's inability to access resources:

> One issue indirectly caused by government but open to governmental solution is that of documentation. Many of the poor interviewed, especially in the cities, expressed frustration over the difficulties of getting access to programs, services, or even employment for lack of needed documentation. A mother in Mexico City spoke of being denied access to a milk-feeding program for her child because she did not have a birth certificate for the child. Men in the same city talked of being refused employment due to the lack of identity (such as voting) cards. Only 15 percent of the sample of the Mexico City area had legal papers attesting to land ownership. ... If they didn't follow their leader and give him the support he sought, he could arrange it that they be evicted from their place of residence.
> —Mexico 1995

Document requirements represent only part of the barrier. Other barriers to entry include the hostility and unfairness that excluded people face when dealing with bureaucracy. Documentation, in this sense, becomes the device through which certain groups are socially excluded, a device that allows the state to humiliate and deny services:

> While access to the judicial system was perceived to be extremely important, officials are generally said to be extremely rude and unhelpful. Transport availability and costs were also said to be major factors inhibiting such access. "It is difficult to get to the court. It costs R10 to return by taxi from the farm to Patensie, and then R3.50 from Patensie to Hankey." Further, systemic problems also inhibit access to the judicial system. In the case of maintenance grants poor women are expected to obtain maintenance from absent fathers if they can locate them. This system places an unreasonable burden on these women, who face hostile and obstructive officials,

widespread administrative incompetence, lackadaisical sheriffs who fail to find absent fathers even when given correct addresses. —South Africa 1998

Corruption

If I had not given them money and presents, I would not have received normal care. I understood that when no one came to care for me the first three days of my stay in the hospital, and my neighbor in the ward hinted that I needed to pay for someone to pay any attention to me. —A patient at a hospital in Yerevan, Armenia 1996

In total she received aid from the Executive Committee, the equivalent of one loaf of bread. Real assistance is reserved for friends and family of those Executive Committee workers charged with dispensing aid. —Ukraine 1996

The chiefs and headmen no longer care about the needs of their people and have been separated from them in terms of the Administration Act, No. 38 of 1927. ... These acts encourage bribery, as manifested in the money, brandy and stock that chiefs demand from people for giving them residential sites. This means that of the land allocated to people, [much] is bought and those who cannot afford this resort to squatting. —South Africa 1998

One way for the excluded to gain access to institutions is to pay bribes. This is frequently done in Eastern Europe and the former Soviet Union, where poor people emphasize the importance of connections in getting anything: social security, pensions, jobs, health care, admission to universities, and business licenses. One woman in Donetsk, Ukraine says, "Jobs that pay are only given to relatives or friends" (Ukraine 1996). Connections are often the only means that the excluded have for gaining access to entitlements such as health care or judicial process. Corruption among local officials is noted to be a common problem in all parts of the world. In Madagascar, for example, "the President of the *Firaisana* takes advantage of his position by commercializing common waters. In a region where water is a rare resource, he says, it is a scandal to see truck drivers channeling water to people for whom it is not destined. There, the president of the *Firaisana* is the government. People know about these problems, but they do not say anything. [The respondent] said that this is not an isolated case, but happens in many other regions" (Madagascar 1996).

In Uganda paying bribes for health services seems to be taken for granted. A poor man reports, "In Jinja hospital you first pay Shs 500/ for the book to have your name recorded, then you pay another Shs 500/ for the doctor's consultation. In case you are referred to a Chinese doctor you pay another Shs 1000/. In this case you also have to pay foot allowance to the person who takes you to the Chinese doctor. This one is negotiable. Should you be admitted, then you begin paying Shs 500/ per day. And if you make a mistake of mentioning that you are from Masese, you will simply not be treated at all—we are so poor" (Uganda 1998).

The Moldova PPA describes a man who had been hospitalized for seven months following a brutal beating on the street. "Despite the fact that the police had helped him, he decided not to pursue the case when his attackers threatened his life. They even gave him 80 lei with the demand that he bribe the judge to dismiss the case. [He] complied" (Moldova 1997). Corruption feeds fear and crime.

Corruption is significant, not only because it makes access harder for the poor in financial terms, but also because it erodes the trust that a society needs to function effectively. Corruption makes equal access and fair treatment from the state impossible for the poor and the excluded, and accelerates their disengagement from wider society. Corruption is a central reason why societies grow more insecure. Increasing insecurity leads to deepening social cleavages, increasing social exclusion and societal fragmentation.

Intimidation

> My husband and I are no longer as close as we used to be
> when I was working—I think it is because he knows that I am
> solely dependent on him, especially because the children are
> still young. I am scared of him. ... But I know that I have to
> do my best and listen to what he tells me to do, for the sake of
> the children. —South Africa 1998

Psychological violence is not an uncommon means of isolating individuals and groups. Fifty percent of the PPAs contain some reference to the threat of violence. In general, those with power use the credible threat of harm to maintain their dominance over those without power.

Intimidation is observed at every level of society. As a mechanism of social exclusion, it is often used to reinforce social stereotypes and power relations. For example, a PPA from India reports that there are still deeply entrenched caste exclusions. "Mr. Pichhalu Barik's little granddaughter touched a tube well in the village Khairmal. The villagers refused to take water from that tube well. They called a meeting of the villagers, and gave Barik's family threat of punishment. He had to apologize to the villagers for the act of his granddaughter" (India 1998a).

In another instance local officials use intimidation to undermine new mechanisms of accountability. "Participants made both collectors and local government officials accountable for setting prices arbitrarily, forbidding producers to sell their produce to other agents, determining the timing of when the produce can be sold, and threatening them with a boycott. Sometimes the farmers say that [in retaliation] the collectors prevent rehabilitation of roads and bridges to prevent farmers from getting their crops to the market. They forcibly obstruct the farmers' journeys to places of meetings for farmers' associations" (Madagascar 1994).

Powerful institutions, even when they are obviously helping the poor, can easily slide into use of intimidation to meet their goals and standards. In Bangladesh the Grameen Bank is well known for its work with poor women. Lowest-level bank officials, mostly men, work with women's groups and enforce weekly repayment of microloans. However, sometimes the zeal and rewards for collection can degenerate into intimidation because the collectors know that the beneficiaries have few options. A fieldworker notes, "Khodeja lives in Hogolbaria. She has been a responsible member of Grameen Bank for a while and pays her installments on time. Unfortunately, her husband and brother-in-law died in a road accident, so she missed paying her next installment. The Grameen Bank staff forced the other group members and Khojeda's family to repay the money. 'They were so cruel,' women say, 'If they behave like that again we shall beat them up'" (Bangladesh 1996).

Finally, in South Africa, the threat of violence is reported to be the major form of control by men over women. In discussion around obtaining child maintenance women repeatedly stressed that they were reluctant to insist on pressing for support, even when this is a legitimate claim to be backed up by court action, as this would put them at risk. "It is dangerous to go looking for him, you might get hurt" (South Africa 1998).

Physical violence

> Those juveniles are in another world and don't believe in
> anything. They don't care if you are really tall built, or tiny,
> if they like what you are carrying they will take it from you,
> and if it involves breaking in your home, they'll do it.
> —Venezuela 1998

We don't fear death because we see it every day. —Youth in Greenland, Jamaica 1997

Social exclusion can result in direct physical violence. Fear of repercussions casts a pall of silence around the subject of violence—violence perpetuated by the state and violence against women in the household and in the community. Nonetheless, researchers are still able to record many instances of violence and violence against women. The Jamaican PPA investigated the issue of violence specifically, and notes that community groups identify over 25 distinct kinds of violence including interpersonal, gang, economic, and political violence. All discussion group participants, regardless of age, income, gender, or community agree that violence starts when politicians introduce guns into the areas. People report a shift from political violence to interpersonal and gang-based violence after the introduction of guns. Violence further fragments society: "Costs of violence can range from weak investor confidence, damage to the image-dependent tourism industry, higher health and police costs, the disaffection and migration of the urban middle class, higher mortality and morbidity rates, reduced access to social services, dysfunctional families, deeper oppression of women, to the breakdown of community spirit and participation, and the substitution of a climate of fear" (Jamaica 1997).

In South Africa people say that the high rates of violence in the urban areas result in lower migration to urban areas. Research teams visiting one area were told about a raid the previous night in which three people had been killed. "On the day the discussions were to take place, the youth were preoccupied with ensuring the safety of the community during the coming night. ... After the discussion, a group of youths escorted the researcher out of the township for her own safety" (South Africa 1998).

In Thailand discussion groups identify increased levels of conflict in the household, in the community, and with outsiders. In discussion groups in Bangkok it is reported that many poor people are being attacked by loan sharks because of their inability to pay back loans. This has increased feelings of fear and insecurity in the community. On an individual level, the most recurrent theme on the subject of violence is that of domestic abuse of women and children. Domestic violence is rooted in norms of gender inequity and identity and is often linked to alcohol and drug abuse. A woman in Kenya reports, "Both my parents used to drink, and therefore neglected the children. They could not do anything worthwhile to assist us. I got married in 1982 and divorced in 1987. We divorced because my husband was an alcoholic. He started selling property ... to get money for alcohol. We had no *shamba* [garden plot]. When I stopped him from selling things, he beat me. He chased me, and I came to Korogocho" (Kenya

1996). In Bangladesh when the issue of violence was raised in group discussion, "The women began 'speaking in hushed tones and sometimes ... withdrew from the discussion altogether'" (Bangladesh 1996).

Who Are the Excluded?

The PPAs often refer to the exclusion of particular groups. While the way in which each of these groups is excluded is context-specific, certain social differences continue to arise as grounds for exclusion. These differences include belonging to a particular ethnic, gender, caste, religion, or age group; living in a particular geographic area; or having certain physical disabilities. While we present excluded groups in discrete categories, it is difficult to generalize about which groups are the most likely to be excluded in which society, and from what they are excluded. Various forms of social difference overlap and intersect in complex ways over time. Some of the most frequent categories of excluded groups are described below.

Women

> *Everybody is allowed to voice their opinion. In many cases I'm cut off while I am voicing my opinion.* —A poor woman, South Africa 1998

> *The woman who has lost a husband, the woman who is old and can no longer till the soil, the woman who does not have children, the woman who is neglected by her children ... are the most vulnerable.* —Lubombo, Swaziland 1997

In the overwhelming majority of PPAs studied there are important examples of exclusion of women, suggesting that they experience pervasive exclusion. While the exact nature of exclusion is shaped by the culture of each society, the following similarities emerge from the PPAs.

Women's identity within the household is traditionally centered on their roles as mother and wife. Women speak of their "obligation to feed the family and care for the children, both materially and emotionally, regardless of the contribution of their husbands" (Bangladesh 1996). The primary expected role of family caretaker has made it harder for women to participate in public life. In many societies women are disconnected from ownership of assets and contact with public institutions. In a discussion among women in Uganda some say they "wished to have been born a man" (Uganda 1998). As one PPA explains, "Women's traditionally subordinate position constrains their access to factors of production: they cannot own land, the plots they receive are generally those left over by men. ... they are seldom contacted by extension agents, and they have only residual access to tools and means of transport owned by the household" (Ghana 1995b).

In many cases the role of wife and mother is reported to be so inflexible that women who fall outside this category are ostracized by individuals and discriminated against by state institutions. In three communities in Nigeria, for example, "spinsters, unmarried mothers, and barren women are often harassed and insulted by younger men and women who ... consider them personally responsible for their fate. Hence they ... carry a lifelong stigma and loss of respect. Economically, these categories of women are perceived as being unable to compete on an equal footing with other women as they have a weaker production base. For example, it was pointed out that these women are suspect when it comes to borrowing money for business ventures or self-improvement. They also suffer threats" (Nigeria 1995).

The increasing role of women in low-paid formal and informal job markets has brought new opportunities as well as new burdens to women. New sources of income for women do not lead to a neat shift in their authority within their households or in the communities. Yet despite these inequities and social constraints some women, as seen in earlier chapters, are resisting, walking out of abusive homes and asserting their rights in overt and covert ways.

Children

> *Children ask for uniforms, shoes, pens. We people who labor for others—should we earn to feed ourselves or buy chalkboards? —Poor woman, Pakistan 1993*

> *Why should I study, I know how to add and count, I can count money, rip people off, and cheat on weighing. Nobody is paying me to study, but I make 15–20 lari a month from trade. —A 10-year-old businessperson, Georgia 1997*

> *They reproach me for beating my children. But what should I do when they cry when they are hungry? I beat them to make them stop crying. —A poor mother, Armenia 1999*

Children are among the most vulnerable groups in society. They have little power or influence over the social processes that govern their lives and little ability to protect themselves from abuse. In Togo the PPA notes that "Customary law considers children as property of their family and gives them no individual rights. The widespread acceptance of highly exploitative labor practices and the occurrence of genital mutilation on girls are among the most extreme examples of the vulnerability of children" (Togo 1996). Lacking basic rights, the problems facing poor children that emerge most strongly in the PPAs are exclusion from education and health care; child labor; abuse; and homelessness.

Children are excluded from school for both economic and social reasons. As one report from Nigeria illustrates, the decision to remove boys from school is almost always a result of economic pressures: "Nine children, five girls and four boys, were consulted in the Northeast. All of the boys said that they would like to attend school, but their parents would not send them because they could not afford the fees demanded" (Nigeria 1997). The same report indicates that girls were excluded from education for both social and economic reasons. Similarly, in rural Benin, parents say, "Why should we send our daughters to school? Once they marry they go to their husband, they no longer belong to us" (Benin 1994).

Child labor is another reason for children leaving school. For poor families, the need to provide additional income takes precedence over education. "It is clear from the children's statements that the main cause of school dropout was the need to be involved in remunerative activities. For example, one 14-year-old boy living in a rural area dropped out of school to work in a salt-packing company. Even though he was a good student and he liked school a lot, he stated that he had to leave school due to financial difficulties and the need to contribute to his family's subsistence" (El Salvador 1997).

Children not only work—they are often forced into the most risky forms of employment. Child prostitution is reported in many countries. In Panama "girls who are 12 or 13 years old are already women. Drug dealers give them money, they see that they have developed breasts ... They offer them money, invite them to lunch, and buy them new shoes. ... Fifteen- and 16-year-old girls lure the younger ones who sometimes offer themselves to older men" (Panama 1998). The Panama report summarizes the career prospects of children in this community: "Young girls end up as mistresses of drug dealers, or as prostitutes. Boys run drugs" (Panama 1998).

Similarly, in Benin "the children are basically on their own, without any education and not even proper respect for the elderly: they're like street children. They can't eat regularly, health care is out of the question, and they rarely have real clothes. The girls have no choice but to prostitute themselves, starting at 14, even at 12. They do it for 50 francs, or just for dinner" (Benin 1994).

In rural areas of India researchers note several examples of bonded child labor in the drought-prone areas of western Orissa. The PPA tells about a 16-year-old boy in bonded labor. "Pachawak dropped out of class 3 when one day his teacher caned him severely. Since then he has been working as child labor with a number of rich households. Pachawak's father owns 1.5 acres of land and works as a laborer. His younger brother (11 years old) also became a bonded laborer when the family had to take a loan for the marriage of the eldest son. The system is closely linked to credit, as many families take loans from landlords, who in lieu of that obligation keep the children as *kuthia*. Pachawak worked as a cattle grazer from 6 a.m. to 6 p.m. and got paid two to four sacks of paddy a year, two meals a day, and one *lungi* [wrap-around clothing]" (India 1998a).

As in other countries, in Eastern Europe and the former Soviet Union the stress of poverty also leads to children begging on the streets rather than studying in schools. In Macedonia a poor woman whose children helped her earn a living said that "every day her two children gather bread from garbage containers and then sell it to people who keep cattle. They earn 100 denars a day" (Macedonia 1998). In Georgia researchers report that increasing numbers of children have stopped their education. Many work informally with parents, and many work as traders, loaders, and assistants; some do heavy manual work (Georgia 1997). In Georgia childhood illnesses and injuries have dramatically increased. A doctor from a clinic reports a fourfold increase in childhood asthma as parents can no longer afford to move to drier climates for sick children. As children increasingly take on adult tasks, the rates of injuries have gone up. "Now that children take over adult tasks such as chopping wood, gathering fuel, and cooking on dangerous kerosene heaters, they frequently injure and burn themselves" (Georgia 1997).

Finally, the PPA in Brazil (Brazil 1995) has shown that many street children do have families and are not orphans. Extreme poverty, the father's absence, and mother's struggling alone to make ends meet push children onto the street to earn incomes. Children may work as vendors, car wash guards, shoeshine boys, and grocery carriers. Only a minority of these children engage in criminal acts. However, they are subject to abuse, harassment, and pressures to join gangs as a way of creating a family in the isolation of the streets. The Brazil report includes the following depiction of the life of a destitute child. "He is often the victim of robbery and physical abuse by both peers and adults. He may join a gang as a way of creating a new family in his state of isolation. He may be harassed, bullied, or lured into criminal acts by gangs of youths and criminals. Surrounded by the drug subculture, he may begin to abuse drugs. Many street children develop extremely low self-esteem, apparently in response to the disparagement and abuse they regularly face in the course of making a living" (Brazil 1995). In South Africa children's gangs are reported to revolve around sniffing glue, drinking alcohol, and taking drugs. Yet these activities "enable the child to become part of a supportive group" (South Africa 1998).

Children are in many ways the most ill-equipped to cope with poverty: "The constant emotional stress of being poor and of the struggle for survival is revealed in many of the studies. This is most extreme in the case of street children. Here, analysis of self-portraits drawn by some of the children indicates stress, anxiety, emotional regression and the lack of a real connectedness with the world" (South Africa 1998).

State institutions in South Africa have been ill-equipped for coping with the problems of poor children. Children often must beg, wash cars, and make a living in other ways that are at odds with city by-laws. In addition street children are excluded from the justice system and have few rights. The South Africa PPA notes that poor children are "treated as youth offenders in terms of the Criminal Procedures Act, instead of being identified as neglected children and treated in terms of the Child Care Act. Children claim to have been assaulted by the police, used as informants, and forced to pay bribes" (South Africa 1998).

The poor

The authorities don't seem to see poor people. Everything about the poor is despised, and above all, poverty is despised.
—Brazil 1995

A poor man looks weak and has a big family; daughters from such families are prone to early marriages and pregnancies and usually leave their children with the old poor grandparents.
—Busia, Kenya 1996

While social exclusion and poverty are distinct concepts, they are deeply connected. Poor people remain poor because they are excluded from access to the resources, opportunities, information, and connections the less poor have. For poor people in developing countries this translates into intergenerational poverty. In addition, poverty is socially stigmatized, making it even harder for poor people to gain access to the networks and resources they need for survival. This vicious cycle is difficult to break.

Being disconnected from powerful institutions limits the information that the poor have about entitlements, scholarships for children, and their own earnings. In Armenia, in cash-starved villages, some mothers who give birth at home do not receive child benefits because they cannot pay the nominal fee required for the birth certificate. In Macedonia, despite poverty, women cannot access scholarships or credits for their children because of lack of information and lack of trust in the outcome—if they even bother to do so, since "only those who have the connections in the services" will get them (Macedonia 1998).

Poverty carries with it painful and humiliating stigma and power-lessness. After the complicated birth of her last child, one respondent spent some time in the hospital. "Her husband was out of work at the time. When she was discharged from hospital, she owed more than 20 lats, which was all the savings the family had. The hospital told them that, by law, they were entitled to be refunded this money from the municipality, and they were given a receipt. A few days later, she went to the municipality office to get her money, but the employee on duty threw her receipt at her, refusing to handle it, [saying,] 'You have paid it yourself.' No explanation was given, and no refund was made" (Latvia 1998).

Because norms and networks provide people with self-respect and standing within the community and provide access to local resources and safety nets, being cut off from social networks and unable to comply with social norms is extremely painful and humiliating for poor people. People often prefer to go further into debt than to be excluded from important community activities. "Ceremonies traditionally also entailed important obligations for guests, who were obliged to come with gifts or money. Poor Moldovans say they are now forced to choose between refusing such invitations because they lack appropriate clothing and money for gifts, and borrowing money so they can meet their obligations. [A man] from Ungheni had to decline several wedding invitations last fall, something he says he had never done in his life. But refusing to attend the wedding of his sister's daughter would have been dishonorable. He therefore borrowed 35 lei for the wedding gift" (Moldova 1997).

Similarly in Benin, "There was the case of a man who let his father die to save money for the funeral. He could have spent the money to take his father to the doctor, but then he would not have had enough money for a good funeral, and that would never do. He was too afraid that people could come one day to him and say, 'When your father died, what were you able to do?'" (Benin 1994).

The elderly

> If I lay down and died, it wouldn't matter, because nobody needs me. This feeling of my own powerlessness, of being unnecessary, of being unprotected is for me the worst of all.
> —An elderly woman, Ukraine 1996

> Tell them, ask them to take me. I can't live this way. In an old people's home, no one will blame me for being old. I don't want to accept help from others. —An old woman, Armenia 1995

I'm old and I can't work, therefore I am poor. Even my land
is old and tired, so whatever little I manage to work does not
give me enough. —An old man, Togo 1996

The treatment of old people is culture-specific. In most of Asia, Sub-Saharan Africa, and Latin America and the Caribbean the elderly are treated with deference and respect. In other cultures, however, particularly in Eastern Europe and the former Soviet Union, where the state assumed responsibility for the welfare of the elderly, many elderly have fallen into excluded groups as people fight to survive. With the collapse of social safety nets over the last decade old people have become extremely vulnerable. According to a respondent in Ajara, "In ten years, there won't be one pensioner still alive" (Georgia 1997). The vulnerability of old people is compounded by the rapidity of the social collapse. Where old people could once expect security in retirement, now they see their situation as hopeless: "I worked my whole life. For 42 years I was officially employed. My husband and I never had to deny ourselves anything. We had really exceptional savings. I was at peace. I thought, even if I don't have children, in my old age, I'll be well enough provided for that even if I get sick or something happens, I'll have the money to hire a caregiver or a nurse to look after me. I'll have money for good food, medical care, for my funeral, and for other things. And now I'm a beggar. I don't have anything" (Ukraine 1996). Isolation, loss of status, and powerlessness is reflected in many experiences reported by the elderly. In Armenia an elderly woman recounts:

My husband died a long time ago; we didn't have any children.
In Baku I worked for 40 years as a railroad guard. My sister
was killed in Sumgeut [an industrial town in Azerbaijan and
the site of anti-Armenian violence in February–March 1988].
Her children went to Russia, but I don't know exactly where.
We came to Yerevan, and from there a bus brought us here.
[After privatization], I gave my land to my neighbor. We agreed
that he would work it and give me two sacks (100 kg) of wheat
flour. Autumn came and I went to him, but he kept delaying. I
went ten days without bread. Probably my neighbors gave him
a hint, for he finally took pity on me and sent me two sacks of
barley flour. It was impossible to eat it, but what could I do? I
don't want to live like this. I go into the street, and children
yell, "There goes the beggar!" The children evidently pick this
up from the adults. I have one very kind neighbor, Ashot. He
helps me with everything. He planted my garden, gathered the
harvest and gave it to me. But he wants to emigrate. How will

I live without him? I have asked Ashot and the village chair-
man to help me move to an old people's home. They say,
"Auntie Violetta, why should you go to such a place?" I help
many people—I sew blankets for them, mattresses, they have
even come to see me from Vaik. One day I got up and there
was nothing to eat. It's unbearable to wait, to hope that some-
one will bring something ... I left a note in my house so that
no one would be blamed for my death, and I decided to throw
myself off the cliff. On the road, I ran into the chairman of the
neighboring village. I couldn't help myself; I started to cry. He
calmed me down, for which I am grateful, and convinced me
to return home. I am not complaining about people. Ashot
supports me, but soon even he will leave. They say there's an
old people's home in Yerevan. Tell them, ask them to take me.
I can't live this way. In an old people's home, no one will
blame me for being old. I don't want to accept help from
others. —Armenia 1995

To cope, elderly pensioners in some Eastern European and former
Soviet Union countries cancel their life insurance to save costs (Latvia
1998). In Moldova, with increasing costs of health care, the elderly poor
"tend to ignore their own illness, which they interpret as an inevitable
part of growing old, or simply of less importance given few resources and
the competing needs of younger family members" (Moldova 1997).

In Vietnam one of the main groups identified as poor is the elderly,
especially those who are ill, or who live on their own and have poor children. Lack of savings, a significant indicator of poverty, is found to be particularly acute among the elderly who cannot access the labor of children
and hence are considered poor risks for loans. Leaders of a women's union
that provides credit say, "We cannot give them loans because if they die, they
won't get the money back" (Vietnam 1999a). The strong desire by poor, elderly parents not to be burdens on their poor children—who are already
deep in their own struggles—emerges in many places. "We are nearly dead
now; we do not have any desire for ourselves; we just hope our children will
not be poor" (Vietnam 1999a) In Ecuador, in the Sierra communities, the
elderly, widows, and others left alone are identified as the poorest because
of their inability to adequately exploit their land resources on their own
(Ecuador 1996a). With increasing economic stress and breakdown of family solidarity the elderly are emerging as a new category of excluded poor
in countries across Sub-Saharan Africa and in Asia. Where social networks
are stressed, the most vulnerable resort to begging. In Madagascar,
"Begging is primarily adopted by those who don't fit into the community,

namely divorced wives, widows, old people, the disabled, and those with no children" (Madagascar 1996).

Ethnic groups

> *Most of the dropouts are found among the indigenous people—if they ever start school.* —Vietnam 1999a

> *They have always excluded us Mayas, they have discriminated against us. They cut down the tree, but forgot to pull down the roots. That tree is now sprouting.* —Guatemala 1997a

Social exclusion on the grounds of ethnicity is a common theme running through the PPAs. Power relations in heterogeneous societies always favor some groups at the expense of others. In India exclusion on the grounds of ethnicity is perpetuated by the rigidities of the caste system: "It is observed by Gandas of Khairmal that, even in public institutions like schools, their children take midday meals sitting at a distance from other children. One Anganwadi worker had to leave the job because she did not want to clean the utensils touched by Ganda boys and did not like to take care of the Ganda children. The practice of untouchability was also reported from other villages" (India 1998a).

Some forms of marginalization are geographical. One example is in India, where the native Adivasi tribal population has been pushed to the degraded forests and eroded hill slopes, scrubland, and rocky soil, by caste settlers. They become sources of agricultural labor for others, or encroach on common property resources that are rapidly diminishing (India 1998b).

In Uganda, "After the community had finished drawing its village social map, we wanted to know what future aspirations the community had. One participant proposed that something be done about the poor situation of the Batwa. At this point it emerged that none of the [Batwa] had had their households included on the village map. Worse, not a single person from this small ethnic group had turned up for the meeting. A separate effort was made by the research team to interview some Batwa families. Two women were found in the neighborhood. One summed it up for us thus: 'We only gain value in the eyes of the Bafumbira when we are working their gardens. In other instances we are invisible'" (Uganda 1998).

Social exclusion on the grounds of ethnicity is a key to understanding who gets whatever resources are available. In the Philippines, indigenous people have benefited the least from government rural development programs. "Mostly dominant in the rolling and mountainous areas, the indigenous tribes verbalize feelings of inferiority" (Philippines 1998). In Vietnam, too, ethnic considerations have been key in determining access to education:

"[In the whole district] there are two Chau Ma children going to school. They do not want to go to school, for the Kinh children are beating them up. ... Teachers are available although most of them only speak Vietnamese. The rate of Kinh children going to school is much higher than that of the ethnic groups. Most of the dropouts are found among the indigenous people, if they ever start school. The reasons for the low attendance vary but the most common are labor needed at home, long distances, no roads, dangerous passages over water, no adequate books and clothes, not understanding Vietnamese, not being made welcome by the Kinh children" (Vietnam 1999a).

People with HIV/AIDS

> *A person with AIDS suffers a lot because there will be no communication whatsoever because people will get afraid of him and he will end up without friends.* —South Africa 1998

> *AIDS knows no boundaries.* —Uganda 1998

Myths and stereotypes that surround AIDS have caused sufferers of the disease to be cut off from social networks, the critical survival asset for the poor. Stereotypes against HIV/AIDS sufferers are heavily culture-specific. In Eastern Europe and the former Soviet Union the negative associations ascribed to drug users and homosexuals have excluded sufferers; in Sub-Saharan Africa the disease is associated with prostitutes, women, and truck drivers, and with poverty.

A key problem for those with HIV/AIDS is shame, denial, social isolation, and losing access to the social networks they need in order to cope with the psychological and material consequences of the illness. "A major fear associated with HIV/AIDS is the fear of social isolation that would result for a household and individual if the knowledge of infection became public. ... This causes many to hide the fact of infection, thereby hampering efforts to bring the issue into the open to further public education" (South Africa 1998). Fear also leads to the widespread attitude that "if you just ignore the symptoms ... [then] they will go away," particularly since HIV/AIDS has become associated with death, orphans, and destitution (Uganda 1998). The behavior of health providers, the "rudeness and moralistic attitudes" of clinic staff who work with HIV/AIDS patients, discourages the poor from seeking crucial services (South Africa 1998).

AIDS has consequences beyond the individual. Whole households may face isolation. In Burkina Faso:

> *AIDS widows ... have been chased with their children from their villages. They end up in the city, arriving with nothing,*

knowing almost no one, and looking for work. They share a common stigma with the older women found at the Center Delwende de Taughin, in Sector 24. Both have been accused of witchcraft and chased from their villages after an unexplainable death. [These] new type of young, homeless women are accused of the deaths of their young, seemingly fit, husbands. What makes them different from the older women and much more vulnerable in the city is that they are probably in danger of being infected themselves. Moreover, they arrive not alone, but with small children, too young to help find work and survive. With the increase in AIDS cases over time ... the numbers of these women, socially ostracized, will continue to grow as well.
—Burkina Faso 1994

The issue of HIV/AIDS and its severe consequences for households and society are discussed in most PPA reports from Sub-Saharan Africa including Benin, Burkina Faso, Cameroon, Ethiopia, Mali, Senegal, South Africa, Swaziland, Tanzania, Togo, Uganda, and Zambia. HIV/AIDS is also identified as an issue in Thailand and in Cambodia. (Case study 3.1 in Chapter 3 offers additional information from the PPAs on HIV/AIDS.)

The disabled

Disabled children are not seen as human beings; they are isolated at home and not sent to school. —Kabale focus group, Uganda 1998

Disability is frequently reported as one of the characteristics of the very poor. Issues of access, both to physical and social space, have emerged. A blind woman from Tiraspol, Moldova (1997) reports: "For a poor person everything is terrible—illness, humiliation, shame. We are cripples; we are afraid of everything; we depend on everyone. No one needs us; we are like garbage that everyone wants to get rid of." High health costs exacerbate disability. The report continues: "Families on the edge of indigence or already in debt are often unable to treat [their] chronic or serious illnesses. Maria ... recently discovered several lumps in her breast. The family already has such a large debt from her husband's treatment that she has refused to even consult a doctor, although she realizes she might have cancer. A disabled man in the district of Balti reported similar behavior on the part of his wife: "She has a serious liver disease and even though I tell her to go to the doctor, she won't. She is afraid of paying money." Even when poor people do start treatment, they sometimes find they can't afford to complete it. A woman reported she had come down with pneumonia. She borrowed enough money to buy ten doses of penicillin, but only had nine injections, since she could not afford a tenth syringe (Moldova 1997).

Social exclusion can still continue even when the basic economic concerns of disabled people are met:

> *Before the earthquake, Armenians were unaccustomed and often repulsed to see people with any sort of deformity, regarding birth defects and handicaps as shameful. Families often hid handicapped children at home so they would not reduce the marriage chances for the normal children. Since the earthquake, considerable aid has gone to the disabled. In Giumri's Austrian Quarter, the disabled, along with their able-bodied relatives or guardians, have occupied 100 specially designed apartments well supplied by electricity and cooking gas. The disabled have patrons in Europe who send money and clothing, and even pay for holidays. Yet the disabled remain isolated. Lack of special transport confined them to a single neighborhood, special school, small church, local polyclinic, and small shop. The able-bodied population living in the earthquake zone who lost close family members and remain ill-housed and needy feel they have suffered just as much as the disabled, and consider it unfair that "all the aid" goes to the "handicapped." As a result, the disabled are prey to name-calling and hostility when they venture from their immediate surroundings into Giumri.* —Armenia 1995

Widows

> *Even before the funeral of the deceased husband, some widows are mistreated by the in-laws who take all the property, including the children.* —Mbarara focus group, Uganda 1998

We did not start our analysis with the idea of featuring widows as an excluded group in a case study, but the data suggest that in many cultures, among the poor, becoming a widow is tantamount to social death. Widows are seen as harbingers of death and bad luck, and are considered burdensome, useless, and easy prey, and are often identified as the poorest of the poor. In Swaziland women say that the hardship of widows is made worse by a Swazi custom that regards them as bearers of bad luck and imposes on them social isolation during a prolonged period of mourning (Swaziland 1997). The combination of social prejudices, kinship customs, and lack of accountability on the part of state institutions helps explain why widows face great risk of social exclusion and poverty (see case study 6.2).

Conclusions

Poor women and men in many countries feel further socially excluded and less protected than before. This disintegration of social order is compounded by the fact that for many the old coping mechanisms based on traditional networks are fast disappearing. The poor speak of a loss of community, which was once a partial substitute for the lack of assistance from distant state regimes the poor feel powerless to change. Community solidarity has indeed increased in some places as a form of self-protection, but it is unable to confront—much less change—corrupted state institutions that become aligned with criminality and justice and police protection that can be bought and sold. In this type of environment moving out of poverty is beyond personal control, beyond personal effort. Hence, many poor people see few benefits to increased investment in human capital. Children in Mexico (1995), Latvia (1998), and Vietnam (1999a) freely assert that moving out of poverty is related to neither schooling nor hard work.

For many vulnerable groups—such as the elderly, those with HIV/AIDS, widows, and, in many contexts, women—changes over the last decade have eroded important social safety networks and practices. Caught in cycles of poverty and exclusion, the poor struggle to survive while opportunities to access information, jobs, education, health care, markets, pensions, and other resources elude them. The way the state is organized often exacerbates existing social tensions and cleavages leading to even greater inequality between the rich and the poor (see table 6.1 in appendix 7).

Case study 6.1 The Poor and the Police

The gradual relaxation of state control has reduced some of the functions of the police. But at the same time, it has also had the effect of reducing state control over the police. For this reason, many people are deeply fearful of the police. Because the state is weak, citizens—especially the poor and powerless—feel unprotected against the police. They have no recourse but compliance when police demand bribes or threaten brutality. —Ukraine 1996

The presence of dysfunctional police forces plays a substantial role in the deterioration of social cohesion and trust within a society, and the rise in lawlessness, crime, and violence. Corruption, institutional failure, and social fragmentation are all brought into sharp relief by attitudes toward the police. The police are said to be among the three most repressive institutions in society (the other two being the military and the household) (Gelles and Straus 1988). When the institutional checks and balances on police action disintegrate the police force is capable of immense repression and exploitation.

The precise consequences of this repression, of course, differ from context to context, depending primarily on the extent of preexisting police involvement in society. The countries of the former Soviet bloc, for example, were characterized by an exceptionally pervasive and surveillance-oriented police system. A report from Ukraine explains:

> *In discussing perceptions of the police and their relation to crime and [law] enforcement it should be noted that the Soviet police force was charged with serving the state by monitoring and controlling citizens and preserving order, rather than controlling crime. Soviet citizens obtained their registration (propiska) through the police. It was the role of militia to ascertain that citizens were employed and living where they were registered, and to register marriages and divorces in the internal passports people still use as legal identification. Citizens also applied to the police for foreign passports and visas. —Ukraine 1996*

Around the world police pervade society for a range of reasons, such as to wage a war on drugs, or to address terrorism and antidemocratic forces, and so on. Heightened police presence in communities has noticeable effects. In Jamaica, for example, the development of a special crime-fighting unit has created tremendous social tension:

> *Police are a central part of the everyday life of the urban poor, yet are perceived as reinforcing existing structures based on fear and divisiveness. The actions of the Anti-Crime Squad (ACID) and Rat Patrol (mixed army and police patrol) were singled out as being brutal and intimidating, particularly by young people who perceive themselves to be subjects of wholesale harassment. —Jamaica 1997*

In South Africa the police have historically been associated with repressive minority rule, and there are residual poor relations between the majority population and the police (South Africa 1998). In much of South Asia the police are associated with corrupt politicians, evoking fear rather than respect among poor people.

Police Activities

The police support their families by just showing their shadow.
—Resident, Akhuria, Armenia 1995

The mere presence of the police can cast such a pall of fear that people are willing to make payments just as precautionary measures to be left alone. The power of the police to dominate, threaten, evoke fear, and demand bribes is pervasive in environments where no one is policing the police. The police are mentioned in about 40 percent of the reports reviewed. In none of the documents is the report favorable. At best, the police are reported as "largely inactive" in their policing roles; at worst, they actively harass, oppress, and brutalize. In countries as different as Jamaica, Uganda, India, and Moldova, police brutality is mentioned as a serious problem facing the poor.

Examples of police indifference are particularly prevalent in Eastern Europe and the former Soviet Union. They are considered indifferent because their actions do little to meet people's expectations, as in the following example from Ukraine. An elderly lady, Rosa, reported that once she telephoned the police to report that her Arab neighbor had been badly beaten by armed men demanding money. The police claimed they didn't have enough gasoline to come, although as Rosa pointed out, their station was located only 200 meters from the crime (Ukraine 1996).

This indifference seems particularly prevalent in cases of violence against women. Rape victims in South Africa report, "Even the policemen are not doing anything about this. If we go to report to them, they always say, Go find other people who were raped by that person and come back with all the names of the victims, only then they will know if that person is really a rapist. They will ask you, what did you do to get raped? Did you provoke the rapist? What kinds of clothes were you wearing? They ask you all sorts of questions without giving any help" (South Africa 1998).

Along with the problem of indifference by police, corruption proves to be another major obstacle to ensuring adequate protection and justice. In Madagascar the police and judges, who are supposed to be the guardians of justice, are seen as the most corrupt (Madagascar 1994). The impact of police corruption varies in significance from one context to the next, yet can become pervasive in a particular society because it is self-perpetuating.

Many PPAs also note that the police are largely responsible for making informal sector survival strategies increasingly difficult, by harassing vendors and small traders, especially women. Women who are hawking goods in the informal sector end up constantly on the move to avoid the police, who patrol unauthorized areas in order to collect bribes from traders and kiosk owners. Such bribes are mentioned in many PPAs around the world. In Cameroon, for example, "Traders in food crops mentioned that even where the road is good, because of the numerous road blocks, police harassment, and customs check points 'travel is a real nightmare'" (Cameroon 1995).

In Georgia bribes factor into both formal and informal business activities. Small businessmen are faced with bribes demanded by all officials, including the police, and are faced with extortion from organized crime. Entrepreneurs say that the only way to survive and to protect oneself against "sudden accidents" is to have a *krysha,* a protector, to have good relations with powerful figures in the police force, and to publicize this fact to all (Georgia 1997). While police actions can range from indifference and neglect to corrupt activities, the severest form of injustice affecting the poor usually takes the form of violent police harassment of individuals. This can mean being beaten by Moscow police as suspicious "persons of Caucasian nationality" or in some extreme cases, being "returned in a coffin" (Georgia 1997).

Minority or socially excluded groups are particularly vulnerable to police extortion and harassment. In Pakistan researchers find the most extreme case of insecurity among the Bengali community of Rehmanabad, in Karachi. "They had been subject to evictions and bulldozing, and on returning to the settlement and constructing temporary housing of reeds and sacks, have faced ongoing harassment by land speculators, the police, and political movements" (Pakistan 1993). Similarly, in Bangladesh tribal groups stopped filing cases with the police because they know that there will be no action, only further harassment (Bangladesh 1996). In Georgia the internally displaced persons (IDPs), in addition to suffering the humiliation of being labeled beggars, report that even when they had land their poultry was stolen more often than that of others, and that the police refused to take an interest (Georgia 1997).

Coping Strategies

As the formal state deteriorates local agents of the state are increasingly able to exercise power arbitrarily and with impunity. Those poor people who are able to solicit the patronage of the police fare substantially better than those who are unable to enlist this kind of support (India 1998d). Two kinds of coping mechanism are identified in the reports, which correspond to two roles of the police force: maintaining justice and protecting the public.

Coping with the absence of justice

Police forces are relatively new phenomena in many countries, and most have a variety of social mechanisms for preserving order that predate official police activities. In India, for example, village quarrels and conflicts are often resolved by the *mukhia* (village head) joined by four other village members to form an informal committee called a *panch*. The aggrieved parties usually respect the decision of this body, and decisions are almost never reported to the police or taken to the courts (India 1997a).

Some forms of informal justice follow traditional lines. In other cases popular courts are established. While these tend to be more democratic than their predecessors, there is no guarantee that they will be free of repression or injustice. A Jamaican PPA notes that informal justice systems within poor communities have developed as a response to the lack of law and order. These alternative systems, mainly hierarchical in structure in the form of councils, committees, or even ad hoc groups are headed by dons or other powerful leaders to hand out justice informally. In one instance a cocaine addict was beaten up and driven out of an area, in another an accused child-beater was "tried by the people" and forced to leave the community (Jamaica 1997). Neither of these mechanisms for dispensing justice is ideal. In times of institutional crisis certain groups can become "judge, jury, and executioner"—an exceptionally dangerous state of affairs, particularly for those without power.

Coping with the absence of security

In times of institutional breakdown those with greater power or resources are able to claim the attention of the police more successfully than those without. If the police are unwilling or unable to provide the protection sought by those in power, they create their own solutions. In Ukraine, for example, businessmen frequently feel compelled to have bodyguards because the police are not willing or able to protect private citizens or private property. As a result, a mutual dependency between police and business interests is forged. Moreover, many people consider that the local "mafia" (including ethnic and local gangs, organized crime, and corrupt government institutions) have penetrated law enforcement agencies, and that criminals generally operate with the knowledge and protection of the police (Ukraine 1996). The bond between the police and formal business interests also contributes to the frequent reports of the police harassing those involved in informal sector business.

Those without resources to pay for added security sometimes agree to combine their efforts in an attempt to secure greater protection. In some villages in Tanzania where cattle theft is prevalent and police presence low, people have banded together to create *sungusungu,* or security groups within their communities. All the men and women in the village above age 20 are required to join. The young men are responsible for security, and at night patrol the village to make sure that people are not loitering around.

Women take turns to prepare food for the guards (Tanzania 1997). Similarly, in rural Georgia, because of frequent theft of livestock and harvest, farmers take turns watching the fields before the harvest. They have found themselves confronting armed thieves at night (Georgia 1997).

When protection from the police is up for sale the poor in urban slums are often trapped between two evils: corrupt and preying police on the one hand, and slumlords and gangs on the other. In Bangladesh slum dwellers note the lack of assistance from law enforcement agencies. In the slums of both Chittagong and Dhaka men report that musclemen regularly harass teenage girls and even kidnap and rape them. Musclemen demand money from the slum dwellers, and threaten that they will burn down their houses if any complaints are lodged against them (Bangladesh 1996).

Consequences for the Poor

The police cannot patrol; they are corrupted. —Panama 1998

When the actions of an ineffective police force reduce people's trust in it, this lack of trust contributes in turn to a further deterioration in the police force's reputation and effectiveness. But it is important to stress that the corruption of the police has consequences well beyond this. Many reports, across all regions, mention that reduced trust between groups and individuals occurs as a consequence of an impaired police force, and the associated increase in crime. The absence of trust in the police prejudices future cooperation both within communities and among groups. Without trust in fellow community members, there is little hope for positive change. In Jamaica, for example, the PPA notes that existing social institutions in the communities studied have largely failed to reduce violence, leaving an institutional vacuum in many cases. Consequently, the only major mechanism to control or reduce violence is the visible presence of different branches of the police force, with widespread accusations of brutality, as well as accusations of human rights violations (Jamaica 1997).

In Moldova increased crime, from pilfering fields to rape and assault, makes poor people fearful of venturing out of their homes in villages, towns, and cities. People feel they are vulnerable to threats, intimidation, and abuse from those in power. Lack of trust within communities, lack of trust between citizens and their officials, collusion between local officials and police, and perceptions of a two-tier system of justice, along with distrust of the banking systems, which have also been corrupted—all these put "severe constraints on citizens' initiative and grass-roots activity" (Moldova 1997).

Conclusion

There are no quick fixes. The problems associated with the police are embedded in the problems of state dysfunctionality. Given the impact of crime, lawlessness, corruption, and police harassment on poor people's lives, poverty reduction strategies can no longer ignore the role police play—either through their activities or the lack of activities that can lead to lawlessness—in impoverishing poor men and women. Women are particularly vulnerable. Consideration should be given to the creation of police stations run by women for women which have similar power, resources, and status as male police stations as has been suggested in the Republic of Yemen (Republic of Yemen 1998).

Case study 6.2: Widows

This case study addresses two questions: How and why are widows excluded, and how do they cope?

How and Why are Widows Excluded?

> When my husband died, my in-laws told me to get out. So I
> came to town and slept on the pavement. —A middle-aged
> widow, Kenya 1996

> If the woman has no children at the time of widowhood, she is
> asked to leave immediately, sometimes blamed for the death,
> and even labeled a witch. Relations ensure that she leaves with
> nothing but her clothes. —Tanzania 1997

The PPA reports suggest that there are four main reasons for widows to find themselves excluded. It is felt that they cannot contribute economically, they have no assets, they are expected to play certain social roles, and formal safety nets rarely provide for them.

They cannot contribute

> They do not possess any kind of skill. —India 1997b

As an Indian report notes, widows are assumed to be an economic burden on the household: "They are wholly dependent on their family for care and support as they do not have any earnings of their own. Socially, they are often neglected and considered a burden on the family. The general perception is that they do not make any significant economic contribution to the family and that they do not possess any kind of skill" (India 1997b).

Despite this perception, widows frequently do work, but their range of possible activities is often severely limited by childcare responsibilities. The lack of economic productivity, in other words, may have more to do with the constraints placed on widows than with the women themselves. A widow in Guatemala observed, "The widows don't have anyone to help them, and they don't have even a small piece of land—not even to have a house, never mind to grow crops" (Guatemala 1994a). Further, many cultural traditions and legal systems deny widows access to the resources once controlled by the household. She often cannot fall back on her original social networks for support, because she is expected to sever those ties on marriage.

For many women, finding socially acceptable remunerated work is challenging enough without the stigma, childcare responsibilities, and grief of widowhood. Yet in the absence of assets, opportunities, and social support, widows must work endlessly to survive. One widowed mother of six who weaves textiles, collects wood to sell, and works occasionally as a laundress, says, "We are poor because our work does not permit us to eat. What we earn from our work is sufficient for one or two days and then we have to look for work for the next days. We have pain every day. We never rest, ever" (Guatemala 1994a).

They do not possess assets of their own

> *After the death of my husband, his brother married my husband's second wife and took all documents related to the house that my husband owned. Now I'm neither owner nor renter, he rents four of the six rooms and he keeps the rent. My brother-in-law has rented some of my children. I work as a maid and sell sand that is used for washing dishes. I collect this sand around the neighborhood. I eat what I can find and it is not every day that I eat.* —A widow in a neighborhood of Bamako, Mali 1993

In many traditional societies widows are often expropriated of the family assets when their husbands die. This means that they experience a drastic fall in income at a time when they can least afford it. The economic hardship suffered by widows is exacerbated by the discrimination against them in credit markets, which makes it harder for them to reacquire assets. This theme is highlighted in women's discussion groups:

In the case of widows, male relatives of the husband (generally his brothers) will claim rights on household property unless the male children are old enough to inherit, taking away means of production and transport, and even their house. In some areas of Africa, widows are supposed to stay inside their house for a whole year, thus being practically forced to abandon whatever income-generating activity they had and to depend on charity. The custom whereby brothers-in-law "inherit" widows along with property represents one of the best outcomes, as it affords women the possibility to maintain the usufruct rights over their household property and provides them the protection and status deriving from a husband. —Benin 1994

And in Nigeria "it was pointed out that these women are suspect when it comes to borrowing money for business ventures or self-improvement. They also suffer threats to their privacy and property. In particular, widows and barren women lose their husband's property to relations of the husband in accordance with traditional family rules" (Nigeria 1995).

They are expected to fulfill social responsibilities

Bereavement and funerals can cause poverty. —Kenya 1997

Despite the economic loss resulting from a husband's death, widows are often expected to participate in expensive community undertakings, the most obvious of which is paying for the husband's funeral. Funeral costs can be exceptionally high, especially as a percentage of a poor person's income. In some countries arrangements exist for a kinship network to contribute to fees. If no such network exists, however, the widow will sometimes have to pay for the appropriate expenses herself: "Bereavement and funerals can cause poverty. In Kisumu the widow(s) and children are often left bankrupt. This marks the beginning of poverty for the bereaved family members" (Kenya 1997).

In South Asia social obligations include finding a dowry for a daughter's marriage:

Rehala lives in Mahya Bagra. She is 35 years old. Rehala's husband died 10 years ago, leaving her three children to bring up alone. Her son married and went away, having squandered all her savings. She works as a maidservant. Both her daughters have married, the eldest to a rickshaw puller and the second to a day laborer. When they married, Rehala said she could not give dowry. Every day the men are demanding it.

*They want gold, furniture, utensils, and mattresses. She
thought her son would help out but he is only concerned for
himself. She already has an outstanding loan of Tk 30,000
and feels she will never be able to repay the loan and give the
dowry demanded by her two sons-in-law.* —Bangladesh 1996

They are poorly provided for by state or community safety nets

*If assistance ... comes at all, no one ever knows what happens
to it.* —Moldova 1997

There are very few assistance programs that directly assist widows. Often
widows have to find assistance by qualifying for a second category of assistance, such as pensions or government transfers to the poor.
Furthermore, widows, like other poor and excluded groups, are poorly positioned to influence government policies; powerlessness in the face of political indifference and corruption contributes to their economic hardship.

How Do Widows Cope?

Widows try to cope in many ways. Those most commonly reported in the
PPAs include informal employment, taking children out of school, drawing
on entitlements where they exist, returning to parents, migrating, and
becoming sex workers.

They seek informal employment

For a woman it is a problem to start life afresh.
—Tanzania 1997

As noted above, widows work to help mitigate their situation. They are
often barred from formal employment due to gender discrimination, and
widows are forced to find work in the informal sector (MacEwen Scott
1995). A group of women in rural Tanzania report, "For a woman it is a
problem to start life afresh. ... Sometimes women engage in businesses like
selling food in the open markets, do piecework, or prostitution. Many lacking education do not know their legal rights and end up moving with drivers of long-haul trucks along the Dar-Malawi or Rwanda roads. They
come back when they are pregnant" (Tanzania 1997).

In Macedonia (1998) a widow explains that she begs. "Every day she
goes to buildings or stands in crossings and begs with her three-year-old-
child. She earns around 150 denars a day. She goes to beg by bus, but she
does not pay her fare because the drivers already know her, and they do not

ask for money ..." Her children do not go to school because she doesn't have enough money.

The struggle to live touches widows in many countries. "Mai is a 37-year-old widow whose husband died when she was three months pregnant. Unable to work while pregnant, and struggling to raise two other young children, she quickly fell into debt and had to mortgage their land to buy food. Mai currently works as a domestic servant, but she is still 2 million VND in debt. She currently goes to work from 6:30 a.m. to 5:00 p.m. and lists her main difficulties as having the money to buy back her land and then loneliness. Her dream now is to save enough capital to raise pigs and ducks, while her daughter's dream is freedom of debt for her mother" (Vietnam 1999a).

They withdraw their children from school

We simply have to survive. —Moldova 1997

One way in which widows survive is to make the difficult choice of taking their children from school. In this event girls are more likely than boys to be withdrawn so that they can provide income through child labor or do housework while the mother works. "One young mother of four keeps her three school age children out of school so they can help scavenge cardboard. She explained, 'We simply have to survive. If we had nothing to burn, we would die. My children can't go to school because, without them, I wouldn't be able to gather enough cardboard every day'" (Moldova 1997).

They access state or community entitlements, where they exist

Without pensions ... many households and communities would collapse. —South Africa 1998

If widows are elderly, pensions can be a vital source of income, not only for the widow, but also, through multiplier effects, for the community in which she lives. A South African PPA notes "Without pensions, it was apparent that many households and communities would collapse. Pensions are shared by households and communities and are used to invest in the development of household assets, and their utilization. Moreover, pensions are very frequently a primary source of support for grandchildren, with the pensioner [providing childcare] in the absence of the child's parents. Pensions also help to make old people secure in the family (or enable them to leave households if they so choose). As such, they give the elderly some measure of control over their own lives" (South Africa 1998).

In a few cases there are even direct entitlements for widows. "The collective welfare fund is for taking care of the five-guarantee households, that is, the aged, the infirm, old widows and widowers, and orphans with five types of help (food, clothing, medical care, housing, and burial expenses), and an allowance for especially poor households, and so on" (China 1997).

Yet the state, in general, does not directly target social safety nets to widows. In some cases widows have the option of accessing community and household entitlements:

> Widows and the elderly have a respected place in Pakistani society and those who are part of a social network are afforded some degree of support and care. In return they provide help with childcare, domestic tasks, and income generating activities. Nevertheless, support is usually extended by people who are themselves deprived, with very little—or nothing—to spare ... Despite widows being a locus of most social safety-net programs, on the whole the problems of the elderly have not been given high priority by the social sectors, and widows are not necessarily among the elderly. —Pakistan 1993

They return to their parents' home

> Even her father hesitates in welcoming her because she cannot inherit anything from the family. —Tanzania 1997

The extent to which a widow can expect her family to provide support after her husband's death depends on the culture. In Eastern Europe and the former Soviet Union this is mentioned much less than in other parts of the developing world. In Sub-Saharan Africa where the kinship networks otherwise serve as social safety nets, widows are not included in their scope. In Kenya, for example, widows report that, since they would not be welcome in their father's homes, they often just went to the nearest town, eking out a living, often moving in and out of prostitution (Kenya 1996). In Tanzania women say, "It is tragic for women, because when she comes back with nothing, even her father hesitates in welcoming her because she cannot inherit anything from the family. A divorced or separated family will be buried at the church compound, not on her father's farm. In some areas they bury her at the boundary of the farm, as she has no place in the farm. The farm is for her son" (Tanzania 1997).

They migrate

> I have been everywhere, carrying these children with my teeth.
> —South Africa 1998

Given the relative unavailability of socially acceptable work for widows living in rural areas, many widows become migrants, heading for urban zones. This makes them potentially more vulnerable; while kinship networks may extend into urban areas, often they do not. One elderly widow says, "Oh, in those years [after being evicted from a farm] I was tossed around, getting knocks here and there. I have been everywhere, carrying these children with my teeth. I moved toward the coast to a place near Port Alfred. I sought some way of supporting myself by working for some sort of whites in the area, spending a year here, two or so there, and another one elsewhere. I then came back to Manly Flats to work on a chicory form, but then had to join my daughters in Grahamstown because the children with me found the farm work exhausting" (South Africa 1998).

They become sex workers

> *After the death of my husband, I tried to make money in different ways, but prostitution was the most cost-effective.*
> —Widow with two children, Macedonia 1998

In order to generate an income some widows find work as sex workers. Given the risk of disease and the social stigma attached to the work, this is generally seen as a last resort coping strategy for widows and for poor women. In Cameroon, "Two main reasons were given for the high rate of prostitution: (a) high unemployment, and (b) retrenchments and massive salary cuts. ...Commercial sex workers interviewed in Yaounde and Douala confirmed this. In East Province teenage girls and women out of general employment would say in despair, 'We have food to sell, but no one will buy [it]. Those that try to buy, pay cheaply for it [so] that it is no longer worth the effort to farm. In the face of this double bind, what else is there left for a woman to sell?'" (Cameroon 1995).

Conclusion

These findings suggest four areas where policy changes could improve the lives and livelihoods of widows and their families: (1) enforced property rights; (2) employment opportunities; (3) improved safety nets; and (4) community level interventions.

Enforcing property rights challenges the economic basis for the exclusion of widows. If widows own resources, others are more likely to find reasons to support them and work with them. Such social and economic assets also provide a better guarantee against future risks.

Employment opportunities are essential. Widows find themselves discriminated against in the employment market, and are forced into the informal sector, which pays less and is more insecure. In Bangladesh one of the most important priorities for all women is the opportunity to work. It is therefore essential to remove discrimination against widows and women more generally in the formal market, and especially to improve conditions in the informal sector into which most poor women are thrown. Assistance with self-employment opportunities is especially valuable, as it would ease their cash flow, give them enhanced social status, provide them with psychological security, help them to send their children to school, and enable them to access health care. Many women express the view that they are not looking for charity, but looking for employment opportunities. This way they will not have to ask or beg for any outside assistance (Bangladesh 1996).

State- and community-funded safety nets can provide widows with a modicum of security. Baseline security is necessary if widow-headed households are to take the risks necessary for long-term economic improvements. These safety nets should work to ensure that widows have access to the opportunities and freedom necessary to get out of poverty and to redefine their role in society.

Interventions at the community level are needed, given the persistence of social norms, to address some of the social and economic pressures that widows face. The need for direct assistance emerges strongly in these PPAs. Community-based programs that bring widows together in economic and social solidarity can transform their lives.

Chapter 7

Conclusions:
The Way Forward

*Tell the officials in the city that the money
meant for the poor never reaches us. If they
want to give assistance, they must give it directly
to us and not through those men.*

—A poor woman, Pakistan 1993

The central story of this book is about the tenacity of social norms, the unequal distribution of power, and the indomitable spirit of poor people. Despite the hard work of the poor themselves, the commitment of thousands of dedicated people within developing countries and international development agencies, and billions of dollars spent by national governments and international development organizations, there are more poor people today than there were at the beginning of the decade. Fifty-six percent of the world's population is currently poor: 1.2 billion people live on less than $1 a day and 2.8 billion live on $2 a day.[1] For the vast majority of the poor, development programs, however well intentioned, seem ineffective and irrelevant. There are of course examples of programs that work—pockets of excellence—but their impact is modest indeed in the face of the huge scale of the poverty problem.

"Although there is widespread disappointment with the government's performance, communities have not concluded that it has no role in development. Rather, they point to the need for change in responsibilities, under which money would be channeled to communities as implementers, with government providing technical assistance and supervision" (Nigeria 1996). The core message from poor people is a plea for direct assistance to them, for support to their organizations so they can negotiate directly with governments, NGOs, and traders without exploitative and corrupt "middlemen." They want governments and NGOs to be accountable to them. This requires systemic change. How this can be accomplished is the central challenge that confronts us at the dawn of the twenty-first century.

This final chapter is not a blueprint for action. Rather it suggests directions for change that need to be further developed by those engaged in making a difference in poor people's lives. The first section briefly discusses the power of institutions and social norms and recapitulates key findings from the PPA analyses. The second section identifies four elements of a strategy for change.

Institutions and Power

We poor people are invisible to others. Just as blind people cannot see, they cannot see us. —Pakistan 1993

People now place their hopes in God, since the government is no longer involved in such matters. —Armenia 1995

Sen coined the term "economic and social regress" to describe increased destitution and decreased well-being among poor groups in an age of unprecedented global prosperity (Sen 1993). The stark reality of this regress is given form and context throughout the narratives in the PPAs. Social norms and institutions are the key obstacles faced by poor women and men as they attempt to eke out a living against the odds. Poor people's experiences demonstrate again and again that informal rules or social norms are deeply embedded in society, and that the rules in use invariably override formal rules.

It is precisely because social norms are deeply embedded that change in one part of a social system cannot bring about systemic changes. In fact, a change in one part of a system merely creates resistance in the system until "order" is restored. This phenomenon is evident in all kinds of social systems, from the household to the nation state.

Poor people's experiences reflect fundamental inequities in power among different social groups, and the lack of bridges or horizontal linkages between those more powerful and those less powerful. It is no surprise that in this institutional environment the experiences of poor people are characterized by the lack of power and by voicelessness. In these circumstances promotion of voice and empowerment of poor people become the central tasks of development policies and agencies.

Findings

This section highlights eight findings that emerge from the content analyses of 81 Participatory Poverty Assessments (PPAs) conducted in 50 countries. Whether the topic was poverty, institutions, or gender relations, the process did not start with a presumed set of answers—the patterns emerged through objective analysis of poor people's descriptions of their realities.

Powerlessness and Poverty

> *Poverty is humiliation, the sense of being dependent, and of being forced to accept rudeness, insults, and indifference when we seek help.* —Latvia 1998

Poor people—including the newly impoverished in Eastern Europe, Central Asia, and the former Soviet Union—describe poverty as the lack of food and assets, the powerlessness that stems from dependency on others, and the helplessness to protect themselves from exploitation and abuse because of their dependence on the same groups for survival. Lack of food and unemployment are mentioned as key problems almost everywhere. The rich are defined as those with only one job, while the poor are rich in many dangerous jobs (Pakistan 1996, South Africa 1998). In rural Sub-Saharan Africa and Asia the poor are defined as those who have to sell their produce at low prices to the rich because they need immediate cash and lack storage facilities, and who later are obliged to buy it back at high prices. They are also those who work long hours for low wages because they have no bargaining power. Agricultural wage laborers are seen as the most exploited, often trapped in intergenerational debt. Poor people say that they are treated with rudeness, and experience deep humiliation in their interactions with both the state and with their employers. In Georgia people equate poverty with the lack of freedom—they feel enslaved by their crushing daily burdens, by depression, and by fear of what the future will bring (Georgia 1997).

Our analysis of definitions of poverty reveals that these psychological dimensions are central to poor people's definitions of poverty. Tranquility and peacefulness are important to poor people, even when poverty does not decrease (Guatemala 1997b). Maintaining social traditions, hospitality, reciprocity, rituals, and festivals is central to poor people's self-definitions as humans, despite dehumanizing economic and environmental realities. *"Without these simple humane signs of solidarity, our lives would be unbearable,"* says a poor woman in Ukraine (1996).

The lack of basic infrastructure—particularly roads, transportation, and water—is seen as a defining characteristic of poverty. *"Where a road passes, development follows right on its heels,"* says an old man in Cameroon (1995). Roads and transportation both increase physical and social connectedness and increase prices obtained for crops and products. Roads—even roads to the next village—are seen as expanding people's options, increasing their negotiating power, and increasing their access to markets and services. Access to clean drinking water and water for irrigation frequently emerges as a characteristic difference between the poor and the rich.

Illness is dreaded all over the world. Because poor people live on what they earn from their daily labor, with few cash or other reserves, severe illness can throw a whole family into destitution. *"If you don't have money today, your disease will take you to your grave,"* says an old man in Ghana (1995a). Medical fees, transport costs, the need to bribe health staff to receive treatment, and the humiliation of putting up with rude and callous behavior emerge as major problems throughout the world. In the Philippines a young mother who did not have access to a faraway clinic found herself *"holding and singing lullabies to my baby until she died in my arms"* (Philippines 1999). In Vietnam a poor woman says that the death of one person allows the others to live, while in Central and Eastern Europe poor people say that they have to choose between spending money on medical services that may not cure the patient, and spending it on burial expenses. In Georgia residents in one area have a new saying: *"The sick do not have the right to live"* (Georgia 1997).

Literacy is universally valued as a means to survive, to avoid exploitation, and to maintain mobility. *"I am illiterate, I am like a blind person,"* says a poor mother in Pakistan (1993). However, education, even primary education, receives mixed reviews in many countries, including those in Eastern Europe and the former Soviet Union. While poor people value education, official and unofficial spending required even for so-called "free" primary education is considered high, and its potential returns low. People speak of absent teachers, low teacher motivation and skills, contributions required from the families—such as chalk, heating fuel, and gifts—and costs related to school uniforms, textbooks, and transportation. In addition, many poor parents and children calculate that in a tight economy and corrupt society education does not lead to jobs. *"Getting a job has nothing to do with what you learn in school"* (Uganda 1998).

Poor people speak extensively of the important role of assets in reducing their vulnerability. There are strong gender differences: poor women in most countries have less access to assets than do men. These include physical assets, particularly land and housing; human assets, such as health and entrepreneurial skills; social assets or social networks; and environmental assets. In the absence of personal savings or state-provided assistance, social relations are poor people's only social insurance. Poor people also highlight their greater vulnerability to both seasonal and catastrophic environmental shocks and to increased social strife. Physical vulnerability—the fear of physical and sexual assault—is a concern expressed by poor women in many countries.

This combination of limited assets and voice results in poor people feeling powerless to defend themselves and their families. Poor women dependent on collection of nontimber forest products report shrinking resources due to unsustainable clear-cutting of trees and their inability to stop the large-scale felling. *"Little by little the environment is dying and people don't understand that the problem comes from the fact that man is killing the environment,"* says a poor mother of seven children in Guatemala (1997b).

Relations within the Household

He scolded her and physically assaulted her for not preparing his meal. —Bangladesh 1996

Many poor households are stressed and crumbling, but gender norms and inequity remain intact both within the household and in institutions of society. The household is the fundamental building block of society, and the place where individuals confront basic livelihood concerns, norms, values, power, and privilege. Men's identity and roles are associated with being the breadwinner and the rule-maker, and women's identity and roles are associated with being the caregiver of the family. Social norms still support men's authority, and indeed men's right, to beat women, and social norms still dictate that women suffer in silence. While many households manage to survive intact, many are crumbling under the weight of social, political, and economic dislocations. However, the responses of men and women to these dislocations are dramatically different. Many men are collapsing, falling into domestic abuse and violence, turning to alcohol and drugs, or abandoning their families. Women, on the other hand, seem to swallow their pride and hit the streets to do demeaning jobs to bring food to the family table. "*Rather than suffering from poverty, we should better go sweep up the garbage in other people's houses*" (Moldova 1997).

Faced with discrimination in the labor market, including age discrimination and a lack of opportunities in the formal sector, women have entered the informal market in large numbers, thereby exposing themselves to additional risk. Women's increased income is not necessarily empowering them. "*Men own everything because when they were born they just found it like that*" (Tanzania 1997). Women in many countries are still treated as legal minors regarding ownership of land and property. In times of trouble, "*The first thing to be sold is invariably women's jewelry*" (Pakistan 1993). The death of the husband often leaves widows destitute.

Relations with the State

A person remains unprotected; he is oppressed by a feeling of being humiliated, beaten, insulted, and robbed.
—Ukraine 1996

"*Nobody wants you to come with empty hands*" (Macedonia 1998). Poor people experience the state as ineffective, irrelevant, and corrupt. While they appreciate the importance of government-provided services, poor people experience corruption in every part of their daily lives. "*If the government passes a loan of Rs.10,000 only half of it reaches the beneficiary. The rest is taken away by the government people. If we make a hut, the men from the Forest Department will start harassing us for money, asking from where we got the wood and saying the wood belongs to the Forest Department and so on*" (India 1997d). In health, education, finance, the distribution of water, land, and seeds, the availability of pensions and unemployment benefits, and even the distribution of relief during emergencies, states are often experienced as corrupt, callous, and uncaring. *"The poor are those who suffer. Because in our country there are resources. The authorities don't seem to see poor people. Everything about the poor is despised, and above all poverty is despised"* (Brazil 1995).

Lack of information and the need for documents, which state officials make difficult to obtain, limit poor people's access to state-provided services. Institutional practices reflect gender norms, making it difficult for women and girls to access education, health care, loans, and property. Women's access is further limited by the fact that many programs target heads of households, invariably presumed to be men. To qualify, women need documents issued only to men. In Ukraine the unemployed say that the *"humiliation experienced at the unemployment office is designed to chase the unemployed away"* (Ukraine 1996). In Kenya men, women, and youths say that they are "treated worse than dogs" at the health clinic (Kenya 1996). In many countries of Eastern Europe and the former Soviet Union privatization is equated with theft (Georgia 1997). In Thailand poor people say, *"It was the rich who benefited from the boom ... but we the poor pay the price of the crisis"* (Thailand 1998).

Relations with the Elite

> The leaders have the power, but they have no interest in the community. —Venezuela 1998

The local elite and local leaders act as effective gatekeepers to government-provided assistance, either diverting resources to their own use or further deepening their power over the poor by becoming the resource distributors. Poor people speak about collusion between local officials and the local elite. In Panama people say, *"The community has no voice"* (Panama 1998). In Eastern Europe and the former Soviet Union people report an increase in patronage ties, and say that without such protectors survival would be difficult. In India the *Panchayat Raj*—with authority and resources devolved to the village council—despite problems, is viewed as breaking the hold of local elites in some areas, although caste-based organizations remain strong in other areas, as does bonded labor (India 1998d). Despite obvious wrong-doings and excesses by the elite, without a secure means of livelihood and access to justice the poor remain silent witnesses.

Cooperation across class and caste occurs primarily when a problem affects the rich just as much as the poor, such as when floods threaten, or when a road must be built to reduce isolation.

Relations with NGOs

> *Even the nongovernment initiatives have at best provided*
> *marginal access to Gandas [tribal people].* —India 1997c

NGOs have limited presence and outreach. Where they are present NGOs are often praised as the only groups concerned about poor people. In the absence of state services, they have become important providers of basic services and charity to poor people. In many places NGOs are clearly more trusted than the government. However there are also accounts of NGO ineffectiveness, irrelevance, and favoritism. In Togo "briefcase NGOs" affect the credibility of all NGOs. In Bangladesh the urban poor are upset with NGOs because *"NGOs promise much and do little"* (Bangladesh 1996). Poor people in many countries lack information about NGO activities in their areas. NGOs also suffer from the "tarmac bias" (that is, they work most frequently with the poor who live close to roads), despite their best intentions to reach the poorest.

Some of the problems experienced by NGOs are due to uncertain and short-term funding and limited capacities. Some NGOs involved with delivering services financed by international organizations are criticized for "dispensing financing with little local participation" (Senegal 1995). The potential of NGOs to support poor people's organizations, function as independent watchdogs, and keep the state accountable at the local level remains largely unfulfilled.

Networks and Associations of the Poor

> *These days nobody gets enough fish, so it's no use to expect*
> *your brother or neighbor to help you out; he doesn't have*
> *enough either.* —Benin 1994

Informal networks and associations of poor people are common in rural and urban communities. In the absence of connections to state resources these informal networks become critical for survival; they become poor people's lifelines. *"If it hadn't been for help from the village, the children would have died of hunger"* (Armenia 1995). Poor people also recognize the limits of their networks. *"If one man is hungry and doesn't have any food, how can he help another hungry man?"* (Pakistan 1993). In times of shared economic stress the resources of these networks are further depleted. Rich people's networks are more cohesive and cut across village boundaries as well as social, economic, and political activities. Poor people's networks in many parts of the world do not transcend community boundaries and rarely enter the political domain.

There are important differences between men's and women's networks. Men are more embedded in formal patron-client relations, whereas women, lacking access to formal systems, invest heavily in social relations with other women, both for social solidarity and for informal sharing of limited resources. Most of these women's organizations remain disconnected from any external resources. Associations are stronger in rural than in urban areas, where they are more likely to be organized around occupational groups.

Community-based organizations provide basic services in the community and build social cohesion. Women are generally excluded from community-level decisionmaking. *"Men have a better place in the community"* (El Salvador 1997). Some community-based organizations reflect local power relations and often involve fees. A poor woman in Togo says, *"If you are as poor as I am and can't contribute regularly, you can't participate"* (Togo 1996). Given economic stress, the introduction of fees for services forces poor people to make choices. With limited resources they very often try to continue their membership in burial societies, to ensure they will be taken care of, at least in death. Burial societies are found worldwide, particularly in Sub-Saharan Africa and in Eastern Europe and the former Soviet Union. *"They will not put you free of charge even in a grave,"* says a pensioner in Macedonia (1998).

Organizations of the Poor

There is surprisingly little mention of organizations of poor people that cut across communities or that have succeeded in accessing resources that were meant for the poor. In Ecuador, over a 20-year period, federations of indigenous organizations have emerged at regional and national levels and now work with governments on local and national policy issues, including land reform. In some places in India NGOs are involved in organizing women's credit groups and work groups to help purchase raw materials in bulk, and eventually to raise awareness and to mobilize women around their rights and economic activities (India 1997a). In Vietnam NGOs are involved in helping set up poor people's production organizations to change poor people's bargaining power. In Nigeria a widow's organization started by a Catholic priest has changed widows' lives dramatically in a society where widows had been scorned, hated, and were vulnerable to assault. The reports are relatively silent on collective movements and on poor people's cooperatives, trade unions, or health associations.

Social Fragmentation

> *Respect is lost. If someone wants to do something always someone steals the money.* —Panama 1998

Poor people report living with increased crime, corruption, violence, and insecurity amidst declining social cohesion. They feel helpless against the forces of change. Many poor people report a decline in economic opportunities, and report that new opportunities are only available to those with connections. This perpetuates vicious cycles of exclusion. Even in rural areas people feel that sharing and reciprocity have declined as people struggle for survival. "*What is mine is mine, and what is yours is yours, in this community people are very stingy*" (Ecuador 1996a). In the Republic of Yemen people feel that businessmen are betraying traditional solidarity (Republic of Yemen 1999). In country after country—Ethiopia, Jamaica, Kenya, South Africa, and Thailand—poor people draw strong links between crime and unemployment. This is most extreme in the countries of the former Soviet Union. People report that seedlings planted in the ground are stolen overnight (Ukraine 1996), that violence has become so pervasive that "the streets have invaded the classroom" (Armenia 1996), and that brutal attacks on both men and women are common because police protection is no longer available (Moldova 1997).

Few poor people feel they have access to justice and the police, and officials and criminals are often accused of being in collusion. Instead of being seen as protectors, where they are mentioned at all the police are largely viewed negatively for their indifference, for their role in intimidation, corruption, and crime, and for their ability to instill fear, to harass, and to brutalize. "*The police support their families by just showing their shadow*" (Armenia 1995).

Elements of a Strategy for Change

Poor people's encounters with institutions should provide opportunities and essential services. Instead — and despite the efforts of many committed individuals within governments, civil society, and international organizations that work in partnership with poor people — these institutional encounters often leave poor people disempowered, excluded, and silenced. This institutional crisis, combined with so many well-intentioned efforts to reduce poverty, has created the opportunity for rethinking development strategies to reach the poor.

Poor people do not want charity but opportunity. In Macedonia, 95 percent of poor young people see employment as the only way out. A young man said, "*I don't want to be servant to no one for 3,000 denars. I do not want to be humiliated*" (Macedonia 1998). Any changes must be supported by economic growth that creates livelihood opportunities for the poor. While further research and evaluations are needed to discern which programs work best in which institutional environment, poor people's voices urge us to act now, to innovate, and to learn by doing. Changing poor people's lives for the better is inherently complex because poverty is never caused by the lack of only one thing. It involves many interrelated elements, and without shifts in power relations poor people cannot access or shape the resources aimed to assist them. A strategy for change must have four critical elements. It must:

1. Start with poor people's realities
2. Invest in the organizational capacity of the poor
3. Change social norms
4. Support development entrepreneurs

1. Start with Poor People's Realities

When development interventions and government performance are approached from the perspectives and experiences of poor people, the world of development assistance looks different. The challenge for outsiders is to look at the world through the eyes and spirit of the poor, to start with poor people's realities and then trace upwards and outwards to identify, and then make, the changes needed to impact poor people's lives. When we view the world from the perspectives of poor people six areas call for action.

Poverty diagnosis by the poor and expansion of poverty measures

Poor people's definitions of poverty do not only include economic well-being, but also include vulnerability, powerlessness, the shame of dependency, and social isolation. The degree of dependency emerges as a classification criterion of poverty. In fact, poor people do not talk much about income, but focus instead on the range of assets they use in coping with their vulnerability and in overcoming shocks. What you measure is what you see. Poor people's experiences urge an expansion of poverty measures to include voice and power, vulnerability, and accumulation of assets.

Poor women and men have detailed knowledge and have context-specific criteria about who is poor and not poor. This knowledge should be used in programs that require identifying poor people. The participatory methods to measure poverty such as those used in many of the PPAs can become a powerful complement to household surveys to monitor and evaluate change over time. Sampling frameworks will need to be clearly defined and merged where possible.

Future PPAs need to adopt an explicitly institutional approach to understanding poverty from the perspective of poor people. It is also critical to adopt a gendered approach in the PPAs. This will bring about a better understanding of how men's and women's lives are embedded in institutions—from the household to national levels—in specific contexts, and how this differentially affects their freedom to pursue a life with dignity. Much more work needs to be done to understand the attitudes, interests, and values of service providers and the local elite in order to design strategies that are more likely to be supported by them or not immediately hijacked.

Informal livelihoods

Concern about insecure livelihoods is widespread. Most of the poor who are not involved in agriculture acquire their livelihoods in the informal sector, yet most government and international attention is focused on formal employment opportunities. There appear to be no large-scale programs of assistance that focus on the needs of poor women and men in the informal sector. There are very few trade unions of the poor that focus on the problems of poor workers in the informal sector. Much can be learned from the work of the Self-Employed Women's Association (SEWA) in India, which focuses on organizing women in informal employment and is experimenting with schemes to provide health and life insurance to workers in the unregulated sector of the economy.[2]

Health protection

Health is affected by many factors, including people's homes and environments. Examples of ill health throwing poor families into destitution emerge all over the world and cannot be ignored. Programs that provide poor people with health coverage and yet do not drain the national treasury are desperately needed.[3] While domestic violence has many causes, health-care staff has an important role to play in care, documentation, and support of women who have been physically abused. The World Health Organization now recognizes gender-based violence as a major public health concern.[4] The spread of HIV/AIDS (particularly in Africa), and the silence and stigma associated with the disease, need to be broken for effective prevention and treatment.

Lack of infrastructure

Lack of infrastructure such as roads, transport, and water emerges as a characteristic that distinguishes the poor from the rich. From the perspective of poor people the order of improvements in roads needs to be reversed, with much more emphasis on roads connecting villages to each other and the nearest town. In the domestic water supply sector much innovative work has been undertaken around the world, and this needs to expand.[5] Private toilet areas to prevent assault and harassment of women emerge as a high priority in Bangladesh and Pakistan.

Literacy and skills

Poor people give high priority to literacy and skills acquisition and the value of education, but are interested in education only when their immediate survival needs have been met. There are exceptions. For example, in Kenya parents often express a willingness to sell everything they have to ensure children get through at least primary education (Kenya 1996). But in many countries poor people will invest in education only if the costs are lowered, if the structure and quality are relevant to their lives, and if they feel that the chances of finding employment are fair. The hidden and not-so-hidden costs of education are too high for many poor parents. Innovations such as scholarship programs for poor girls are radically changing the decision to send girls to schools in a few countries. New thinking is required to bring basic education within the reach of all poor children.[6]

Lawlessness and corruption

Poor people feel powerless to change the behavior and actions of state officials, the police, and the local elite. Corruption and a decline in personal safety are real and widespread issues for poor people. Since these issues cannot be dealt with in isolation, systemic interventions are needed to create local government councils that are accountable to poor people, an accountable police force that protects rather than harms the poor, justice systems, and legal aid within the reach of poor men and women. Local-level accountability can be increased through public access to information. Innovative use of information technology to connect poor people to markets, the media, and to each other can help shift the bargaining power of poor people vis-à-vis their governments, civil society, and the private sector.

2. Invest in the Organizational Capacity of the Poor

Organizational capacity or social capital has rightly been called the asset of the poor, yet our analysis shows that this asset is on the decline, eroded by economic pressure and by economic and physical dislocation. The analysis also shows that, given the pressures to survive and their dependency on the rich, the networks of poor people become atomized and serve a survival and social function rather than a transformational or political function. There are relatively few poor people's organizations that have the bargaining power to negotiate with local elites and participate in local, national, or global governance and decisions.

It is only when poor people can draw on the strength of their numbers and organize themselves that their voices can be heard, that they can negotiate with buyers and sellers, and that they can participate effectively in local governance and in government programs intended to serve them. Much remains to be done to support organizations of the poor at the local level. Developing organizational capacity of the poor is a long-term process that may take 10 to 20 years. It requires long-term financing, trust, and flexibility. This has to be done with care, because it is very easy for impatient outsiders to take over local processes and leadership. Taking a stand is risky. When funding is through intermediary organizations of uncertain duration, the poor and their families who take action bear all the risk.

Grassroots coalitions of poor people's organizations and intermediary organizations are needed to ensure that poor people's voices and interests are reflected in decisionmaking beyond the community. Information technology has a critical role to play. Global, regional, and national policy networks of poor people's organizations are crucial to influence decisions being made outside the community but that have an important bearing on the lives of poor women and men.

Implement community-driven approaches

Many countries are introducing radical decentralization in attempts to create accountable and responsive governments. Governments, international development agencies, NGOs, and the private sector need to support community-driven development strategies on a large scale. Community-driven development involves giving community groups authority and control over funds, resource allocation, and decisionmaking. This radically changes the incentives of service providers to be accountable to community groups that are representative of poor men and women. Neither radical decentralization nor community-driven development will work effectively, however, unless poor people's organizational capacity is strengthened for effective bargaining, and methods are found to encourage the rich to support the poor—or at least to minimize their negative impact on poor communities.

Developing local organizational capacity requires facilitators who work with poor men and women to inform them about programs, rules, and assets. Poor people need organization to demand local-level transparency and accountability, a process that may also require protection from punitive actions taken by the local elite. So far, governments and most development assistance have focused on the rules, resources, and capacities of the formal systems of governance, and not on mechanisms to build the capacity of poor women and men to participate in local governance and to demand local-level transparency and accountability. There are promising examples of programs that invest in local organizers and organizations chosen by the poor that are unlocking information about budgets and wages and putting them in the public domain, and that are developing government procedures that deliver timely assistance without distorting local priorities.[7] An independent press that investigates local governance and prints information about wrongdoing can create pressure for accountability and good local governance.

Partnership with civil society

NGOs and civil society can play key roles in building up organizations of poor people and in serving a watchdog function. To be effective, NGO monitors accountable to poor people need long-term funding, media support, and space to develop. Local and national laws and finances must support this effort. In any environment it is easy for well-intentioned, powerful, and articulate outsiders to take over, thereby diminishing the very local-level processes they want to support. Organizing among the poor, letting leadership among the poor emerge, and acting on local-level priorities are all processes that have their own rhythm. They require patience, listening, and strong norms of service and humility. All are difficult for highly educated outsiders to practice.

3. Change Social Norms

A norm is a shared expectation of behavior that connotes what is considered desirable and appropriate (Marshall 1994). Poor people's interactions with landlords, traders, moneylenders, state officials, local council members, local elite, politicians—and women's encounters within the household with husbands, mothers-in-law, other relatives, other women, traders, financiers, police, educators, and employers—are not governed primarily by the laws of the land, but by the social norms that dictate who has what value in each interaction. These pervasive and interconnected norms hold the entire edifice of society and governance in place. Changed social norms can lead to sustained change in behavior, which is then reinforced by formal rules and laws. Changes in social norms about cigarette smoking in the United States in the last few years are a case in point. In contrast, dowry, domestic abuse, and bonded labor persist in India despite changes in laws because social norms support these practices. Laws create the space for change, but social practice does not change without supportive changes in social norms.

Change in social norms means changing mindsets, combining the power of the individual and the power of the institution, and facing up to pervasive gender inequalities.

Changing the mindset

After 50 years of development assistance it is clear that policies and projects are not implemented in a vacuum. They are formulated by bureaucrats and planners and implemented by people with a particular mindset in a particular culture and with particular social norms, reinforced by metaphors, stories, proverbs, and films. The power of social norms has been overlooked. The persistence of untouchability in India, female genital mutilation in Africa, and theft of state resources with impunity all suggest that technocratic fixes will continue to be defeated by social norms. Similarly, if officials and the political elite believe that poor people are lazy, stupid, undeserving, and pampered, poverty policies are unlikely to be formulated or implemented in ways that serve poor people. If it is assumed that poor people lack agency and cannot make wise spending decisions, policymakers are unlikely to seek the poor as partners in their own development programs.

Changing the mindset of service providers, the elite, and the press is not simple, but it can be done. Much can be learned from the market penetration strategies of the private sector. Development communication still remains a stepchild in poverty reduction strategies, in terms of both the resources invested and the technical expertise brought to bear.

Power of the personal

Communism was a societal experiment to create a more equitable world. It failed because human nature eventually subverted even the power of a coercive state. Development assistance, with its focus on the enormity of the problem, has lost sight of the power of the individual. Individuals in interaction with other individuals bring about change, one step at a time. Hence individual commitment, values, and behavior matter, and can be the most potent sources of change as committed individuals interconnect. Without tapping into the power of the individual, or personal, the best-intended plans go astray. With change in personal commitment, small miracles happen as people start to use their skills, positions, and power for the collective good.[8]

Power of the personal, combined with the institutional

To bring about large-scale change will require the power of both individual and institutional action, but attention has first to be given to the personal over the institutional. The evidence shows clearly that rules in use about bribery and behavior subvert formal rules that promote accountability and public commitment. India, for example, has progressive laws, but protection under these laws is nearly impossible, not only for the poor, but even for the well-to-do. If personal norms change in favor of the poor and their rights, clever minds will just as creatively subvert outdated rules and laws to support resource allocation decisions that serve the poor.

The best strategy is to combine the power of the personal with the power of the right institutional incentives in a reformed state. Much has already been written about reform of the state.[9] Examples abound—such as the design of irrigation departments in water resource management, rural roads and markets, community-based education and health clinics, social investment, and community-driven projects. Everywhere, while case studies highlight the institutional, there are always individuals who set personal examples and lead the way to reform. Such champions cannot be created or programmed by development assistance, and their critical role remains unsung.

Facing gender inequities

Gender inequality is learned in every household around the world. Expectations about gender roles are internalized by both men and women from early childhood, and become such a deep part of the psyche that they are resistant to change and hard to overcome. The very way in which the PPA studies were conducted reflects the fact that development still follows a *women in development* (about women) approach rather than a gendered (about women and men) approach. The PPAs reflect remarkably little knowledge about men's lives and quite extensive information about women's lives.[10] Since men's and women's lives are intertwined, changing women's lives means changing men's internalized norms about women and their behavior toward women. Only then will equitable laws be put into practice. To enable both men and women to make the necessary transitions with fewer traumas, innovative approaches are needed to assist men with their fears of "emasculation and social impotence" when women step outside the house.

All poverty reduction programs impact gender relations within the household, and should include awareness-raising and psychological support to both men and women, together and separately, to navigate the difficult path of changing power relations. A poor woman in Uganda suggests one possibility: "*Women and men should sit at a round table to discuss their rights. Unless men are included, these things will not be understood. It will be like bathing in mud again*" (Uganda 1998).

4. Support Development Entrepreneurs

New alliances must be formed between the state and the poor, civil society, and international development agencies. The lessons from the literature on social movements, including such concepts as new political opportunity structure and political allies, need to be applied to transforming defunct bureaucracies.[11] Raka Ray has recently added the concept of political fields, "the socially constructed environment within which organizations are embedded to which organizations constantly respond" (Ray and Kortweg 1999: 21–36). This environment includes all parties, the media, religious organizations, and pressure groups. Social movements bring about realignments of power, change social norms, and create new opportunity structures. Out of this will emerge a mindset that applies "liberalization not only for the rich but also the poor" (Bhatt 1998).[12] In Ethiopia, for example, even though free-market policies have been adopted, poor people in some rural areas note that regulation of certain types of trade has made the search for a livelihood more difficult. This includes bans on firewood cutting, street trading, and on trading in the traditional market (Ethiopia 1998).

Development leaders or entrepreneurs are found at all levels in society, from the woman in a village who takes a stand on behalf of her neighbor being beaten up by her husband, to technical innovators in electrical companies. Their social energy creates momentum for an improved quality of life for poor people.[13] Yet their scale and impact remains limited. Venture capital funds are needed for development entrepreneurs.

Recent research by Alan Khazei and Vanessa Kirsch based on interviews with more than 350 social entrepreneurs, business people and government leaders in 20 countries came to the same conclusions: limited impact and problems of scaling up. They conclude that there is plenty of start-up money for nonprofit work and funds for really big established groups, but almost no money for those in-between groups that need bridge money to survive and grow. They point to the need for a second-stage capital market for nonprofits. Since their research Kirsch has created a venture capital fund to finance carefully selected organizations that will be nurtured and monitored using "balanced scorecards" and dropped if they do not post measurable social returns (Dahle 1999). Venture capital funds for poor youth are also being tested in India.[14]

Find allies within and outside the system

Allies are needed to initiate change in social norms, from both within the system and outside it. Within the system development entrepreneurs are needed to initiate change in behavior and actions. The power of the media, of news stories, advertisements, music, and theatre is needed to start a new conversation about a just and equitable society for all, and to change specific social norms about the poor, gender, and corruption. For example, to fight corruption it is critical to re-establish honesty—not corruption—as the norm. Faith-based organizations have a particularly important role to play in the struggle against corruption, in giving voice to the poor, and in building social cohesion.

Create new heroes

The paradox of large organizations is that the corrupt and the honest live side by side.[15] The PPA studies also mention cases of honest officials or caring local leaders and elite surrounded by corruption. The challenge is to recognize, support, and empower these individuals so that their social energy is more effectively harnessed for the collective good. At the same time, we need to broaden and deepen our understanding of the institutional environments that create and reproduce both corruption and commitment, so that committed individuals can be supported at the same time that institutional environments are redesigned. Only then will it be possible to turn institutional cycles from vicious to virtuous.

Support the committed

Development assistance is geared to move large amounts of money through inefficient and frequently corrupt bureaucratic systems with little flexibility. Rules and audits are needed to keep systems accountable. Transforming a government department or ministry through social movement, on the other hand, requires empowering development entrepreneurs with authority, finances, and supportive resources to implement programs and to deliver results both in changed social norms and in services. It is equally important that these heroes be celebrated through the media, and that they become household names and new role models. Checks and balances will, of course, still be needed, with results from monitoring studies of client satisfaction made widely available.

Poor people's lives will improve by building on their priorities, realities, and networks. This will involve long-term support to civil society to facilitate the emergence of people's organizations that enhance the ability of poor men and women to share in economic growth, participate in democratic governance, ensure fair distribution of government resources, and protect themselves from exploitation. Governments have important roles to play by adopting economic and social policies that open economic opportunities for the poor, provide basic infrastructure, and protect citizenship rights. International agencies have important roles in supporting intermediaries that work directly with poor people.

The Voices of the Poor

For poor people empowerment, security, and opportunity must all be experienced at the local level. Without physical, psychological, and economic security, participation and empowerment remain meaningless slogans. Poverty is experienced at the local level, in a specific context, in a specific place, in a specific interaction. Those who plan for poverty reduction are far away. While participatory poverty assessments such as those reviewed here give us some idea about poor people's realities, the danger is that development agencies will simply continue "business as usual." When we go into poor people's homes as outsiders, poor people open their lives, their joys, and their suffering to us, and we experience their dignity, their wisdom, and their warm hospitality. It is difficult for us to practice direct reciprocity, but we can communicate their voices. Researchers in the South African PPA write: *"After we had lunch with them, they sang for us. It is really amazing how they used songs to express themselves and their thoughts, expectations, fears, and anxieties. The words of the final song were: 'Here they are, yes we agree, here they are, our visitors who were sent by the World Bank, yes, here they are, they are here to help us ... and we hope they won't forget us'"* (South Africa 1998).

Will we remember?

Notes

1. The decline in numbers is almost exclusively due to reductions in the number of poor people in East Asia, most notably in China. In South Asia the number of people in poverty has increased steadily although there was a modest decline in the share of people living in poverty. In Africa, both the share of the population in poverty and the absolute numbers of poor people increased. Africa is now the region with the largest share of people living below $1 per day. In Latin America the share of poor people remained roughly constant over the period but the number of people in poverty increased. In the countries of the former Soviet bloc, poverty rose markedly — both the share and numbers of people in poverty increased. For more detail see *Poverty Trends and Conditions*, World Bank 1999.

2. The Self-Employed Women's Association (SEWA) is a registered trade union with 250,000 women members who are self-employed vendors, home-based workers, and laborers in the informal sector. To protect these workers SEWA started the Integrated Social Security Program, the largest and most comprehensive contributory social security scheme in India, presently insuring over 32,000 female informal sector workers in India. The scheme covers health insurance, life insurance, disability insurance, and asset insurance (loss or damage to house or work equipment). SEWA works with two nationalized companies—the Life Insurance Corporation of India and the United India Insurance Company. The scheme works through risk-pooling by women who already know and can monitor each other. The scheme is financed by the interest paid on a grant provided by the Deutsche

Gesellschaft für technische Zusammenarbeit (GtZ), one-third through direct contributions by female workers, and one-third through a scheme subsidized by the government of India through the Life Insurance Corporation. The total health and asset insurance premium is rupees 60 (US$1.50) per year, and life insurance can be added for a higher premium. The coverage is rupees 3,000 for natural death, rupees 25,000 for accidental death, rupees 2,000 for lost assets, and rupees 3,000 for a lost or severely damaged house. Currently SEWA is thinking of expanding to pension plans for older workers and increasing coverage and health benefits. For more information see Srinivas (1999).

3. A health insurance scheme started by Grameen Bank is promising. Grameen Kalyan, Grameen Bank's health-care program, acts as both an insurer and health provider. The health centers are attached to the Grameen Bank centers and offer curative outpatient and door-to-door services. A center is started after thorough discussions with members. Premiums are based on a sliding scale. Health centers have recovered approximately 65 percent of costs, and already 66 percent of Grameen Bank members participate in the scheme. The annual premium in 1996 was Taka 12 (US$2.50) per family for a maximum of eight family members. As village health workers have been added to the centers' staffs, the pricing structure is currently being refined (Srinivas 1999).

4. See Lori Heise, M. Ellsberg, and M. Gottemoeller, *Ending Violence Against Women*. Population Reports, Series L, No. 111. Baltimore, John Hopkins University School of Public Health, Population Information Program, December 1999. For more information see http://www.genderhealth.org and http://www.jhuccp.org

5. See the Water and Sanitation Program, a multidonor program executed by the World Bank, searchable at www.wsp.org

6. The Indian state of Madhya Pradesh has received an amazing response from the government's offer of "a teacher and books" if the village applies for a school within 90 days of the announcement. The teachers are from the village and the school may be under a tree.

7. Recent analyses of success stories all point to long-term investment, evolving, adapting, and learning by doing (see Krishna, Uphoff, and Esman 1997; Narayan and Ebbe 1997). Recent examples of World Bank-financed community-driven programs include poverty-focused projects in Northeast Brazil, the Kecematan Development Project in Indonesia, the Uttar Pradesh Water Supply Project in India, and a Village Community Support Project in Guinea, among others.

8. Robert Chambers has written extensively about the importance of personal change. See Chambers (1997).

9. The World Bank's *World Development Report 1997* focused on the role of the state and reviewed extensive literature and experiences from around the world.

10. A computerized search for men's networks or groups yielded almost nothing, whereas a mound of paper resulted from a search for women's networks.

11. For an excellent history and review of social movements, see Tarrow 1994.

12. Speech by Ela Bhatt at the World Bank, January 1998. Ela Bhatt is the founder of SEWA, a trade union in India that serves women working in the infor-

mal sector. Her work has also led to the creation of WIEGO, a global network for "Women in Informal Employment, Globalizing and Organizing."

13. This is the motivating principle for the Ashoka Foundation, which identifies and supports individuals, leaders, and practical visionaries who have the entrepreneurial drive and creativity to transform systems to bring about large-scale change. Over 1,000 fellows have been financed in 34 countries since 1981.

14. The Bharatiya Yuva Shakti Trust (Business and Youth Starting Together) provides venture capital in the range of US$1,000, training, and mentoring to poor unemployed or underemployed youth between the ages of 18 and 35. Founded in 1991, it has spread to several Indian states and helped over 450 youth with business ideas to start up businesses. Many have not only lifted themselves out of poverty but now employ others. Even as the nonprofit trust is growing, every business start-up is provided active one-to-one mentoring by an experienced business person living in the same city.

15. Although not a new observation, this paradox was sharpened by a conversation with Norman Uphoff in June 1999.

APPENDIXES

Appendix 1: Regions and Countries of PPA Reports

REGION	COUNTRY	NUMBER OF REPORTS
Sub-Saharan Africa; and the Middle East and North Africa (subtotal = 31)	Benin	1
	Burkina Faso	1
	Cameroon	1
	Ethiopia	1
	Gabon	1
	Ghana	2
	Guinea-Bissau	1
	Kenya	2
	Madagascar	2
	Mali	2
	Niger	1
	Nigeria	3
	Rwanda	1
	Senegal	1
	South Africa	1
	Swaziland	1
	Tanzania	1
	Togo	1
	Tunisia	1
	Uganda	2
	Yemen, Republic of	2
	Zambia	2
Eastern Europe; and the former Soviet Union (subtotal = 11)	Armenia	3
	Azerbaijan	1
	Georgia	1
	Kyrgyz Republic	1
	Latvia	2
	Macedonia	1
	Moldova	1
	Ukraine	1
East Asia (subtotal = 9)	Cambodia	1
	China	1
	Indonesia	2
	Philippines	1
	Thailand	1
	Vietnam	3
Latin America and the Caribbean (subtotal = 16)	Brazil	1
	Costa Rica	1

REGION	COUNTRY	NUMBER OF REPORTS
	Ecuador	2
	El Salvador	2
	Guatemala	5
	Jamaica	1
	Mexico	1
	Nicaragua	1
	Panama	1
	Venezuela	1
South Asia	Bangladesh	1
(subtotal = 14)	India	10
	Nepal	1
	Pakistan	2
Project Totals:		81

Appendix 2: List of PPA Authors

Armenia 1995   Dudwick, Nora. 1995. "A Qualitative Assessment of the Living Standards of the Armenian Population, October 1994–March 1995." World Bank, Washington, D.C.

Armenia 1996   Gomart, Elizabeth. 1996. "Social Assessment Report on the Education and Health Sectors in Armenia." World Bank, Washington, D.C.

Armenia 1999   Bertmar, Anna. 1999. "Children's De-Institutionalization Initiative: Beneficiary Assessment of Children in Institutions." World Bank, Washington, D.C.

Azerbaijan 1997   World Bank. 1997. "Poverty Assessment." Washington, D.C.

Bangladesh 1996   UNDP (United Nations Development Programme). 1996. "UNDP's 1996 Report on Human Development in Bangladesh: A Pro-Poor Agenda—Poor People's Perspectives." Dhaka, Bangladesh.

Benin 1994   World Bank. 1994. "Toward a Poverty Alleviation Strategy." Washington, D.C.

Brazil 1995   World Bank. 1995. "A Poverty Assessment." Washington, D.C.

Burkina Faso 1994   World Bank. 1994. "Visual Participatory Poverty Assessment." Draft. Washington, D.C.

Cambodia 1998   Robb, Caroline M., M. Shivakuma, and Nil Vanna. 1998. "The Social Impacts of the Creeping Crisis in Cambodia: Perceptions of Poor Communities." World Bank, Washington, D.C.

Cameroon 1995   World Bank. 1995. "Diversity, Growth, and Poverty Reduction." Washington, D.C.

China 1997   World Bank. 1997. "Anning Valley Agricultural Development Project: Summary of a Social Assessment (Annex 10)." Washington, D.C.

Costa Rica 1997   World Bank. 1997. "Identifying the Social Needs of the Poor: An Update." Washington, D.C.

Ecuador 1996a   Hentschel, Jesko, William F. Waters, and Anna Kathryn Vandever Webb. 1996. "Rural Poverty in Ecuador—A Qualitative Assessment." Internal Document. World Bank, Washington, D.C.

Ecuador 1996b   World Bank. 1996. "Poverty Report." Washington, D.C.

El Salvador 1995   Pena, Maria Valeria Junho. 1995. "Social Assessment: El Salvador Basic Education Modernization Project." World Bank, Washington, D.C.

El Salvador 1997   Pena, Maria Valeria Junho, Kathryn Johns Swartz, Tania Salem, Miriam Abramovay, and Carlos Briones. 1997. "Stakeholder Consultation and Analysis: Second Phase of the Social Assessment for the El Salvador EDUCO Program and the Basic Education Modernization Project." World Bank, Washington, D.C.

Ethiopia 1998   World Bank. 1998. "Participatory Poverty Assessment for Ethiopia." Draft. Washington, D.C.

Gabon 1997	World Bank. 1997. "Poverty in a Rent-Based Economy." Washington, D.C.
Georgia 1997	Dudwick, Nora. 1997. "Poverty in Georgia: The Social Dimensions of Transition." World Bank, Washington, D.C
Ghana 1995a	Norton, Andy, Ellen Bortei-Doku Aryeetey, David Korboe, and D.K. Tony Dogbe. 1995. "Poverty Assessment in Ghana Using Qualitative and Participatory Research Methods." World Bank, Washington, D.C.
Ghana 1995b	World Bank. 1995. "Poverty Past, Present and Future." Washington, D.C.
Guatemala 1993	World Bank. 1993. "Guatemala Qualitative and Participatory Poverty Study, Phases I and II." Internal Situation Report. Washington, D.C.
Guatemala 1994a	Webb, Anna Kathryn Vandever. 1994. "Interim Evaluation Report: Guatemala Qualitative and Participatory Poverty Study, Phase II." Rafael Landívar University, Guatemala City, and World Bank, Washington, D.C.
Guatemala 1994b	Instituto de Investigaciones. 1994. "La Pobreza: Un Enfoque Participativo: El Caso de Guatemala." Rafael Landívar University, Guatemala City.
Guatemala 1997a	Traa-Valarezo, Ximena. 1997. "Social Assessment for the Guatemala Reconstruction and Local Development Project." World Bank, Washington, D.C.
Guatemala 1997b	Gómez, Marcela Tovar. 1997. "Perfil de los Pueblos Indígenos de Guatemala (FONAPAZ)." Internal Document. World Bank, Washington, D.C.
Guinea-Bissau 1994	World Bank. 1994. "Poverty Assessment and Social Sectors Strategy Review." Washington, D.C.
India 1997a	Centre for Community Economics and Development Consultants Society (CECOEDECON). 1997. "Report on Social Assessment for the District Poverty Initiatives Project: Baran District." Institute of Development Studies (IDS), Jaipur, India.
India 1997b	Indian Institute of Rural Management. 1997. "A Report on Findings of Fieldwork (DPIP) in Todaraisingh and Uniara Blocks of Tonk District." Indian Institute of Rural Management, Jaipur, India.
India 1997c	Reddy, S. Sudhakar, K. S. Reddy, P. Padmanabha Rao, and G. Santhana Babu. 1997. "District Poverty Initiatives Project: Strategy and Investment Plan for Poverty Alleviation in Adilabad." Centre for Economic and Social Studies, Hyderabad, India.
India 1997d	Operations Research Group. 1997. "Draft Fieldwork Report: Raisen District." Environment Planning and Coordination Organisation, Bhopal, India.
India 1997e	Operations Research Group. 1997. "Draft Fieldwork Report: Sagar District." Environment Planning and Coordination Organisation, Bhopal, India.

India 1998a	PRAXIS. 1998. "Participatory Poverty Profile Study: Bolangir District, Orissa." U.K. Department for International Development, New Delhi.
India 1998b	World Bank. 1998. "District Poverty Initiatives Project, Social Assessment Fieldwork Report: Guna District Main Report." Washington, D.C.
India 1998c	World Bank. 1998. "District Poverty Initiatives Project, Social Assessment Fieldwork Report: Rajgarh District Main Report." Washington, D.C.
India 1998d	World Bank. 1998. "District Poverty Initiatives Project, Social Assessment Field Report: Shivpuri District Main Report." Washington, D.C.
India 1998e	Kozel, Valerie, and Barbara Parker. 1998. "Poverty in Rural India: The Contribution of Qualitative Research in Policy Analysis." World Bank, Washington, D.C.
Indonesia 1998	Evers, Pieter J. 1998. "Village Governments and Their Communities: Allies or Adversaries." World Bank, Jakarta.
Indonesia 1999	Chandrakirana, Kamala. 1999. "Local Capacity and Its Implications for Development: The Case of Indonesia. A Preliminary Report: Local Level Institutions Study." World Bank, Jakarta.
Jamaica 1997	Moser, Caroline, and Jeremy Holland. 1997. "Urban Poverty and Violence in Jamaica." World Bank, Washington, D.C.
Kenya 1996	Narayan, Deepa, and David Nyamwaya. 1996. "Learning from the Poor: A Participatory Poverty Assessment in Kenya." World Bank, Washington, D.C.
Kenya 1997	Nyamwaya, David (editor). 1997. "Coping Without Coping: What Poor People Say About Poverty in Kenya." African Medical and Research Foundation and the Government of Kenya, Nairobi.
Kyrgyz Republic 1998	Scott, Kinnon, Salman Zaidi, Zhong Tong, and Dinara Djoldosheva. 1998. "Update on Poverty in the Kyrgyz Republic." World Bank, Washington, D.C.
Latvia 1997	Hofmane, L. 1997. "Report on the Qualitative Analysis Research into the Living Standards of Inhabitants in Aluksne District." World Bank, Washington, D.C.
Latvia 1998	Institute of Philosophy and Sociology. 1998. "Listening to the Poor: A Social Assessment of Poverty in Latvia." Institute of Philosophy and Sociology, Riga, Latvia.
Macedonia 1998	Institute for Sociological and Political-Legal Research. 1998. "Qualitative Analysis of the Living Standard of the Population of the Republic of Macedonia." Institute for Sociological and Political-Legal Research, Skopje, Macedonia.
Madagascar 1994	Moini-Araghi, Azadeh. 1994. "Participatory Poverty Assessment: Synthesis Report." World Bank, Washington, D.C.
Madagascar 1996	World Bank. 1996. "Poverty Assessment." Washington, D.C.
Mali 1992	World Bank. 1992. "Qualitative Study on the Demand for Education in Rural Mali." Washington, D.C.

Mali 1993	World Bank. 1993. "Assessment of Living Conditions." Washington, D.C.
Mexico 1995	Salmen, Lawrence. 1995. "The People's Voice: Mexico—Participatory Poverty Assessment." World Bank, Washington, D.C.
Moldova 1997	De Soto, Hermine G., and Nora Dudwick. 1997. "Poverty in Moldova: The Social Dimensions of Transition, June 1996–May 1997." World Bank, Washington, D.C.
Nepal 1999	South Asia Partnership Nepal. 1999. "Country Report: Nepal." Ottawa: South Asia Partnership Canada, Kathmandu.
Nicaragua 1998	Fuller, Bruce, and Magdalena Rivarola. 1998. "Nicaragua's Experiment to Decentralize Schools: Views of Parents, Teachers, and Directors." World Bank, Washington, D.C.
Niger 1996	World Bank. 1996. "Poverty Assessment: A Resilient People in a Harsh Environment." Washington, D.C.
Nigeria 1995	Todd, Dave. 1995. "Participatory Poverty Assessment." World Bank, Washington, D.C.
Nigeria 1996	World Bank. 1996. "Poverty in the Midst of Plenty: The Challenge of Growth with Inclusion." Washington, D.C.
Nigeria 1997	Francis, Paul A., with S. P. I. Agi, S. Ogoh Alubo, Hawa A. Bin, A. G. Daramola, Uchenna M. Nzewi, and D. J. Shehu. 1997. "Hard Lessons: Primary Schools, Community, and Social Capital in Nigeria." World Bank, Washington, D.C.
Pakistan 1993	Beall, Jo, Nazneen Kanji, Farhana Faruqi, Choudry Mohammed Hussain, and Mushtaq Mirani. 1993. "Social Safety Nets and Social Networks: Their Role in Poverty Alleviation in Pakistan." Unpublished report for the Overseas Development Administration (U.K.).
Pakistan 1996	Parker, Barbara. 1996. "Pakistan Poverty Assessment: Human Resources Development—A Social Analysis of Constraints." World Bank, Washington, D.C.
Panama 1998	Pena, Maria Valeria Junho, and Hector Lindo-Fuentes. 1998. "Community Organization, Values and Social Capital in Panama." World Bank, Washington, D.C.
Philippines 1999	World Bank. 1999. "Mindanao Rural Development Project Social Assessment: Key Findings for Cotabato and Sultan Kudarat." Washington, D.C.
Rwanda 1998	World Bank. 1998. "Etude Participative Sur L'Evolution de la Pauvreté au Rwanda." Washington, D.C.
Senegal 1995	World Bank. 1995. "An Assessment of Living Conditions." Washington, D.C.
South Africa 1998	May, Julian, with Heidi Attwood, Peter Ewang, Francie Lund, Andy Norton and Wilfred Wentzal. 1998. "Experience and Perceptions of Poverty in South Africa." World Bank, Washington, D.C., and Praxis Publishing, Durban.
Swaziland 1997	Ministry of Economic Planning and Development of the Kingdom of Swaziland and the World Bank. 1997. "Swaziland: Poverty Assessment by the Poor." Washington, D.C.

Tanzania 1997	Narayan, Deepa. 1997. "Voices of the Poor: Poverty and Social Capital in Tanzania." Environmentally and Socially Sustainable Development Network. World Bank, Washington, D.C.
Thailand 1998	Robb, Caroline and Chaohua Zhang. 1998. "Social Aspects of the Crisis: Perceptions of Poor Communities in Thailand." World Bank, Washington, D.C.
Togo 1996	World Bank. 1996. "Overcoming the Crisis, Overcoming Poverty: A World Bank Poverty Assessment." Washington, D.C.
Tunisia 1995	World Bank. 1995. "Poverty Alleviation: Preserving Progress while Preparing for the Future." Washington, D.C.
Uganda 1998	McClean, Kimberley, and Charles Lwanga Ntale. 1998. "Desk Review of Participatory Approaches to Assess Poverty in Uganda." The Ministry of Planning and Economic Development, Kampala, Uganda.
Uganda 1999	Ministry of Finance Planning and Economic Development. 1999. "Participatory Poverty Assessment—Poor People's Perspectives." Draft. Kampala, Uganda.
Ukraine 1996	Wanner, Catherine, and Nora Dudwick. 1996. "Ethnographic Study of Poverty in Ukraine, October 1995–March 1996." World Bank, Washington, D.C.
Venezuela 1998	Walker, Ian, with Rafael Del Cid, Fidel Ordoñez, and Felix Seijas. 1998. "Evaluación Social del Proyecto Promueba, Caracas, Venezuela." World Bank, Washington, D.C.
Vietnam 1996	World Bank. 1996. "Social Issues." Washington, D.C.
Vietnam 1999a	ActionAid Vietnam. 1999. "Ha Tinh Participatory Poverty Assessment." Draft. ActionAid Vietnam and the Hanoi Research and Training Centre for Community Development, Hanoi.
Vietnam 1999b	Save the Children (U.K.). 1999. "Pilot Participatory Poverty Assessment: Ho Chi Minh City-District 11, Wards 5 and 7." Hanoi.
Yemen, Republic of 1998	La Cava, Gloria, Sharon Beatty, Renaud Detalle, Thaira Shalan, Nagib Zumair, and Angelica Arbulu. 1998. "Republic of Yemen Civil Service Modernization Program: Social and Institutional Assessment." World Bank, Washington, D.C.
Yemen, Republic of 1999	Volpi, Elena. 1999. "Yemen Child Development Project: Social Assessment." World Bank, Washington, D.C.
Zambia 1994	World Bank. 1994. "Poverty Assessment." Washington, D.C.
Zambia 1997	Francis, Paul A., John T. Milimo, Chosani A. Njobvu, and Stephen P. M. Tembo. 1997. "Listening to Farmers: Participatory Assessment of Policy Reform in Zambia's Agricultural Sector." World Bank, Washington, D.C.

Appendix 3: Systematic Content Analysis Using QSR NUD*IST

Once a text is formatted as a QSR NUD*IST file, that text can be retrieved and assigned coding. After an entire file is coded, QSR NUD*IST can be queried concerning frequencies of certain themes and how they occur in conjunction with other themes. For instance, in the course of the analysis one might want to know everything that women said about exclusion from informal credit associations. A preliminary inquiry would likely search for the intersection of the nodes: women's voices, social exclusion, and informal credit associations. QSR NUD*IST then searches automatically through every coded text unit in each of the reports to identify and retrieve all text units assigned this combination of codes. Once coding is completed, the program generates matrices showing the frequencies of theme intersections within text units. This makes it possible to determine the frequency with which certain themes appear in proximity to one another. These frequency matrices guided the analyses.

The index tree in QSR NUD*IST allowed each coder to assign a given text unit a string of codes to provide maximum detail regarding unit content, depth, and tone. For example, a discussion of women expressing distress over the inadequacy of access to drinking water infrastructure in their village may be coded in a string containing nodes (3 1) women's voice (if there is quoted speech); (4 1) women as subject; (5 4) water; (6 7) access; (7 2) unhappiness or dissatisfaction; (7 4) negative; (F 6) infrastructure. Because the nodes were not mutually exclusive, it was expected that coding would vary somewhat from coder to coder. In the above example, for instance, one coder may have coded for "infrastructure" while another may not have done so (since lack of access can, on the one hand, be an implied lack of infrastructure, but, on the other hand, there may not have been a specific mention of infrastructure). Similarly, one may have coded for "security" as well, as a way of indicating an issue of water security. In this way the nodes were used to reveal patterns across text units in an iterative, structured process of node intersection examination. (See appendix 5.)

The index tree itself is the result of several iterations. One of QSR NUD*IST's strengths is its capacity to incorporate emergent themes in the analysis through coding tree modifications and additions. Because of this, the coding schema changed considerably over time as nodes were added (and occasionally merged if the conceptual overlap was too great). We confronted the problem of coding stability principally by making inquiries of texts using multiple methods (such as string searches) and making multiple intersection searches using a series of related nodes. For example, when the research team revisited their original "definitions of poverty" node, they noticed a great many references to the psychological effects of poverty. A new node, psychological effects, was developed. When this node was revisited, the research team noted that humiliation was a constant theme throughout the reports. A text search for the word "humiliation" confirmed this particular dimension of poverty. In this way, QSR NUD*IST was used as a tool to deepen the understanding of the definition of poverty and to "let the data speak."

The iterative exploration of the data involved a process of consistently examining whole sets of related codes and coding intersections. For instance, in looking for examples of humiliation, we not only looked at that particular node, but also at other related nodes, such as psychological effects, conflict and crime, culture and identity, and others that might fall within a larger conceptual domain. We also used the string search capabilities of QSR NUD*IST to locate key words and phrases related to the concept under investigation. And finally, throughout the analysis we referred to the original documents themselves. Clearly there is always a degree to which the researcher is present in the interpretation of what the poor say. But we believe that through sensitive and reflective analysis, the voices of the poor may be amplified, not muffled, by the researcher.

Appendix 4: "Consultations with the Poor" Index Tree

(F)   Free Nodes

(F 1)   **Space and Population:** Used to code mentions of crowding and overpopulation at either the household or community level.

(F 2)   **Sanitation:** Used to code mentions of lack of access to clean water and sanitation facilities.

(F 3)   **Traditional Health Care:** Code for mentions of health care sought through modes other than health-care professionals or through clinics. Includes home remedies and use of traditional healers.

(F 4)   **Quality:** A general coding category used in conjunction with specific mention of quality (positive or negative).

(F 5)   **Seasonality and Climate:** Used to code mention of seasonality and/or climate directly impacting the lives and livelihoods of the report subjects.

(F 6)   **Infrastructure:** Used to code mentions of various types of physical infrastructure.

(F 7)   **Communication:** Used to code mentions and discussions of communications infrastructure, including media.

(F 8)   **Tradition:** Codes mentions of cultural traditions structuring the experience of poverty (e.g. exclusion of women from paid labor force).

(F 9)   **Rights:** Used to code mentions of rights and rights violations.

(F 10) **Geography:** Codes mentions of geographical features that affect the experience of poverty (e.g. poor infrastructure in mountainous areas, and so on).

(F 11) **Corruption:** Codes mentions of corruption in business and/or government.

(F 12) **Social Capital:** Used to mark points in the text at which the researcher made reference to the concept of social capital in relation to the research setting.

(F 13) **Alcohol, Drugs, Gambling:** Used to code mentions of these three items.

(F 14) **Prostitution/Sex Work:** Used to code mentions of these two items.

(F 15) **Counterintuitive:** A subjective coding used to reference text that appeared unusual, counterintuitive, or otherwise worthy of a special mention.

(F 16) **Agricultural Productivity:** Codes mentions of agricultural productivity levels.

(F 17) **Forest Resources:** Codes mentions of forest-resource use.

(F 18) **Definitions of Poverty:** Used to code information about how the poor define, understand, and interpret poverty, its causes, and its effects.

(F 19) **Informal Economy:** Codes mentions of participation in or presence of informal economy.

(F 20) **Social Assistance, Aid:** Used to code mentions of the presence or effect, or both, of social assistance and aid programs or benefits.

(F 21) **Change:** Used to code mentions of social, cultural, or institutional change over time.

(F 22) **Belief Systems:** Codes mentions of sociocultural belief systems influencing actions.

(F 23) **Shocks:** Used to code mentions of events and occurrences that pose severe physical and/or psychological shocks to the subjects within the report.

(F 24) **Reproduction, Women's Health:** Used to code specific mentions of women's health and reproductive health issues

(F 25) **Psychological Health:** Used to code mentions of psychological health.

(F 26) **Love:** Used to code mentions of love.

(F 27) **Status:** Used to code mentions of status and status differentials.

(F 28) **Time Allocation:** Used to code mentions of time allocation of respondents.

(F 29) **Cash:** Used to code mentions of participation in monetized economy.

(F 30) **Social Mobility:** Used to code mentions of the possible amount of social mobility.

(F 31) **Safety:** Used to code mentions of the physical safety of a given living environment.

(1) **Cases:** The header for case information nodes; contains no data.

    (1 1) **Report Rating:** After reading and coding a document in QSR NUD*IST, coders assigned a subjective rating to the report using a scale of 1–5, with 1 indicating "poor" and 5 "excellent." The rating is based on the utility of the report for the purposes of this study. A report rich with information on the experience of poverty as expressed by poor people received a high rating, while one focused principally on aggregate economic indicators or macrolevel poverty analysis received a lower rating.

    (1 2) **Gender Rating:** As with the report rating, coders assigned a rating to the report for its coverage of gender. A report that was heavily disaggregated by gender was rated higher than a report that failed to explore the ways in which experiences of poverty are gendered.

    (1 3) **Methods:** Cites references to methodology used to gather data presented in the document.

        (1 3 1) **Number of Communities in Sample:** References to the number of communities included in the sampling frame for the document.

        (1 3 2) **Number of Regions:** References to the number of regions in a particular country covered in the document.

        (1 3 3) **Number of Groups:** References to the number of groups from a particular community included in data collection. For example, researchers may conduct focus groups with several separate informant groups in a single community, including women's groups, men's groups, community leaders, and so on.

        (1 3 4) **Selection Methods:** References to the methods employed for selecting the regions, communities, or groups included in data collection.

(2)   **Institutions:** The header for the group of nodes referencing institutional structures identified and discussed in the documents.

(2 1)   **Formal/Governmental Institutions:** All references to any formal institution was assigned this code. If the institution was identified more specifically, a second institution code was assigned to identify the specific type of formal/governmental institution being discussed. This node assumes that most state institutions discussed in the documents are also associated with a governmental structure, which differentiates them from civil society institutions below. Nongovernmental organizations are considered formal institutions for the purposes of this study.

(2 2)   **Informal Institutions:** This code was assigned to institutions not associated with formal governing structures or organizational management, such as community-based revolving credit associations.

(2 3)   **Village:** Institutions identified as functioning primarily at the village or community level were assigned this code in combination with either (2 1) or (2 2).

(2 4)   **Ward/District:** Institutions identified as functioning primarily at the ward or district level were assigned this code in combination with either (2 1) or (2 2).

(2 5)   **Regional:** Institutions identified as functioning primarily at the regional level were assigned this code in combination with either (2 1) or (2 2).

(2 6)   **National:** Institutions identified as functioning primarily at the national level were assigned this code.

(2 7)   **International:** Institutions identified as functioning primarily at the international level were assigned this code. International development organizations or funding institutions are included in this node.

(2 8)   **NGOs:** Institutions identified as nongovernmental organizations were assigned this code. These are almost exclusively considered formal institutions.

(2 9)   **Political Parties:** Institutions identified as functioning primarily as political organizations or parties were assigned this code.

(2 10)   **Law:** Institutions identified as functioning primarily in law enforcement or administration were assigned this code. These include police, civic order, and judicial institutions.

(2 11)   **Economic:** Institutions identified as functioning primarily as financial institutions, such as banks, were assigned this code. Formal financial policies, such as Structural Adjustment Programs (SAPs), were also assigned this code.

(2 11 1)   **Credit Groups:** Formal or informal patterns of borrowing and lending were assigned this code.

(2 11 2)   **Other Economic Associations:** Formal or informal associations focused on economic association, but not specifically for providing credit, were assigned this code.

(2 12)   **Social Groups/Associations:** Groups such as clubs, cooperatives, and other informal associations were assigned this code. The subnodes for this code allow the researcher to distinguish between these groups as they serve women, men, the elderly, or religious groups.

(2 12 1)   **Women's**

(2 12 2)   **Men's**

(2 12 3)   **Elderly**

(2 12 4)   **Religious**

(2 13)   **Family/Household:** References to household social processes were assigned this code.

(2 13 1)   **Marriage:** References to marriage and social institutions related to marriage were assigned this code. These include references to issues such as dowry, bride price, and other marriage-related social norms and institutions.

(2 14)   **Community-Based Organizations (CBOs):** References to community-based organizations were assigned this code. These are distinguished from NGOs by their scale: NGOs are assumed to have scope and coverage beyond a single locality, whereas CBOs are assumed to be community-based.

(3)   **Voices:** The header for this group of nodes is used to identify voice in the documents. Each represents a direct quotation from a subject as coded below. Reported speech coded both the voice of the researcher (3 12) and the voice of the identified speaker. For example, (3 5) and (3 1) would be used to code the reported speech of a poor woman. A code was only assigned if a speaker was explicitly identified by that category in the text. No inferences as to whether a speaker was rich or poor, minority or majority, and so on, were made.

(3 1)   **Female:** Used to code reported speech of women.

(3 2)   **Male:** Used to code reported speech of men.

(3 3)   **Unspecified Gender:** If a direct quote is provided but the gender of the speaker is unspecified, this code was assigned.

(3 4)   **Children:** Used to code the reported speech of children (with a gender coding as appropriate).

(3 5)   **Poor:** Used to mark text units in which the speaker is identified as poor.

(3 6)   **Rich:** Used to mark text units in which the speaker is identified as rich.

(3 7)   **Minority:** Used to mark text units in which the speaker is identified as a member of a minority social group.

(3 8) **Majority:** Used to mark text units in which the speaker is identified as a member of a majority social group.

(3 9) **Rural:** Marks text in which the speaker is identified as resident of a rural area.

(3 10) **Urban:** Marks text in which the speaker is identified as a resident of an urban area.

(3 11) **Proverbs:** Proverbs and sayings reported in the text were assigned this code.

(3 12) **Researcher:** This node was used to identify speech reported by the researcher or assertions made by the researcher that may not otherwise be clearly understood as the researcher's voice.

(3 13) **Other:** This node was used to mark the direct speech of a person not fully described using the above voice codes.

(4) **Subjects:** The header for the group of nodes identifying topics addressed in a given text unit.

(4 1) **Female:** Used to code discussions pertaining to women.

(4 2) **Male:** Used to code discussions pertaining to men.

(4 3) **Unspecified Gender:** Used to code discussions pertaining to people whose gender is unspecified.

(4 4) **Children:** Used to code discussions pertaining to children.

(4 5) **Poor:** Used to code discussions pertaining to people identified as poor.

(4 6) **Rich:** Used to code discussions pertaining to people identified as rich.

(4 7) **Minority:** Used to code discussions pertaining to people identified as belonging to a minority group.

(4 8) **Majority:** Used to code discussions pertaining to people identified as belonging to a majority group.

(4 9) **Rural:** Used to code discussions pertaining to rural areas.

(4 10) **Urban:** Used to code discussions pertaining to urban areas.

(4 11) **Religious Group:** Used to code discussions pertaining to religious groups.

(4 12) **Caste, Tribe, Indigenous Group:** Used to code discussions pertaining to people identified by their caste, tribe, or indigenous identity.

(4 13) **Race, Ethnicity:** Used to code discussions pertaining to people identified by their race or ethnicity.

(4 14) **Age Group (specific; not children or elderly):** Used to code discussions pertaining to people identified as belonging to a specific age group that is neither children nor elderly.

(4 15) **Occupational Group:** Used to code discussions pertaining to people identified as belonging to a specific occupational group.

(4 16) **Disability:** Used to code discussions pertaining to people identified as disabled.

(4 17) **Sexual Orientation, Practice:** Used to code discussions pertaining to people identified by their sexual orientation.

(4 18) **Migrant:** Used to code discussions pertaining to people identified as migrants.

(4 19) **Community:** Used to code discussions pertaining to a community as a social group.

(4 20) **Unemployed:** Used to code discussions pertaining to people identified as unemployed.

(4 21) **Elderly, Pensioner:** Used to code discussions pertaining to people identified as elderly or pensioners.

(4 22) **Refugee:** Used to code discussions pertaining to people identified as refugees.

(4 23) **Other:** Used to code discussions pertaining to people whose identification is not captured by the above nodes.

(5) **Themes:** The header for the group of nodes identifying themes addressed in a given text unit.

(5 1) **Basic Needs:** Used when general references to basic needs were made. In most cases, a more specific need was identified; in these cases, the nodes below were used:

(5 1 1) **Food**

(5 1 2) **Shelter**

(5 1 3) **Clothing**

(5 1 4) **Water**

(5 2) **Health Care:** References to health and health care were assigned this code.

(5 2 1) **Reproductive Health:** References to contraception, maternity, and women's reproductive health were assigned this code.

(5 2 2) **Mortality:** Used to mark references to mortality.

(5 3) **Education:** This code marks any references to education. In combination with a code from group 2 (Institutions), the node can represent a formal educational system. It was also used to mark discussions of training and other types of information dissemination discussed in the documents.

(5 4)   **Economic Livelihood:** This code was used broadly to mark references to economic security and well-being. References to employment, income generation, and general participation in the formal cash economy were assigned this code.

(5 5)   **Culture, Identity, Dignity, Self-Respect:** References to community-specific norms, values, and self-identification were assigned this code. Discussions of individual dignity were also assigned this code.

(5 6)   **Livable Environment:** References to environmental quality and access to natural resources were assigned this code.

(5 7)   **Choices and Options:** References to the degree of control people describe over the social processes in which they are involved. For example, choices regarding children, marriage, political participation, expression, association, mobility, speech, thought, and others were assigned this code.

(5 8)   **Conflict and Crime:** References to war, violence, and crime were assigned this code. This category includes domestic violence and organized criminal activity.

(5 9)   **Property and Land:** This node contains references to land and land rights or access, as well as any form of material property. Discussions of soil quality and soil fertility were coded (5 9) in combination with free nodes for agricultural productivity (F 16) and quality (F 4).

(5 10) **Coping Strategies:** Discussions of strategies for meeting basic needs were assigned this code. An example would be seasonal migration in response to food scarcity.

(5 11) **Migration:** References to migration were assigned this code.

(5 12) **Information:** References to information access or dissemination were assigned this code; assertions about people's level of awareness about existing food assistance programs, for example, would be coded for food (5 1 4), access (6 7), and information, among other nodes.

(6)   **Social Relations:** The header grouping nodes referring to specific types of social relations and interactions.

(6 1)   **Social Exclusion:** Discussions of a systematic denial of access or services to a specific social group or individual were assigned this code.

(6 2)   **Risk and Vulnerability:** Mentions of a particular sensitivity to an event or occurrence that poses an immediate threat to health and social and/or economic well-being were assigned this code.

(6 2 1)   **Particular Groups or Individuals Affected**

(6 2 2)   **Everyone Affected**

(6 2 3)   **Periodic**

(6 2 4)   **Constant**

(6 2 5)   Not Catastrophic

(6 2 6)   Catastrophic

(6 3)   **Social Cohesion:** This code was assigned to mentions of social cohesiveness, particularly within the family or community.

(6 4)   **Social Fragmentation:** Used to code passages in which there is reference to the disintegration of social groups, particularly at the household or community level.

(6 5)   **Effectiveness:** Used to refer to the overall level of capacity of a given institution, usually a formal institution, with a specific mandate to provide some type of service. It is almost always used with an Attitude coding.

(6 6)   **Trust and Confidence:** Used to code text in which trust and confidence (or lack thereof) is specifically referred to. It is almost always used with an Attitude coding.

(6 7)   **Access:** Used to refer to access to services, institutions, and/or infrastructure. This coding is almost always used with an Attitude coding.

(6 8)   **Security:** Often used in conjunction with the Basic Needs codes to indicate issues of food security, and so on. Also used in reference to issues of general safety and predictability of physical well-being.

(6 9)   **Power:** Used in reference to power imbalances between people or people and institutions, or in reference to specific powers ascribed or denied to specific people and/or institutions.

(6 10)   **Gender Relations:** Used in reference to mentions of socialized norms of behavior concerning relations between men and women, particularly differential roles, treatments, preferences, and access to opportunities and services among men and women.

(7)   **Attitudes:** The header for nodes identifying qualitative assessments, by the subjects or author of the reports, of a variety of institutional and interpersonal relationships.

(7 1)   **Happiness and Satisfaction:** Indicates happiness or satisfaction on the part of the subject.

(7 2)   **Unhappiness and Dissatisfaction:** Indicates unhappiness or dissatisfaction on the part of the subject.

(7 3)   **Positive:** Indicates a positive assessment on the part of the researcher.

(7 4)   **Negative:** Indicates a negative assessment on the part of the researcher.

Appendix 5: Sample Analysis Procedure: Institutions

For the purposes of this study, data coded for references to any or all of the following are included in the category of formal institutions: "formal institutions," "political parties," and "law."

Community or social groups are differentiated from the informal category to highlight data coded for any or all of the following: "social groups," "women's associations," "men's associations," "elderly associations," "religious associations," "nongovernmental organizations," and "community-based organizations." Data coded for "family, household" or "marriage," or both, are included in the set of text units for this category.

Data sets were generated by assembling text units with intersecting coding; that is, text units coded for "formal institutions" and "effectiveness," "informal institutions" and "effectiveness," "community associations" and "effectiveness," and so on were queried and analyzed. The data sets were disaggregated by gender in order to distinguish between men's and women's reports of their experiences with institutions. The tables below indicate a general pattern of topical coverage in the data. Formal institutions, for example, appear to be discussed far more frequently than informal institutions or social groups and associations in the PPAs.

In general, discussions about institutions focused on access, effectiveness, trust, and power. These dimensions of institutional interaction were often addressed in negative terms. Topics of access emerged in every institutional category, while people tended to emphasize power in the formal and informal spheres and safety in the informal and household spheres. Data coded for references to men tend to focus on issues of quality and access in the formal and informal spheres, while data coded for women concentrate on formal institutions and the household on access, trust, and effectiveness. In the household category there are also many references to security and safety.

The matrices below indicate the number of text units in the data set coded for the listed variables. Text unit counts should be read with a note of caution, however, since the size of a text unit was not uniform throughout the data. In addition, since the coding categories were not designed to be mutually exclusive, values in different cells in the table may represent the same text unit coded for multiple variables. These matrices should be used as a heuristic tool rather than be read as a definitive statement of which topics were reported most frequently by respondents.

Variables were assigned the values "positive" and "negative" when there were explicit references to these values in the text. Otherwise, data was coded as "neutral." A discussion of the effectiveness of a government housing subsidy program, for instance, would be coded for "effectiveness" and "formal." In most cases, an explicit reference to the positive or negative effectiveness of the program would be coded accordingly.

Data Output Matrices: number of text units coded at each intersection: Neutral Node 3 and Institutions, no gender coding

Indicators	Formal, Government	Informal	Social Groups, Associations	Family, Household
+ive effective	10	0	3	0
-ive effective	67	35	19	13
Effective neutral	115	19	47	6
+ive trust	2	0	2	1
-ive trust	60	16	12	15
Trust neutral	110	16	20	20
+ive access	7	4	1	2
-ive access	107	136	5	71
Access neutral	197	194	61	133
+ive security and safety	4	0	0	0
-ive security and safety	13	38	2	15
Safety neutral	39	55	21	86
+ive power	0	2	1	1
-ive power	8	23	6	2
Power neutral	90	67	43	21
Change	19	12	0	32
Quality	69	42	2	22
Information	39	55	16	3

Node 3 and Institutions, coded for men

Indicators	Formal, Government	Informal	Social Groups, Associations	Family, Household
+ive effective	0	0	0	0
-ive effective	3	0	0	3
Effective neutral	7	3	1	0
+ive trust	0	1	0	0
-ive trust	0	0	1	3
Trust neutral	6	1	3	3
+ive access	6	6	6	0
-ive access	3	1	0	5
Access neutral	2	16	0	9
+ive security and safety	0	0	0	0
-ive security and safety	0	0	0	4
Safety neutral	0	1	0	1
+ive power	0	0	0	0
-ive power	0	0	0	1
Power neutral	2	0	0	6
Change	0	0	0	2
Quality	12	14	8	2
Information	0	0	0	0

Node 3 and Institutions, coded for women

Indicators	Formal, Government	Informal	Social Groups, Associations	Family, Household
+ive effective	1	0	0	0
-ive effective	18	1	0	4
Effective neutral	26	10	8	1
+ive trust	0	0	0	0
-ive trust	19	1	1	6
Trust neutral	39	1	1	6
+ive access	6	7	6	2
-ive access	18	18	8	39
Access neutral	28	15	9	27
+ive security and safety	0	1	0	1
-ive security and safety	0	6	0	35
Safety neutral	20	2	1	23
+ive power	0	0	0	0
-ive power	2	1	0	4
Power neutral	23	9	2	16
Change	1	0	1	6
Quality	11	12	6	8
Information	45	0	6	5

Sample Summary Table—A selection from a table of summarized text units
Summary: Node 3 and Institutions/Restricted for Women

Intersection	Country	Comments	Theme
Negative effective and formal institutions	Ukraine	Official insults a woman who has too many children	Humiliation in service delivery
Formal and effectiveness	Ukraine	Shame of poverty fading ...getting used to it	
Formal and trust	Moldova	Poor feel abandoned by the authorities who once looked out for them	Trust
Informal and effectiveness	Togo	Shame at selling peanuts on the street with a university degree	Pride
Formal and effectiveness	Pakistan	Complaints as risky	Corruption and options
Formal and trust	Pakistan	Money taken from widows by officials	
Formal and effectiveness	Ukraine	Quote about the government taking away whatever it gives	Inaccessibility of social services or government or effectiveness.
Formal and effectiveness	Costa Rica	Women confront more barriers to access agricultural support services	
Formal and negative access	Moldova	Woman is unaware of the entitlements due to her for her children	
Formal and trust	Pakistan	Widows and disabled get insufficient support that's unreliable	
Formal and negative safety	India	Pregnant women not eating as much to make room for embryo	Health-care institutions/health
Family and negative access	Latvia	"Women don't complain about their health"	
Family and access	Moldova	Afraid to go to the doctor due to anticipated expense	
Informal and negative access	Kenya	Women treat most illnesses with traditional herbs	

Intersection	Country	Comments	Theme
Formal and access	Pakistan	Women can't go to hospital without a man's permission and accompaniment	
Informal and negative access	Kenya	Access to health care for female-headed households is a challenge ... mothers use credit or borrow from friends and family	
Formal and negative access	Vietnam	Women cannot afford health care they desire for themselves or their children	
Formal and safety	Zambia	Women access land through their husbands	Land
Family and access	Bangladesh	Access to land as a priority for poor women	
Family and access	Uganda	Women completely alienated from land they used to be able to access through males	
Formal and access	Guinea-Bissau	Land resources are owned by the state and women cannot inherit or have direct rights over land	

Appendix 6: Listing of Poverty Assessment Reports Analyzed for This Research

Africa and the Middle East

Country, Year, and Title	Sample	Methods
Benin 1994 **Toward a Poverty Alleviation Strategy**	Four urban communities and 22 villages were drawn from five regions. Poorest communities were selected based on a comparison of soils, road networks, poverty levels, and levels of food expenditures.	Group discussions with village elders, young people, handicapped, and widows; life histories of participants, semi-structured interviews, social mapping, interviews with key informants, and children's drawings.
Burkina Faso 1994 **Visual Participatory Poverty Assessment (draft)**	Households and villages from four regions (Toussiana, Damesma, Boureye, and Ouagadougou) were selected according to ecological and ethnic variation, community size, and accessibility. Choice was influenced by the presence of local NGOs to act as intermediaries. Up to 10 males per village were chosen to take pictures to be discussed by all. Total of 125 Burkinabe took pictures, and a much larger number were interviewed, either individually or in groups.	Visual PPA that included photography, conversations, focus groups, written interviews, and triangulation with NGOs who were active in the village.
Cameroon 1995 **Diversity, Growth, and Poverty Reduction**	There were 1,559 households and 150 key informants, selected across five zones. Villages were selected according to the frequency with which key informants ranked them as poor. Within the selected villages the sample was representative according to age, gender, occupation, and rural and urban zones.	Conversational interviews, focus groups, transect walks, mapping, participant observation, and case histories.
Ethiopia 1998 **Participatory Poverty Assessment for Ethiopia (draft)**	There were 10 sites representative of various agro-ecological zones, ethnic compositions, and livelihoods: six rural in the Oromia, Amhara, and SNPPR regions, and four urban in the Addis Ababa region. Six sites were poor, two were middle-income, and two were affluent. In urban areas the sample included those living in shantytowns or substandard dwellings whom neighborhood and village leaders considered poor. Managers and development workers in various government representatives were also interviewed.	Social mapping, wealth-ranking, livelihood analysis, trend and seasonality analysis, institutional diagrams, matrix ranking and scoring, timelines, and interviews.

Africa and the Middle East, Cont.

Country, Year, and Title	Sample	Methods
Gabon 1997 Poverty in a Rent-Based Economy	The sample included 277 individuals and 48 focus groups of 6 to 10 people each. Various age groups were represented (55 percent women and 45 percent men).	Open-ended interviews and focus groups.
Ghana 1995a Poverty Assessment in Ghana Using Qualitative and Participatory Research Methods	There were 15 communities selected to be representative of different geographical, agro-ecological, socioeconomic zones, ethnic/cultural groupings, level of access to services and infrastructure, and level of integration with markets (including Upper East, Upper West, Western, Greater Accra, Volta, Northern, Brong Ahafo, and Central Regions).	Conversational and semi-structured interviewing, wealth-ranking, matrix ranking and scoring, institutional diagramming, seasonality diagramming, and participatory mapping.
Ghana 1995b Poverty Past, Present, and Future	Conducted over three phases; a total of 15 communities were involved. Different socioeconomic groups were selected from both rural and urban sites.	Participatory Rural Assessments techniques (PRAs), semi-structured interviews and focus groups to collect data on the community's assessments of its own needs.
Guinea-Bissau 1994 Poverty Assessment and Social Sectors Strategy Review	Synthesis of recent studies and reports by the World Bank and other institutions, also informed by the Guinea-Bissau 1991 Household Income and Expenditure Survey.	Desk review, and case studies of poor households by a local sociologist.
Kenya 1996 Learning from the Poor: A Participatory Poverty Assessment in Kenya	Five communities were randomly selected in each of seven of the poorest rural districts and one low-income urban area. Total sample was 3,500, including interviews with 15 households ranked poor or very poor from each community. In addition, 150 female-headed households from two Nairobi slums were interviewed.	Mapping, wealth-ranking, seasonal analysis, trend and price analysis, focus group discussions, key informant interviews, problem identification, gender analysis, household and school questionnaires.
Kenya 1997 Coping Without Coping: What Poor People Say About Poverty in Kenya	Ten study sites were selected across agro-ecological zones in each of seven districts (Kajiado, Kisumu, Makueni, Mombasa, Nakuru, Nyeri, and Taita Taveta). Mombasa was the only urban area included.	Open-ended research techniques, including social mapping, Venn diagram and three-pile sorting, focus group discussions, interviews, gender analyses, and case studies.

310

Country, Year, and Title	Sample	Methods
Madagascar 1994 Participatory Poverty Assessment: Synthesis Report	Four regions selected (Tulear, Antananarivo, Soavinamdriana, and Sambave and Brickaville) to represent different agro-ecological zones, levels of income, and modes of livelihood. There were 2,582 poor households involved in focus groups or one-on-one interviews. In addition, approximately 100 interviews were conducted with community leaders, service providers, and government officials.	Structured conversational interviews, focus group interviews with locals, participant observation, and institutional appraisal.
Madagascar 1996 Poverty Assessment	Same as above.	Same as above.
Mali 1992 Qualitative Study on the Demand for Education in Rural Mali	There were 12 villages in four different regions, chosen according to their levels of demand for education, measured by average enrollment ratios.	Participant observation and interviews, open-ended conversations with a random sample.
Mali 1993 Assessment of Living Conditions	The study took place in Kayes, Sikasso, and Mopti (as an RRA) and in Bamako (as a Beneficiary Assessment).	Beneficiary Assessment, semi-structured interviews, participatory exercises, and children's drawings.
Niger 1996 Poverty Assessment: A Resilient People in a Harsh Environment	Rural and urban areas and the poorest sections of the capital city, Niamey. In-depth interviews with approximately 100 people including married women, young unmarried women, the unemployed, students, street children, groups of beggars, cooperatives of the disabled, a neighborhood patrol, a savings group, women engaged in petty trade, and migrants. Approximately 200 people were interviewed in urban areas, plus approximately 190 villagers, either individually or in focus groups, from 12 villages in three rural areas.	Informal interviews, open-ended questionnaires, participatory tools, and discussion groups.

Country, Year, and Title	Sample	Methods
Nigeria 1995 Participatory Poverty Assessment	Interviews with the poorest individuals and households within certain communities in 10 states (Akwa Ibom, Benue, Cross River, Kaduna, Kwara, Lagos, Ondo, Osun, Oyo, and Sokoto)—37 urban areas and 58 rural areas. Local leaders helped researchers identify and contact the poorest groups.	In-depth interviews and focus group discussions covering seven topics, surveys, field observation, case studies, and secondary review.
Nigeria 1996 Poverty in the Midst of Plenty: The Challenge of Growth with Inclusion	Over 2,000 people in 95 communities from 45 LGAs, based on the proportion of poor people they contained. Sample included sites in Oyo, Benne, and Osun States, selected by 14 teams of experienced Nigerian researchers with help from state and local government leaders.	Individual and group discussions, interviews with government leaders.
Nigeria 1997 Hard Lessons: Primary Schools, Community, and Social Capital in Nigeria	There were 18 local government education leaders, 540 parents, and 180 pupils sampled purposively to represent the main ecological and sociolinguistic categories in 54 schools selected from six zones.	Semi-structured interviews, focus groups, participant observation, brief questionnaires, and documentary analysis.
Rwanda 1998 Etude Participative Sur L'Evolution de la Pauvreté au Rwanda	There were 12 areas of 12 municipalities in 9 prefectures selected according to 11 criteria (agro-ecological zone, socioeconomic level, economic potential, rural, urban, migration, effects of the war, population density, access to services, roads, and types of employment).	Social mapping, wealth-ranking, matrices, transects, Venn diagrams, impact trees, chapatti diagrams, focus group discussions, home visits, and secondary data.
Senegal 1995 An Assessment of Living Conditions	The material in this report is based on the findings of a mission to Senegal led by the World Bank. Additional information comes from the first household Priority Survey that was completed in 1993.	A household survey, desk review, and key informant interviews.
South Africa 1998 Experience and Perceptions of Poverty in South Africa	There were approximately 1,400 respondents in 25 communities (10 of which were in KwaZulu-Natal, 7 in Eastern Cape, and 4 in Northern Province). These are the poorest provinces in South Africa, excluding Gauteng and the Free State.	This study used PRA methods in 17 of the communities. Elsewhere, this study used combinations of participant observation, focus group discussions, conversational and semi-structured interviewing, literature review, and workshops.

Country, Year, and Title	Sample	Methods
Swaziland 1997 Swaziland: Poverty Assessment by the Poor	There were 63 communities in four agro-ecological regions, involving more than 600 households, 100 focus groups, and 100 key informants. The site selection was based on the ecological zones rather than social formations, and actual sites were thus chosen based on the land tenure system.	Focus groups and semi-structured interviews, social mapping, trend analysis, wealth-ranking, preference ranking of sources of finance, institutional diagrams, and gender analysis.
Tanzania 1997 Voices of the Poor: Poverty and Social Capital in Tanzania	More than 6,000 participants in 87 villages were chosen to be nationally representative of rural areas spread throughout the country. Fifteen households from each village were selected for a household survey—households that had also contributed to the national agricultural survey. In addition, researchers convened groups for discussion.	This study used two participatory methods: PRA and SARAR. Tools included mappings, wealth-ranking, seasonal analysis, price analysis, Venn diagrams, problem identification, gender analysis, key informant interviews, household surveys, and District-level workshops.
Togo 1996 Overcoming the Crisis, Overcoming Poverty: A World Bank Poverty Assessment	The sample included individuals and households from rural communities and urban neighborhoods. The sample comprised 40 villages covering five regions and urban neighborhoods in Lomé.	Semi-structured interviews; issues covered include: problem hierarchies, perceived solutions, survival strategies, and life histories.
Tunisia 1995 Poverty Alleviation: Preserving Progress while Preparing for the Future	The poverty assessment prepared in 1995 was based on the 1990 National Household Survey. The sample size was 7,734.	The primary methodological tool in this report is the survey.
Uganda 1998 Desk Review of Participatory Approaches to Assess Poverty in Uganda	The report was based on a desk review of 56 studies that have used participatory approaches of data collection to assess poverty in Uganda.	The reports used for the study used approaches including PRA, RRA, household surveys, and secondary documented information sources.
Uganda 1999 Participatory Poverty Assessment: Poor People's Perspectives	Twenty-four rural and 12 urban sites in nine of the most disadvantaged districts were purposively selected in order to capture the multiple facets of poverty in Uganda. In each district at least one urban and up to three rural communities were chosen.	PRA methods, including focus group discussions, case studies, and key informant interviews.

Country, Year, and Title	Sample	Methods
Yemen, Republic of 1998 Republic of Yemen Civil Service Modernization Program: Social and Institutional Assessment	Respondents were from six ministries in five governorates (Sana'a Capital and governorate, Taiz, Aden, and Lahej). Sixteen focus group discussions were held, including 110 respondents (67 men and 43 women); there were also 78 in-depth interviews. An attitudinal Survey of Civil Servants was carried out for a stratified sample of 403 respondents (71 percent male and 29 percent female).	Survey instruments (with both closed and open-ended questions), focus group discussions, and direct observation.
Yemen, Republic of 1999 Yemen Child Development Project: Social Assessment	The study sample included 12 village clusters and six districts in two Northern governorates. The villages involved are among the most geographically isolated and are severely lacking in social services and infrastructure.	Project stakeholders were asked to discuss their problems and coping strategies, and to suggest solutions to several pertinent issues, such as health, female education, and water and sanitation.
Zambia 1994 Poverty Assessment	The study was based on six rural and four urban areas, each comprising at least one and often several rural villages, urban slums, or shanty compounds. Sites were selected to represent different livelihoods, cultural/ethnic groups, agro-ecological zones, access to infrastructure and services, and integration with markets.	Unstructured or semi-structured interviews, focus group discussions, mapping, time lines, wealth-ranking, seasonal calendars, and livelihood analysis.
Zambia 1997 Listening to Farmers: Participatory Assessment of Policy Reform in Zambia's Agricultural Sector	There were 10 low-income communities selected across regions to represent different livelihoods, ethnic groups, agro-ecological zones, levels of access to infrastructure, and levels of integration with markets.	Conversational interviewing, focus group discussions, case studies, and participant observation.

Country, Year, and Title	Sample	Methods
Armenia 1995 A Qualitative Assessment of the Living Standards of the Armenian Population	There were approximately 700 poor and medium-income households (the majority were poor); there were also interviews with key informants such as village, district, and city officials; medical personnel; psychologists; teachers; and NGOs. The six districts were considered to be moderately poor to poor (Akhurian and Spitak, Tashir, Vardenis, Vaik, Goris, and Yerevan).	Semi-structured interviews, focus groups, street conversations and spontaneous street meetings, and direct observation.
Armenia 1996 Social Assessment Report on the Education and Health Sectors in Armenia	Three urban and four rural sites were chosen to represent various differences around the country, including Yerevan, Gumri, Sisian Town in urban zones, and Lusarpiur (Shirak Region), Darbas (Sunik Region), Lor (Sunik Region), and Shahap (Ararat Region) in rural zones. Qualitative research involved 12 focus groups of users, plus open-ended interviews with users and service providers.	Quantitative and qualitative research, including focus groups, open-ended interviews, and observation.
Armenia 1999 Children's De-Institutionalization Initiative: Beneficiary Assessment of Children in Institutions	The study was based on two boarding schools, including one for the mentally ill. Within each school target groups were organized to include 60 families, 52 children, nine ex-boarders, and various service providers, institutional staff, and members of the general community.	Qualitative open-ended, one-on-one interviews and focus groups with families, key informants, and other groups in society identified as relevant to the study.
Azerbaijan 1997 Poverty Assessment	There were community assessments in 91 communities (25 cities, 5 towns, and 61 villages) and a Social Assessment involving 140 poor or vulnerable respondents (pensioners, internally displaced persons, students, unemployed, educational or medical workers, and agricultural workers).	Semi-structured focus groups of five to eight respondents lasting 1.5 to 2 hours, and also community surveys. Done in tandem with a 1995 national household survey.
Georgia 1997 Poverty in Georgia: The Social Dimensions of Transition	The study was based on 600 households, chosen on the basis of poverty and vulnerability, in nine regions, including various ecological zones, agricultural conditions, urban and rural settings, ethnic communities, and population groups. There were also interviews with local officials, doctors, teachers, and other members of the community.	Observation, informal discussions, and interviews.

Country, Year, and Title	Sample	Methods
Kyrgyz Republic 1998 Update on Poverty in the Kyrgyz Republic	The study was based on 1,950 households across urban and rural regions in northern and southern sectors of the country (information from household and community questionnaires under the Kyrgyz Poverty Monitoring Survey [KPMS], carried out by the National Statistical Committee in the fall of 1996).	Household and community questionnaires.
Latvia 1997 Report on the Qualitative Analysis Research into the Living Standards of Inhabitants in Aluksne District	The study was based on fewer than 100 in-depth interviews with poor families in the Aluksne district and the urban Livani region. Participants were selected across age, gender, and professional and employment experience.	Surveys and interviews about the conditions facing families and surrounding areas on livelihoods, social assistance programs, education, health, and food issues.
Latvia 1998 Listening to the Poor: A Social Assessment of Poverty in Latvia	The study was based on semi-structured interviews with 400 households and 20 local experts. Purposive sampling ensured that different geographic, economic, and cultural regions were included, as well as household types most likely to be poor.	Qualitative data collected through semi-structured interviews.
Macedonia 1998 Qualitative Analysis of the Living Standard of the Population of the Republic of Macedonia	The study was based on 400 poor households reflecting the urban-rural distribution of the country. There were 100 households from each of four regions; 200 were under the poverty line, the other 200 were randomly selected.	Questionnaires and semi-structured interviews.
Moldova 1997 Poverty in Moldova: The Social Dimensions of Transition	The study was based on 200 poor individuals and households from six districts, selected to include a range of ages, occupations, and household types.	Qualitative open-ended interviews and careful observation of those interviewed.
Ukraine 1996 Ethnographic Study of Poverty in Ukraine	The study was based on 500 poor households selected across five urban and rural regions (Donetsk, Crimea, Kiev, Kharkiv, and Ivano-Frankivsk Oblasts). In all regions except the Crimea 50 interviews were conducted in the largest city, and 50 in the villages. About 28 percent of respondents were male and 72 percent were female	Observation and semi-structured interviews.

Country, Year, and Title	Sample	Methods
Cambodia 1998 The Social Impacts of the Creeping Crisis in Cambodia: Perceptions of Poor Communities	Rapid field research undertaken in April–May 1998 in Phnom Penh and the provinces of Battambang, Siem Reap, Kompong Cham, and Kandal. Community groups, NGOs, and government officials were interviewed individually and in groups.	Semi-structured interviews, focus group discussions, observation during field visits, and a range of participatory techniques.
China 1997 Anning Valley Agricultural Development Project: Summary of a Social Assessment (Annex 10)	This project area involved a total of 15 county-level administrative units and 615,580 households.	Survey techniques.
Indonesia 1998 Village Governments and Their Communities: Allies or Adversaries	The study was based on 1,200 households in 48 villages in three provinces (Jambi, Central Java, and Nusa Tenggara Timur). Interviews were conducted in each village with 25 households randomly selected; discussions were held with village officials, and project sites were visited.	Household survey, observation, key informant interviews, and discussion groups.
Indonesia 1999 Local Capacity and Its Implications for Development: The Case of Indonesia. A Preliminary Report: Local Level Institutions Study	Same as above.	Same as above.
Philippines 1999 Mindanao Rural Development Project Social Assessment: Key Findings for Cotabato and Sultan Kudarat	The study was based on 2,000 community residents from 90 Barangays randomly selected after clustering based on agro-ecological zones. There were 1,350 households participating in the survey and 120 focus group discussion in 60 Barangays.	Household survey and focus group discussions.

Country, Year, and Title	Sample	Methods
Thailand 1998 Social Aspects of the Crisis: Perceptions of Poor Communities in Thailand	Six focus groups (Labor and Slums NGO Networks; Women, Children, and AIDS NGO Networks; Slum dwellers of Teparak Terminus, Khon Kaen, NE Province; Government extension departments; Handicapped NGO Networks; and Slum Dwellers in Bangkok); and in-depth interviews with four NGOs, three communities, four associations, two academic institutions, three donors, the chamber of commerce, and the government.	Focus groups, rapid assessment techniques, and participatory exercises.
Vietnam 1996 Social Issues	Undertaken to explore the consequences of establishing protected areas. There were 13 villages selected in the provinces of Dong Nai, Lam Dong, and Song Be, based on their vicinity to parks and reserves and their different ethnic composition.	Rapid Rural Appraisal (RRA) and Participatory Rural Appraisal (PRA) methods; interviews with farmers, key informants, commune and district staff; and workshops.
Vietnam 1999a Ha Tinh Participatory Poverty Assessment (draft)	The study was based on 302 households in 13 villages in six districts. One commune from each district was randomly selected, and the richest and the poorest villages from each commune were then chosen (the ranking was carried out by commune leaders).	Household discussions and exercises, group discussions, separate and combined meetings with men and women.
Vietnam 1999b Pilot Participatory Poverty Assessment: Ho Chi Minh City–District 11, Wards 5 and 7	The study was based on 120 households from two specified residential quarters (out of four) in District 11, an urban area three kilometers west of Ho Chi Minh City's center. There were 15 poor households, and three to five "rich" households selected for interview in each of eight clusters. A group of six to eight children were also interviewed in each cluster, and 37 interviews were held with separate groups of local leaders, men, women, and children in the same districts. In total, there were approximately 160 interviews.	Semi-structured interviewing, focus groups, observation, and key informant interviews.

Country, Year, and Title	Sample	Methods
Brazil 1995 A Poverty Assessment	The report was based on 17 background papers and the 1990 national household income survey (PNAD), conducted by Fundação Instituto Brasileiro de Geográfica e Estatística (IBGE).	Beneficiary Assessment and data from the PNAD, plus background papers involving a variety of quantitative, qualitative, and participatory techniques.
Costa Rica 1997 Identifying the Social Needs of the Poor: An Update	The study was based on 262 households in selected urban areas (Sarapiqui), rural areas, and secondary cities (Buenos Aires and Puntarenas) and the Central Valley (Guarco and Cartago and Rincón Grande de Pavas). Local community leaders, NGO leaders, and service providers were also interviewed.	Interviews with individuals and groups (elders' councils, women's organizations, and local committees); focus group discussions, and unstructured interviews with teachers; local government, health and education personnel; NGOs; extension agents.
Ecuador 1996a Rural Poverty in Ecuador—A Qualitative Assessment	The Rural Qualitative Assessment was undertaken in seven small rural communities: four in the Sierra (Chimborazo and Cotopaxi provinces), two in the Costa (Manabi) and one in the Oriente (Napo). All communities were located in cantons classified as very poor in the Poverty Map of the Consejo Nacional de Desarrollo. The sample is not representative at a national or regional level, but there is reasonable certainty that the characteristics of selected households reflect those at the community level. There were a total of 176 interviews, in addition to focus groups, of which 92 were with women, 84 with men.	Four methodologies were used: (1) key informant interviews with community leaders (such as teachers and physicians); (2) semi-structured household interviews with men and women, following a thematic guide; (3) focus groups that separated men and women; and (4) direct observation.
Ecuador 1996b Poverty Report	Quantitative data was based on the 1994 Ecuador Living Standard Measurement (LSMS) that included 1,374 rural households. The data was also informed by 10 working papers, some of which reflected qualitative work. One study was conducted in Cisne Dos, a low-income neighborhood in Guayaquil. Another study reflected the view of poverty in seven poor rural communities in the Andean highlands, the Costa, and the Amazon jungle.	Key informant interviews with community leaders, semi-structured household-level interviews with men and women, focus groups, and direct observation. A Rural Qualitative Assessment (RQA) was used for the study in seven poor rural communities.

Country, Year, and Title	Sample	Methods
El Salvador 1995 Social Assessment: El Salvador Basic Education Modernization Project	There were 24 focus groups: eight with teachers in urban areas, four with teachers in rural areas, eight with parents in urban areas, and four with parents in rural areas. A case study of one school was conducted in Chalchuapa, and in-depth interviews were conducted with the government, school staff, NGOs, and donors.	Institutional assessment, community participation, focus group discussions, in-depth interviews, and a case study of an EDUCO school.
El Salvador 1997 Stakeholder Consultation and Analysis: Second Phase of the Social Assessment for the El Salvador EDUCO Program and the Basic Education Modernization Project	There were 56 randomly chosen public schools in El Salvador: four from each department—half rural and half urban. Structured interviews were held with 281 randomly chosen parents, 57 teachers (30 rural, 27 urban); there were six focus groups of 36 public school children (selected by their teachers); there were interviews with eight boys from an all-male, religious, semi-private urban school, and there were interviews with 13 school dropouts under 15 years old.	Questionnaire-led structured interviews, open-ended interviews, and focus group discussions.
Guatemala 1993 Guatemala Qualitative and Participatory Poverty Study, Phases I and II	The study was based on 447 families living in the poorest marginal urban areas, rural villages, and hamlets within a given municipality in three regions, and identified by others as poor. In addition, researchers interviewed institutional personnel and other individuals who were knowledgeable about the poverty groups under investigation.	Interviews using a thematic guide for case studies. Interviews were conducted with family units, talking with as many family members as possible to obtain varied perceptions.
Guatemala 1994a Interim Evaluation Report: Guatemala Qualitative and Participatory Poverty Study, Phase II	The study was based on 223 interviews with individuals, families, institutional personnel, and local leaders. Other community members identified the individuals and families as among the poorest in each place. These interviews lasted three hours each; interviews with key informants lasted an average of five hours each. About 49 percent of those interviewed were chosen from marginal urban areas, and 51 percent from poor rural areas. There were 22 focus group discussions conducted, mostly with local government leaders.	Conversational interviews that followed a thematic guide, meetings, focus groups, and larger forums.

Country, Year, and Title	Sample	Methods
Guatemala 1994b La Pobreza: Un Enfoque Participativo—El Caso de Guatemala	The study was based on 627 interviews with families in eight regions, using the Poverty Map of Guatemala (1993) to select the poorest municipalities. Focus groups and interviews were held in the municipal capital; in addition, key informants identified the poorest two settlements, where further interviews were carried out. Other communities were also visited, and the poorest persons in them were interviewed. Interviews were also conducted with key informants, such as government authorities, poor persons, nurses, schoolteachers, ministers, and community leaders.	Conversational interviews, focus groups, and controlled observation.
Guatemala 1997a Social Assessment for the Guatemala Reconstruction and Local Development Project	The study was based on key informants representing eight municipalities: five in San Marcos and three in Huehuetenango. Consultations included representatives chosen by the communities. In total, 760 persons participated in 8 workshops; there were 96 focus group discussions, 24 general assemblies, 8 focus groups with the Mayor and Municipal Corporation, 32 interviews with government agencies, and 48 interviews with NGOs, cooperatives, and community organizations.	Workshops with semi-structured group, consultations with 20 to 25 representatives, including two to three from each village. Also a complete range of PRA exercises with focus groups at three levels, the largest being the municipal.
Guatemala 1997b Perfil de los Pueblos Indígenas de Guatemala (FONAPAZ)	The study included a large historical analysis of indigenous marginalization in Guatemala, using data from interviews with community leaders, village elders, and indigenous leaders to obtain information on the current state of the indigenous people.	Conversational interviews with community leaders, village elders, and indigenous leaders; survey participation; and meetings including focus groups and larger forums.
Jamaica 1997 Urban Poverty and Violence in Jamaica	The study was based on five urban communities that are broadly representative of Jamaica's poor urban areas. The study included focus groups of different types (older men, men in a football club, youths, women), as well as semi-structured interviews.	Participatory Urban Appraisal (PUA) methodology.

Country, Year, and Title	Sample	Methods
Mexico 1995 The People's Voice: Mexico— Participatory Poverty Assessment	The study was based on 722 persons, divided roughly equally by gender and region, from towns or neighborhoods in Ciudad Juarez, Zacatecas, Mexico City and its surrounding areas, and Oaxaca, selected as representative of the places where large concentrations of the poor live. There were also 47 key persons (teachers, health workers, community leaders, and government officials) interviewed. There were several focus groups, collective interviews, and three to five case studies in each region.	Conversational one-on-one interviews, collective interviews, case studies, and focus groups.
Nicaragua 1998 Nicaragua's Experiment to Decentralize Schools: Views of Parents, Teachers and Directors	The study was based on 12 primary and secondary schools. At each there was a 60–90 minute interview with the entire council, supplemented by focus groups of three to five teachers or parents and interviewers with professional staff and school directors. A total of 82 interview sessions (individual or group) were conducted.	Interviews and focus groups with teachers, directors, and parents lasting two to three days in each school.
Panama 1998 Community Organization, Values, and Social Capital in Panama	Quantitative data from the Living Standards Measurement Survey (LSMS) were collected in 1997, and qualitative information from focus groups. A composite Social Capital Index was constructed, on the basis of which 16 focus groups were selected: four with low social capital, one with medium social capital, and 11 with high social capital. There were 244 people participating in these focus groups, of whom 107 were indigenous.	Community questionnaires, statistical analysis, and focus groups.
Venezuela 1998 Evaluación Social del Proyecto Promueba, Caracas, Venezuela	The study was based on 2,312 households selected across various regions, plus interviews with 20 key informants and community leaders (priests, teachers, businessmen, and NGO workers) in the three Universidades de Planificación Físca (UPFs). There were also 16 focus groups organized, of four types: community leaders, women, men, and mixed, for structured discussions.	Household interviews, focus groups, and interviews with key informants.

Country, Year, and Title	Sample	Methods
Bangladesh 1996 UNDP's 1996 Report on Human Development in Bangladesh: A Pro-Poor Agenda—Poor People's Perspectives	Eight rural communities and two urban slum areas were chosen to represent the range of community-level economic impoverishment. A total of 3,385 persons participated in 159 PRA discussions, which involved 58 urban villages and 22 slum areas.	Time lines, oral histories, a seasonal calendar, problem scoring, institution ranking, and so on. Women and men were sometimes interviewed together and sometimes separately. Results were triangulated.
India 1997a Report on Social Assessment for the District Poverty Initiatives Project: Baran District	The sample comprised 36 villages in two tehsils, based on criteria such as the number of families living below the poverty line, literacy rates, and access to roads.	Small and large group discussions, informal interviews with specific groups, wealth-ranking, seasonal analysis, social and resource mapping, gender analysis, case studies, and workshop meetings.
India 1997b A Report on Findings of Fieldwork (DPIP) in Todaraisingh and Uniara Blocks of Tonk District	Thirty-three of the poorest villages from the two blocks in the Tonk District were purposively selected for field inquiry. The sample then stratified villages by size and individuals by wealth and leadership position. Ten of the poorest families were randomly selected for a detailed inquiry in each village, and eight other poor groups were given special attention.	A multi-method approach that included focus groups and structured personal interviews.
India 1997c District Poverty Initiatives Project: Strategy and Investment Plan for Poverty Alleviation in Adilabad	Out of a total of 52 mandals, 20 of the most backward were chosen (16 in the forest and dry zone, two in the mineral zone, and two in the irrigation zone). One village from each mandal was selected, and households within the 20 chosen villages were ranked (with the help of local leaders) according to infrastructure, family size and composition, assets, social status, cropping pattern, and housing condition. Ten percent of the households ranked poorest were randomly selected for the study.	Interviews with key informants, focus groups, community interviews, direct observation by researchers, and a formal survey of selected households.
India 1997d Draft Fieldwork Report: Raisen District	Four districts and nine blocks were covered during the course of study. In the first phase, a total of 1,685 households in 183 villages were sampled. In the second, qualitative phase the least developed villages were selected for study.	Quantitative household surveys, and PRA techniques such as resource mapping, Venn diagrams, transect walks, mapping, and focus group discussions.

Country, Year, and Title	Sample	Methods
India 1997e Draft Fieldwork Report: Sagar District	Four districts and nine blocks were covered during the course of this study. Across the nine blocks selected a total of 95 Gram panchayats were identified. In Phase II, 44 representative gram panchayats were subject to qualitative and participatory analysis.	Participants were identified to be representative of a population that is considered the poorest of the poor.
India 1998a Participatory Poverty Profile Study: Bolangir District, Orissa	The study was based on 29 villages, spread across the Bolangir district. The study used a combination of random and purposive sampling models based on characteristics such as skewed land distribution and lack of work.	Social mapping, rural mapping, matrix scoring or ranking, trends analysis, semi-structured interviewing, focus group discussion, and Venn diagrams.
India 1998b Social Assessment Field Report: Guna District Main Report (Madhya Pradesh)	Poor or very poor communities and villages were selected based on the occupation and caste of the community members. The number of households selected in each village varied from 40 to 200.	PRA tools such as focus group discussions, key respondent interviews, transect walks, occupational calendars, timeline, key informants, and wealth-ranking.
India 1998c Social Assessment Fieldwork Report: Rajgarh District Main Report	The study was based on members of poor households and marginal communities within chosen villages in "pockets of poverty" located in Rajgarh, Khilchipur, Jirapur, and Biaora blocks. The site selection was based on criteria enumerated in the Desk Review of District Poverty.	PRA tools including transect walks, village mapping, wealth-ranking, occupational calendars, timelines, focus group discussions, and key respondent discussions.
India 1998d Social Assessment Fieldwork Report: Shivpuri District Main Report	The study was based on members of poor households and marginal communities within selected villages in the major "pockets of poverty" located in Pohri, Kolaeas, Shivpuri, and Pichhore blocks. Site selection was based on criteria enumerated in the Desk Review of District Poverty.	PRA tools such as transect walks, village mapping, wealth-ranking, occupational calendars, timelines, focus group discussions, and key respondent discussions.
India 1998e Poverty in Rural India: The Contribution of Qualitative Research in Policy Analysis	The qualitative instruments were applied and developed in 30 villages in eastern Uttar Pradesh and north and central Bihar. Each village was visited for a period of one week by a four- to eight-person research team. A series of research instruments was developed to capture the views of a wide range of villagers—poor, middle-income, well-off, male, and female.	Qualitative exercises included a wealth-ranking exercise, a social mapping exercise, a social capital inventory, discussions of availability, quality and usage of government programs and services, household case history interviews, and a women's roles/gender issues exercise.

Country, Year, and Title	Sample	Methods
Nepal 1999 Country Report: Nepal	Poor men, poor women, poor youth, lower caste, Kamaiya (bonded labor), and helpless people were the participants in the dialogues in five sites. There were 14 to 27 poor people taking part in the dialogues conducted at various places.	Qualitative open-ended participatory PRA methods, using the Methodology Guide for the Consultations with the Poor study.
Pakistan 1993 Social Safety Nets and Social Networks: Their Role in Poverty Alleviation in Pakistan	The study was based on 10 micro-studies of villages and urban settlements in eight districts of Sindh and Punjab. The districts were in the most poverty-intense zones, and show a range of different ethnic, agro-ecological, cultural, and production systems.	Interviews and discussions, PRA tools, and focus groups. Interviews were also held with government officials, NGOs, and research organizations.
Pakistan 1996 Pakistan Poverty Assessment: Human Resources Development—A Social Analysis of Constraints	Households were chosen on the basis of their low-income status and the presence of a woman of child-bearing age and school-age children of both sexes. Members of the Pakistan Federal Bureau of Statistics (FBS) identified low-income houses by noting the appearance of the house, or else they were identified by local members of the community. A total of 101 parents participated.	Interviews and focus groups with families, teachers, health workers, and family planning providers, separated by gender but not by caste.

Appendix 7: Tables and Figures

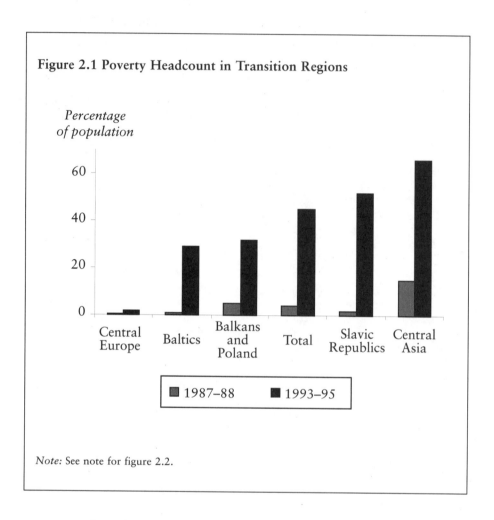

Figure 2.1 Poverty Headcount in Transition Regions

Percentage of population

Note: See note for figure 2.2.

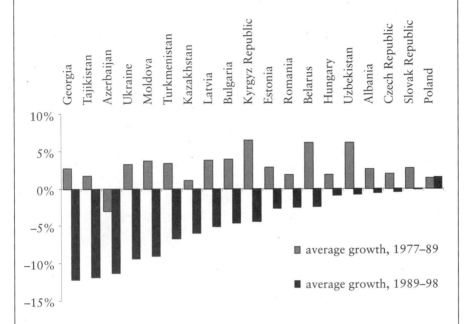

Figure 2.2 Average GDP Growth: Transition Economies 1977–98

■ average growth, 1977–89

■ average growth, 1989–98

Note: Figures 2.1 and 2.2 illustrate the increasing level of poverty and decreasing economic growth in transition economies in the past 10 years. The poverty headcount, or the proportion of poor people, in these countries has increased dramatically between 1987–88 and 1993–95. These countries have also regressed in growth rates: the average GDP growth in transition economies has reversed from a positive trend to a negative trend over the past 10 years. Together, figures 2.1 and 2.2 illustrate a downward trend in living standards and overall economic well-being.

Source: Milanovic 1998.

Table 3.1 Indicators of Corruption, Security of Property Rights, and the Existence of Law and Order

Country	Corruption (0–10, 0=entirely corrupt)	Property rights and governance (1–6, 1= unsatisfactory)	Law and order (0–6, 0=no law and order)
Cameroon	1.4	3.0	3.0
Niger	1.9	1.0	3.0
Ecuador	2.3	2.5	4.0
Kenya	2.5	2.0	4.0
Uganda	2.6	3.5	4.0
Latvia	2.7	4.0	
Pakistan	2.7	3.0	3.0
Ukraine	2.8	2.0	
India	2.9	3.5	4.0
Thailand	3.0	3.5	5.0
Nicaragua	3.0	2.0	4.0
Guatemala	3.1	2.0	2.0
Ghana	3.3	3.5	3.0
Senegal	3.3	3.0	3.0
Mexico	3.3	3.0	3.0
China	3.5	3.0	5.0
El Salvador	3.6	3.0	3.0
Jamaica	3.8	4.0	3.0
Brazil	4.0	3.0	2.0
Tunisia	5.0	4.5	5.0
South Africa	5.2	4.0	2.0
Costa Rica	5.6	5.0	4.0

Note: This table indicates the prevalence of corruption, secure property rights, and legitimacy and order in various nations covered by this review. Corruption is measured from 0–10, with a score of 0 indicating the greatest level of corruption relative to other countries. Cameroon is shown to be relatively the most corrupt, and Costa Rica the least. Property rights and governance are measured from 1–6, with a score of 1 representing the least satisfactory level of secure property rights and governance matters within a nation. Niger is indicated to be the least satisfactory of all in this regard, and Costa Rica the most. The prevalence of law and order is measured from 0–6, with 0 indicating the least (or no) prevalence of law and order. Brazil and Guatemala are shown to have the least prevalence, while Thailand, China, and Tunisia have the greatest.

Source: World Bank, *World Development Indicators 1998;* World Bank, *International Country Risk Guide Database.*

Figure 5.3 Women's Political Representation and Economic Rights

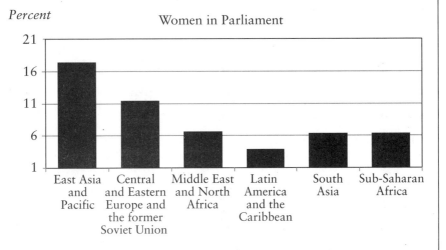

Percent

Women in Parliament

(Bar chart showing percent of women in parliament by region, y-axis from 1 to 21 with marks at 1, 6, 11, 16, 21)

East Asia and Pacific; Central and Eastern Europe and the former Soviet Union; Middle East and North Africa; Latin America and the Caribbean; South Asia; Sub-Saharan Africa

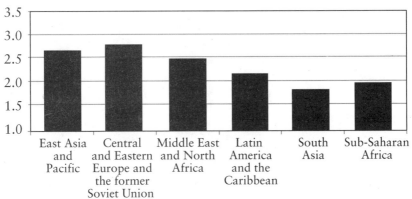

Women's Economic Rights

(Bar chart showing women's economic rights by region, y-axis from 1.0 to 3.5 with marks at 1.0, 1.5, 2.0, 2.5, 3.0, 3.5)

East Asia and Pacific; Central and Eastern Europe and the former Soviet Union; Middle East and North Africa; Latin America and the Caribbean; South Asia; Sub-Saharan Africa

Note: Figures 5.3 and 5.4 illustrate the gender disparity of human capital accumulation, political representation, and economic rights. Figure 5.3 illustrates women's political representation, indicated by the proportion of seats occupied by women in the lower and upper chambers of Parliament, and their economic rights. Women in East Asia and Pacific enjoy the greatest level of political representation relative to the other regions. Women's economic rights illustrate whether women and men are entitled to equal pay for equal work, measured on a 1–4 scale. Women in Central and Eastern Europe and the former Soviet Union enjoy the greatest economic rights relative to other regions. Figure 5.4 illustrates the difference between men and women in educational attainment levels across regions; consistently, more men than women attain secondary education. In East Asia and Pacific and Central and Eastern Europe and the former Soviet Union this difference is nearly 15 percent; 20–30 percent of women attain secondary education, while 35–45 percent of men attain secondary education.

Source: Dollar and Gatti 1995.

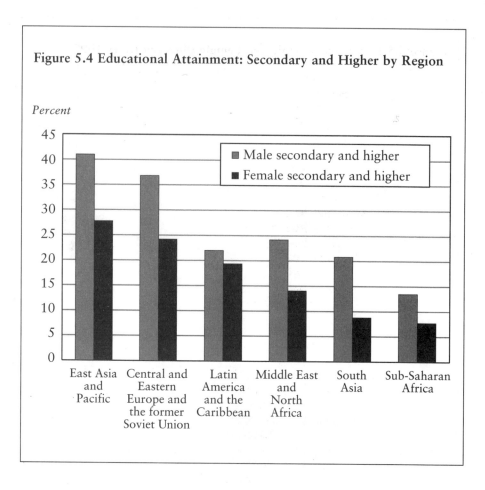

Figure 5.4 Educational Attainment: Secondary and Higher by Region

Percent

Legend:
- Male secondary and higher
- Female secondary and higher

X-axis categories: East Asia and Pacific; Central and Eastern Europe and the former Soviet Union; Latin America and the Caribbean; Middle East and North Africa; South Asia; Sub-Saharan Africa

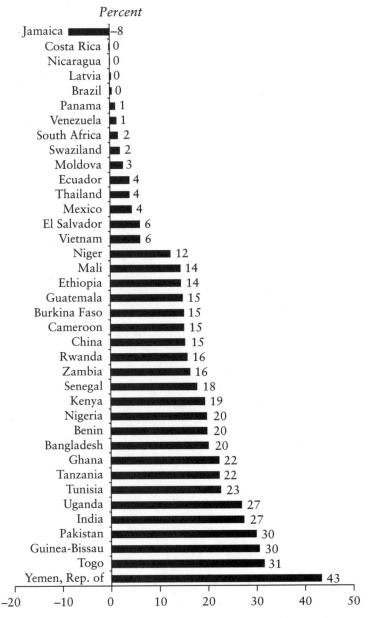

Figure 5.5 Difference in Male and Female Illiteracy Rates 1997

Percent

Jamaica	-8
Costa Rica	0
Nicaragua	0
Latvia	0
Brazil	0
Panama	1
Venezuela	1
South Africa	2
Swaziland	2
Moldova	3
Ecuador	4
Thailand	4
Mexico	4
El Salvador	6
Vietnam	6
Niger	12
Mali	14
Ethiopia	14
Guatemala	15
Burkina Faso	15
Cameroon	15
China	15
Rwanda	16
Zambia	16
Senegal	18
Kenya	19
Nigeria	20
Benin	20
Bangladesh	20
Ghana	22
Tanzania	22
Tunisia	23
Uganda	27
India	27
Pakistan	30
Guinea-Bissau	30
Togo	31
Yemen, Rep. of	43

Note: This figure shows the difference in male and female illiteracy rates for individuals above age 15. Most countries show a positive difference, indicating that more women than men are illiterate. Yemen has the highest difference of 43 percent. Jamaica is an exception, with a negative difference, showing that Jamaican women are more literate than men.

Source: World Bank, *World Development Indicators 1998.*

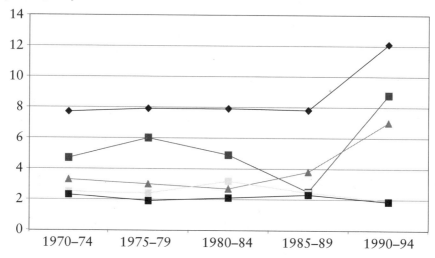

Figure 6.1 Median Intentional Homicide Rates by Region, 1970–94

Intentional homicides per 100,000 persons

Legend:
- Latin America and the Caribbean
- Asia
- Sub-Saharan Africa
- Middle East and North Africa
- Central and Eastern Europe and the former Soviet Union

Note: This figure illustrates the trends in crime, measured by intentional homicides per 100,000 persons, across regions. The trend in Latin America and the Caribbean is a stark illustration of high crime levels increasing over time. Between 1970 and 1989 this region's crime rates were among the highest in the world; it became even more violent in 1990–94. Sub-Saharan Africa exhibited a decreasing trend from 1975–89, then a sharp increase. Central and Eastern Europe and the former Soviet Union had relatively low crime rates in the early 1970s, showed a decrease through the mid-1980s, then exhibited a sharp rise in the late 1980s and early 1990s. Asia and the Middle East and North Africa had small changes in crime levels, relative to other regions, through the 1970s and 1980s, and showed a decreasing trend in the 1990s.

Source: Fajnzylber et al. 1998.

Table 6.1 Growth, Inequality, and Poverty: Indicators of Relative Inequality and Absolute Poverty

Country	1995–96 GNP per capita growth (avg. annual percent)	Gini Index[a]	Population below $1 a day (percent)[a]
Armenia	7.4	39.4	
Azerbaijan	−1.3		
Bangladesh	3.8		
Benin	3.2		
Bolivia	2.6	42.0	
Brazil	6.7	59.6	23.6
Burkina Faso	3.3	39.0	
Cambodia	3.9		
Cameroon	4.5	49.0	
China	8.9	37.8	22.2
Costa Rica	−2.0	46.1	18.9
Ecuador	1.2	43.0	30.4
El Salvador	0.0	48.4	
Ethiopia	7.2	44.2	46.0
Gabon	−1.2	63.2	
Georgia			
Ghana	2.3	33.9	
Guatemala	8.6	59.1	53.3
Guinea-Bissau	3.7		
India	5.1	32.0	47.0
Indonesia	5.8	31.7	7.7
Jamaica	−1.6	37.9	4.3
Kenya	3.1	54.4	50.2
Kyrgyz Republic	4.1	35.3	18.9
Latvia	3.5	27.0	
Macedonia	0.6		
Madagascar	0.5	43.4	72.3
Mali	1.2	54.0	
Mexico	4.7	50.3	14.9
Moldova	−9.7	34.4	6.8
Nepal	4.6	30.1	50.3
Nicaragua	4.2	50.3	43.8
Niger	−0.1	36.1	31.1
Nigeria	1.9	37.5	61.5
Pakistan	0.3	31.2	11.6
Panama	4.1	56.5	25.6
Philippines	4.5	45.0	26.9
Rwanda	7.8	28.9	45.7
Senegal	3.2	54.1	54.0
South Africa	1.0	62.3	23.7
Tanzania	1.7	38.1	
Thailand	4.4	51.5	3.9
Togo	4.3		
Tunisia	−0.4	40.2	
Uganda	6.2	40.8	69.3
Ukraine	−8.5	25.7	
Venezuela	−3.7	53.8	11.8
Vietnam	7.3	35.7	
Republic of Yemen	−7.8		
Zambia	3.4	52.4	84.6

Note: This table illustrates growth, inequality, and poverty across countries. Growth is measured by average annual 1995–96 growth of GNP per capita. Inequality is measured by the Gini coefficient: the higher the number, the greater the inequality. Poverty is indicated by the proportion of people living below $1 a day.

[a]The Gini Index and Population below $1 a day represent currently available data, not necessarily of the same year, and hence may not be comparable across countries.

Source: World Bank, *World Development Indicators 1998;* World Bank, *World Development Indicators 1999.*

References

Agarwal, Bina. 1992. "Gender Relations and Food Security: Coping with Seasonality, Drought and Famine in South Asia." In Lourdes Benería and Shelley Feldman, eds. *Unequal Burden: Economic Crises, Persistent Poverty, and Women's Work.* Boulder, Colo.: Westview Press.

———. 1997. "Bargaining and Gender Relations: Within and Beyond the Household." *Feminist Economics* 3(1): 1–51.

Akerlof, George A., and Rachel E. Kranton. 1999. *Economics and Identity.* Washington, D.C.: Brookings Institute.

Alkire, Sabina. 1999. "Operationalizing Amartya Sen's Capability Approach to Human Development: A Framework for Identifying 'Valuable' Capabilities." Ph. D. diss., Oxford University.

Baulch, Bob. 1996a. "Neglected Trade-Offs in Poverty Measurement." *IDS Bulletin* 27(1): 36–42.

———. 1996b. "The New Poverty Agenda: A Disputed Consensus." *IDS Bulletin* 27(1): 1–10.

Bebbington A., and T. Perreault. 1999. "Social Capital, Development and Access to Resources in Highland Ecuador." *Economic Geography.* October.

Benería, Lourdes. 1989. "Gender and the Global Economy." In Arthur MacEwan and William Tabb, eds. *Instability and Change in the Global Economy.* New York: Monthly Review Press.

Berelson, Bernard. 1954. "Content Analysis." *Handbook of Social Psychology.* Vol. 1. Reading, Mass.: Addison-Wesley.

Bhatt, Mihir. 1999. "Natural Disasters as National Shocks to the Poor and Development." Disaster Mitigation Institute, Ahmedabad, India.

Booth, David, Jeremy Holland, Jesko Hentschel, Peter Lanjouw, and Alicia Herbert. 1998. *Participation and Combined Methods in African Poverty Assessment: Renewing the Agenda.* Department for International Development (DFID), U.K.: Social Development Division and Africa Division.

Bradley, Christine. 1994. "Why Male Violence against Women is a Development Issue: Reflections from Papua New Guinea." In Miranda Davies, ed. *Women and Violence: Realities and Responses, Worldwide.* London: Zed Books.

Brunetti, Aymo, Gregory Kisunko, and Beatrice Weder. 1997. "Institutions in Transition: Reliability of Rules and Economic Performance in Former Socialist Countries." Policy Research Working Paper 1809. Washington, D.C.: World Bank.

Carvalho, Soniya, and Howard White. 1997. "Combining the Quantitative and Qualitative Approaches to Poverty Measurement and Analysis: The Practice and the Potential." Technical Paper 366. Washington, D.C.: World Bank.

Castellas, Manuel. 1997. *The Power of Identity.* Malden, Mass.: Blackwell Publishers.

Cernea, Michael 1979. "Entry Points for Sociological Knowledge in the Project Cycle." Agricultural and Rural Development Department. Washington, D.C.: World Bank.

———, ed. 1985. *Putting People First.* New York: Oxford University Press.

Cernea, Michael, with the assistance of April Adams. 1994. "Sociology Anthropology and Development: An Annotated Bibliography of World Bank Publications 1975–1993." Environmentally and Sustainable Development Studies and Monograph Series 3. Washington, D.C.: World Bank.

Cernea, Michael, and Ayse Kudat. 1997. "Social Assessments for Better Development: Case Studies in Russia and Central Asia." Environmentally Sustainable Development Studies and Monograph Series 16. Washington, D.C.: World Bank.

Chambers, Robert. 1989. "Editorial Introduction: Vulnerability, Coping and Policy." *IDS Bulletin* 20: 1.

———. 1994. "The Origins and Practice of Participatory Rural Appraisal." *World Development* 22 (7). Washington, D.C.: World Bank.

———. 1997. "Whose Reality Counts?: Putting the First Last." London: Intermediate Technology Publications.

Chambliss, William J. 1999. *Power, Politics, and Crime.* Boulder, Colo.: Westview Press.

Charmes, Jacques. 1998. "Informal Sector, Poverty and Gender: A Review of Empirical Evidence." Contributed paper for *World Development Report 2000.* Washington, D.C.: World Bank. October.

Dahle, Cheryl. 1999. "Social Justice—Alan Khazei and Vanessa Kirsch." Fast Company, Issue 30, December 1999, www. fastcompany.com.

Dasgupta, Partha, and Ismail Serageldin. 1999. *Social Capital: A Multifaceted Perspective.* Washington, D.C.: World Bank.

Davies, Miranda, ed. 1994. *Women and Violence: Realities and Responses Worldwide.* London: Zed Books.

Dollar, David, and Roberta Gatti. 1995. "Gender Inequality, Income, and Growth: Are Good Times Good for Women?" Policy Research Report on Gender and Development, No. 1. Washington, D.C.: World Bank.

Economist Intelligence Unit. 1997. *Armenia Country Profile, 1996–97.* London: The Economist Intelligence Unit, Ltd.

Edwards, Michael, and David Hulme, eds. 1992. *Making a Difference: NGOs and Development in a Changing World.* London: Earthscan Publications.

Edwards, Robert, and Michael W. Foley. 1997. "Social Capital and the Political Economy of Our Discontent." *American Behavioral Scientist,* 40(5): 669–78.

Esman, Milton J., and Norman Uphoff. 1984. *Local Organizations: Intermediaries in Rural Development.* Ithaca, N.Y.: Cornell University Press.

Fajnzylber, Pablo, David Lederman, and Norman Loayza. 1998. *What Causes Violent Crime?* Office of the Chief Economist, Latin America and the Caribbean Region. Washington, D.C.: World Bank.

Floro, Maria Sagrario. 1995. "Economic Restructuring, Gender and the Allocation of Time." *World Development* 23: 1913–29. Washington, D.C.: World Bank.

Folbre, Nancy. 1991. "Women on Their Own: Global Patterns of Female Headship." In Rita S. Gallin, Anne Ferguson, and Janice Harper, eds. *The Women and International Development Annual.* Vol. 4. Boulder, Colo.: Westview Press.

Foley, Michael W., and Robert Edwards. 1996. "The Paradox of Civil Society." *Journal of Democracy* 7(3): 38–52.

Foster, James, and Amartya Sen. 1997. "On Economic Inequality after a Quarter Century." 2d ed. Oxford: Clarendon Press.

Fox, Jonathan. 1993. *The Politics of Food in Mexico: State Power and Social Mobilization.* Ithaca: Cornell University Press.

Galtung, Johan. 1994. *Human Rights in Another Key.* Cambridge, U.K.: Polity Press.

Gelles, Richard J., and Murray Straus. 1988. *Intimate Violence.* New York: Simon and Schuster.

Giddens, Anthony. 1984. *The Constitution of Society.* Oxford: Blackwell.

Goetz, Anne Marie. 1998. "Women in Politics and Gender Equity on Policy: South Africa and Uganda." *Review of African Political Economy* 76: 241–62.

Greeley, Martin. 1994 "Measurement of Poverty and Poverty of Measurement." *IDS Bulletin* 25(2).

Grootaert, Christiaan. 1998. "Social Capital: The Missing Link?" Social Capital Initiative Working Paper No. 3. Social Development Family. Washington, D.C.: World Bank.

———. 1999. "Social Capital, Household Welfare, and Poverty in Indonesia." Policy Research Working Paper 2148. Social Development Family. Washington, D.C.: World Bank.

Grootaert, Christiaan, and Deepa Narayan. 1999. "Local Institutions, Poverty and Household Welfare in Bolivia." Social Development Family. Environmentally and Socially Sustainable Development Network. Washington, D.C.: World Bank.

Holland, Jeremy, and James Blackburn, eds. 1998. *Whose Voice? Participatory Research and Policy Change.* London: Intermediate Technology Publications.

Hyden, Goran. 1997. "Civil Society, Social Capital, and Development: Dissection of a Complex Discourse." *Studies in Comparative International Development* 32: 3–30.

Jackson, Cecile. 1996. "Rescuing Gender from the Poverty Trap." *World Development* 23: 489–504.

Jain, Devaki. 1996. "Panchayat Raj: Women Changing Governance." Gender in Development Programme. United Nations Development Programme, New York.

Kabeer, Naila. 1997. "Women, Wages and Intra-household Power Relations in Urban Bangladesh." *Development and Change* 28(2): 261–302.

Kabeer, Naila, and Ramya Subrahmanian. 1996. *Institutions, Relations and Outcomes: Framework and Tools for Gender-aware Planning.* University of Sussex, U.K.: Institute of Development Studies.

Kaufmann, Georgia. 1997. "Watching the Developers: A Partial Ethnography." In R. D. Grillo and R. L. Stirrat, eds. *Discourses of Development: Anthropological Perspectives.* Oxford: Berg Press.

Korten, David C. 1990. *Getting to the 21st Century: Voluntary Action and the Global Agenda.* West Hartford, Conn.: Kumarian Press.

Krishna, Anirudh, and Norman Uphoff. 1999. "Mapping and Measuring Social Capital: A Conceptual and Empirical Study of Collective Action for Conserving and Developing Watersheds in Rajasthan, India." Social Capital Initiative Working Paper No. 13. Washington, D.C.: World Bank.

Krishna, Anirudh, Norman Uphoff, and Milton J. Esman (eds). 1997. *Reasons for Hope: Instructive Experiences in Rural Development.* West Hartford, Conn.: Kumarian Press.

Leach, Melissa, Robin Mearns, and Ian Scoones. 1997. *Community-Based Sustainable Development: Consensus or Conflict?* University of Sussex, U.K.: Institute of Development Studies.

Lipton, Michael, and Martin Ravallion. 1995. "Poverty and Policy." In Jere Richard Behrman and Thirukodikaval Nilakanta Srinivasan, eds. *Handbook of Development Economics.* Vol. 3. Amsterdam: Elsevier Press.

MacEwen Scott, Alison. 1995. "Informal Sector or Female Sector? Gender Bias in Urban Labor Market Models." In Diane Elson, ed., *Male Bias in the Development Process.* 2d ed. Manchester, U.K.: Manchester University Press.

Marshall, Gordon. 1994. *The Concise Oxford Dictionary of Sociology.* New York: Oxford University Press.

Max-Neef, Manfred. 1993. *Human Scale Development: Conception, Application, and Further Reflections.* London: Apex Press.

Milanovic, Branko. 1998. *Income, Inequality, and Poverty during the Transition from Planned to Market Economy.* Regional and Sectoral Studies. Washington, D.C.: World Bank.

Milimo, John T. 1995. "An Analysis of Qualitative Information on Agriculture: from Beneficiary Assessments, Participatory Poverty Assessments and Other Studies which used Qualitative Research Methods." Ministry of Agriculture, Food, and Fisheries. Lusaka, Zambia.

Moore, Mick, and James Putzel. "Thinking Strategically about Politics and Poverty." IDS Working Paper 101. University of Sussex, U.K.: Institute of Development Studies.

Moser, Caroline. 1998. *The Asset-Vulnerability Framework: Reassessing Urban Poverty Reduction Strategies.* Washington, D.C.: World Bank.

Moser, Caroline, Annika Tornqvist, and Bernice van Bronkhorst. 1998. "Mainstreaming Gender and Development in the World Bank: Progress and Recommendations." Washington, D.C.: World Bank.

Narayan, Deepa. 1999. "Bonds and Bridges: Social Capital and Poverty." Policy Research Working Paper 2167. Policy Research Department. Washington, D.C.: World Bank.

Narayan, Deepa, and Katrinka Ebbe. 1997. "Design of Social Funds: Participation, Demand Orientation, and Local Organizational Capacity." Discussion Paper no. 375. Washington, D.C.: World Bank.

Narayan, Deepa, and Lant Pritchett. 1999. "Cents and Sociability: Household Income and Social Capital in Rural Tanzania." *Economic Development and Cultural Change* (47)4: 871–8.

Narayan, Deepa, and Lyra Srinivasan. 1994. *Participatory Development Tool Kit: Training Materials for Agencies and Communities.* Washington, D.C.: World Bank.

Narayan, Deepa, and Michael Cassidy. 1999. "A Dimensional Approach to Measuring Social Capital: Development and Validation of a Social Capital Inventory." Draft. Washington, D.C.: World Bank.

Narayan, Deepa, and Talat Shah. 2000. *Gender Inequity, Poverty, and Social Capital.* Policy Research Report on Gender Development, Working Paper Series. Washington, D.C.: World Bank.

North, Douglas. 1990. "Institutions and their Consequences for Economic Performance." In Karen Schweers Cook and Margaret Levi, eds. *The Limits of Rationality.* Chicago, Ill.: University of Chicago.

Norton Andy, and Thomas Stephens. 1995. "Participation in Poverty Assessments." Social Development Papers 9. Washington, D.C.: World Bank.

Orbach, Susie. 1999. "Psychoanalysis and Social Policy." Seminar paper presented to the World Bank, Washington, D.C., April.

Patton, Michael Quinn. 1990. *Qualitative Evaluation and Research Methods.* Newbury Park, Calif.: Sage Publications.

Portes, Alejandro. 1998. "Social Capital: Its Origins and Applications in Modern Sociology." *Annual Review of Sociology* 22: 1–24.

Pottier, Johan. 1997. "Towards an Ethnography of Participatory Appraisal and Research." In R. D. Grillo and R. L. Stirrat, eds. *Discourses of Development: Anthropological Perspectives.* Oxford, U.K.: Berg Press.

Putnam, Robert, Robert Leonardi, and Raffaella Y. Nanetti. 1993. *Making Democracy Work: Civic Traditions in Modern Italy.* Princeton, N.J.: Princeton University Press.

Ravallion, Martin. 1995. "China's Lagging Poor Areas." *American Economic Review, Papers and Procedures* 89: 301–5.

Ray, Raka, and Anna Kortweg. 1999. "Women's Movements in the Third World: Identity, Mobilization and Autonomy." *Annual Review of Sociology* 25: 47–71.

Rietbergen-McCracken, Jennifer, and Deepa Narayan. 1998. "Participatory Tools and Techniques: A Resource Kit for Participation and Social Assessment." Social Policy and Resettlement Division, Environment Department. Washington, D.C.: World Bank.

Robb, Caroline. 1999. "Can the Poor Influence Poverty? Participatory Poverty Assessments in the Developing World." Washington, D.C.: World Bank.

Rodrik, Dani. 1998. "Globalization, Social Conflict and Economic Growth." *World Economy* 21(1): 43–58.

Rupesinghe, Kumar, and Marcial Rubio. 1994. *The Culture of Violence*. New York: United Nations University Press.

Salmen, Lawrence. 1987. *Listen to the People*. New York: Oxford University Press.

———. 1995. "Participatory Poverty Assessment: Incorporating Poor People's Perspectives into Poverty Assessment Work." Social Development Paper No. 11. Washington, D.C.: World Bank.

———. 1998. "Toward a Listening Bank: A Review of Best Practices and the Efficacy of Beneficiary Assessment." Social Development Paper No. 23. Washington, D.C.: World Bank.

Sartori, Giovanni. 1997. "Understanding Pluralism." *Journal of Democracy* 8(4): 58–69.

Schuler, Sidney Ruth, Syed M. Hashemi, and Shamsul Huda Badal. 1998. "Men's Violence against Women in Rural Bangladesh: Undermined or Exacerbated by Microcredit Programmes?" *Development in Practice* 8(2): 148–57.

Schwartz, S. H. 1994. "Are There Universal Aspects in the Structure and Contents of Human Values?" *Journal of Social Issues* 50(4): 19–45.

Sen, Amartya K. 1981. *Poverty and Famines*. Oxford: Clarendon Press.

———. 1983. "Poor, Relatively Speaking." *Oxford Economic Papers* 35: 153–69. Reprinted in *Resources, Values and Development*.

———. 1984. "Rights and Capabilities." In Amartya K. Sen, ed., *Resources, Values and Development*. Oxford, U.K.: Blackwell.

———. 1985. "A Sociological Approach to the Measurement of Poverty: A Reply to Professor Peter Townsend." *Oxford Economic Papers* 37: 669–76.

———. 1992. *Inequality Reexamined*. Cambridge, Mass: Harvard University Press.

———. 1993. "Economic Regress: Concepts and Features." *Proceedings of the World Bank Annual Conference on Development Economics*, 315–54.

———. 1997. *On Economic Inequality*. 2d ed. Oxford: Clarendon Press.

———. 1999. *Development as Freedom*. New York: Knopf Press.

Shah, Shekhar. 1999. "Coping with Natural Disasters: The 1998 Floods in Bangladesh." Seminar paper presented in June to the World Bank, Washington, D.C.

Shapiro, Gilbert, and John Markoff. 1997. "A Matter of Definition." In Carl W. Roberts, ed., *Text Analysis for the Social Sciences*. Mahwah, N.J. Lawrence Erlbaum Associates.

Silverman, David. 1993. *Interpreting Qualitative Data: Methods for Analyzing Talk, Text and Interaction*. Thousand Oaks, Calif.: Sage Publications.

Srinivas, Smita. 1999. *Social Protection for Women Workers in the Informal Economy*. Draft. Washington, D.C.: World Bank and Geneva: International Labour Office.

Standing, Guy. 1999. "Global Feminization through Flexible Labor: A Theme Revisited." *World Development* 3(27): 583–602.

Stone, P. J., D. C. Dunphy, M. S. Smith, and D. M. Ogilvie. 1966. *The General Inquirer: A Computer Approach to Content Analysis*. Cambridge: MIT Press.

Strauss, Anselm L. 1987. *Qualitative Analysis for Social Scientists*. New York: Cambridge University Press.

Tarrow, Sidney. 1994. *Power in Movement: Social Movements, Collective Action and Politics*. Cambridge, U.K.: Cambridge University Press.

Tendler, Judith. 1997. *Good Government in the Tropics*. Baltimore, Md.: Johns Hopkins University Press.

Townsend, Peter. 1971. *The Concept of Poverty*. London: Heinemann Educational.

Tripp, Aili Mari. 1992. "The Impact of Crisis and Economic Reform on Women in Urban Tanzania." In Lourdes Bería and Shelly Feldman, eds. *Unequal Burden: Economic Crises, Persistent Poverty, and Women's Work*. Boulder, Colo.: Westview Press.

Uphoff, Norman. 1986. *Local Institutional Development: An Analytical Sourcebook with Cases*. West Hartford, Conn.: Kumarian Press.

Uphoff, Norman, Milton J. Esman, and Anirudh Krishna. 1997. *Reasons for Success: Learning from Instructive Experiences in Rural Development*. West Hartford, Conn.: Kumarian Press.

Visaria, Leela. 1999. "Violence against Women in India: Evidence from Rural Gujarat." In *Domestic Violence in India: A Summary Report of Three Studies*. Washington, D.C.: International Center for Research on Women.

Weber, Robert Philip. 1990. *Basic Content Analysis*. 2d ed. Newbury Park, Calif.: Sage Publications.

WHO (World Health Organization). 1997. *Violence against Women*. Geneva.

Woolcock, Michael. 1998. "Social Capital and Economic Development: Toward a Theoretical Synthesis and Policy Framework." *Theory and Society* 27(2): 151–208.

Woolcock, Michael, and Deepa Narayan. 2000. "Social Capital: Implications for Development Theory, Research, and Policy." *World Bank Research Observer* 15(2), Washington, D.C.: World Bank.

World Bank. 1996a. *From Plan to Market: World Development Report 1996.* Washington, D.C.

————. 1996b. *Sourcebook on Participation.* Washington, D.C.

————. 1997a. *Poverty Assessment: A Process Review.* Operations Evaluation Department Document 15881. Washington, D.C.

————. 1997b. *World Development Report 1997: The State in a Changing World.* New York: Oxford University Press (for the World Bank).

————. 1998. *World Development Indicators.* Washington, D.C.

————. 1999. *World Development Indicators.* Washington, D.C.

————. 2000. *Poverty Trends and Voices of the Poor.* Poverty Reduction Group. Washington, D.C.

Wratten, Ellen. 1995. "Conceptualizing Urban Poverty." *Environment and Urbanization* 7: 11–36.

Abbreviations and Acronyms

ACID	Anti-Crime Squad
AMREF	African Medical and Research Foundation
BPL	Below the Poverty Line
CBO	Community-Based Organization
COPEI	Comité de Organización Política Electoral Independiente
EDUCO	Educación con Participación de la Comunidad
IBGE	Fundação Instituto Brasileiro de Geográfica e Estatistíca
IDP	Internally Displaced Person
IRDP	Integrated Rural Development Program
LINTCO	Cotton Marketing Organization
LSMS	Living Standard Measurement Survey
PDS	Public Distribution System
PNAD	Pesquita National por Amostra de Domicilios
PPA	Participatory Poverty Assessment
SEWA	Self-Employed Women's Association
STD	Sexually Transmitted Disease
WDR	World Development Report
WIEGO	Women in Informal Employment: Globalizing and Organizing

Currencies

Country	Local currency	Year	Exchange rate
Armenia	Dram	1999	540 Dram/US$ (June 1999)
		1996	414 Dram/US$
		1995	406 Dram/US$
Bangladesh	Taka	1996	41.794 Tk/US$
Benin	CFA Franc	1994	555.2 CFA Fr/US$
Ecuador	Sucre	1996	3,191.3 SU/US$
Ethiopia	Birr	1998	7.12 Birr/US$
Georgia	Lari	1997	1.3 Lari/US$
Guinea-Bissau	Peso	1994	12,892 P/US$
India	Rupee, Rs	1998	41.26 Rs/US$1
		1997	36.6 Rs/US$
Kenya	Kenyan Shillings	1997	56.4 KSh/US$
		1996	57.1 KSh/US$
Latvia	Lat	1998	0.59 LVL/US$
		1997	0.58 LVL/US$
Macedonia	Denar	1998	54.46 Den/US$
Mexico	Peso	1995	Ps 6.419/US$
Moldova	Lei	1997	Lei 4.61/US$
Nicaragua	Córdoba	1998	C 10.58/US$
Niger	CFA Franc	1996	511.6 CFA Fr/US$
Pakistan	Rupee, Rs	1996	33.57 PRs/US$
		1993	N/A
Panama	Balboa	1998	1 B/US$
South Africa	Rand, R	1998	R 5.5316/US$
Togo	CFA Franc	1996	511.6 CFA Fr/US$
Uganda	Ugandan Shilling	1999	1,380 NUSh/US$ (March 23, 1999)
		1998	1,240 NUSh/US$
Vietnam	Dong	1999	D 13,917/US$ (June 18, 1999)
		1996	D 11,100/US$
Yemen, Republic of	Yemen Riyal	1999	160 YR//US$ (October 1999)
		1998	135.9 YR/US$

Note: Exchange rates are annual averages, local currency per US$, unless a date is specified in lieu of an annual average.
Source: Economist Intelligence Unit.